Promises and Predicaments

Promises and Predicaments

Trade and Entrepreneurship in Colonial and Independent Indonesia in the 19th and 20th Centuries

Edited by
Alicia Schrikker and Jeroen Touwen

NUS PRESS
SINGAPORE

Published by:

NUS Press
National University of Singapore
AS3-01-02, 3 Arts Link
Singapore 117569

Fax: (65) 6774-0652
E-mail: nusbooks@nus.edu.sg
Website: http://www.nus.edu.sg/nuspress

ISBN 978-9971-69-851-5 (Paper)

National Library Board, Singapore Cataloguing-in-Publication Data

Promises and predicaments: trade and entrepreneurship in colonial and independent Indonesia in the 19th and 20th centuries/edited by Alicia Schrikker and Jeroen Touwen. – Singapore: NUS Press, National University of Singapore, [2015]
pages cm
Includes bibliographical references and index.
ISBN: 978-9971-69-851-5 (paperback)

1. Indonesia – Economic conditions – 19th century. 2. Indonesia – Economic conditions – 20th century. 3. Indonesia – Commerce – History. 4. Entrepreneurship – Indonesia – History. I. Schrikker, Alicia, editor. II. Touwen, Jeroen, 1964-, editor.

HC447
330.9598022 — dc23 OCN893179303

Cover image: 'N.V. De Nederlandsch-Indische Industrie, Fabriek van Stoom- en Andere Werktuigen aan de Kalimas te Soerabaja' (Dutch-Indies Industry, factory of steam and other machinery on the Kalimas river in Surabaya), photo made by G.P. Lewis (presumably), ca. 1902–07. Image code 107271. Courtesy of KITLV Leiden.

Printed by: Mainland Press Pte Ltd

Contents

II. Entrepreneurship in the Colonial and Post-colonial Economies

III. Trade and Economic Growth under Changing Regimes

List of Tables

List of Figures

Preface

In preparing this book, we sought to bring fresh perspectives to one of the fastest growing economies in Southeast Asia by inviting a mix of young scholars and senior academics to revisit key issues in the economic history of Indonesia during the nineteenth and twentieth centuries.

The study of Indonesia's economy has passed through a number of stages. In the early twentieth century, Dutch writers such as G.F.E. Gonggrijp and J.H. Boeke wrote much appreciated studies that provided valuable data, but with a strong emphasis on the European side of the political economy. Their views and their conclusions were embedded in issues linked to the era in which they wrote. In the immediate post-war decades, a group of Australian scholars, notably Bruce Glassburner and Jamie Mackie, adopted somewhat different perspectives and started a tradition of Australian economic historiography of Indonesia that remains active to the present day. What might be called the Australian school is represented in this volume by Hal Hill, Robert Cribb, Howard Dick and Roger Knight. Still later, a statistically-based econometric approach emerged, represented in this volume by Hill, Anne Booth, Thee Kian Wie and Jan Luiten van Zanden. The contributions by several younger scholars, among them Ewout Frankema, Pim de Zwart, Alexandra de Pleijt and Daan Marks, also draw on this tradition.

Other historians deal with questions that econometrics cannot answer and use non-quantitative source materials to explore questions relating to ethnicity, spatial developments, economic policy and economic nation-alism, as well as new types of entrepreneurship (represented in the chap-ters by Leonard Blussé, Bambang Purwanto, Farabi Fakih and Pham van Thuy). In the chapters on wages, monetization and the trade in rice, Freek Colombijn, David Henley, Alexander Claver and Pierre van der Eng, combine statistical evidence with discussions of policies, institutions and ideas, asking new questions of old material, and suggesting answers that combine fresh insights with older conclusions. Their work moves away from periodization based on a strict delineation between political regimes in favour of an understanding that while many things changed along with a change of regime, much remained the same. This perception is particularly significant in the economic realm, where transitions are long term processes, and need to be studied accordingly.

The contributors to this book include scholars who have helped build the field over the past 30 years along with representatives of a new generation of researchers. Our goal was to highlight themes and questions that will help readers unfamiliar with Indonesia's economic history understand and explore the subject as an exciting and challenging field of study. We were inspired in part by the publications of Thomas Lindblad, whose work exemplifies the value of searching for continuities that extend across the colonial-postcolonial divide and transcend political regimes. Lindblad's insights provide a foundation for the articles in this volume, and without the groundwork laid in his many seminal publications, our book would not have been possible. For that reason we are dedicating the collection to him.

We would like to thank all contributors, our colleagues at NUS Press, Elizabeth Stone at Bourchier Services, the Unger-Van Brero Fonds, the Institute for History at Leiden University, the Leiden Institute for Area Studies, and the Royal Netherlands Institute of Southeast Asian and Caribbean Studies (KITLV) for their support.

INTRODUCTION

1

Building Bridges between Themes and Approaches in Indonesian Economic History

Jeroen Touwen and Alicia Schrikker

Indonesia's economic history is an important and fast-developing field that has attracted many talented scholars over recent decades. It is a challenging theme as it covers a large heterogeneous region, with extensive natural resources, multiple ethnicities, a vibrant political economy and a rather capricious path-dependency. The histories that have been produced in this field can serve as inspiration for historians whose interest lies beyond the Indonesian Archipelago, such as scholars working on late colonial and independent Malaysia and the Philippines, as well as historians of other Southeast Asian regions such as Thailand, Vietnam, Laos, Cambodia and Myanmar.

This collection of essays explores the economic development of Indonesia before and after decolonization from three angles: the impact of trade, the changes in entrepreneurship and the changing political regimes. Economic history is arguably one of the best-developed fields in Indonesian history, thanks to the dedicated commitment of and co-operation between scholars worldwide—from Indonesia, Australia, the Netherlands and elsewhere. The volume is dedicated to J. Thomas Lindblad who has made an indispensable contribution to the field over the past thirty years.[1]

Since the nineteenth century, trade in the Indonesian Archipelago has been expanding in various forms. It is typical for Indonesia that diverse ethnic groups participated in this developing world trade. Some of these groups were successful in creating new opportunities to earn an income, combining more traditional forms of agriculture and trade with the cultivation of export crops. Entrepreneurial activities thrived under the aegis of the late colonial regime, from the end of the cultivation system to the late colonial state of the 1930s. After independence new economic actors gradually took the stage, next to those who remained in place. Economic decolonization was a slower process than political decolonization and presented different problems, while the subsequent post-1945 regimes placed varying priority to economic growth. These variables shaped a remarkable mixture of promises and predicaments in a resource-rich economy.

The essays in this book build upon the insights that we find in *The Emergence of a National Economy*.[2] In this well-received textbook (published in 2002) Dick, Houben, Lindblad and Thee present an integrated approach to Indonesia's economic history in which the interconnection between globalization, state formation and the development of a national economy takes a central position. To start with, they show that Indonesia's outward orientation has to be understood in the light of the centuries-old globalization process that constituted long-term interaction between the region and the world economy. This outward orientation is used as a prism through which the trade activities in the Indonesian Archipelago can be viewed and which explains much of its historic dynamism. In contrast with the continuous outward orientation, state formation in Indonesia followed a capricious path. Before the arrival and intervention of the European colonial powers, the archipelago was connected to the larger Southeast Asian economy though myriad small-scale trade flows.[3]

One could say that trade was a predecessor to state formation. During a protracted era of expanding world trade, the colonial state gradually manifested more strongly—in the nineteenth century in Java and after 1870 increasingly in the Outer Islands, reaching the remote corners of the archipelago. Although in the early twentieth century this was still a bureaucratic construction based on trial and error, it eventually shaped the outline of the modern Indonesian nation state. After independence, Indonesia again followed a remarkable trajectory in which political and economic priorities seemed to change intermittently through the decades. But, despite its regional diversity, the state still clung together and gradually consolidated.

Dick, Houben, Lindblad and Thee show how the two processes of globalization and state formation contributed to the emergence of a national Indonesian economy. Unlikely as it seems, the national economy arose from the many local economies that once constituted the Malay Archipelago, in which many actors ignored the bureaucratic state borders and developed substantial transnational flows of commodities and people. It was the interaction of many local economies that gave Indonesia's modern economic history its unique character.[4]

A number of important themes follow from this perspective. Below, we briefly comment on these themes, in order to provide a context for the essays collected in this book. We address the development of economic institutions that facilitate economic development, the connection between the political economy and macro-economic analysis of trade and investment, the periodization across different regimes, the economic roles of specific ethnic and social groups, and the spatial distribution of economic activity in the archipelago. The contributions to this volume all relate to one or more of these aspects, as will be discussed in the latter part of this introduction.

Economic historians have increasingly combined distinct approaches to economic history in their analysis. They connect a macro-economic focus on economic development, based on the statistical analysis of trade, income or investment, to the political economy of power, policy priorities and economic institutions. This is certainly a very fruitful approach. In addition to the economic structure, there is a demand to develop a better understanding of the economic institutions, which, formally and informally provide the backdrop of the market economy. For example, in the period between roughly 1914 and 1942, the late colonial state constrained the bottom-up processes of institution building—the organization of societies, unions, political parties with a mass following—hindering the development of a stronger civil society.[5]

At yet another level, economic historians have developed a keen eye for the economic actors themselves (both men and women) such as the entrepreneurs, traders, smallholders, credit suppliers and consumers, but also politicians, government officials, the military and households. The role of historical economic actors is essential for understanding the larger picture of stagnation and growth. But conversely, national growth and trade statistics may underpin or inspire local and regional histories, or more thematically oriented studies. It has become clear that the agency of economic actors provides an explanation of economic change within the structure of the political economy. For example, even under colonial rule, certain non-privileged groups found space to expand their business. In the early independence period rights and rules were often disputed, while economic roles were generally fluid, which created unexpected outcomes.[6]

Increasingly, we observe a tendency to analyse Indonesian economic history from a long-term perspective and to look across regimes and the dominant historiographical periodization. Many scholars position their research in one of the obvious periods: delineating, for example, the pre-colonial period, the VOC period (roughly between 1600 and 1795), the cultivation system (1830–70), the liberal and late colonial period (1870–1942), the early post-war independence period of Sukarno (1945–65), the new order period under Suharto (1965–98) and the post-Suharto period up until the present. However, economic performance and characteristics in earlier periods had strong effects in later periods. One may think of path dependencies, when specific firms, sectors or local economies are receptive to the legacies of earlier times. There are also various types of resemblances, for example when different regions share a similar tradition of trade openness, or when the political economy displays similarities under different regimes.[7] A recent study crosses five of the above-mentioned periods and seeks to explain long-term Indonesian growth by analysing specific factor inputs and structural institutional and geographic forces over a period of two hundred years.[8] Not all contributions to this volume place such a long time frame at the centre of their analysis, but a perspective that traverses separate periods is generally present, even when figuring in the background.

Decolonization can be viewed as a radical breaking point but also as a process of gradual transition. After the protracted political struggle, the economic side of the Indonesian revolution still had to begin and took more than a decade.[9] At the core of economic decolonization lies nationalism, as an aspiration to own and control the productive assets of the country. The strive for *Indonesianisasi* was a conscious effort to bring the economic leadership into Indonesian hands. This example shows how trade, entrepreneurship and political regime were closely interrelated, but the regime's influence was not straightforward, since human capital and ownership had their own characteristics and structures.[10]

In this volume, we aim to analyse economic development as a result of the interplay between foreign trade, new forms of entrepreneurship and the political economy. Historians, in their analysis of specific economic roles of various actors in the Indonesian economy, have increasingly shown sensitivity towards the cross-cultural interaction between various ethnic groups. This forms an important approach to economic development. It may outline different types of factor inputs by these groups, supplying labour, capital and credit, and entrepreneurship. Forming intricate networks, Indonesian population groups interacted with Chinese, Japanese, Europeans and others. We may think of networks in export and retail trade, but also firm owners of one ethnic group hiring workers of another group, or the initiation of new entrepreneurial activities by specific groups. These mechanisms added a specific flavour to the economic development of the Indonesian Archipelago, which has had both advantages and disadvantages, at times creating political or social tensions. The central government has attempted to find policy answers to these tensions since the nineteenth century. Indonesia's unity in diversity almost forms a model to scale of globalization at large.

It is clear that, in the long run, exports of raw materials had positive effects on Indonesian economic development, but there may have been an opportunity cost of export-oriented activities. Historians such as Booth and Dick argue that foreign exports resulted in double colonial drain to European and Chinese overseas destinations.[11] This constituted a downside to the fascinating story of oil and tin exploration and the substantial agricultural exports that in the long run have benefited the economy. Export gains were earned by specific and diverse groups. During the late colonial period, spin-off effects in European industry and commerce were important, but parallel to the capital-intensive industries and the large agricultural estates, local initiatives on a much smaller scale were important to sustain and propel the local economy. Lindblad has shown in his book on Southeast Kalimantan how in the late colonial period the large export-oriented Western-dominated industries existed alongside widespread indigenous economic activities in commodities, such as rubber and copra. There was an Asian trading network that was small-scale, ethnically diverse and technically rather primitive—and that was dynamic and resilient.[12]

Finally, we observe a growing interest in the spatial distribution of economic activity across the archipelago. The trading links between key regions and the trade centres provide insight into the strengths and weaknesses of the emerging Indonesian national economy. Owing to the large distances, the construction of infrastructure was costly, but the region accommodated rich natural resources and a dynamic domestic market. These characteristics result in a tension between opportunities and threats, which in the course of time explain the economic development of stagnant regions and regions that profited more from trade and investment. In the late nineteenth century the configuration changed, and while Java remained a dominant centre, certain regions in the Outer Islands became growth centres, and were oriented towards other hubs, such as Singapore and Macassar. In the New Order era, the influence of Japan as a dominant economic centre expanded. The Indonesian exports of oil and gas led to a strong regional concentration of exports, but when oil and gas prices decreased in the 1980s the manufacturing sector gained way, facilitating the Indonesian entry into the post-1980 period of modern globalization.[13]

The debate on the national economy has focused on the role of government policy and the impediments to successful economic growth. A predecessor to this debate was the search for the reasons and motives for Dutch expansion in the Indonesian Archipelago, a debate that was carried out long ago but is far from unimportant. The effects of the disruption of intra-Asian trade by the arrival of the VOC—and the manner in which during the nineteenth century the 'pax neerlandica' expanded—are significant, because they influenced later developments. Lindblad has shown that, although there was an explicit political agenda, in the background the economic interests were always present.[14]

In sum, the recent literature builds various bridges: between state formation and the development of a national economy, between a variety of ethnic groups, and also in the temporal perspective, between the colonial and independent periods. Colonial Indonesia and independent Indonesia are no longer viewed as separate entities but rather as two halves of a continuing historical narrative. The national economy is connected to the outside world in a number of ways, which in turn are strongly influenced by the economic policies pursued by the government. Another bridge that we observe is that between econometric and ethnographic or socio-political scholarly traditions. And finally there is a bridge towards the larger region of Southeast Asia, when Java and the Outer Islands are explicitly positioned in the wider context of a region that in the globalized world had become one of the most promising and dynamic areas. Furthermore, Indonesia's long-term economic performance has become subject to innovative South–South comparisons, in particular in relation to African regions.[15]

These trends have left their mark on the contributions to this volume, which we have grouped along three leading themes. The first is: what were the economic and socio-cultural effects of trade and investment in the short run and in the long run? Trade and foreign investment can be viewed as forces that propel national income, but they also have an impact on economic institutions. They constitute engines driving change, following the traditional view of classical economists such as David Ricardo and Adam Smith. Second, we zoom in on the economic actors and ask how entrepreneurship in the colonial and post-colonial economies adapted to the changing context and initiated new changes. The changes in the political economy are the subject of the third question: what types of interaction can we observe between the political economy and economic development? In this way we have defined three clusters that together address the interplay between entrepreneurship, the colonial and post-independence political economy, and economic development.

I. Economic or Socio-cultural Effects of Trade and Investment

In the first part, focusing on the economic effects of trade and foreign investment, Anne Booth addresses the impact of changes in patterns of trade and investment on regional development in Indonesia. This particularly had an effect on the economic balance between Java and the rest of Indonesia, when the Outer Islands took a leading role in providing exports for the colony. Booth draws a continuous line between the late colonial period and the post-independence period, surveying the role of oil and gas during the Suharto era and indicating that the post-1990 increase of Javanese exports was contingent on the fall in oil and gas prices. She surveys the resource drain and persisting poverty in some areas, particularly Papua Barat. Next, Hal Hill addresses the turning points in recent structural economic change in Southeast Asia. He examines the various patterns in the Southeast Asian economies in sector size, in relation to the rate of economic growth, natural resource endowments, demographic transitions, labour market adjustments and policy interventions. De Zwart, Marks, De Pleijt and Van Zanden analyse the statistical relationship between trade openness and development, using a long-term time-series analysis. They focus on two dimensions of development: the increase of total factor productivity, and the real wage of an unskilled labourer. They find that the link between trade and the alleviation of mass poverty is not straightforward: in some periods there was a clear relationship between waves of globalization and productivity growth, but it depended on the broader institutional and economic context. Only after decolonization did living standards improve, mainly as a result of productivity growth in agriculture. This, in turn, was stimulated by government investment, facilitated by the exports of oil and gas.

Alex Claver focuses on a narrower theme, but one that also forms an important part of the institutional context. Having earlier studied indigenous trade flows, Claver analyses the contribution of the colonial coinage system to trade in the indigenous economy. He focuses on the circulation of copper coins (*duiten*) in the colonial economy and the monetary stabilization efforts by the colonial administration. He concludes that the monetary developments within the colony were erratic, but, paradoxically, in Java the coinage system basically worked well.

II. Entrepreneurship in the Colonial or Post-colonial Economies

The second part of this book deals with the economic actors and addresses entrepreneurship in the colonial and post-colonial economies. Here, we hope that contrasting the late colonial period and the independent period will shed new light on the economic roles of specific groups. It seems as if groups adapt, under all circumstances, to new economic roles. The most remarkable example is, of course, the economic role of the military (as studied by Purwanto in this book).

One of the important conclusions of the Indonesian economic historiography of the last decades is that the Chinese played such an important role in the development of the indigenous trading network, facilitating exports and providing credit. Leonard Blussé takes an out-of-the-box view on the Chinese community by studying Chinese sailors in the service of the VOC. Inspired by a painting, he describes the recruitment of Chinese sailors on VOC ships and emphasizes the harsh conditions under which they were working on the ships. This provides a fresh angle on a very early division of economic roles, which is picked up at a much later stage by Freek Colombijn, who examines housing construction in the 1930s and 1950s. Colombijn focuses on the economic relationship between the Indonesians and the Dutch. He postulates that actors from different ethnic groups each occupy a niche and complement each other. These niches could be held by Asian entrepreneurs and point at a richer variety of roles and responsibilities than would be surmised by overemphasizing dualist divisions. Apart from the construction sector, this type of co-operation was also found in inter-island shipping and urban public transportation.

Knight focuses on the international sugar trade between Java and Japan between the 1880s and the mid-1940s. He analyses why the trade-nexus between Java and Japan came under duress after 1920—having first developed into a 'sugar empire' through the agency of European, Japanese and Chinese-Indonesian merchant houses and banks. In the 1920s, competition with new suppliers such as the Taiwanese put the empire under strain; later it came into the crossfire of the war. Again we see a strong example of co-operation between ethnic groups and different nationalities in trading networks, and how regime changes forced changes upon these networks.

Purwanto concentrates on a relatively unknown subject in Indonesian economic development: the increasing economic role of the military in post-independence Indonesia. He concludes that the military did not only take hold of large-scale enterprises, but also made much money by facilitating sports and entertainment, supplying transports, locations and facilities. Their prime motivation to do so, next to earning additional income, was to gain popular support.

Henley concludes the section on entrepreneurship by looking at how transaction costs, determined in turn by institutional structures, are determinants of economic development. He shows how these transaction costs and the effect of institutions—that are central to the New Institutional Economics literature—had unexpected forerunners in Asian historiography in the writings of two anthropologists: Roy Franklin Barton, who worked in the Philippines between 1916 and 1930, and Alice Dewey, who studied peasant markets in Java in the 1950s. Their understanding of the centrality of market institutions shows how the institutional approach is vital and enriching in Southeast Asia, where general economic principles are complemented with other co-ordinating principles such as trust, kinship and pact holding.

III. Trade and Economic Growth under Changing Regimes

In the third part of the book we address the interaction between political economy and economic development. The continuities and discontinuities of trade and economic growth under changing regimes is addressed as a theme separate from trade and investment (the macro-economic view) and entrepreneurship (the micro-economic view). Rice trade and basic food production form a major thread throughout this section, as do economic planning and political plotting.

First, Robert Cribb focuses on the rice trade of the Republic of Indonesia during the Indonesian revolution. It is a short and understudied period in Indonesian economic history and one that forms a strange interlude with a somewhat dramatic character. The decision made by the republic to export rice to India is central to this analysis of the economy of the revolution. Until the revolution the region had relied on rice imports. The export of rice was now possible because the republic did not feel responsible for feeding the urban centres that were still in the hands of the colonial government. It was a decision that seemed erratic from the point of view of an Indonesian national economy, and which angered the Dutch government, but made sense within the political economy of the republic at the time.

Thee Kian Wie analyses the fragile Indonesian economy immediately after independence, and the fateful choices made by President Sukarno who valued political priorities higher than economic problems. When the United States offered to provide financial aid for Indonesia's economic development programme, it was a final effort to improve its important relations with Indonesia. But President Sukarno had little interest in accepting foreign aid, certainly not from the USA, even though it might have enabled the Indonesian government to deal with Indonesia's serious economic problems. As a result, the Indonesian economy deteriorated steadily, experiencing crippling hyperinflation.

Pham van Thuy looks at the practical side of Indonesia's economic nationalism and asks the question why, despite early political claims made by Haji Agus Salim, actual *Indonesianisasi* started late. By addressing this theme, Pham Van Thuy stays close to the work of Thomas Lindblad. He shows how practical circumstances, the limited capital and knowledge in Indonesian society, simply made early nationalization of colonial companies impossible.

Farabi Fakih's study looks at a group of Indonesian economists who were trained at prestigious institutes in the US in the 1950s and 1960s. He shows how limited their influence was on the 'old order' regime, despite their exclusive knowledge. Regardless of the quality of their advice, their training in the US made them suspicious and it was considered impolitic to give them serious positions in government circles. Fakih thereby underlines the point made by Thee Kian Wie, that political ambitions overruled economic ambitions.

Van der Eng explores the reasons why food aid to Indonesia increased quickly after the mid-1960s, a period in which international food aid is less often studied than in the period since the 1970s. At the time, Indonesia was the world's biggest rice importer and also a budding major market for wheat-based food products. This is related to the failure of achieving the desired reorientation of the Indonesian economy during the 1950s, as was also pointed out by Lindblad.[16]

Frankema disentangles the success of Indonesia's 'green revolution', a period in the late 1960s and 1970s when agricultural production received a boost from technological and research-based innovations. He aims at assessing which aspects of it could be replicated in other parts of the world. Several aspects were context-specific and, according to his view, should be attributed to the specific Indonesian historical and ecological conditions.

Finally, Dick takes on a methodological approach by highlighting the important role of statistics in Indonesia's modern economic history as the basis of perceived economic changes. He reviews the evolution of government statistics under different regimes, from its colonial origins to its present form, and discusses the limitations of national accounting. He provides us with a critical note to the use of such statistics by policy-makers and us, historians.

This book addresses many different themes and questions, each of which can (and should) be explored in much more depth than is possible here. It may serve as a survey of scholarly outcomes of the past four decades and as an introduction to new angles of research. We are pleased to present the reader with this nuanced and multivalent collection of essays on a topic well worth studying.

Notes

1. We are grateful to Xu Xiaodong for assisting us in the task of editing the manuscript.
2. Dick et al., *The Emergence of a National Economy*.
3. Ibid., 35–7. See also Knaap, 'Shipping and Trade in Java'.
4. Dick et al., *The Emergence of a National Economy*, 2. This unique character can also clearly be observed in: Lindblad and Thee, *Festschrift for A. Booth, Special Edition of Masyarakat Indonesia* 13: 2 (2013).
5. Van Zanden and Marks, *An Economic History of Indonesia*, 125–32.
6. Booth, *The Indonesian Economy in the Nineteenth and Twentieth Centuries*, 312–8; Lindblad, *Bridges to New Business*, 15–7, 139–47. See also the essays by Colombijn and Purwanto in this volume.
7. Booth, *The Indonesian Economy in the Nineteenth and Twentieth Centuries*, 320.

8. Van Zanden and Marks, *An Economic History of Indonesia*, 6–28; see also De Zwart et al. in this volume.
9. Lindblad, *Bridges to New Business*, 2.
10. See also Pham van Thuy in this volume.
11. Dick et al., *The Emergence of a National Economy*, 143; Booth, *The Indonesian Economy in the Nineteenth and Twentieth Centuries*, 213–4.
12. Lindblad, *Between Dayak and Dutch*; Touwen, *Extremes in the Archipelago.*
13. Booth, *The Indonesian Economy in the Nineteenth and Twentieth Centuries*, 320–3. See also Booth in this volume.
14. Lindblad, 'Economic Aspects of the Dutch Expansion'.
15. Lindblad (1998), *Foreign Investment in Southeast Asia*; Hal Hill, 'Foreign Investment and East Asian Economic Development'; Neilson, 'Value Chains, Neoliberalism and Development Practice'.
16. Lindblad, 'The Political Economy of Realignment in Indonesia', 158.

I

ECONOMIC AND SOCIO-CULTURAL EFFECTS OF TRADE AND INVESTMENT

2

Trade and Growth in the Colonial and Post-colonial Periods

Anne Booth

Introduction

The view that 'history matters' in the study of economic development has recently been stressed in several papers.[1] These authors point out that, in recent years, development agencies have become more aware of the importance of institutions in promoting or retarding economic development. Institutions, whether economic, legal, social or political, are often the product of slow evolutionary change, and any attempt to understand them must involve a close study of their history. It has also been argued that when colonial, or, more recently, national, governments have tried to impose rapid institutional change from above, the results have not infrequently failed, or produced unintended results, at least in part because of a failure to understand the historical underpinnings of the institutions involved.[2]

Thomas Lindblad hardly needs to be persuaded that history matters in the study of economic development. His work has been very much in the spirit of a number of distinguished 'pioneers of development' who were preoccupied with the lessons of history. He has made important contributions to the quantitative study of economic development in Indonesia and elsewhere in Southeast Asia, with particular emphasis on international trade and investment flows. This article will focus on one aspect of Thomas Lindblad's contribution: the impact of the changes in patterns of trade and investment on regional development in Indonesia, and particularly on the economic balance between Java and the rest of the country. I begin with an overview of the development of the Indonesian export economy from 1830 to 1942, and discuss the implications of changing patterns of trade on regional development across the archipelago. I then look at the post-independence evolution of the export economy, from the 1950s to the early twenty-first century, and discuss both changes and continuities compared with the colonial era.

The Evolution of the Export Economy in Indonesia: 1830–1942

The broad facts of export and economic growth in Java from the early nineteenth century to 1900 are well known. In the 1830s, export volume growth was rapid, at around 13.5 per cent per annum, and export prices were also rising, so income terms of trade grew rapidly over the decade.[3] But GDP growth was much slower, partly because the export/GDP ratio was low when export growth accelerated, and partly because the rapid growth of both sugar and coffee cultivation took labour away from the domestic production of other agricultural products. In addition, manufactures such as textiles were displaced by cheaper imports. Van Zanden and Marks estimate that GDP growth over the 1830s was only 2.1 per cent per annum, and 0.7 per cent in per capita terms.[4] Between 1840 and 1873, export volume growth was only 1.5 per cent per annum. GDP growth per capita was negative between 1840 and 1860, and although it was positive from 1860 onwards it was never much above 1 per cent per annum.

The development of the Cultivation System had important implications for both the Indonesian and the Dutch economy. Van Zanden and Van Riel have described the growth of a 'colonial complex' in the Netherlands, in which industries such as shipbuilding, sugar refining and textiles benefited from the growth in trade between the Netherlands and Indonesia.[5] In the case of textiles, the Dutch restricted exports from Britain into Java in order to protect the market for Dutch products.[6] The budget of the Netherlands also benefited from the *batig slot*, which was the term used for the remittances on the government account to the home budget. Van Zanden and Van Riel estimate that, in the 1830s, the remittances already accounted for around 32 per cent of tax income in the Netherlands, rising to 53 per cent by the 1850s, and almost 4 per cent of Dutch GDP.[7] Indeed, Van Zanden and Marks call it the most extreme example of extractive institutions introduced in any colony in the nineteenth century.[8]

By the 1860s pressure was mounting in the Netherlands for a reform of the system. While moral outrage at the exploitation of native labour may have been one reason for this pressure, another was the realization that a system based on coercion was expensive to maintain, especially as, with a growing population, free wage labour was becoming more abundant. The population of Java in 1850 has been estimated at 14 million, compared with only 7.5 million in 1800.[9] Part of this growth was due to higher birth rates, and part to public health measures, especially vaccination against smallpox, which reduced death rates. The growing population in Java was used by the reformers as a reason for a root-and-branch change in the organization of the export economy, based on a greater reliance on markets for both exports and labour.

What was happening outside Java? Lindblad has pointed out that, for much of the nineteenth century, 'the colonial state scarcely existed in the Outer Islands except in the Moluccas'.[10] Dutch officials were mainly based in the port towns, and, in contrast to Java, there was little attempt to collect information on population or production. Trade figures do exist, especially from Singapore, which, after its foundation in 1819, rapidly became the main *entrepôt* for the entire Malay Archipelago. Apart from forest and sea products, the main exports from outside Java consisted of pepper and other spices, coffee and cloves. Rice was an important export from Lombok, and tin from Bangka and Billiton. Lindblad uses the data compiled by Wong to demonstrate the considerable growth in the value of exports from Indonesia to Singapore over the nineteenth century; there was a marked increase in the decades from 1850 to 1870.[11]

In spite of the expectations of the liberal reformers, the immediate impact of the legislation in the early 1870s was disappointing. Export growth in the archipelago did accelerate to around 3 per cent per annum, but total output growth in Java was slower, and in per capita terms GDP grew at only about 1 per cent per annum between 1880 and 1900.[12] But outside Java, and especially in Sumatra, dramatic changes were taking place. The expansion of estate agriculture on the north-east coast of Sumatra has been well documented; to begin with the main crop was tobacco but by the first decade of the twentieth century other crops were grown, especially rubber.[13] By the 1920s, palm oil estates were also being established. Demand for crops such as palm oil and rubber, and tin, grew as a result of rapid industrialization in both Europe and the US. One consequence of this was a major change in the direction of exports. In 1874 over 60 per cent of exports went to the Netherlands; by 1910 the proportion had dropped to 26 per cent.[14]

The century from 1830 to 1930 witnessed a considerable growth in Indonesia's export trade as a percentage of total Asian trade, excluding Japan, from 6.5 per cent in 1830 to 16.5 per cent in 1928.[15] This was a period when Asian trade was also increasing as a proportion of total trade from the tropical world. The figures compiled by Lewis show that total exports from Indonesia were the highest in Asia after India in 1883, and rose more than sevenfold between 1883 and 1929, from $80 million to $582 million.[16] But in per capita terms, exports were lower than in some

Table 2.1: Exports from and imports to Java as a percentage of total exports and imports from/to Indonesia, 1911/15 to 2006/10

	Exports	*Imports*
1911/15	57	70
1916/20	60	71
1921/25	53	71
1926/30	49	64
1931/35	45	67
1936/40	35	65
1956/60	14	68
1961/65	13	78
1966/70	12	75
1971/75	13	70
1976/80	11	76
1981/85[a]	18	70
1986/90	28	78
1991/95	43	82
1996/2000	48	80
2001/05	48	81
2006/10	41	78

Note: a. After 1981, the CBS revised the export data; total exports increased by around 13 per cent but exports from Java increased more than threefold. It is probable that the percentage of exports from Java between 1950 and 1980 was understated.

Sources: Until 1936/40: Lindblad (1992: 21). From 1956/60, *Statistical Pocketbook of Indonesia*, various issues between 1959 and 1968/69; *Statistical Yearbook of Indonesia*, various issues from 1975; and *Indikator Ekonomi*, various issues until April 2012.

other colonial territories, especially British Malaya. Two forces drove the growth in agricultural export revenues in Indonesia from the 1880s onwards: one was the introduction of new crops on land which had not previously been used for export agriculture, especially outside Java. The second was the growth of the smallholder producer. A further important development was the increase in non-agricultural exports from the mining sector.

The increase in exports from outside Java continued until the end of the 1930s. By the second decade of the twentieth century, the rise of estate agriculture and mining, especially in Sumatra, meant that over 40 per cent of all exports originated from outside Java.[17] While the commodity terms of trade began to decline after 1913, the income terms of trade for Indonesia continued to improve until 1928, and although they declined in the early 1930s, they recovered after 1934.[18] Export volume also recovered after 1934, especially outside Java, and, by the latter part of the 1930s, the proportion of exports originating from outside Java had increased to 65 per cent (Table 2.1). Part of the growth was the result of increased smallholder production; by 1940 Creutzberg estimated that smallholder exports accounted for almost 40 per cent of total agricultural exports by value, compared with little more than 10 per cent in 1895.[19]

The rise of the smallholder producer was not uniform by crop. Rubber, which had been introduced on large estates at the end of the nineteenth century, began to be cultivated by smallholders in the second decade of the twentieth century, and by 1936/40, smallholders accounted for over 40 per cent of total production.[20] By 1936/40, smallholders accounted for 87 per cent of coffee production, 68.5 per cent of tobacco production and almost 16 per cent of tea production. Production of sugar and palm oil remained almost entirely dominated by estates until 1940, while crops such as pepper and copra were entirely produced by smallholders. In addition to agricultural exports, whether estate or smallholder, production of tin and petroleum products also grew rapidly after 1900, and by the end of the 1930s accounted for around 27 per cent of all exports by revenue.

Although the impact of these changes in the export economy was to increase the share of the Outer Islands in total exports, much of the export growth was concentrated in only a few regions, while others remained largely insulated from the international economy. Touwen suggests that the various regions outside Java could be divided into four groups.[21] One group, where both European companies and indigenous smallholders were active in export production, comprised East Sumatra,

Table 2.2: Per capita Outer Islands exports and imports by region, 1926/30 (guilders per capita)

Region	*Only Foreign*		*Including Regional*	
	Exports	*Imports*	*Exports*	*Imports*
Belitung	441	101	458	176
Bangka	81	49	308	93
East Sumatra	150	65	155	76
S/E Kalimantan	97	27	113	45
Palembang	74	42	99	55
Riau	86	50	92	54
Jambi	88	36	91	45
Lampung	51	5	80	45
West Kalimantan	55	27	61	36
Bengkulu	17	9	53	27
Outer Islands	40	n/a	52	26

Source: Touwen (2001: 355–6).

Southeast Kalimantan and Palembang; over the four decades from 1900 to 1940 these three regions accounted for almost 63 per cent of all foreign exports from outside Java. A second group comprised Riau, Bangka and Belitung; in these three regions most of the exports came from mining companies run by Dutch and other companies. They accounted for 11.4 per cent of total exports. A third group consisted of regions where only smallholder exports were important; this group included North and South Sulawesi, West Kalimantan, West Sumatra, Aceh and Jambi. Together they accounted for around 21 per cent of export value. The final group, comprising Lampung, Bali, Lombok, Tapanuli, Ambon, Bengkulu, Ternate, Timor and New Guinea accounted for only 5 per cent of all exports over 1900–40.[22]

Touwen's estimates also show how much variation existed in exports and imports per capita across the regions outside Java. In 1926/30, foreign (excluding regional) exports amounted to 441 guilders per capita in Belitung and 150 guilders in East Sumatra, compared with an average for all regions outside Java of only 40 guilders per capita (Table 2.2). The imbalance between exports and imports was particularly marked in both these regions, and in Southeast Kalimantan. Although the addition of inter-regional trade reduced the imbalances somewhat, Touwen's estimates show clearly that, in the ten regions where total exports per capita

Table 2.3: Outer Island share in population and government expenditures, 1930

Region	*% Share of Outer Islands Total*		*Government Expenditure (Guilders/Person)*
	Population	*Government Expenditure*	
Belitung	0.4	0.6	12
Bangka	1.1	1.7	13
Jambi	1.3	2.3	14
Riau	1.6	2.2	11
Bengkulu	1.7	2.0	9
Lampung	1.9	2.3	10
West Kalimantan	4.2	4.3	8
Palembang	5.8	9.6	14
S/E Kalimantan	7.2	7.6	9
East Sumatra	8.8	14.9	14
	As % of Indonesian Total		
Ten Provinces	10.6	14.1	11
Outer Islands	31.2	29.7	8
Java	68.8	70.2	9

Sources: Touwen (2001: 392); Boomgaard and Gooszen (1991: tables 16–18).

exceeded 50 guilders, exports were often more than double imports (Table 2.2). It should also be noted that, using the 1930 census data, these ten provinces accounted for only 34 per cent of the total population outside Java, although 83 per cent of the Chinese population outside Java were located in these provinces. By the 1920s, a minority of the total population outside Java was responsible for much of the export production (Table 2.3).

How much of the growth in export production outside Java was the result of deliberate government policies and how much a response on the part of private companies and individuals to the opportunities generated by growing international markets for a range of agricultural and mineral products? Large estate and mining companies no doubt viewed themselves as responding to market opportunities, but at the same time they used their often considerable influence with both the home and the colonial governments to change policies to their advantage. This was true of land policies and also taxation policies, although it should be noted that, in contrast to British Malaya, both corporations and individuals were subject to income taxation. It has been argued that neither in Indonesia nor

British Malaya did the government provide much support to the smallholder cultivators; indeed, in both colonies much of the production took place in areas which were remote from direct government control.[23] There is evidence that 'ethically minded' officials in the decades after 1900 did appreciate the dynamism of smallholder export producers outside Java, and some argued for greater spending on infrastructure, credit and the Agricultural Extension Service. But assistance to these cultivators was hampered by the government focus on improving food production in densely settled Java. Also, the sheer size of the regions outside Java and the scarcity of officials made it difficult for the government to do very much.[24]

It can be argued that cultivators outside Java coped very well on their own without direct government aid. One example concerns land tenure. The colonial legal system provided large estates with long leases, but small farmers relied on traditional land tenure systems which seem to have functioned quite well. It is unlikely that families would have invested their labour and cash in the back-breaking work of clearing jungle land and planting tree crops if they had not been reasonably confident that the land and the trees would be theirs to cultivate as they wished, and to pass on to their heirs. Farmers who planted tree crops which took several years to mature (seven years in the case of rubber) would not have invested their time and money had they expected the land to be seized before the trees even reached maturity. In Java, the colonial government had precise knowledge about planted area of both food and non-food crops. They calculated a land tax for all agricultural land, and farmers used the land tax document as proof of ownership. But, with the exception of Bali and Lombok, the authorities had very little data on land under smallholder cultivation outside Java. A registration of land under smallholder rubber in 1939 came up with a figure of 1.3 million hectares, which was far higher than previous estimates, but still probably lower than the actual figure.[25] In many regions, even less was known about land under other crops, including food crops.

If the approach of the Dutch government to the growth of smallholder producers was mainly one of benign neglect until the early 1930s, policies became more hostile to export producers after the onset of the global slump. World prices of most commodities fell sharply, and the decision of the Dutch government to stay on the gold standard meant that producers did not even have the assistance afforded to export producers in those British and American colonies where the currency depreciated. The decision to keep the guilder on gold did mean that imports became cheaper, especially from Japan where the yen was sharply devalued. But the selective controls imposed from 1934 onwards had the effect of curbing Japanese imports, although Indonesia remained an important market for Japanese textiles until 1940.

Export trade was subject to increased regulation, as the Dutch government joined various international schemes to restrict the output of tropical crops.[26] Quotas were imposed on estate companies, but smallholder output was far more difficult to control. A special export tax on native rubber was imposed in 1934; by 1936 it amounted to almost 19 per cent of the total tax revenue. The incidence of this tax fell almost entirely on domestic producers and probably had some impact on reducing output but it was deeply unpopular. Government claims that the revenues would be used to assist producers through public works were not believed, and by 1936 the tax had been rescinded. In this year the guilder was also devalued. Export revenues in guilders almost doubled between 1935 and 1937, although they fell again in 1938 and 1939. Over the 1930s the balance on commodity trade fell compared with the previous decade, although it remained positive, as did the current account balance.

The growth in smallholder export production undoubtedly led to some improvement in incomes and living standards for many Indonesians outside Java in the last four decades of colonial rule. People had some cash income to spend on both food and non-food items; some even managed to buy motor vehicles, or go on the *hajj*. In addition, large estates and mines provided incomes to large numbers of indigenous workers as well as to Chinese. Even if working conditions were harsh, many Javanese who owned little agricultural land benefited from employment on sugar estates, and tens of thousands moved to Sumatra in search of incomes. But in spite of the opportunities afforded by the growth in export production, living standards for the great majority of Indonesians remained low until 1942, and almost certainly below the Philippines, British Malaya and Thailand.[27]

Outside Java, poor infrastructure, illiteracy, high infant and child mortality and inadequate nutrition still characterized populations—even in those regions where exports per capita were much higher than the national average, such as Southeast Kalimantan, Northeast Sumatra, Palembang, Riau and Jambi. Elsewhere, living standards were probably worse, although lack of data make precise estimates impossible. The central government did increase expenditures outside Java; Touwen's estimates show that, by 1929/30, around 30 per cent of total expenditures which could be attributed to regions took place outside Java, which was not much lower than the population share. In the ten regions with the highest exports per capita, government expenditures per capita were higher than in Java and higher than the national average (Table 2.3). But many in the exporting regions must have felt that they were not receiving back enough to compensate them for their contribution to the national budget. The highly centralized fiscal system meant that there was little scope for regional governments to provide infrastructure or services. These legacies were bequeathed to an independent Indonesia, and were to cause major problems in the 1950s and 1960s.

The Transition to Independence: Challenges, Achievements and Failures

The 1940s were a bad decade for Indonesia, and for much of the rest of East and Southeast Asia. In spite of being welcomed as liberators by many Indonesians in 1942, the Japanese proved no more capable of ruling in the interests of the indigenous population than the Dutch. As transport links, both within Indonesia and with other parts of the region, deteriorated, rice supplies were badly affected, and the Japanese army took increasing amounts from farmers to feed their troops. By 1944 famine conditions prevailed in some parts of Java, and mortality increased sharply. The surrender of the Japanese in 1945 was swiftly followed by the declaration of independence on 17 August 1945, a declaration which the Dutch refused to recognize. Four more years of struggle took place before the Dutch finally transferred sovereignty, under circumstances which were hardly favourable to the infant republic.[28]

In 1949, total GDP was only 69 per cent of the level reached in 1941.[29] But there was quite rapid growth after 1949, at least until 1957, when total GDP had returned to the level of 1941. But population also grew rapidly, at around 2 per cent annually, and by 1960 per capita GDP was still below pre-war levels. Export growth was also quite rapid; although it is often argued that Indonesia became 'inward-looking' after 1949, in fact the index of export volume was 30 per cent higher in 1957 than it had been in 1940.[30] Over almost three decades, from 1938 to 1966, export volume grew by 47 per cent while GDP grew by only 30 per cent. Paauw argued that the growth in export volume was mainly the result of growth in oil exports, which, in turn, was the result of the so-called let-alone contracts that had been negotiated by the Dutch with the oil companies in the late 1940s.[31] These contracts allowed the companies to repair infrastructure damaged by the Japanese in return for some freedom in the disposition of foreign exchange earnings.[32] They were unpopular with most nationalists but were honoured after 1949 until they expired.

While it is certainly true that oil output did grow after 1950, rubber and tin exports also increased, although, in the case of tin, there was a sharp decline in export volume after 1957.[33] The rubber story illustrates both the resilience of the export sector and also the problems it faced after 1949. By the late 1930s, smallholder production accounted for almost half of total production. In the years from 1954 to 1960, the proportion rose to 65 per cent. Total rubber exports in 1954–56 reached almost 700 million metric tons, compared to just over 400 million tons in 1938–40. While both estates and smallholders received a boost from the high prices in the early 1950s, it was the smallholders who were better able to weather the price falls after the temporary boom was over. They were also far less vulnerable to the political problems of the late 1950s, which resulted in the nationalization of the Dutch estates and labour difficulties for others.

The years after 1949 also saw some progress in reforming the tax system. The revenue system developed by the Dutch was more diversified than that prevailing in other parts of Asia; trade taxes accounted for only 16 per cent of total revenues and both corporate and personal income taxes were assessed. The Natsir government brought in a general sales tax, which, in principle, should have further diversified the revenue system. But the fall in per capita GDP, together with administrative problems caused by the departure of Dutch officials, meant that real per capita revenues were considerably below 1938 levels by 1954.[34] By 1954, the impact of the Korean War boom on export revenues and export taxes had declined, but trade taxes were still a higher percentage of total government revenues than in the 1930s. The increasingly hostile policy to foreign enterprises led to the departure of several large multinationals, even before the wholesale nationalization of Dutch enterprises in the late 1950s, which further affected the revenue base. By the end of the decade, government deficits were increasing and were funded by borrowing from the central bank, which fuelled inflation, leading to hyperinflation by the mid-1960s.

Several studies of economic policy-making in the 1950s have stressed that the newly independent government inherited a highly restrictive set of regulations from the Dutch era, which affected not just foreign trade but other aspects of the economy as well.[35] But in the early post-independence era, there were some attempts at liberalization, at least in part motivated by a desire to get rid of regulations which were considered to favour Dutch enterprises. Nor were attitudes to foreign investment and foreign enterprises uniformly hostile. In a statement to parliament in 1950, Natsir stressed that foreign expertise and capital would still be needed in some sectors of the economy for many years to come. It is also untrue that most private business people were Chinese, with well-connected Indonesians functioning only as sources of access to import licences and bank loans. As the 1950s progressed, Lindblad has argued that a number of businesses owned and managed by Sumatrans and Javanese did emerge, both in manufacturing and in trade.[36] Some did not survive the turbulence of the 1960s, although at least one quarter of the large indigenous businesses identified in the early 1990s had their origins in the Sukarno era, or even earlier.

There was also progress in the provision of education and health care. The 1961 population census showed that the percentage of the population claiming to be literate was much higher for both males and females in the under-25 age group than for older Indonesians.[37] This suggests that, especially after 1950, access to at least primary education did increase in rural as well as urban areas. Even if central or provincial funds were restricted, many villages took matters into their own hands, and built schools, and even hired teachers, using locally generated funds. Access to post-primary education was far more difficult for many young people, especially in rural areas, while university education was still available only to a tiny proportion, many of them the children of civil servants.[38]

To set against these achievements there were major problems which successive governments after 1950 could not tackle, let alone solve. Much infrastructure, both in Java and elsewhere, had deteriorated and few funds were available for rehabilitation. Marks has shown that temporal fluctuations in rice prices increased sharply after 1950, compared with the years from 1920–40.[39] He argues that markets became more fragmented as transport systems deteriorated, which would have had a serious impact on incomes and living standards in more remote regions. After 1957 export volume also fell and inflation accelerated. In several of the major producing regions outside Java, illegal trade grew, much of it the result of deliberate mis-invoicing of legal trade.[40] Indeed, Pitt argues that, by the mid-1960s, so much trade was conducted illegally that, for many exporters outside Java, the trade regime was not too different from that which would have prevailed under a more open regime, with market-determined exchange rates.

Even if that was the case, the export-producing provinces still had legitimate grievances from the 1950s onwards. In 1956/60 the percentage of exports from Java had fallen to only 14 per cent, compared with 35 per cent in the late 1930s (Table 2.1). The main reason for this decline was the demise of sugar exports: sugar production was only around 40 per cent of the average for 1938–40 by the mid-1950s and almost all went into the domestic market. At the same time, the proportion of imports going into ports in Java grew. While some of these imports would have been shipped out again to smaller ports outside Java, many stayed in Java. This was because both government and private demand for imports of capital and consumption goods was higher in Java. In addition, it is probable that government expenditures became more skewed towards Java, although this is more difficult to quantify.

By the mid-1950s there were constant complaints by the exporting regions that, although they were the main generators of the nation's wealth, they were neglected when decisions were made on its expenditure.[41] The whole issue of regional finance was subjected to detailed investigation in the mid-1950s by a committee headed by M. Nasroen, a senior civil servant in the Department of the Interior, and composed of fiscal experts from various government agencies. The committee's report proposed a complex system which would fund local governments through two streams: one would be exclusively local and the other composed of a share of central government revenues from income, company and wages taxes, stamp taxes, property taxes, and customs and excise duties.[42]

The Nasroen proposals were criticized by Paauw on the grounds that they neither simplified the tax structure nor attacked the problem of an extremely complex administrative system.[43] He pointed out that most of the taxes assigned to local governments were never going to yield much revenue. This was a criticism which was to recur again in most assessments of regional finance in Indonesia up to the present day. In addition, he argued that there were some taxes which could have yielded substantial revenues to local governments, but governments lacked the incentives to assess them effectively, as the revenues had to be sent on to Jakarta. Furthermore, the formulae suggested for distributing central revenues did not appear to be based on either the needs or the capacity of the local governments. In spite of these criticisms, many of the findings of this committee were incorporated in Law No. 32 of 1956, concerning financial relations between the centre and the autonomous regions. This law did make some important concessions to the regions in that it allowed the proceeds of both income taxes and foreign trade taxes to be shared between provinces where the tax revenues originated and the centre, but, as Legge pointed out, implementation of this law was slow.[44] In particular, little progress was made in laying down rules for the sharing of the most important taxes between the centre and the regions.

The New Order and After

The economic technocrats appointed by Suharto after he took effective power in 1966 faced huge challenges. The first priority was to reduce inflation, through reducing the budget deficit. It proved possible to do this without massive cuts in expenditures, which had already fallen to below 10 per cent of GDP in 1966. Government revenues increased partly because of increased aid flows and partly because an acceleration in growth after 1968 increased tax revenues. The acceleration in growth was, in part, due to improved export performance; between 1966 and 1972, export volume more than doubled. The commodity terms of trade did not greatly improve; it was only after global oil prices increased in 1973 that there was a substantial increase. The main reason for the growth in export volume until 1972 was the successful reform of the complex exchange rate system which had evolved since the 1950s. By 1970, the exchange rate was unified under a single rate determined by market forces.[45]

In the latter part of the 1960s and early 1970s, there was little change in the percentage of total exports being shipped from Java ports. With the increase in the price of oil after 1973, and the growth in crude oil production, the proportion of exports coming from Java fell to only 11 per cent in the latter part of the 1970s (Table 2.1). Almost half of exports by value were originating from one port in Riau. Suharto had spent part of his army career fighting against rebels in South Sulawesi, and was sensitive to the development needs of regions outside Java. He used the oil revenues to fund a series of development grants to provincial and district levels of government, collectively known as *Inpres* grants. They were mainly used for the rehabilitation and extension of infrastructure, and for building schools and health clinics, both in Java and in many parts of the Outer Islands.[46] Key agricultural inputs such as fertilizer were heavily subsidized; cheap fertilizer, improved irrigation and the availability of new rice varieties together led to a substantial increase in rice output and rice consumption in the latter part of the 1970s and into the 1980s.[47]

Even after oil and gas prices started to fall in the early 1980s, over 80 per cent of exports were being exported from outside Java. Four provinces accounted for a high proportion of total exports: Aceh, Riau, East Kalimantan and Irian Jaya. By the early 1980s all these provinces experienced significant resource drains. Just how significant these drains had become was clear after regional income accounts began to be published in the 1980s. In all four provinces, the export surplus as a proportion of GDP was at least 50 per cent on average in the years from 1983 to 1987 (Table 2.4). Changes did occur through the 1990s, and into the 2000s, and by 2003–07, the export surplus as a ratio of GDP had fallen quite markedly in three of the four provinces. The reasons varied by province. In Aceh, the sharp rise in imports relative to exports after 2004 was the result of the influx in aid funds in the wake of the tsunami. In Riau the decline could be partly due to the decentralization legislation, although, even in the 1990s, the surplus was falling as a result of the slowdown in oil production. In Irian Jaya (now Papua and West Papua) the decline in the export surplus in the 1990s was the result of higher consumption and investment expenditures within the province. Again, the decentralization measures which came into force in 2001 do not seem to have had a dramatic effect: the surplus in 2003–07 was, in fact, higher than in the 1990s. In East Kalimantan, where, by the early 2000s, the value of exports was far higher than in any other province outside Java, the export surplus was higher than in the 1980s.

Table 2.4: Export surplus as a percentage of GDP: Aceh, Riau, East Kalimantan, Papua/West Papua and Indonesia: 1983/87, 1992/96 and 2003/07

Region	*1983/87*	*1992/96*	*2003/07*
Aceh	67.7	46.4	4.3
Riau	65.4	49.7	36.8
East Kalimantan	64.4	43.6	65.6
Papua/West Papua	54.3	11.7	15.6
Indonesia	1.2	0.9	5.1

Sources: CBS (1994, 1995, 1997b, 2008).

The issue of resource drains from the major export-producing regions outside Java needs to be reviewed in the context of another important development which began in the latter part of the 1980s—with the increase in Java's share of total exports by value (Table 2.1). In the decade from 1996 to 2005, mainly as a result of the growth in manufactured exports, Java accounted for close to half of total exports (Table 2.1).[48] While this percentage could be overstated, to the extent that exports from outside Java have been re-exported through Java ports, there can be little doubt that, by the early 2000s, exports from Java were a much higher proportion of the total than at any time since the 1920s. There was a decline after 2005, mainly due to the growth in exports of coal and palm oil; both these and other commodities also benefited from some increase in prices, while manufactured exports struggled against increasing competition, especially from China. But on balance it seems unlikely that, in the immediate future, there will be a return to the extreme imbalance in export production by region which characterized the years from the 1950s to the 1980s.

Does this mean that the problem of imbalance between per capita GDP on the one hand and levels of poverty and living standards on the other will also become less serious in the future? In 1993, when the Central Bureau of Statistics (CBS) first began to publish the headcount measure of poverty for each province, there was a negative correlation between per capita GDP and poverty but the correlation coefficient was quite low (−0.342). The main outlier was the province then known as Irian Jaya, where the per capita GDP was the fifth highest in the country (after East Kalimantan, Riau, Aceh and the DKI) but where the headcount measure of poverty was almost twice the national average, and higher than in any other province except East Timor and West Kalimantan. In Aceh, Riau and East Kalimantan, the headcount measure of poverty was around the national average in 1993. Among the high-income provinces, only in the DKI was the headcount measure markedly lower than the national average.[49]

By 2009, when the decentralization measures had been in force for several years, the negative correlation between the headcount measure of poverty and per capita GDP had increased somewhat (−0.433). But the problem of poverty in what were now two provinces (Papua and West Papua) had not gone away. These two provinces were ranked fifth and sixth in terms of per capita GDP in 2009, after East Kalimantan, DKI, Riau and Riau Islands. But the headcount measure of poverty in 2009 in these two provinces was higher than in any other province.[50] These high levels of poverty persisted in spite of the evidence that the drain from Irian Jaya and then from Papua and Papua Barat had fallen since the 1990s (Table 2.4). To the extent that, by the early 2000s, a higher proportion of provincial GDP was remaining in the two provinces, this did not appear to have had a dramatic impact on poverty levels.

Conclusions

Lindblad and Touwen have shown that, by the last decade of Dutch rule in Indonesia, the proportion of exports accruing from Java had fallen to around 35 per cent, and that the majority of exports from the 'Outer Islands' were derived from a relatively small number of regions outside Java. In the early post-independence years, mainly as a result of the collapse in sugar exports, the proportion of total exports from Java fell even further. Yet most imports were still coming in to Indonesia through ports in Java, and although some would have been re-exported, most imports of both consumption and capital goods stayed in Java. This gave rise to demands for a different approach to the sharing of government revenues, but the recommendations put forward over the 1950s were never implemented.

During the first two decades of the Suharto era, most export revenues were derived from a small number of commodities dominated by oil and gas. The geographic concentration of exports became even more extreme. Only with the fall in oil and gas prices on world markets in the 1980s and the growth in manufactured exports did the proportions change. Throughout the 1990s, there was a sharp increase in the share of Java in total exports. The evidence also shows that there was some decline in the resource drain in three of the four provinces outside Java where the ratio of exports to regional GDP was extremely high. But problems of poverty persisted, especially in what was the province of Irian Jaya, which became the provinces of Papua and Papua Barat after Suharto left office. Here, the headcount measure of poverty has remained high. It appears that, so far, the decentralization measures implemented after 2001 have made little difference to living standards for the majority of the population in these two provinces.

Primary Sources

Central Bureau of Statistics (CBS).

Notes

1. See e.g. Woolcock et al., 'How and Why Does History Matter for Development Policy?'
2. Easterly, 'Institutions: Top down or Bottom up?'
3. Booth, *The Indonesian Economy in the Nineteenth and Twentieth Centuries*, Table 2.1.

4. Van Zanden and Marks, *An Economic History of Indonesa*, Table 4.1.
5. Van Zanden and Van Riel, *The Strictures of Inheritance*, 143.
6. Booth, *The Indonesian Economy in the Nineteenth and Twentieth Centuries*, 138.
7. Van Zanden and Van Riel, *The Strictures of Inheritance*, Table 5.1.
8. Van Zanden and Marks, *An Economic History of Indonesia*, 72.
9. Boomgaard and Gooszen, *Changing Economy in Indonesia*, vol. 11, 82.
10. Lindblad, 'The Outer Islands in the Nineteenth Century', 84. The VOC did control the port of Makassar in South Sulawesi to safeguard the transport of spices to Europe.
11. Wong Lin Ken, *The Trade of Singapore.*
12. Van Zanden and Marks, *An Economic History of Indonesia*, Table 4.1.
13. Thee Kian Wie, 'The Development of Sumatra', 136–41.
14. Booth, *The Indonesian Economy in the Nineteenth and Twentieth Centuries*, Table 5.4.
15. Ibid., 205.
16. Lewis, *Aspects of Tropical Trade*, 48.
17. Lindblad, 'Regional Patterns in the Foreign Trade of Java, 1911–1940', 21.
18. Booth, *The Indonesian Economy in the Nineteenth and Twentieth Centuries*, Table 2.1.
19. Creutzberg, *Indonesia's Export Crops*, 142.
20. Ibid., 94.
21. Touwen, *Extremes in the Archipelago*, 64.
22. Ibid., 358.
23. Barlow and Drabble, 'Government and the Emerging Rubber Industries', 197.
24. Touwen, *Extremes in the Archipelago*, 279–81.
25. Thee, 'The development of Sumatra, 1820–1940', 144.
26. Van Gelderen, *The Recent Development of Economic Foreign Policy.*
27. Booth, 'Measuring Living Standards in Different Colonial Systems'.
28. Lindblad, *Bridges to New Business*, 178.
29. Van der Eng, 'Indonesia's Growth Performance in the Twentieth Century', 172–3.
30. Rosendale, 'The Indonesian Terms of Trade, 1950–1973', 73.
31. Pauw, *Financing Economic Development*, 570–1.
32. Hunter, 'The Indonesian Oil Industry'.
33. Rosendale, 'The Indonesian Terms of Trade, 1950–1973', 74.
34. Booth, 'Colonial Revenue Policies', 58–9.
35. Pitt, 'Indonesia', 11; Booth, *The Indonesian Economy in the Nineteenth and Twentieth Centuries*, 156–7.
36. Lindblad, 'Economic Growth and Decolonisation', 107.
37. Booth, 'Government and Welfare', 71.
38. Ibid., 64–5.

39. Marks, 'The Lost Decades', 87.
40. Pitt, 'Indonesia', 76.
41. Feith, *The Decline of Constitutional Democracy*, 487–8.
42. Paauw, *Financing Economic Development*, Appendix D; Legge, *Central Authority and Regional Autonomy*, 189–200.
43. Paauw, *Financing Economic Development*, 411.
44. Legge, *Central Authority and Regional Autonomy*, 193.
45. Pitt, 'Indonesia', 91–2.
46. De Wit, 'The Kabupaten Programme'.
47. Mears, 'Rice and Food Self-Sufficiency', 126.
48. Hill, *The Indonesian Economy since 1966*, 114–6.
49. CBS, *Produk Domestik Regional Bruto Propinsi-Propinsi di Indonesia menurut Penggunan 1993–96*, 572.
50. CBS, *Statistical Yearbook of Indonesia 2009*, 182. The headcount measure of poverty for Papua was 37.5 per cent and that for Papua Barat was 35.7 per cent. The national figure was 14.2 per cent.

3

Structural Change and 'Turning Points': The Southeast Asian Experience

*Hal Hill**

Introduction

It is a well-established empirical proposition that major structural changes occur during, and are driven by, the process of socio-economic development. The most important of these changes relates to the changing structure of the economy—the shift of economic activity out of the agricultural sector and into the industrial and service sectors. This process occurs in one form or another in practically every economy that has experienced rising per capita income. In turn, it has led to the identification of 'turning points' in the long sweep of economic development. Three widely cited points have been those where industrial sector output exceeds that of agriculture, where industrial employment exceeds that in agriculture, and where agricultural output and employment begin to decline in absolute terms. Moreover, consistent with this theory, it has also been

*I am most grateful to Michael Cabalfin for his able research assistance in the preparation of this chapter.

established empirically that the faster the rate of economic growth, the faster is this process of inter-sectoral relocation of productive resources. Over time, the differences in returns to factors between the sectors begin to narrow, as mechanization and technological progress spread beyond the modern industrial and service sectors to agriculture, and as production and factor markets become more integrated.

There is general agreement on the fundamental drivers of this process, even if their relative importance may vary over time and across countries. On the demand side, there are the relative price effects, driven mainly by Engel's Law, namely that the percentage of household expenditure devoted to food declines as incomes rise. On the supply side, differential rates of technological progress across sectors, and changes in relative factor endowments of land, physical capital and human capital are identified as the major factors.

The bare bones of this theorizing have been extended in several directions, both empirical and theoretical. Models of economic development incorporating provision for international factor mobility, and its interaction with the process of structural change, have been developed. The labour market and demographic dimensions have been explored, particularly related to the famous Lewis model of surplus labour.[1] These transitions are of course interrelated. Central to the transfer of resources from agriculture to industry and services is the process of rising productivity and living standards. That is, the structural change is partly driven by the transformations in the labour market, as the phase of 'unlimited labour' is completed, and economic growth then begins to push up real wages. Demographic variables are an important element of the supply side of this conceptual framework, with more rapid fertility declines hastening the labour market adjustment. The policy framework is particularly relevant in this phase of development, as investments in human capital, including advanced research and development (R&D), determine the speed of adjustment into high value-added activities.

Thus there is a complex set of interactions involving the rate of economic growth, sectoral size and natural resource endowments, demographic transitions, labour market adjustments and a wide array of policy interventions. The purpose of this chapter, in honour of our good friend and colleague Thomas Lindblad, is to examine these various patterns in the Southeast Asian economies, as a means of deepening our understanding of the region's development dynamics and its drivers.

* * *

In the next section we examine the process of structural change in Southeast Asia between the three main sectors: agriculture, industry and services, including trends in relative productivities across these sectors. The following section provides a narrative on some additional dimensions of structural change, focusing on the labour market and demographic variables. The final section extends the discussion and sums up.

Several caveats should be mentioned at the outset. First, structural change is a long-term process stretching over decades. Its study therefore requires long-term data series. This poses an immediate constraint for our study, as reliable, consistently measured national accounts and labour force data on a long-term basis are not available for all these economies. Modern national accounts of the four transitional economies of mainland Southeast Asia commence around 1990. Labour force data are also problematic. For consistency, we draw on the World Bank's World Development Indicators database and the analysis commences at 1980, or as early as is feasible. Country sources, of course, provide longer series, although they are not necessarily consistent for inter-country comparisons. This study is therefore confined to the six large economies—Indonesia, Malaysia, the Philippines, Singapore, Thailand and Vietnam, recognizing also that the Vietnamese data are reliable only from about 1990.

Second, owing to the length constraint, this chapter focuses primarily on the sectoral dimensions of structural change, together with a narrative overview of labour market and demographic adjustments. The analysis could be extended in various directions. One is to investigate the changing comparative advantage associated with these structural changes, particularly the transition from labour-intensive production and trade patterns to those that are skill- and capital-intensive. Another approach would be to focus on intra-sectoral changes, such as that from hand-powered to mechanized technologies within the main sectors.[2]

Related to this point, the analysis is confined to the three main sectors: agriculture, industry and services. Following convention, industry includes mining, manufacturing, construction and utilities. For the two resource-rich economies in the group, Indonesia and Malaysia, the interpretation of the shift from agriculture to industry has to accommodate the fact that the dynamics of the four industrial sub-sectors vary. Two occurrences are of particular significance. One is a mining boom, of the sort that occurred in the 1970s and again in the past decade. This inflates the share of industry both through the immediate price effects [the gross domestic product (GDP) sector shares below are measured at current prices] and as these higher prices elicit a supply response. The real exchange-rate effects of these booms also have implications for the shares of the tradable goods sectors (that is, agriculture and manufacturing). The other event is the switch from import-substituting to export-oriented manufacturing, which has implications for both the trajectory and the labour intensity of this sector, and therefore for industry as a whole. Owing to this sector's size and dynamism, some analyses of structural change identify manufacturing separately. This chapter does not, again owing to space constraints.

Third, although we discuss the effects of various policy interventions on the process of structural change, we eschew the broader issue of major regime change and longer-term growth trajectories.[3] Four of the economies implemented fundamental economic reforms that reversed economic decline, sometimes decades in duration, and led to strong economic growth. These 'policy' turning points, which are arguably the most important of all, occurred in Indonesia in the mid-1960s, and Vietnam (and subsequently its two small neighbours) in the second half of the 1980s. The effects of these turning points are analysed only insofar as the accelerated economic growth that resulted from them also generated rapid structural change. In addition, all of the economies have become more internationally oriented over time. This could also be said to constitute a 'turning point', particularly when it is pronounced and part of an overall reform programme. As we will argue below, it too has shaped the process of structural change.

Structural Change: A Sectoral Perspective

Output Shares

Figure 3.1 shows the sectoral shares of GDP for the six Southeast Asian economies, since 1970 for Indonesia, Malaysia, the Philippines, Singapore and Thailand, and 1985 for Vietnam. We first provide a short description of patterns, followed by an interpretation of these outcomes.

Indonesia experienced very rapid structural change in the 1970s. The share of agriculture fell by more than half, in spite of rapid growth, while that of industry more than doubled, driven mainly by manufacturing catch-up and the oil boom of that decade. This was the period of greatest structural change in the country's modern economic history. Thereafter, agriculture continued to decline, but at a much slower rate, and with two noticeable reversals, during the Asian financial crisis, 1997–99, and the period of buoyant commodity prices from 2005. The industry share

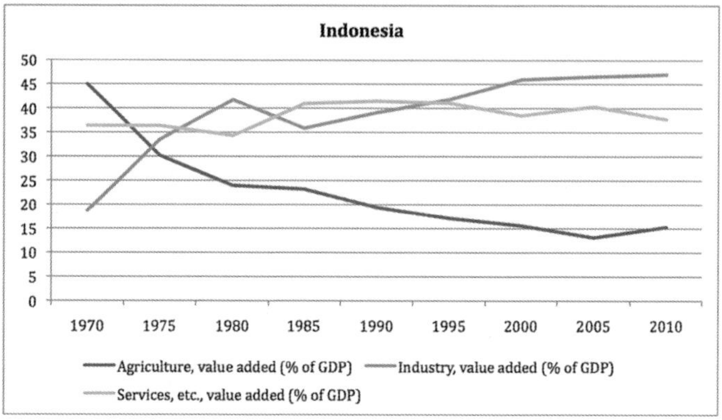

Source: WDI.

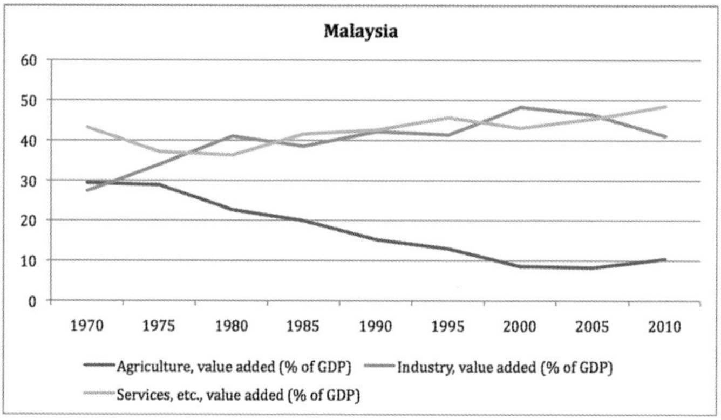

Source: WDI.

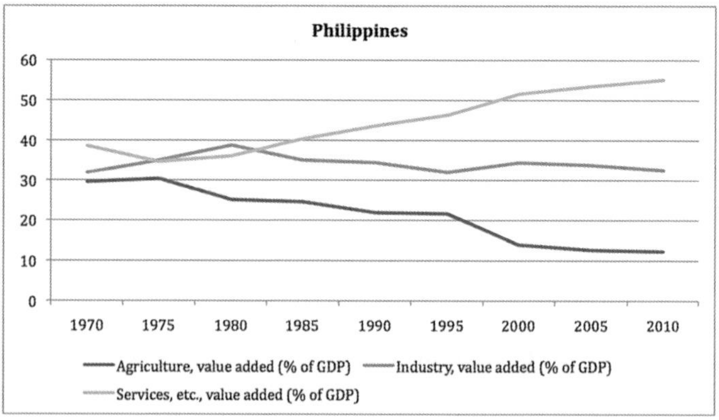

Source: WDI.

Figure 3.1: Sector shares of GDP for Indonesia, Malaysia, Philippines, Singapore, Thailand and Vietnam, 1970–2010 (percentages)

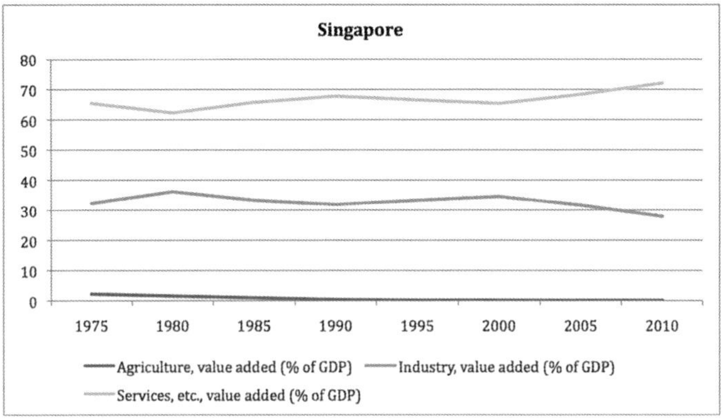

Source: WDI.

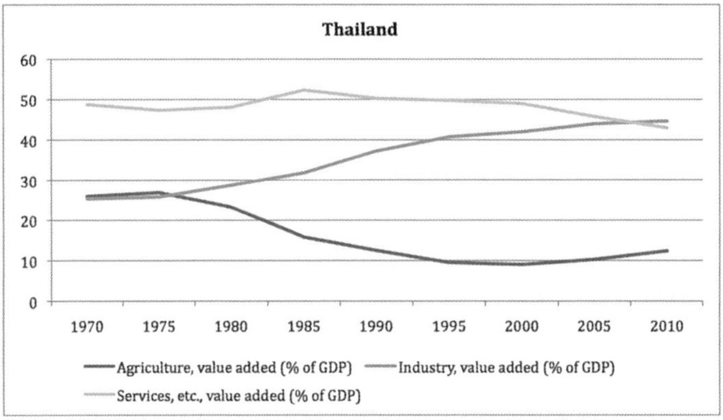

Source: WDI.

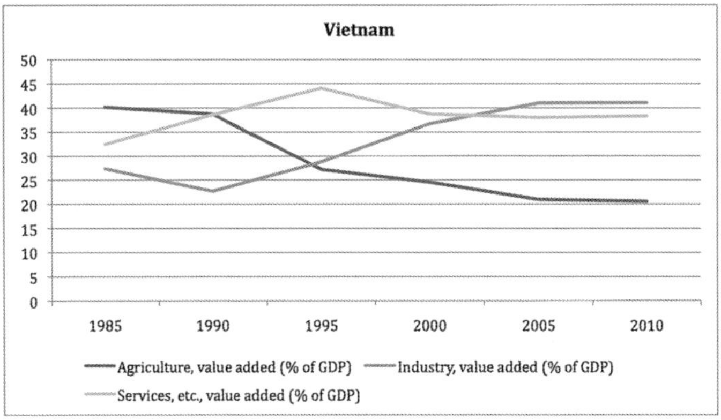

Source: WDI.

Figure 3.1: *continued*

fell sharply in the early 1980s, by about five percentage points, as energy prices declined. Thereafter, it rose steadily, driven initially by export-oriented industrialization, and subsequently by higher energy and mineral prices. Its share has exceeded 40 per cent since the early 1990s, and is trending towards 50 per cent. The services share has been remarkably steady since 1970, at close to 40 per cent throughout the period. In terms of turning points, the industry share has exceeded agriculture from 1973 onwards, as has services. Industry first overtook services in the late 1970s, and has remained above it continuously since 1994.

There are some similarities in the Malaysian pattern, with industry overtaking agriculture in 1971. Agriculture's share actually rose in the mid-1970s, and again in the late 1990s, as well as in the first decade of the twenty-first century. Here too commodity price movements and economic crisis had an effect. After rising by more than 10 percentage points in the decade through to the early 1980s, the industry share was flat for most of that decade, again owing to lower commodity prices, before rising by a further 10 percentage points to almost 50 per cent through to the late 1990s, owing to the dynamic manufactured export performance. In the past decade, however, the share has declined back to about 40 per cent, in spite of high energy prices, owing mainly to the slower export growth, as Malaysia shifted out of labour-intensive manufactures, and in response to intensified competition from China. The services share rose steadily to almost 50 per cent, signalling the country's transition to a post-industrial economy, especially as services sector liberalization proceeds.[4]

By 1970 the Philippines had already passed the turning point at which industry exceeds agriculture. This reflected its early and persistent promotion of import substitution, and its increasingly poor relative resource endowments. Thereafter, agriculture continued its steady downward trend, except for a brief reversal in the mid-1980s, again crisis-related. There are two distinctive features of the Philippine pattern compared with its neighbours. The first is the steady decline in the industry share from about 40 per cent in the early 1980s to just over 30 per cent in 2010. The second is the inexorable rise in services, overtaking industry in the early 1980s, and rising a further 20 percentage points in the following three decades. The Philippine literature has focused on the likely explanations for these trends.[5] The declining manufacturing share can be explained by the failure to make the transition from import substituting to export-oriented industrialization, at least until the reforms of the late 1980s and early 1990s resulted in an export dividend. Agriculture's share, as noted, was declining mainly for comparative advantage reasons, compounded by inadequate rural infrastructure and conflict in the agricultural frontier region of Mindanao, and in spite of the fact that trade policies increasingly favoured this sector over manufacturing. Several factors explain the rising services sector. One is the success of some internationally oriented traded services, principally IT-based back-office processing services, call centres and the like, which now employ more than 700,000 workers, and in which the country is an acknowledged international leader. Another is the rapidly growing international labour exports and remittances, which appear to have significant service-sector linkages, particularly in their spending effects, in areas such as small-scale restaurants, transport and the like. However, the sector appears to have been as much one of 'last-resort' economic activity as of dynamism, given that both agriculture and industry has not been high-growth sectors for much of this period. It is also worth noting that two possible explanatory factors for the high services share have not been present: tourism, which in spite of the country's potential has underperformed (owing to infrastructure constraints and occasional security and related country-reputational problems), and an appreciating real exchange rate, except for a period in the mid-1990s.

The patterns in Singapore are straightforward. For as long as national accounts have been available, agriculture has always been insignificant, and it has become more so over time. The country's role as the region's *entrepôt* and provider of high-value services has continued, with the services share gradually rising over time, to account now for almost three-quarters of GDP.

In Thailand, industry overtook agriculture in the mid-1970s, a process briefly delayed by the exceptionally high prices of grain (relevant for this major rice exporter) in the early 1970s. Over the next decade and a half the agricultural share fell by more than half, to just over 10 per cent. It has maintained that share ever since, with slight increases from 2004 onwards as real food prices have increased. The industrial share rose steadily during the 1970s and 1980s, as manufacturing grew strongly, and the country engineered a successful transition from a relatively mild period of import substitution to export orientation, including its emergence as the region's key automotive production hub. The share of the services sector has hovered around 50 per cent, with no clear long-term trend. Tourism has been consistently important, while Bangkok has traditionally served as a major services centre for the broader Mekong region.

Vietnam's modern national accounts have been measured with reasonable accuracy only from the late 1980s, and thus the analysis commences at this point. Its structural change has been a largely conventional one from the early 1990s, as the relative price distortions and output restrictions of the socialist era—including the undervaluation of services output and agricultural price suppression—were gradually removed. In spite of its rapid growth, the agriculture share declined by more than half in the two decades from the late 1980s. The share then rose slightly during the very high food prices around 2007, since by now Vietnam has also emerged as a major rice exporter. The industrial sector share declined in the late 1980s, as the state-owned enterprises (SOEs) began to lose their preferential access to input supplies and markets. However, the reforms produced rapid industrialization from the early 1990s, boosted further by the rise of the energy sector following the discovery of offshore oil supplies, and its share rose by almost 20 percentage points in the next two decades. Industrial output began to exceed that of agriculture around 1993, a full two decades or more later than its then higher-income neighbours. The share of the service sector rose by almost 15 per cent in the country's first decade of liberalization, partly as a result of more accurate measurement of its output. Thereafter its share has declined somewhat, unable to keep pace with the more dynamic goods sectors, and also held back in some sectors in which the SOEs continue to receive favourable treatment. Vietnam's service sector remains relatively small by regional standards. Vietnam and the Philippines are the two regional outliers in this respect, with similar per capita incomes but a difference in service sector shares of almost 20 percentage points.

Employment Shares

We now examine the patterns of structural change as viewed from the perspective of the labour market, keeping in mind that the comparative data series commence only in 1980, and later still for Vietnam (Figure 3.2). We would expect to observe the same general trends, but the timing of the turning points will likely differ. This is because the release of labour from the agricultural sector proceeds more slowly than the changing output shares, resulting in large inter-sectoral differences in labour productivity (the subject of the next section). Moreover, agricultural employment is often measured less accurately, to the extent that seasonal and part-time workers in the sector are recorded as 'agricultural', whereas in reality they are also engaged in services and manufacturing (particularly agricultural processing) for at least some of the year, or in home duties.

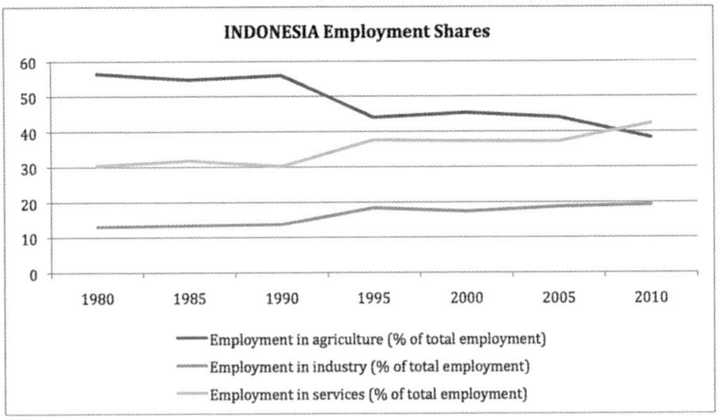

Source: WDI.

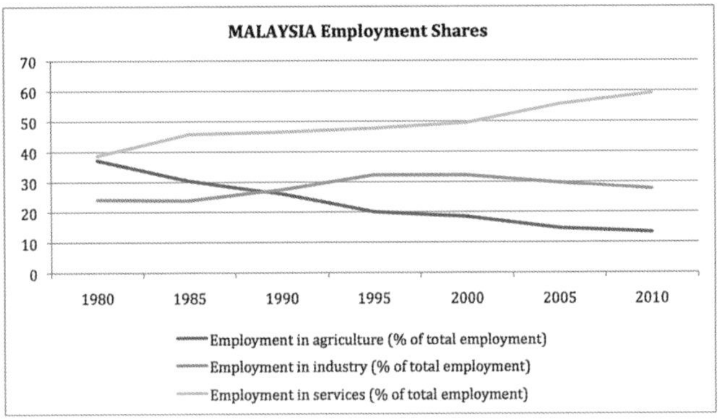

Source: WDI

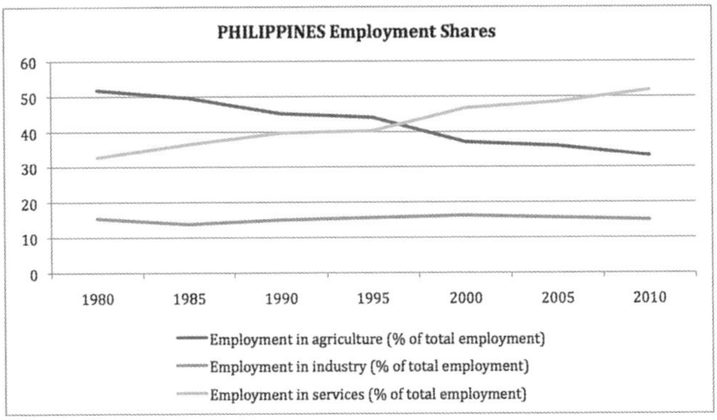

Source: WDI.

Figure 3.2: Employment shares by sector for Indonesia, Malaysia, Philippines, Singapore, Thailand and Vietnam, 1980–2010 (percentages)

(cont'd overleaf)

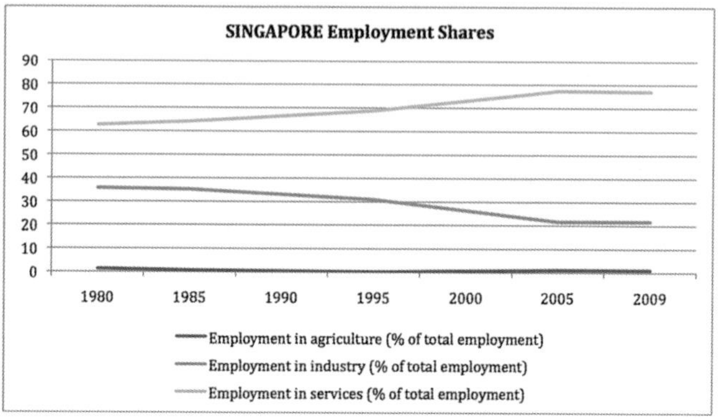

Source: WDI.

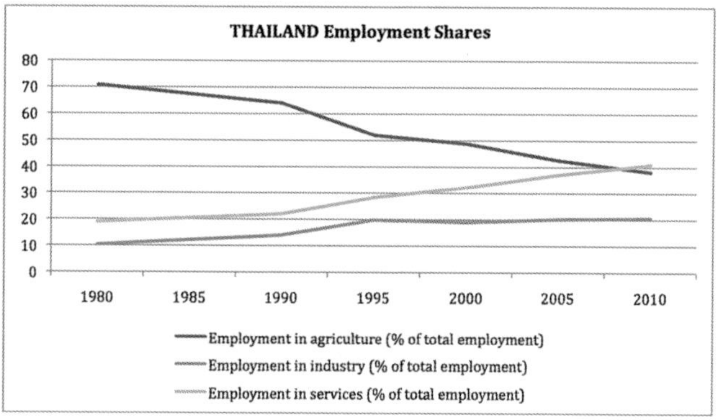

Source: WDI.

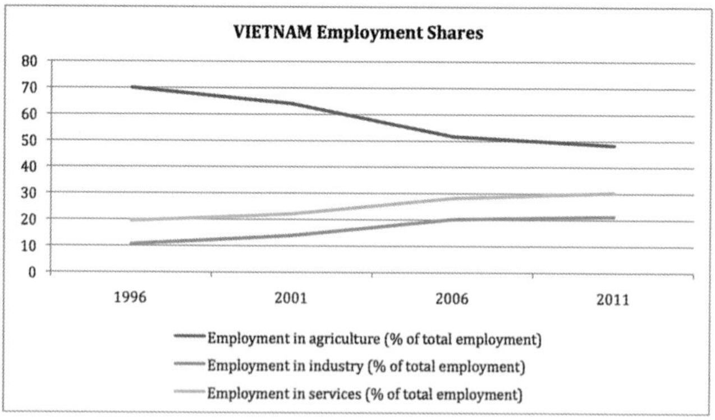

Source: WDI.

Figure 3.2: *continued*

In the case of Indonesia, agriculture remained the largest sector of employment until 2007, when it was overtaken by services. It is still about 35 per cent of the workforce, almost double that of industry. By contrast, in Malaysia the industrial workforce overtook that of agriculture in the early 1990s, while services have been the largest sector of employment throughout the period since 1980. To the extent that the very large migrant workforce, variously estimated to be around 25 per cent of the total, has been engaged primarily in labour-intensive activities, such as domestic service, hotels and restaurants, this dominance is likely to continue. The Philippine agricultural workforce, although declining by almost 20 percentage points since 1980, continues to be about twice as large as that of industry. The industrial share has remained virtually unchanged, while employment in services overtook that of agriculture in 1996. Over the entire period 1980–2010, the major transition has been the switch from agriculture to services, with a 20 percentage point differential between the two sectors at both the start and end points.

For Singapore, the inexorable rise in services has resulted in that sector's share now being close to 80 per cent, with the 15 percentage points increase in its share since 1980 mirrored by a similar decline in industry. The movement out of agriculture in Thailand has apparently occurred quite late in the development process, reflecting its relatively strong comparative advantage in this sector, and possibly also an overstated agricultural employment statistic. Its share is still reported at almost 40 per cent, higher even than Indonesia, and it was overtaken by services only in 2009. Industrial employment has been fairly stable at about 20 per cent, well below the other two sectors. By contrast, almost half of Vietnam's workforce is still in agriculture, with its industrial and service workforces increasing only gradually. This country has by far the highest share in agriculture among the six, and the lowest in services.

Inter-sectoral Labour Productivity

Combining these two series—sector share of GDP and employment shares by sector—generates relative inter-sectoral labour productivity by sector for each country. For ease of presentation, these are given for each sector relative to the economy-wide average (Figure 3.3). The series commences in 1980 for Indonesia, Malaysia, the Philippines, Singapore and Thailand—the ASEAN-5 (Association of Southeast Asian Nations)—and the mid-1990s for Vietnam. To repeat, we would expect there to be substantial inter-sectoral differences in labour productivity, with agriculture

Source: WDI.

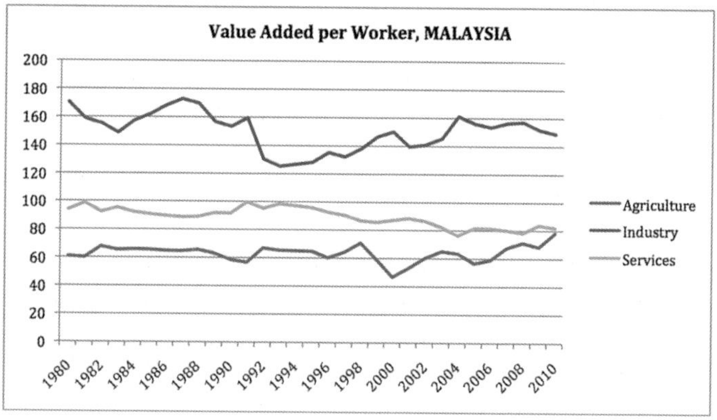

Source: WDI.

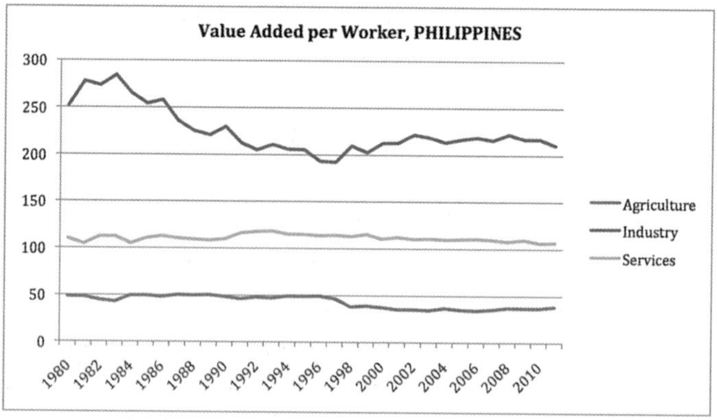

Source : WDI.

Figure 3.3: Relative labour productivity by sector for Indonesia, Malaysia, Philippines, Singapore, Thailand and Vietnam, 1980–2010 (constant 2005 US$)

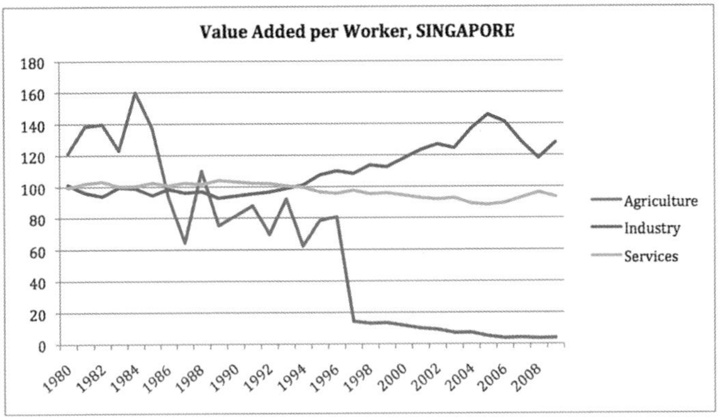

Source: WDI.

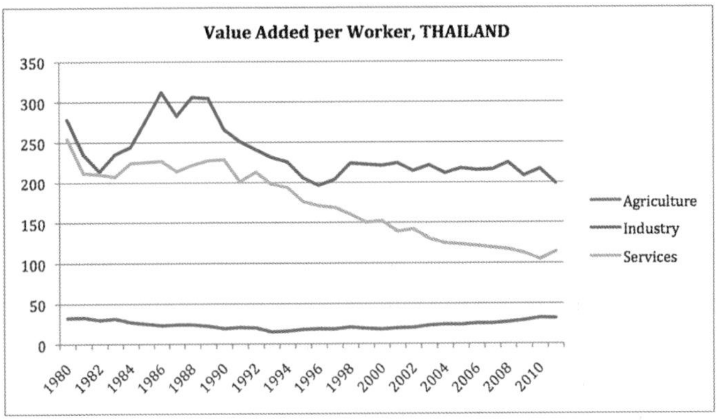

Source: WDI.

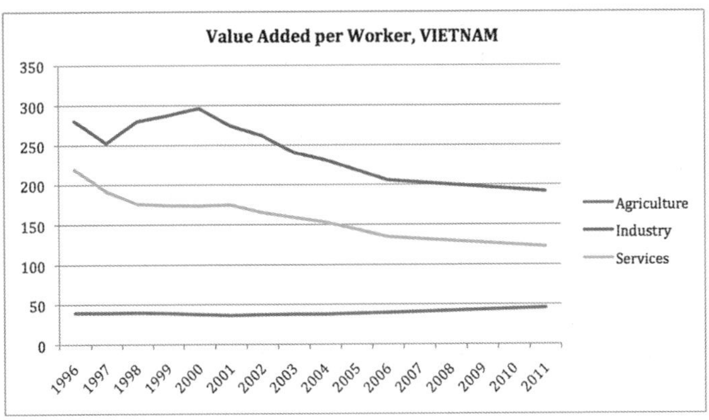

Source: WDI.

Figure 3.3: *continued*

lagging. This, after all, is the driver of structural change: that is, it induces workers to migrate out of agriculture and into higher productivity—and hence wages—in industry and services. We conjecture that these differences would be expected to converge as countries become more economically advanced, as inter-sectoral and spatial mobility increase, and as the economy sheds its 'dualistic' features. It may be, however, that except for Singapore and possibly Malaysia, the Southeast Asian economies have not yet reached this stage of development.

For Indonesia, industrial labour productivity is consistently about 2.5 times the national level, with that relativity declining only gradually. The capital intensity of the energy sector explains much of this result. Agriculture is less than half the national average throughout, with no clear trend, while services has declined from somewhat above the average to slightly below, and putting aside the aberrant hump in the early 1980s. The agricultural trend is not surprising, as large-scale mechanized agriculture is still uncommon. However, the slightly falling ratio for services is unexpected, in view of the rapid growth of modern sector services in the retail trade, finance, transport and telecommunications. Presumably the explanation is that the services sector still has a large informal employment-elastic component, especially in trade, and also an array of personal services. Tighter labour market regulations since the turn of the century may have increased the dualistic nature of the labour market.

In the case of Malaysia, the sectoral rankings are similar, but the differences are smaller, indicative of that country's more developed, less 'dualistic' economy, including its more technologically advanced agriculture sector. Labour productivity in agriculture and services has now converged to about 80 per cent of the economy-wide average, the highest of all the economies, reflecting both agricultural advance and the labour intensity of some service sub-sectors where lower-wage migrant workers predominate.

The relativities in the Philippines have been fairly stable since around 1990, with the industrial sector almost always at least double the national average, while the convergent agriculture and service sectors are somewhat less than half the figure. The 1980s reforms and crisis had a major effect of depressing the relativity for manufacturing, as this sector switched to a more labour-intensive growth path. The low figure for the Philippine services—the lowest relatively among the six—confirms anecdotal evidence that, in spite of pockets of recent dynamism, much of it serves as a sector of last-resort, low-wage employment.

Industry and services ratios are fairly similar in Singapore, but over time the former has been drawing ahead, and is now about one-third higher. This indicates that the process of upgrading has been faster in manufacturing than in services in aggregate, despite the latter's high-value orientation. Here also, the concentration of lower-skill migrant workers in pockets of services is the most plausible explanation for these trends. The large fluctuations in the tiny agricultural sector have little analytical meaning.

The Thai figures suggest very large inter-sectoral differences, possibly exaggerated, as noted, to the extent that its labour force surveys overstate agricultural employment. That is, the industry figure is about double the national average, while that for agriculture is just one-third. Since 1991, the services sector has declined from about double the national average to being similar to it, with the large influx of migrant workers from neighbouring poor economies (principally Myanmar) into low-skill services a likely explanation. Such a large industry–agriculture gap points in turn to a large rural–urban income gap, and hence to a continuing challenge of high inequality.

Vietnam had the largest gap between industrial and agricultural productivity through to the turn of the twenty-first century, at about 7:1. But it has begun to narrow significantly, owing to the success of the country's agriculture and the more labour-intensive manufacturing growth. The earlier high ratio for services is also converging to the economy-wide average.

Summing up, what can we conclude about turning points from these comparisons? Table 3.1 summarizes the results.[6] First, these economies passed the turning point where industrial output begins to exceed that of agriculture quite early after the onset of rapid economic growth, and at quite low levels of per capita income. This occurred in the period 1970–76 for Indonesia, Malaysia and Thailand, and in the 1960s in the Philippines, at significantly different levels of per capita income. For example, the per capita income at Malaysia's turning point was more than double that of Thailand and three times Indonesia. It occurred about twenty years later for Vietnam, shortly after it commenced its phase of modern economic growth. The interplay of relative resource endowments, per capita income and inter-sectoral incentives explain much of these outcomes. In terms of employment, only in Malaysia has industry overtaken agriculture, a reflection of that country's more advanced development, its more technologically advanced plantation sector and its still

Table 3.1: Summary turning point indicators (years; GDP per capita in constant 2005 US$)

	A<M in GDP		*A<M in Employment*		*S of GDP >40%*		*S of Employment >40%*	
Country	*Year*	*GDP per capita*	*Year*	*GDP per capita*	*Year*	*GDP per capita*	*Year*	*GDP per capita*
Indonesia	1974	413			1985	655	2008	1,452
Malaysia	1971	1,427	1990	3,147	1982	2,498	1982	2,498
Philippines	1960s	<800			1985	907	1995	993
Singapore	na		na		1975	6,814	1980	9,645
Thailand	1971	595			1960	359	2009	2,940
Vietnam	1994	339			1993	317		

Notes: A = Output in Agriculture, M = Output in Manufacturing; S = share of; GDP = Share of Services in Gross Domestic Product

Source: World Development Indicators (WDI), accessible at: World Bank, data.worldbank.org.

relatively labour-intensive manufacturing sector. In no country in the region has agricultural output or employment began to decline in absolute terms, reflecting their middle-income status and, in most cases, the persistence of comparative advantage.

It is even more difficult to generalize on trends in the services sector. The turning-points literature has—perhaps mistakenly—focused less on this sector. Taking an arbitrary benchmark of 40 per cent of output and employment, Indonesia, Malaysia and the Philippines passed this point during the 1980s; Thailand earlier, in part owing to its large tourism sector; and Vietnam later. The range of per capita incomes at this point was larger still. The employment shares are similarly dispersed, with Malaysia crossing the 40 per cent figure in 1982, Indonesia and Thailand only very recently (2008 and 2009 respectively), while Vietnam is still below it. However, the corresponding incomes per capita varied less. Subsequently, the Philippines has continued to evolve as the most services-oriented economy among the five.

Structural Change: Additional Dimensions

As noted, structural change is a multidimensional phenomenon. We now focus on the labour market and demographic dimensions, and then link any observable turning points to those identified in the sectoral analysis. Owing to space constraints, and the difficulty of obtaining reliable wage data, this draws mainly on the relevant literature in these fields.

The literature on labour markets and demographic trends also identifies key turning points. In the case of the labour market, the seminal contribution of the Lewis model was premised upon a dual economy, the low-productivity traditional sector alongside the high-productivity modern sector, and the transfer of labour between them.[7] During the surplus labour phase, this transfer occurs at constant real wages, a process that continues until the labour surplus dries up, and real wages in the traditional sector begin to rise, converging towards those in the modern sector. The speed of this transition depends on the rate of growth in the modern sector, the labour intensity of that growth and the relative size of the two sectors.

Manning and Posso examine these labour market transitions, posing the question as to why real wages rose more quickly in the Newly Industrialized Economies (NIEs) as compared with the Southeast Asian economies (the latter proxied by Indonesia, Malaysia and Thailand, and appropriately placing Singapore in the former group).[8] The faster growth in the NIEs is one obvious explanation, but Manning and Posso stress that there are others. One was the stronger and earlier adoption of labour-intensive, export-oriented industrialization in the NIEs. Another was relative resource endowments, in particular the larger agricultural sectors and richer natural resource endowments in Southeast Asia. The NIEs' larger investments in education, including more recently R&D, facilitated the transition of workers into the modern, technologically advanced sector, and was a further differentiating factor.

Turning to demographic trends, Jones provides a comprehensive survey for Southeast Asia, drawing attention to the transition from high to low rates of fertility and mortality, and by implication various demographic turning points.[9] He dates the early beginnings of fertility decline to the late 1950s in Singapore, the mid-1960s in Malaysia and Thailand, the late 1960s in Indonesia and the Philippines, and the early 1970s in Myanmar and Vietnam. However, the transitions have varied sharply across the region, with Singapore and now increasingly Thailand moving into a phase of 'ultra-low' fertility, while that in the Philippines remains stubbornly high.[10] As a result of these transitions, Southeast Asia has generally been enjoying a period of 'demographic bonus', as the share of the working-age population (notionally and arbitrarily assumed to be those aged between fifteen and sixty-four years) has declined steadily. The dependency ratio of course comprises two groups—the youth and the elderly ratios. The dependency ratio declines because, with the onset of fertility decline, the youth dependency ratio declines, but there is considerable delay before the elderly ratio begins to rise significantly. Thus the period of demographic bonus is defined by the interaction between these two variables, and it generally lasts for some decades.

However, the countries that experienced an earlier fertility decline are now approaching the end of this phase, and are therefore entering the period of 'demographic burden', when the dependency ratio rises. Based on the analysis and projections of Komine and Kabe,[11] Singapore's fertility rate appeared to fall below replacement levels (that is, 2.1) in 1975–80, Thailand in 1995–2000 and Vietnam in 2005–10.[12] That phase is projected to be reached later in Indonesia (2015–20), Malaysia (2020–25) and the Philippines (2035–40). The countries with earlier and sharper declines in fertility will also be the ones that exhibit the same pattern for ageing, and the point at which the labour force, and eventually the population, begins to decline. Of course these projections need to also incorporate the effects of international migration, retirement age (and associated pension policies) and also female workforce participation.

Drawing on the theory of the demographic transition, Jones attributes these declines to a range of economic, institutional and ideological factors.[13] While socio-economic factors are typically seen as the most important, as evidenced by the generally lower fertility in richer countries, a broader set of explanatory variables is required, especially to understand intra-country differences. For example, fertility differs significantly among Malaysia's ethnic groups, as it does among Indonesian regions. The Philippines continues to be the region's major outlier.

It is beyond the scope of this chapter to examine empirically the demographic and labour force variables, which are presented in detail in the Komine-Kabe and Jones papers. The wage data are particularly problematic, and difficult to assemble in a form that is amenable to testing turning-point theories.[14] For present purposes, we can get a summary indication of approximate trends from two series, unemployment rates (Figure 3.4) and R&D expenditure (Figure 3.5).

The unemployment data show clearly that the more advanced economies in Southeast Asia—Singapore, Malaysia and Thailand—have become 'labour scarce', as indicated by their low rates of unemployment, while the much higher rates for Indonesia and the Philippines indicate that these are still very much in the labour surplus phase. (An additional indication for these two is that they are significant labour exporters, the Philippines on a very large scale.) The Singapore transition generally dates from the late 1970s, when the government explicitly adopted a

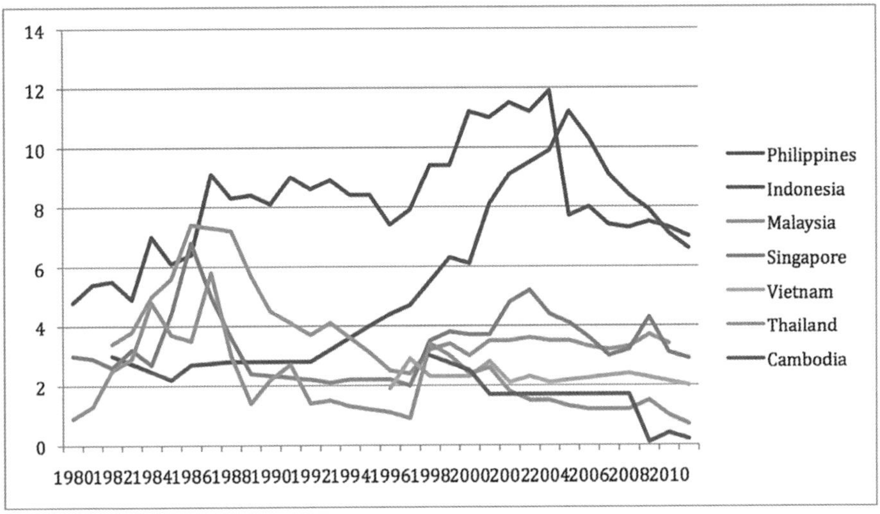

Source: WDI.

Figure 3.4: Unemployment rates in Southeast Asia (total unemployment as a percentage of total labour force)

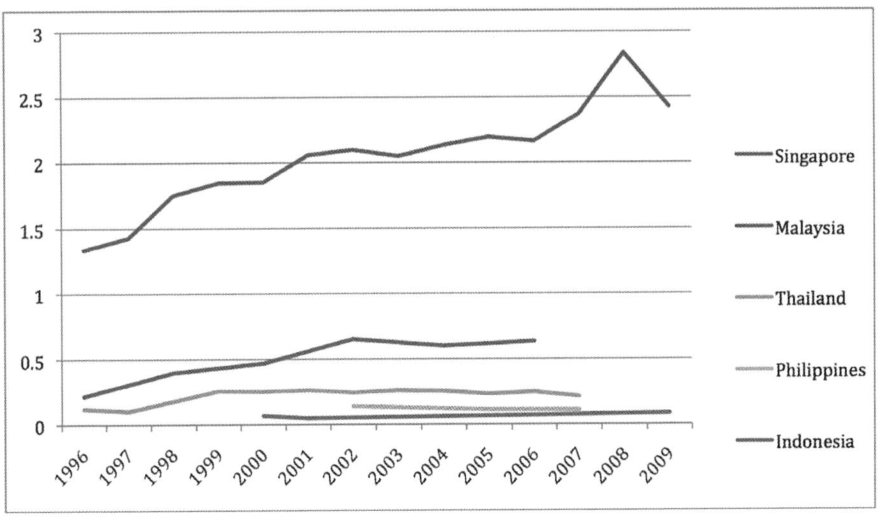

Source: WDI.

Figure 3.5: R&D expenditure in Southeast Asia (percentage of GDP)

'high-wage' policy in order to phase out labour-intensive activities. That process was delayed by the mid-1980s recession, but resumed again decisively later in that decade. In Malaysia the point was around 1990, again with a subsequent delay occasioned by the Asian financial crisis of 1997–98, while in Thailand it was about to commence when that crisis hit, and it has now become more evident since the mid-2000s. All three countries kept wages low in the earlier period, either by fiat or through a largely unregulated labour market. Trade unions were allowed to exert only limited market power. As the labour surplus dried up, large-scale in-migration was permitted, indeed encouraged, in order to moderate the scale of wage increases, particularly in labour-intensive activities.[15]

These are crude but nonetheless plausible conclusions. They are crude because the unemployment data are weak and sometimes ambiguous. They are a very imperfect indicator of labour market conditions, and for countries with virtually no social security system—such as Cambodia—they tell us even less. But they are plausible because the labour market and migration data do combine to give an approximate picture of turning points.

Rising real wages have to be supported by productivity growth, which in turn requires higher rates of physical and human capital accumulation. Some idea of the transition towards a more technologically advanced economic structure can be gleaned from trends in R&D investment. The data (Figure 3.5) are incomplete but they generally accord with a priori expectations. That is, at low levels of per capita income, R&D is minimal. But it generally begins to rise with the approach of labour scarcity, as firms and governments adapt to the commercial imperative of having to compete with firms from more technologically advanced nations. Thus, the always proactive Singapore government began to invest substantially in R&D from the late 1980s, as did multinational corporations that established regional headquarter operations there for high-end activities. Singapore's R&D effort now approximates the Organisation for Economic Co-operation and Development (OECD) average, with its per capita income at the higher end of the range. Malaysia also is beginning to invest more in R&D, although it has been slower to commence this reorientation.

Discussion and Conclusions

The purpose of this chapter has been to identify and explain patterns of structural change, including the various dimensions of turning points, in the six large Southeast Asian economies since the 1970s. The main arguments are summarized here.

Structural change, in the sense of the transfer of resources out of agriculture and into industry and services, has generally been rapid. The agricultural sectors are now very much smaller than they were a generation or two ago. Several factors have shaped the variety of outcomes observed. The first is the rate of economic growth. The faster is the rate of growth, cet. par., the faster the increases in per capita income, and therefore in the rate of structural change.

The second factor is natural resource endowments. Countries with strong natural resource endowments, including high land–labour ratios, generally retain a stronger comparative advantage in agricultural and mining activities than do resource-poor economies. The obvious Southeast Asian example is Singapore, where agriculture had virtually disappeared by 1980, apart from a small, high-value horticulture sector. Among the larger economies, the Philippines is now becoming a resource-poor economy. It hit the land frontier for agricultural expansion in the 1960s, while it has continued to experience rapid population growth.[16] Thus, in spite of its lower growth, the shift out of agriculture has been quite rapid, at a pace similar to that of Indonesia and Thailand, both higher-growth economies but with more favourable land–labour ratios.

The shares of the natural resource sectors—both agriculture and mining—are also sensitive to international prices. Thus, in a period of strong agricultural commodity prices, these sectors attract resources and, assuming that governments do not interfere in the market, the domestic value of their output also increases. This effect is evident in much of Southeast Asia. For example, the high grain prices of 2007–08 boosted the agricultural sector's share in major rice exporters such as Thailand and Vietnam, while high palm oil prices since around 2005 have had a similar effect in Indonesia and Malaysia. Conversely, lower prices accelerate the process of structural change out of agriculture. Where the commodity boom is mainly concentrated in the mining sector, which was more the case in the 1970s than since 2005, the effects are ambiguous. Typically, high energy and mineral prices pull up agricultural prices, at least cash crops such as rubber and palm oil, as supply substitutes. But high mineral prices also push up the real exchange rate, thus squeezing the other tradable sectors, including agriculture.

A third set of factors is a range of policy interventions. The most important are inter-sectoral variations in the structure of incentives. In the era of import substitution, trade policy typically favoured the manufacturing sector over agriculture. That is, agriculture was taxed, and therefore resources flowed to the non-agricultural sectors, and agriculture's share of value added at distorted domestic prices was depressed. The major trade liberalizations that began to sweep through the region in the 1980s nullified these effects, especially in formerly high-protection economies of Indonesia and the Philippines. In fact, the inter-sectoral incentives have been reversed in some countries, with agriculture now receiving more protection than manufacturing, following the policy settings in much of north-east Asia, particularly Japan and South Korea, although not to the same degree.[17]

Other policies may affect the speed of structural change. Movements in the real exchange rate affect the relative profitability of tradable and non-tradable activities, with the latter proxied as the services sector.[18] For example, during the Asian financial crisis of 1997–98, real exchange rates in the crisis-affected economies fell sharply. Combined with the collapse of the domestic market-oriented manufacturing sector, and several modern sector services, most notably finance and construction, there was a return to agriculture. Conversely, for much of the period since 2005, governments have been attempting to restrain the appreciation of their currencies. To the extent they have been successful, the pace of structural change has thereby been lower.

A further set of policies relate to fiscal incentives, infrastructure expenditure priorities and R&D policies. All of these may have significant, if unintended, sectoral implications. For example, in the 1970s Malaysia successfully implemented a programme of export-oriented industrialization, including generous fiscal incentives and strategically located infrastructure to induce multinational enterprises to relocate there. The result was very rapid industrialization. Singapore has also adopted aggressive incentives policies, including a very large R&D programme, initially focused mainly on manufacturing but since the 1990s also including services.

Labour market policies also have implications for structural change. Very open labour markets, as in Singapore, Malaysia and now Thailand, slow the rate of wage increases and therefore the appreciation of real exchange rates associated with the transition to labour scarcity.[19] The sectoral composition of these labour flows may also affect the process of structural change, especially if labour markets are segmented. In fact, there has been a tendency for governments to regulate labour markets in the modern sector of the economy, particularly the formal manufacturing and service components, which has had the effect of retarding the process of inter-sectoral labour market adjustment.[20]

The differences across countries are also revealing. Although agriculture has shrunk everywhere, it has not been an even process, even allowing for differences in growth rates and incomes. Moreover, there has not been a smooth adjustment from agriculture to industry and then to services. The Philippines has evolved quite quickly into a services-oriented economy, with a relatively small industrial sector as compared with twenty-five years earlier. Although its per capita income is now similar to that of Vietnam, the Philippine service sector share in GDP is almost 20 percentage points higher. In fact, these two countries are the service sector outliers, reflecting their very different development trajectories and policy histories.

There are also very large differences in relative labour productivities across sectors and countries. The still very low figures for agriculture in some countries suggest that their earlier 'dualistic' features persist to some extent, pointing in turn to continuing challenges of interpersonal and interregional inequality, and to the fact that the process of national economic integration is in its infancy from a longer-term development perspective. It may also be suggestive of the need to intensify policies aimed at promoting agricultural productivity. In this respect, Malaysia stands out as far more advanced than its middle-income neighbours.

Finally, it needs to be emphasized that this analysis is positive, not normative, in orientation. There is no 'desirable' economic structure or rate of structural change. Turning points should not necessarily occur at particular stages of economic development. Rather, as demonstrated, they vary with economic growth, resource endowments, policies and institutions. Indeed, one of the major fallacies of economic policy-making has been based on a misinterpretation of the process of structural change, namely the association between higher levels of per capita income and shares of the industrial sector. The view that the direction of causality between these two variables flowed from the latter to the former was, of course, the basis for misdirected industrial policies in much of the developing world during the second half of the twentieth century.

Notes

1. Lewis, 'Economic Development with Unlimited Supplies'.
2. It is also important to remember that the distinction between the three sectors is not always clear-cut, both conceptually and empirically. This applies,

for example, to a range of agricultural and mineral processing activities, and to various service activities embodied in the goods sectors, such as repairs and product design.

3. These are the turning points that economic historians typically emphasize. See for example, Reynolds, 'The Spread of Economic Growth', and his attempt to identify approximate years when 'intensive growth' (that is, sustained increases in per capita income) commenced.
4. Tham and Loke, 'Services Liberalization: The Need for Complementary Policies'.
5. See for example, Balisacan et al., *The Philippine Economy.*
6. For obvious reasons we exclude Singapore from the following discussion.
7. Lewis, 'Economic Development with Unlimited Supplies'.
8. Manning and Posso, 'Trade and Labour Market Outcomes'.
9. Jones, 'The Population of Southeast Asia'.
10. For example, noting that a total fertility rate (TFR) of 2.1 live births per woman generates a stable population, for the period 2005–10 the TFR's for Singapore and Thailand were estimated to be 1.25 and 1.63 respectively, while that for the Philippines was 3.27 (ibid., Table 6).
11. Komine and Kabe, 'Long-term Forecast of the Demographic Transition'.
12. Note that the total population continues to grow beyond this date, independent of trends in migration, owing to age distribution effects.
13. Jones, 'The Population of Southeast Asia'.
14. The major difficulty is obtaining a reliable long-term, cross-country series for unskilled wages, in agriculture, labour-intensive manufacturing or the informal sector, one which measures hourly wages and abstracts from issues of changing skill composition and capital intensity. See Manning and Posso, 'Trade and Labour Market Outcomes', and the earlier writings on Indonesia by the first author.
15. Athukorala and Manning, *Structural Change and International Migration.*
16. The Philippine case is complicated by the fact that commercial agriculture has had limited scope for expansion in major parts of the key agricultural frontier of Mindanao owing to protracted conflict.
17. For detailed discussion of the changing agricultural trade regimes, see Anderson, *Distortions to Agricultural Incentives.*
18. This is of course an over-simplification. A number of services are traded, such as tourism, while others are increasingly so, notably health, education and a plethora of IT business activities. Conversely, a number of perishable agricultural and manufacturing products are quasi-tradable, owing to high transport costs.
19. Athukorala and Manning, *Structural Change and International Migration.*
20. Manning and Posso, 'Trade and Labour Market Outcomes'.

4

Trade and Economic Development: Indonesia in the Long Run

Pim de Zwart, Daan Marks, Alexandra de Pleijt and Jan Luiten van Zanden

Introduction

One of the constant themes in Thomas Lindblad's research is the link between international trade and economic development. This topic was already the focus of his PhD thesis on Swedish trade with the Dutch Republic in the eighteenth century, and continued to interest him when he reoriented his research to Indonesia in the nineteenth and twentieth centuries.[1] One aspect of the literature on this topic concerns the connection between openness and economic development. Classic economic treatises by Adam Smith and David Ricardo showed early on the potential gains of trading between nations and, more recently, advocates of globalization claim that trade promotes growth, and in turn growth reduces poverty.[2] Such voices also resonate in the public domain; in 2013 an article in *The Economist* claimed that capitalism and free trade were the most important factors in the alleviation of poverty in the past decade as they 'enabled economies to grow—and it was growth, principally, that has eased destitution'.[3]

Much of the evidence in support of and against globalization has been based on cross-country growth regressions. T.N. Srinivasan and Jagdish Bhagwati argue that 'while such regressions can be suggestive of new hypotheses and be valuable aids in thinking about the issue at hand, we would reiterate that great caution is needed in using them at all as plausible "scientific" support'.[4] Therefore they call for nuanced and in-depth case studies to get a better understanding of the relationship between trade and economic development.

In this chapter we respond to this call by a long-term time-series analysis of this relationship, focusing on one case study.[5] The case of Indonesia is a good candidate. Lindblad observed that while the process of globalization generated impressive export-led economic expansion, 'dependence on external markets increased the vulnerability of the emerging economy'.[6] Trade growth may also have led to increased segmentation between the indigenous and immigrant populations, as he showed in the case of southeast Kalimantan.[7] Furthermore, as Anne Booth argues:

> Indonesia's involvement in the world economy did transform the local economies of the producing regions through the provision of infrastructure and the growing demand for inputs and services. And yet, the transformation of Indonesia into an open export-oriented economy in the nineteenth and twentieth centuries did not lead to rapid structural change, and sustained economic development.[8]

These observations point to the ambiguous role that the trade sector has played in the process of economic development in Indonesia. Indonesia's export orientation seems to have enhanced economic growth in some periods, but may have failed to do so in other periods.

We try to find out when 'openness'—the share of trade in the total economy—had a positive impact on growth and the standard of living, and when this link was less evident, or even negative. We focus on two dimensions of development: the increase of total factor productivity (TFP) and the real wage of an unskilled labourer. The next section introduces the data on openness on which we will base our analysis. After that we combine those data with the data on TFP and real wages. In the fourth section we examine the relationship between the openness, TFP and real wages via time series analysis. We find a long-term relationship between TFP and openness in sub-periods 1825–65, 1866–1913 and 1966–97, and in all periods there is evidence of a feedback mechanism between these factors (as evident from Granger causality tests).[9] Only after 1960 do we find a consistent rise in living standards, which was not directly caused by trade, but rather by rising productivity levels. It is demonstrated that, depending on the institutional and broader economic context, the expansion of trade and the increase in openness may have different consequences for productivity and living standards.

Indonesia's International Trade

Indonesia's involvement in international trade goes back to (at least) the 'age of commerce' between 1400 and 1650.[10] However, the degree of openness during the VOC (Dutch East India Company) period (1600–1800) was rather limited. Maddison estimated eighteenth-century export by the VOC at less than 2 per cent of gross domestic product (GDP),[11] but the VOC covered only about 50 per cent of total exports of Java;[12] if imports were of a similar magnitude, the openness ratio would be between 5 and 8 per cent. The first stage of opening the Javanese economy may therefore have coincided with the gradual disappearance of the VOC monopoly. Employing GDP data from recent work by Jan Luiten van Zanden (the period 1824–1913) and Pierre van der Eng (1900–2003), it is possible to estimate the share of trade in total GDP between 1820 and 2003.[13]

For the early 1820s, we estimate an openness ratio of about 15 per cent. Since then, exports and imports have grown exponentially, and the share of them in GDP has increased from about 15 per cent in the early 1820s to 60 per cent or more in recent decades (Figure 4.1). The next phase of export expansion occurred during the Cultivation System [the system of cultivation of export crops (sugar and coffee) based on forced labour by the Javanese peasantry], which led to a rise of the degree of openness of the Javanese economy from about 15 per cent to almost 40 per cent. Yet, in this period, the state regulated the export sector of the economy, exports were monopolized and market forces were much weaker than before 1830.

During the 1860s and 1870s reforms of the Cultivation System led to declining levels of exploitation and a significant change in the colonial trade regime. Openness continued to grow steadily, but at a slower pace. With the elimination of restrictions on trade in 1874, trade flows also began shifting to other destinations. Whereas more than 60 per cent of the Indonesian exports were destined for the Netherlands, this had

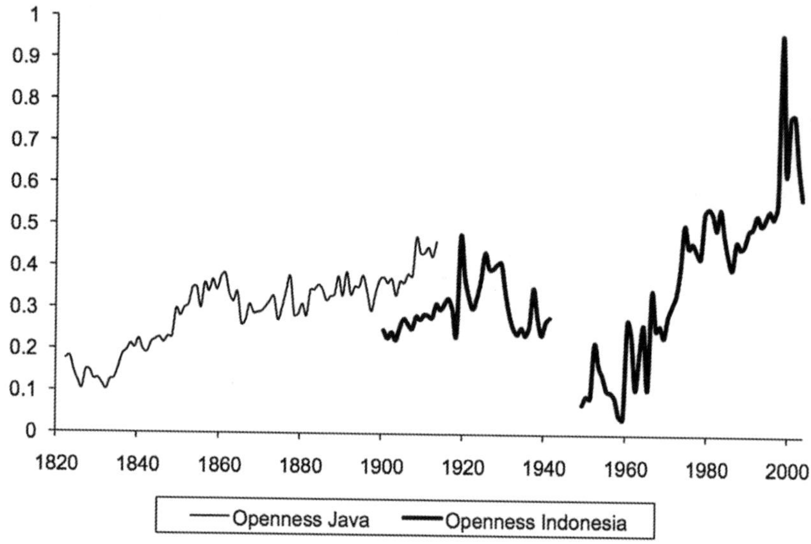

Figure 4.1: Openness in Java (1824–1913) and Indonesia (1913–2003)

declined to about 30 per cent in 1913. Similarly, the share of imports from the Netherlands declined from 55 per cent to 26 per cent of the total imports in 1913.[14]

During the interwar period (1919–39) the trend in openness is more or less flat and is distorted by large fluctuations. Perhaps most remarkable is the poor performance of the export sector during the first decades after independence, when openness fell to very low levels: less than 10 per cent of GDP, which is even less than at the beginning of the nineteenth century. There was some growth in export volume in the early 1950s above the level achieved in the late 1930s.[15] However, compared with the dramatic expansion of world trade that occurred in the 1950s and 1960s, Indonesia's trade performance was disappointing. Whereas world trade grew by about 7 per cent per annum between 1953 and 1966, Indonesian export volume grew by less than 1 per cent per annum.[16] What caused this failure of Indonesia to profit from booming international trade?

In the 1950s and early 1960s foreign trade was tightly controlled by the state, which used its powers to allocate trade to its own citizens (whereas before independence it had been monitored by Dutch firms). Therefore, exports had to be approved and originated from state enterprises, while imports required licences that were held by state trading companies. Moreover, import and export taxes were also of fundamental importance for the financing of the new state. The importance of this kind of taxation is illustrated by the fact that government revenue from taxes on trade fluctuated between 32 and 66 per cent of total tax revenue between 1951 and 1957.[17] Following the takeover of Dutch enterprises in 1957, and the subsequent period of 'Guided Democracy', trade policies only intensified, with an emphasis on indigenous Indonesian control over all aspects of economic activity. In April 1959 government trading houses obtained monopoly rights to import nine categories of goods, which comprised 75 per cent of all imports.[18] Private importers could import only non-essential goods and the number of importers was restricted to 400.[19] Moreover, government intervention in the retail trade, which was traditionally handled by Chinese and Indian traders, resulted in disruption in the distribution of goods and a scarcity of most consumer goods. The impact of government intervention in the trade sector is further reflected by the fact that in 1963 and 1964 about 70 per cent of government revenue came from foreign trade taxes.[20]

After the regime change of 1966–67, barriers to international trade were quickly lowered. As a result of a series of packages introduced by the New Order government, by 1970 many of these barriers had been removed. Most export taxes were reduced, tariffs became the primary instrument of import protection and the tariff structure was simplified.[21] This leads Hill to conclude that 'the late 1960s ushered in a period of economic liberalism in Indonesia'.[22] During the 1970s sentiment changed. Import bans began to reappear and regulation intensified after the oil boom, mainly to protect non-oil tradable activities. The second oil boom led to further trade restrictions with outright prohibitions and an 'authorized importer system' (*Tata Niaga Impor*). However, the revenue motive of foreign trade regulations was no longer important. The contribution of taxes on trade to total revenue declined from 38.2 per cent in 1968 to only 7.3 per cent in 1982. This fall was mainly due to a significant rise of taxes on oil companies, which provided more than 70 per cent of domestic revenue in 1982.[23]

The liberalization measures resulted in a dramatic increase in foreign trade as a percentage of GDP. Starting at only 14 per cent in 1965, this proportion increased to more than 20 per cent in 1970, and then more than doubled to 46.8 per cent in 1980. In 1990 the total trade as percentage of GDP reached 54.7 per cent, even rising to over 70 per cent in 2000. Thus trade growth took place under different institutional conditions. How did this affect the relationship with economic development?

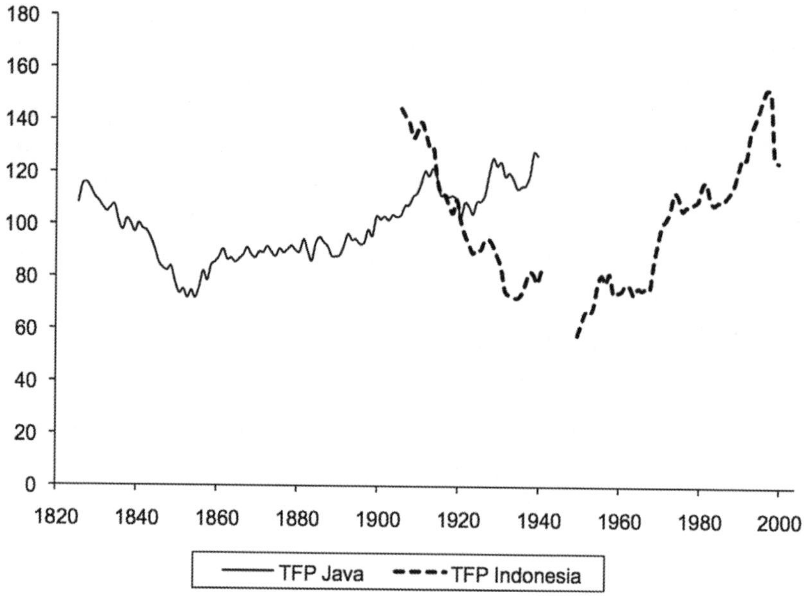

Sources: Van Zanden and Marks, *An Economic History of Indonesia, 1800–2012*; Van Zanden, 'Economic Growth in Java, 1815–1939'; Van der Eng, 'The sources'.

Figure 4.2: TFP in Java (1824–1913) and Indonesia (1900–2003)

Trade, TFP and Real Wages

As already said, we apply two measures of development: TFP and real wages. The concept of TFP, defined as the ratio between real output and real factor inputs, can be traced back to Solow.[24] TFP is not measured directly, but is a residual and reflects the part of the output growth that is not explained by the increases in input factors such as physical capital and labour. It captures omitted factors in the growth equation and the combination of errors in the data.[25] The concept is often used because it is regarded as an important driver of economic growth. Figure 4.2 shows the TFP data, which are again derived from the GDP estimates by Van Zanden and Van der Eng.[26]

Until the 1850s, TFP declined while openness grew which points to the increasing inefficiencies as a result of the Cultivation System. Export production went up, but at the cost of a strong increase of inefficiency as a result of the misallocation of resources on a vast scale. Indigo cultivation did not produce net profits to the state, needed large amount of labour and had negative consequences for the fertility of the soil. Similarly, the first generations of sugar contracts were poorly designed, leading to inefficient forms of cultivation and processing in regions unsuitable for sugar. At the same time, the availability of cheap coerced labour also meant that much labour was wasted.[27] Furthermore, Indonesia provided an important market for Dutch textile manufactures in this period. As a result Indonesia de-industrialized, with its manufacturing sector declining from 15 per cent of GDP around 1815 to 6–7 per cent of GDP in the 1850s. In the late 1840s and 1850s the system was gradually reformed, allowing price mechanisms to do their work and enhance efficiency. This eventually led to the recovery of TFP.

Between 1860 and 1914, TFP increased continuously at a modest rate, as did openness. The period was characterized by a gradual liberalization of labour markets (the abolishment of coerced labour), the construction of modern infrastructure (railways, steamships in inter-insular trade), the inflow of European and Chinese entrepreneurship and capital, and the integration of markets within Java.[28]

During the interwar period trends were less clear—violent fluctuations in both openness and TFP dominate the picture. But the turn to a more inward looking economy immediately after independence clearly led to very low levels of openness and productivity. After 1949, in a few years exports and imports accounted for less than 10 per cent of GDP; even less than at the beginning of the nineteenth century! The phase of rapid growth beginning in the second half of the 1960s witnessed another strong correlation between openness and productivity—both trends were, however, crudely broken off by the Asian financial crisis of 1997–98.

While TFP tells us much about efficiency, technological progress and economic growth, it provides little information about the standard of living of the general population. In recent years, a lot of development has taken place in the computation of comparable real wages across the globe.[29] Pioneered by Robert Allen a methodology has been developed in which real wages are expressed as absolute values relative to subsistence level, based on a consumption basket that reflects the minimum for survival and a family of four. The basket contains around 1,940 calories and 50 grams of protein per day, mainly based on the main staple (rice in this case), some small quantities of other foodstuffs (oil, fish and beans), as well as some clothing and fuel. In order to incorporate costs to sustain a family and pay rent, the budget has to be multiplied by 3.15. Finally, 250 work days per year are assumed. For Java (1825–1940) real wages series were thus computed on the basis of wage and price statistics from

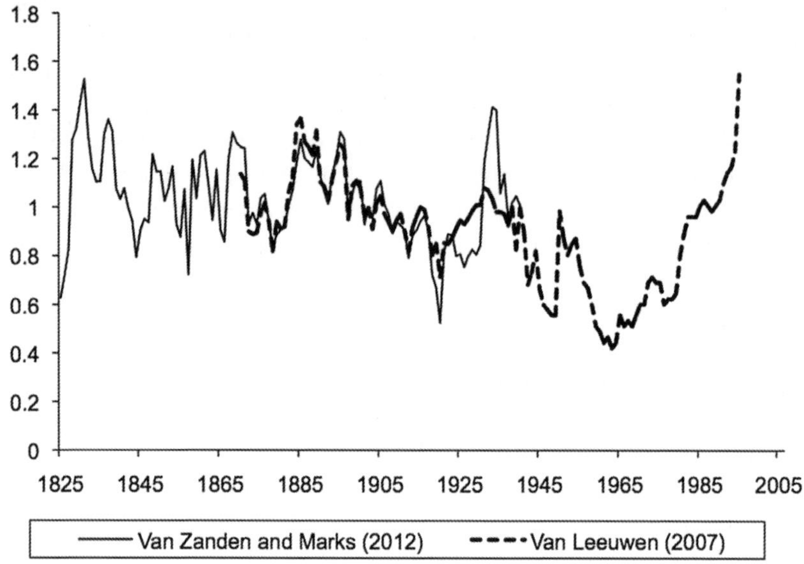

Figure 4.3: Real wages in Indonesia, 1820–1940

the statistical *Changing Economy in Indonesia* series.[30] In order to expand the series to include the post-colonial period, we linked these real wages with those constructed by Bas van Leeuwen.[31] His price index is based on slightly different weights, but Figure 4.3 shows that these series have roughly the same trends between 1870 and 1940.[32] As in all long-run time series, there are problems with the comparability of the data over time. The price index on which the series from the later twentieth century is based is more complex and may thus underestimate increases in real wages vis-à-vis earlier periods. However, as we will investigate the relationship between these variables in different time periods (and we do not change sources in the specific sub-periods), these issues do not affect our results. These are rural wages of indigenous workers, and thus provide no information about the development of living standards of Chinese and European immigrants.

In the period of the Cultivation System the trend in real wages, apart from heavy fluctuations (resulting mainly from the instability in the rice price), is largely flat. While nominal wages increased slightly in this period, real wages were stable as prices also increased. Real wages then increased very slightly until the 1890s as a result of declining prices. After 1895, however, prices increased strongly and, together with the closure of the frontier in Java and the consequent abundance of labour, real wages declined. Figure 4.4 shows that in both these periods there is no relation with openness. Living standards further declined until the late 1920s as a result of inflation. After a short increase of welfare, resultant from wage stickiness and deflation in the 1930s, real wages continue to drop until the regime change of 1966 ushers in a period of fairly continuous welfare growth.

Empirical Analysis

Figure 4.4 shows scatter diagrams between real wages and TFP vis-à-vis openness in three different periods. As can be seen, the relationship between openness, TFP and living standards differed in these different periods, depending on the institutional context. On the basis of the previous sections, we may discern three periods of growth in openness in Indonesia:

1. 1825–65: trade expansion under an exploitative colonial regime,
2. 1865–1913: trade expansion under a liberal colonial regime,
3. 1966–2000: trade expansion after independence.

Due to the large fluctuations in the openness data, and missing observations on TFP for Indonesia and Java, the period 1914–42 is omitted from the analysis. Furthermore, in this period we change sources for both real wages and the GDP estimates on which openness and TFP are based. Including such data may lead to erroneous conclusions.

Figure 4.4 confirms that trade under the Cultivation System had mostly harmful effects on Indonesian development, as it led to increasing inefficiencies and deindustrialization. The growing demand for labour for the production of export crops may have had a slight positive effect on wage levels. However, the price of the consumer basket also increased, as export crops were cultivated at the expense of food production. Consequently, while real wages are trendless, data on rice consumption and heights (a measure of the biological standard of living) suggest a decline in living standards in this period.[33]

Figure 4.4 demonstrates that TFP and openness are strongly positive related in the sub-periods 1865–1913 and 1965–2000, and negatively correlated in the period before 1865. What is more, there seems to exist a clear relationship among openness and living standards in the period after independence.

While the correlations shown in Figure 4.4 are informative, some relations may be driven by a spurious correlation as both variables are

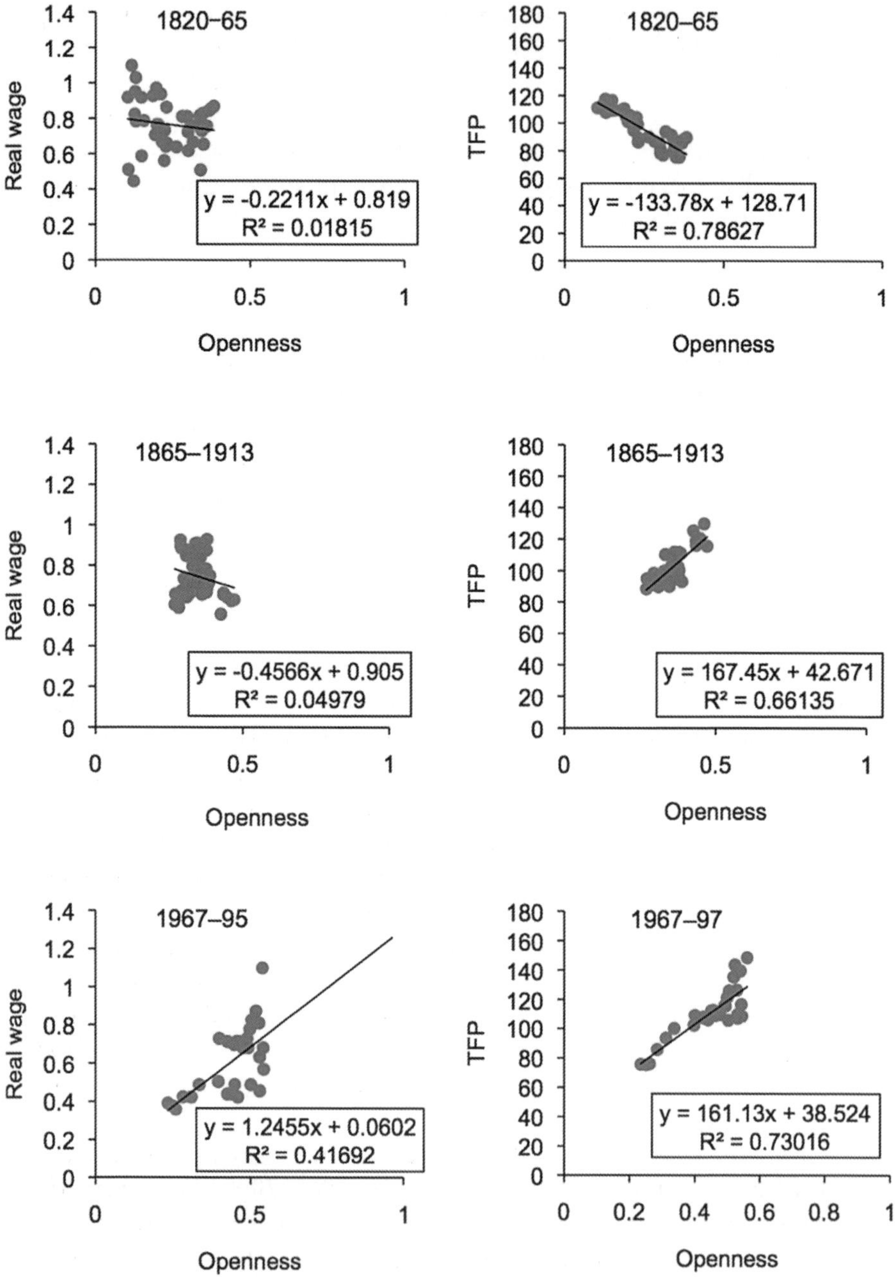

Figure 4.4: Scatter diagrams: real wages and TFP versus openness in Java (1824–1913) and Indonesia (1913–2003)

Table 4.1: Granger-causality between openness, TFP and real wages in Indonesia, 1825–1997

		Dependent variables		
Period	*Explanatory variables*	*Open*	*LnTFP*	*LnRW*
1825–65	Open	–	**0.02**	–
	LnTFP	**0.00**	–	–
1865–1913	Open	–	**0.04**	–
	LnTFP	**0.00**	–	–
1967–97	Open	–	**0.00**	0.95
	LnTFP	**0.00**	–	**0.09**
	LnRW	0.25	0.23	–

Note: Only *p*-values are reported on. The lag-length is chosen according to the Akaike Information Criteria (AIC). Lags are added to the VAR system until there was no indication of autocorrelation at the 5 per cent level.

influenced by a time trend. Therefore, in this section we will empirically test the significant correlations via time series analysis. The analysis relies on vector autoregression (VAR) systems to draw inferences about the direction of short-run causality and examines the possibility of a long-run relationship (co-integration) between openness (Open), TFP (LnTFP) and the real wage of unskilled male workers (LnRW).[34] The sub-periods follow a slightly different periodization than the one discussed above, as it was necessary to remove several shocks from the analysis (such as the Asian crisis of 1997–98).

We follow the Toda-Yamamoto procedure to test for Granger causality, which allows us to examine the short-run causal mechanisms between openness, TFP and real wages.[35] This test makes it possible to test for Granger-causality in the presence of integrated variables and co-integration. The highest order of integration (m) of the variables is identified and the best possible VAR (p) is estimated (the results of the Augmented Dickey-Fuller tests for stationarity can be found below, Table 4.2). The causality tests are in turn performed on the first p lags of a VAR ($p + m$) system. Openness is said to Granger-cause TFP if the past values of openness contain useful information on the current value of TFP. Table 4.1 reports on the results.

The results indicate that there is reverse causality between TFP and openness in all sub-periods. Under the Cultivation System, however, we find a negative feedback mechanism between TFP and openness; increases in trade did not only lead to lower productivity due to the systems inefficiencies, but this also suggests that the reallocation of resources from manufacturing to agriculture further stimulated the export of cash crops in exchange for Dutch textiles (and thus an increase in openness). However, in the 1860s the relationship changed and higher levels of trade started to contribute to TFP, and it worked in the opposite direction as well. Thus, after 1860 we find the patterns predicted by the theoretical literature: the liberalization of the Javanese economy led to increases in efficiency, investments and consequent productivity. We have thus more formal evidence of the positive influence of trade openness on TFP growth in this period. The finding that the growth of TFP in turn stimulates trade is new. This finding might suggest that trade growth between 1865 and 1913 was not purely demand driven (as under the Cultivation System), but also spurred by increasing supply resulting from the advances in productivity.

Figure 4.4 shows only a weak correlation between openness and real wages. The development of living standards in this period has been a subject of some controversy. Since the 1890s the Dutch colonial government implemented 'ethical' welfare policies. While some scholars have suggested this led to an improvement in the standard of living in the early twentieth century,[36] others claim these were generally a failure.[37] Real wages show a decline until the 1920s and only a brief recovery in the 1930s resulting from deflation, while estimates on consumption and GDP per capita show slight increases. Two recent studies on the development of heights have also come to different conclusions for the early twentieth century; while Peter Foldvari et al. find declining heights, the study by Jörg Baten et al. points to a slow recovery of average heights after the cultivation system.[38]

The answer to this puzzle may partly be resolved by differences in the developments between Java and the Outer Islands, as well as differences between population groups, as suggested by Lindblad.[39] In contrast to Java, where 'free' labour had become abundant in the late nineteenth century, and thus relatively cheap, the Outer Islands were still frontier economies and faced labour scarcity.[40] Consequently, living standards were somewhat higher there and declined less (or not at all) over this period. Nonetheless, as Lindblad notes, also in the Outer Islands, Javanese unskilled wage labourers suffered.[41] The increases in consumption and GDP per capita in this period may be explained by the growing wealth of the Europeans.[42] As also observed by others,[43] income inequality probably increased in this period. While trade during this period may thus have increased TFP, which perhaps allowed the accumulation of wealth in the hands of relatively few Europeans (and Chinese), most of the indigenous population did not benefit, and their living standards were possibly even negatively affected by trade.

Jumping forward in time to the post-colonial period, these relationships change slightly, although we find again a reverse causality between openness and TFP as both grow until the 1997 Asian financial crisis (see Table 4.1). Both the growth in the volume of exports and the contribution of exports to GDP were high. In contrast to the earlier periods, when agricultural products and natural resources had dominated exports, manufactured products, which have growth-promoting production functions, now formed a major part of the exports.[44] Structural change took place as the share of agriculture in total employment declined from over 70 to below 40 per cent between 1961 and 2000. While this structural change accounts for part of the overall productivity growth, another part came from productivity growth within each sector.

At the same time, living standards increased, as demonstrated by real wages and confirmed by, for example, the growth in stature and GDP per capita.[45] Table 4.1 shows that increase in openness in this period had no direct effect on the increases in real wages (as indicated by the high *p*-value of LnRW in the last row). Underlying this welfare growth was the 'green revolution' in rice agriculture and the consequential improvement of per capita food supply.[46] Whereas until the 1960s population growth and increases in food supply were always in a somewhat uncomfortable equilibrium, per capita food doubled between 1960 and 2000.[47] To some extent, this 'revolution' was stimulated by trade, as the export of oil for high prices (especially between 1974 and 1986) expanded government funds that were used to stimulate the agricultural sector by investments in irrigation, roads and protection of farmers from international price fluctuations,[48] as well as the introduction of new high-yielding rice varieties.[49] Only via the redistributive activities of the state, did export lead to pro-poor economic growth.[50]

While Granger causality tests are informative about the direction of short-run causality, it is also important to establish whether there is a long-term relationship between trade, TFP and real wages. Do these series follow a similar trend in the long term; that is, are these series said to be co-integrated? A necessary condition for co-integration is that each of the variables should be integrated of the same order (more than zero) and that both series contain a deterministic trend.[51] Augmented Dickey-Fuller tests verify that this preliminary condition is met (see Table 4.2). Given that the integration of the variables is of the same order, Johansen

Table 4.2: Augmented Dickey-Fuller unit root tests

	1825–65		*1865–1913*		*1967–97*	
Variable	*Trend*	*Drift*	*Trend*	*Drift*	*Trend*	*Drift*
Open	–2.49 (0.34)	–0.75 (0.23)	–3.72** (0.02)	–0.68 (0.25)	–1.57 (0.80)	–1.308 (0.10)
Δ Open	–4.93*** (0.00)	–5.00*** (0.00)	–6.96*** (0.00)	–6.83*** (0.00)	–4.56*** (0.00)	–4.671*** (0.000)
LnTFP	–0.77 (0.97)	–1.59* (0.06)	–0.17 (0.99)	1.57 (0.94)	–2.59 (0.29)	–1.51* (0.07)
Δ LnTFP	–6.71*** (0.00)	–6.51*** (0.00)	–8.46*** (0.00)	–8.27*** (0.00)	–3.19* (0.09)	–3.20*** (0.00)
LnRW	–	–	–	–	–2.29 (0.44)	0.09 (0.53)
Δ LnRW	–	–	–	–	–3.12* (0.08)	–3.20*** (0.00)

Note: P-value in parentheses. *, **, and *** denote that we can reject the null-hypothesis of non-stationarity at 10 per cent, 5 per cent and 1 per cent, respectively. For the differences we have also used a test specification constant only. This does not change our results (upon request from authors). The lag-length is based on the AIC.

co-integration tests on the estimated VAR specifications are conducted to examine the possibility of a long-term relationship (Tables 4.3 and 4.4).[52]

The test results suggest a long-term relationship among TFP and openness in the sub-period 1865–1913. Under the Cultivation System, no long-term association can be discerned, as indicated by the results from the trace test in Table 4.3. With respect to the third sub-period (1967–97), we find evidence for one co-integrating vector (Table 4.4). The normalized co-integrating vector in Table 4.4, however, reports on an insignificant long-run coefficient of the real wage, which implies that there was no direct long-run relationship between TFP and living standards. These results of Tables 4.3 and 4.4 suggest that there is a long-run positive relationship between trade and productivity growth (under the condition that price mechanisms are functioning efficiently). However, living standards do not necessarily benefit from trade and productivity directly (and not at all before decolonization), but only indirectly via the channel of productivity (probably caused by state-supported agricultural development, as argued above).[53]

Table 4.3: Results from the trace tests—openness and TFP

	Trace test					
	1825–65		*1865–1913*		*1967–97*	
No. of co-integrating relationships	*Trace statistics*	*Critical value*	*Trace statistics*	*Critical value*	*Trace statistics*	*Critical value*
0	14.60	15.41	26.31	15.41	20.32	15.41
At most 1	3.78	3.76	0.23	3.76	3.66	3.76
	Normalized co-integration vectors					
	–		LnTFP = 3.78 +0.022open (0.003)*		LnTFP = 3.63 +0.024open (0.003)*	

Note: A constant trend is included when modelling the series, because the trends are approximately linear. The VEC models are stable, there is no autocorrelation, and the normality conditions are met. * denotes significance of the long-run coefficient at the 1 per cent level. Standard error in parentheses.

Table 4.4: Results from the trace tests—real wages, TFP and openness

	Trace test	
	1967–97	
No. of co-integrating relationships	*Trace statistics*	*Critical value*
0	31.31	29.68
At most 1	14.22	15.41
	Normalized co-integration vector	
	LnTFP = 4.17 +0.14 (0.1)	LnRW +0.014open (0.003)*

Note: A constant trend is included when modelling the series, because the trends are approximately linear. The VEC models are stable, there is no autocorrelation, and the normality conditions are met. * denotes significance of the long-run coefficient at the 1 per cent level. Standard error in parentheses.

Conclusion

In theory, it is expected that openness will lead to increased exposure to (outside) market forces and increased specialization, which in turn results in economic growth. Critics of globalization have, however, suggested that 'openness will likely exert pressures that widen income and wealth disparities within countries'.[54] While some parts of a society grow richer from the profits of trade, the living standards of a major part of the population may not increase, or may perhaps even decline.

This chapter examined the relationship between openness and economic development in Indonesia over the very long run. TFP and real wages were taken as relevant indicators for economic growth, and openness (imports and exports as a share of per capita GDP) as a proxy for levels of trade. On the basis of openness, we can discern three different periods of trade growth: (1) 1825–65, (2) 1865–1913 and (3) 1966–2000. Due to data limitations, the period between the world wars is outside the scope of this analysis.

There was a clear negative relationship between openness and TFP growth during the first period (1825–65), which was mainly the result of the Cultivation System. The colonial state regulated the export sector of the economy, and created market inefficiencies that were harmful for economic development. In the first wave of globalization (1865–1913), a long-term relationship among openness and TFP emerged. It is furthermore shown that, in the short run, a feedback mechanism occurred: increases in levels of trade enhanced growth TFP, whereas increases in TFP drove further trade expansion. Living standards do not seem to have benefited from this growth. The second wave of globalization took place in the second half of the twentieth century. In this period (1966–97) we again find a long-run relation and feedback mechanism between trade and TFP. We do not find a direct link between trade and real wages in this period, but we do observe short-run causality running from TFP to living standards. This was a period of both export expansion and structural change. While Hal Hill (in this volume) argued that the causality between per capita income and structural change runs from the former to the latter, our analysis also reveals the reverse.

Overall, the results from the time series analysis confirm the existence of a relationship between waves of globalization and productivity growth in some periods. This relationship was, however, clearly dependent on the broader institutional and economic context. Trade did not always lead to growth and poverty reduction. We should also consider the unequal geographical spread of the benefits (and in some regions negative effects) of this trade, which has been discussed in various works of Lindblad, as well as by Booth in this volume. After decolonization living standards improved, not directly as a result of trade, but rather as a result of productivity growth, mainly in agriculture, which in turn was stimulated by government investment. While the latter was made possible by the oil exports, the link between trade and the alleviation of mass poverty is obviously less straightforward than often suggested by globalization enthusiasts.

Notes

1. For example, Lindblad, 'Foreign Investment in Southeast Asia', 61–89; Lindblad, 'Indonesian Economic Development', 193–217; Lindblad, *Bridges to New Business.*
2. Bhagwati and Srinivasan, 'Trade and Poverty in the Poor Countries', 180–3. The literature on globalization, growth and poverty is endless.
3. 'Towards the End of Poverty', *The Economist*, 1 June 2013.
4. Srinivasan and Bhagwati, 'Outward-Orientation and Development', 38.
5. In this chapter we build on Van Zanden and Marks, *An Economic History of Indonesia.*
6. Lindblad, 'The Late Colonial State and Economic Expansion', 111.
7. Lindblad, *Between Dayak and Dutch.*
8. Booth, *The Indonesian Economy in the Nineteenth and Twentieth Centuries*, 203.
9. Granger, 'Investigating Causal Relations'.
10. See Reid, *Southeast Asia in the Age of Commerce.*
11. Maddison, 'Dutch Income in and from Indonesia', 645–70.
12. Knaap, 'Shipping and Trade', 417.
13. Van Zanden, 'Economic Growth in Java'; Van der Eng, 'The Sources of Economic Growth', 294–309.
14. Lindblad, 'De handel tussen Nederland en', 240–98.
15. Booth, *The Indonesian Economy in the Nineteenth and Twentieth Centuries*, 205.
16. Hanson, *Trade in Transition*, 14.
17. Boediono and Pangestu, 'Indonesia: The Structure and Causes of Manufacturing Protection', 3.
18. Ibid., 5.
19. Paauw, 'From Colonial to Guided Economy', 212.
20. Boediono and Pangestu, 'Indonesia', 6.
21. Hill, *The Indonesian Economy*, 114.
22. Ibid., 115.
23. Boediono and Pangestu, '"Indonesia": The Structure and Causes of Manufacturing Protection', 8.
24. Solow, 'A Contribution to the Theory of Economic Growth', 65–94.
25. Chen, 'The Total Factor Productivity Debate', 21–2.
26. Van Zanden, 'Economic Growth in Java'; Van der Eng, 'The Sources of Economic Growth'.
27. Fasseur, *Kultuurstelsel en Koloniale Baten.*

28. Van Zanden and Marks, *An Economic History of Indonesia*, chapter 5.
29. Allen et al., 'Wages, Prices and Living Standards in China', 8–38.
30. Van Zanden and Marks, *An Economic History of Indonesia*, 114–6; wage data: Dros, *Changing Economy in Indonesia*, vol. 13; price data: Altes, *Changing Economy in Indonesia*, vol. 15; Rice prices see: Van Zanden, 'On the Efficiency of Markets for Agricultural Products'; Marks, 'Unity or Diversity?', 310–24.
31. Van Leeuwen, 'Human Capital and Economic Growth in India'. His data are constructed from various sources to estimate a continuous series.
32. As the Indonesian series were differently indexed, these were converted to subsistence ratio through the equation: $y = 2.2561x + 0.241$ ($R^2 = 0.5884$) based on the correlation between the two series.
33. Van Zanden and Marks, *An Economic History of Indonesia*, 52; Baten et al., 'The Biological Standard of Living and Body Height', 103–22.
34. VAR is an econometric model employed to examine linear relationships among multiple time series.
35. Standard Granger-causality tests fit the best possible VAR model on the values of TFP and include past values of openness as independent variables to the specification. Joint significance of the coefficients of the lags of openness implies Granger-causality. These test results can be misleading due to omitted variable bias, non-stationarity of the variables, and/or a wrong choice of the number of lags. Applying a granger-causality test on differenced variables is also prone to errors as it might remove any possible long-run relationship among the variables (see Toda and Yamamoto, 'Statistical Inferences in Vector Autoregressions', 225–50, and Plosser and Schwert, 'Money, Income and Sunspots', 637–60.
36. E.g. Boomgaard, 'The Welfare Services in India'.
37. E.g. Elson, *Javanese Peasants and the Colonial Sugar Industry*.
38. Foldvari et al., 'Indonesia's Regional Welfare', 78–99; Baten et al., 'The Biological Standard of Living and Body Height'.
39. Lindblad, 'The Outer Islands in the 19th Century', 102; ibid., "The Late Colonial State'; ibid., *Between Dayak and Dutch*; Clemens and Lindblad, *Het belang van de Buitengewesten*.
40. Foldvari et al., 'Indonesia's Regional Welfare'.
41. Lindblad, 'The Outer Islands in the 19th Century', 104; Touwen, *Extremes in the Archipelago*, 113.
42. Lindblad, 'The Late Colonial State and Economic Expansion', 113.
43. Leigh and Van der Eng, 'Inequality in Indonesia', 209–12.
44. Van Zanden and Marks, *An Economic History of Indonesia*, 193–4.
45. Foldvari et al., 'Indonesia's Regional Welfare'; Baten et al., 'The Biological Standard of Living and Body Height'; Van der Eng, 'The Sources of Economic Growth'.
46. Van der Eng, 'Food for Growth'.

47. See in this volume: Frankema, 'The Green Revolution in Indonesia'.
48. Van der Eng, 'Food for Growth'.
49. Frankema, 'The Green Revolution in Indonesia'.
50. Henley, 'The Agrarian Roots'.
51. Granger, 'Investigating Causal Relations', 424–38.
52. Johansen, 'Estimation and Hypothesis', 1551–80; ibid., *Likelihood-Based Inference.*
53. These results thus corroborate with Henley, 'The Agrarian Roots'.
54. Rodrik, *Making Openness Work*, 13.

5

A Money Paradox in the Netherlands Indies: Coins, Commerce and Consumers in Late Colonial Life (1800–1942)

Alexander Claver

Capital, credit and remittances figure prominently in the economic history of the Netherlands Indies. Less attention has been paid to the primary means through which business in the colony was conducted, that is, money. Leaving barter trade aside, money transactions have been part and parcel of Indonesia's goods exchange for centuries. Coins were produced and put into circulation in the Indonesian Archipelago long before the presence of the first Europeans. Banknotes did not appear before the second half of the nineteenth century.

Throughout history, coins have been used predominantly for exchanges with a profit motive, for administrative transfers and for religious donations. At the same time, coins are removed from circulation as they get lost, buried, hidden or stolen. They are used in jewellery, melted down or hoarded when the value of their metal content is larger than their circulating value. The availability of money is important to production, modernization and investment. Money enables diversification of production for a more distant market since its availability simplifies the computation of relative values. Barter, on the other hand, is only feasible at close quarters.[1]

In the colonial context of the Netherlands Indies complaints were frequently voiced concerning the availability, size and/or relative value of money in circulation. This chapter examines the way money in the Indonesian Archipelago fulfilled its purpose as a means of exchange in the late colonial economy. The focus will be on coins and their use in commercial transactions. Paper money is excluded here, since the issuance and use of banknotes listened to different rules, answered to different demands and primarily affected the higher echelons of colonial society. Attention will be paid to the major monetary developments and currency reforms in the Netherlands Indies, especially Java, during the nineteenth and early twentieth centuries.

This survey attempts to identify the contribution of the coinage system in supporting the peasant economy in general and the trading sector in particular. First, some remarks on money and society will be made. This is followed by a section on the introduction and circulation of copper coins (*duiten*) in the colonial economy. The next section deals with monetary stabilization efforts by the colonial administration and money purges throughout the Indonesian Archipelago. The last paragraph summarizes the results and presents some tentative conclusions.

Money and Society

Java in the early nineteenth century used to be depicted as a stagnant economy dominated by subsistence agriculture. In this view the countryside consisted of largely self-sufficient villages inhabited by an undifferentiated mass of peasants. Wage labour was virtually absent and the existence of markets and trade fledgling. Money transactions were scarce and money was therefore of limited use. In Java, apart from the *kraton* (court) and other seats of bureaucratic power, coins were not in demand as a medium of exchange. Exchange of goods at village level usually took the form of barter.

This simplified image has been criticized and readjusted accordingly.[2] The Javanese economy around 1800 was indeed characterized by low population density and a limited marketing system. Incentives to increase market production were relatively weak and levels of commercialization and specialization were low. However, indigenous economic diversity was not absent. Research has, for instance, shown non-agricultural economic activities in Java around 1820, the existence of production for the market (both local and supra-local) and the manifold outside contacts of villages.[3]

Although the amount of money in circulation was small, as indicated in Figure 5.1, Javanese society was not moneyless and its economy was not devoid of money transactions.[4] Throughout Southeast Asia a degree of monetization had taken place long before the advent of European traders.[5] Europe could offer few commodities for barter. Purchases therefore had to be made with specie, principally silver coins. With the arrival of these new traders the indigenous money in circulation was supplemented with the Spanish piastre—also known as mat, real or dollar. This currency remained dominant in international trade for a long time.[6]

The Vereenigde Oostindische Compagnie (VOC) likewise bought and shipped silver in ever larger quantities to its trading posts in Asia.[7] Being a remittance medium for international transfers, this kind of silver was scarcely used as a medium of exchange or measurer of value for indigenous Javanese transactions.[8] It did have an impact upon the local Batavian economy, however, as can be judged from the introduction of legal measures in the 1630s for the circulation of 'primitive' money. This legislation appears to have been directed at the business of Chinese traders who had settled in Batavia and the surrounding area.[9]

Over the years money transactions started to assume more importance. Between 1602 and 1811, 458 monetary decrees were promulgated. About 300 were issued during the last quarter of the seventeenth century. In the eighteenth century copper gained more importance as tender.[10] This enabled a penetration of the local economy since the higher-value silver coins were utilized principally among the elite groups.[11] The scarcity of silver, which affected business operations, could now partly be countered.[12]

Still, there was a constant liquidity shortage (both copper coins for small change and silver for larger transactions) because of the hoarding, smuggling and/or export of them for their precious metal content.[13] The monetization of the economy accelerated as well, as did the need for money.[14] After 1800, Javanese domestic demand for money was growing fast and the colonial authorities responded by importing large quantities of copper for circulation as small change. This remained the principle for accommodating local money requirements for years to come.[15]

Copper Coins

During the nineteenth century, a number of coinage acts were issued with the explicit purpose of improving the monetary situation. After the British had left Java, the Coinage Act of 1817 came into effect and, with it, the British Javanese rupee changed its name to the Netherlands Indian guilder.[16] The predilection of the authorities for copper money is striking, and contrasted starkly with the views of the British and the early VOC administrators. The regulation under which copper money did not have to be accepted for payments of over 10 piastres was abandoned. Copper was thus placed on an equal footing with silver. Large amounts of copper coins—so-called *duiten* (doits)[17]—withdrawn from circulation during the British Interregnum, were once again declared legal tender. In 1818 more copper coins, either being shipped from the Netherlands or minted in Surabaya, made their appearance.[18]

Between 1816 and 1826 the money in circulation increased approximately fourfold. This was largely attributable to the introduction of millions of *duiten* (one standard silver guilder coin was divided into 120 *duiten*) flooding the island of Java. A total of 240 million *duiten* was imported by the government in this decade, not counting the huge quantities of copper money minted in Surabaya from 1818 onwards.[19] Copper was considered the most suitable means of exchange. People 'had seen fit to multiply the copper coin as much as possible in the interest of the good people of these countries'. In 1824 it was remarked that copper money was 'the most powerful tool of promoting industry and prosperity amongst the natives'.[20]

The general needs of the indigenous population were considered too limited to justify the use of more precious metals as a general medium of exchange.[21] Political opportunism was present as well. After the British had left Java, a letter to the Minister of Colonies in 1816 stated: 'Send us money, especially small change, in particular *duiten*, so that we, in commencing our rule, can show with deeds how much His Majesty is favourably disposed towards the inhabitants here, and how much the Dutch Government in this respect exceeds all foreign ones.'[22]

Soon the abundance of copper money led to depreciation and inflation. As mentioned, the government made the bulk of its payments in copper money. According to a decree of 1811 monthly military wages were paid in copper coins. Apparently the market demanded small coins for daily payments and wage labourers and soldiers alike did not want to be paid in medium-sized coins.[23] The administration thus injected ever more *duiten* into the economy and persistently followed an inflationary policy.

This damaging policy was maintained even though the inherent dangers had been recognized early on. In 1681, for instance, the monetary situation in Sri Lanka (former Ceylon) led VOC administrators to recommend, in general, that 'from now on no copper money [...] shall be accepted or received [...], but this has to occur in silver money, the rixdollar (*rijksdaalder*), being the standard [...]. We consider it necessary to retain copper money in order to allow the people, mainly those of small stature, to help each other [...], but to fill a complete country with it is utterly ruinous.'[24]

Such objections, voiced in several memoranda, fell on deaf ears.[25] Since silver coins held their value, they were slowly withdrawn from circulation—being hoarded as well as used for remittances—and had all but disappeared by the 1820s.[26] (This is in accordance with 'Gresham's law', which states that 'bad' (relatively less valuable) money will drive 'good' (relatively more valuable) money out of circulation.) Naturally, the Netherlands Indian guilder remained based on silver: the precious metal preferred all over Asia. Silver currencies underpinned domestic and international Asian trade and so different silver coins, like the Indian rupee, the Dutch rixdollar (*rijksdaalder*), the Spanish dollar and the Mexican dollar,[27] circulated alongside each other, especially in trading areas.[28]

The coexistence of different currencies with their own variable exchange rate did not improve the transparency of money transactions. Closer inspection of the variety of coins in circulation shows the complicated monetary situation in Java at the beginning of the nineteenth century. In the 1820s at least twenty sorts of coins of different metal composition were in circulation with such exotic names as *ducaton*, *bonk*, *arcon*, *doubloon* or *tahil*. In addition, a memorandum of 1824 describing the abundance of copper coinage identified no less than fourteen different kinds of *duiten* circulating within Java.[29]

This extreme lack of monetary uniformity and the continuing copper deluge did not see a meaningful response. The Coinage Act of 1826 was rather modest, making the Dutch guilder the standard coin. A renewed limitation on copper payments to a legal maximum of 10 Netherlands Indian guilders constituted the only significant improvement.[30] By now, the stream of copper money had become a huge problem.

In January 1827, the directors of the Batavia Exchange emphasized the great difficulties experienced from 'an absence of a sufficient circulating medium and the excessive amount of *duiten* put into circulation'. They claimed copper coinage had ousted gold and silver specie and before long there would be nothing left but copper and a small number of promissory notes:

> At the Public Cash Offices no copper is accepted, but copper is paid out everywhere. Thus everyone is swamped with copper money which cannot be brought into circulation again. From this, endless conflicts and difficulties arise on a daily basis. Besides, the insufficiency of the copper coin is so huge that it cannot possibly be used for transactions of any importance. Trading transactions have to be cancelled since there are no means of payment.

In conclusion it was said that the consequences 'will result in widespread impoverishment and stagnation of commerce'.[31]

The truthfulness of these assertions is vividly demonstrated in the following outburst of a Batavian businessman in 1827:

> [...] just now some cartloads of copper money are stopping in front of my door, the verification of which will keep me busy the remaining six hours of this day. That money is coming from a Chinese debtor of whom I have demanded payment for a long time to no avail and who is offering me copper money at this time [...] in the hope, that I will reject him, and that he will profit from this rejection later on.[32]

Despite this deplorable situation there was no significant reduction in the amount of copper in circulation. In 1826 *duiten* accounted for no less than 84 per cent of total money in circulation. This percentage would rise to 96 per cent in 1827 and 100 per cent in 1828. In 1829 the percentage came down to 87 per cent and was slightly reduced to 83 per cent in 1830 (Figure 5.2).[33] The trading business depended more and more on credit for its survival. Traders vouched for colleagues and vice versa, reducing the transparency of the concluded deals and invalidating control mechanisms, since it became impossible to judge financial proposals and the probity of those behind them.

In 1823, Candidus ten Brink, an associate in the Batavian trading company Ten Brink & Reynst, would write:

> It is impossible to form an opinion concerning solidity [financial soundness] in a colony if one has not been there; everyone vouches for one

> another [...] In this way someone without a penny in the world, buys houses, estates, etc.[34]

In other words, credit depended more on personal standing than on the security offered, giving a monopoly to what could be considered a 'commercial aristocracy'.

The monetary situation worsened with the advent of the Cultivation System in the 1830s. Private traders were deprived of using export products/crops as a means of remittance since these were mainly exported through the government. Private commitments overseas could only be settled by using an already scarce medium: silver. In addition, exports from the Netherlands Indies were no longer balanced by monetary remittances, as the greater part of the proceeds was spent by the government in the Netherlands; only a small part was returned to the colony. In effect, this new drain to the Netherlands replaced the earlier drain on the money supply by Chinese merchants.[35] After 1830 silver was only sporadically in circulation. If not exported, it was hoarded or melted down to be made into ornaments.[36]

Furthermore, it was decided that the government would effect all payments related to the Cultivation System—crop payments, transport costs, cultivation commission—exclusively in copper. The Javanese economy was thus inundated with copper *duiten*, resulting in a sudden drop in value of the copper currency in the 1840s.[37] Between 1833 and 1843 more than 3 billion *duiten* were put into circulation. In 1832 the restriction on the use of copper for payments was lifted and *duiten* could henceforth be used for unlimited payments.[38] At this point the monetary situation—dubbed the Copper Standard Period—was in total disarray. Money in circulation consisted mainly of *duiten* (approximately 80 per cent), some substitute paper money issued by the government in 1832 and 1842, and the banknotes of De Javasche Bank (DJB) (Figures 5.1 and 5.2).[39]

Monetary policy affected the indigenous economy as well, although the evidence is inconclusive. The Cultivation System provided many Javanese with a regular money income since the export crops they were obliged to grow were paid for in cash. Indigenous monetization proceeded slowly and erratically and was mainly confined to the circulation of *duiten*. Still, the capacity to absorb new money appears to have been large, which indicates an acceleration of the process of commercialization during the first phase of the Cultivation System. By 1850 the rural Javanese economy had been monetized to some extent.[40]

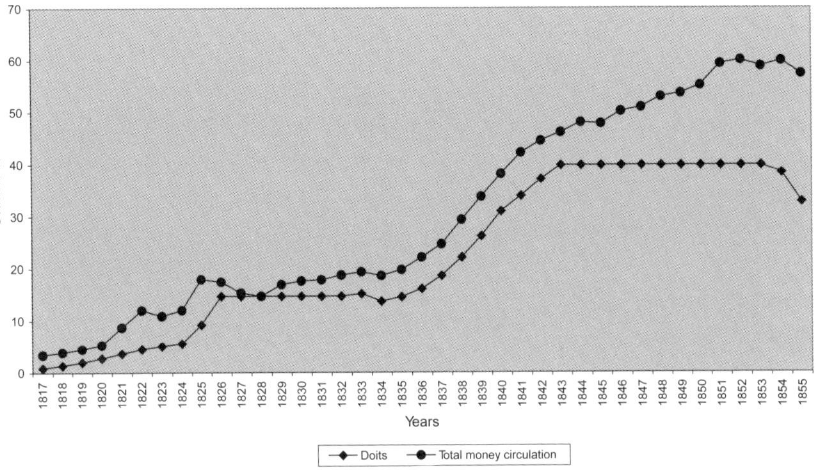

Note: The total amount of money in circulation until 1855 cannot be determined exactly because of the limitations of the available sources. The amount of *duiten* in circulation is most likely underestimated. The often-made assumption that there was no silver money in circulation is probably not true either. Notwithstanding these cautions, Figure 5.1 clearly shows the prominence of copper money in total money circulation for the entire period (see also Figure 5.2). The amount of money in circulation rose steadily after 1816, accelerating in the early 1820s when commodity prices were high. Between 1825 and 1835 the level fluctuated at around *f* 17 million, after which it increased very rapidly to *f* 50 million in 1846. The introduction of huge quantities of *duiten* in response to the Cultivation System's requirements accounted for this.

Pleas for monetary reform, however, did not come from Indonesian peasants, but from merchants, planters and manufacturers. They continued to experience great difficulty in financing their transactions. Commercial transactions also became increasingly expensive since the huge amounts of *duiten* were heavy and costly to store and transport. With the Cultivation System running into trouble in the 1840s, calls for a proper balance between supply and demand money started to be heard.[41]

Source: Van Laanen (1980: 55–60).

Figure 5.1: The circulation of money and doits (*duiten*) in the Netherlands Indies, 1817–55 (million guilders)

Currency Reforms and Money Purges

Towards the middle of the nineteenth century it had become clear that the monetary system was inadequate for domestic use and the expanding international financial traffic.[42] In 1846 a first attempt at purging copper doits from circulation was made. As shown in Table 5.1, some progress

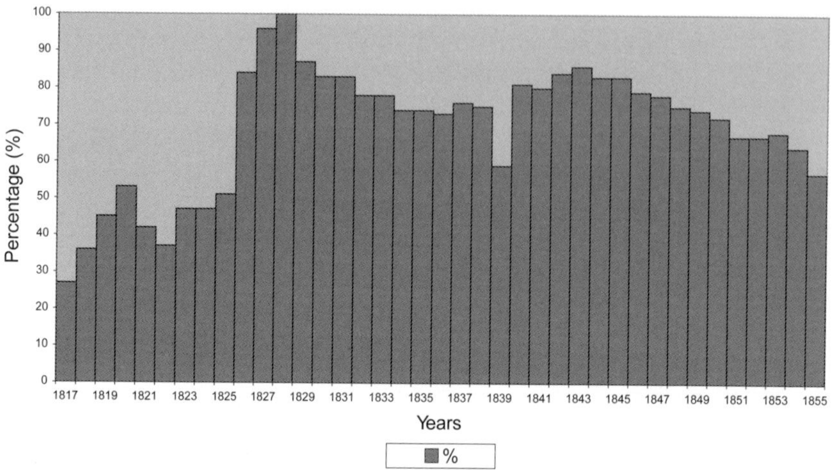

Source: Van Laanen (1980: 55–60).

Figure 5.2: Share of doits (*duiten*) in total money in circulation in the Netherlands Indies, 1817–55

occurred, but in the end the plan failed to achieve its goal. It did pave the way for the introduction of the silver standard as expressed in the Coinage Act of 1854.[43] A monetary union with the Netherlands came into effect and the Dutch guilder became legal tender. Small change, or so-called subsidiary coins, could now only be used for payments up to limited amounts. The standardization and unification of coinage in circulation was attempted but not completely achieved. Most coins were excluded, with the exception of the Spanish piastre, the Mexican dollar and the five-franc piece, which were accepted at Public Cash Offices until 1885.

Table 5.1: Doits (*duiten*) in circulation in the Netherlands Indies, 1846–60 (million guilders)

1846	22.9	1851	11.2	1856	9.8
1847	19.4	1852	11.7	1857	9.5
1848	18.7	1853	11.0	1858	7.8
1849	16.9	1854	8.3	1859	7.3
1850	13.7	1855	9.3	1860	7.3

Source: Van Laanen (1980: 20–1, 60, 69).

Copper pieces remained in circulation with new small coins of 2½, 1 and ½ cent being introduced. The old copper *duiten* ceased to be legal tender in the Outer Islands in 1858 and in Java and Madura in 1859. However, *duiten* had come to enjoy a more or less independent existence in inland Java. Here, it was used for the purpose of payments at local level.[44] Almost 900 million *duiten* with an approximate value of *f* 7.33 million failed to be collected and remained in circulation (see Table 5.1).

Exchanging old *duiten* for new cents put the indigenous population at a disadvantage as the rate did not correspond with the purchasing power of the *duit* at the local market or *pasar*.[45] Unwilling to accept a loss, people simply turned to money changers to obtain the legal subsidiary coins occasionally needed for the payment of taxes. As a result the new copper coins, the only ones accepted by the tax collectors, started to accumulate at the Public Cash Offices and subsequently disappeared from circulation.[46]

Despite all the problems encountered, the monetary system slowly began to meet the requirements of the trading sector. The Coinage Act of 1877 saw a conversion to the gold standard whereby silver remained legal tender. (This construction came to be called the limping gold standard.) Since 1873 the price of silver had gone down and it seemed sensible to have gold support the fiduciary money. However, demonetizing silver would have rendered the large silver reserves of the Dutch central bank worthless as a means of backing its note issue. Selling it would have resulted in unacceptable losses, given the steadily decreasing price. Fortunately, payments between the Netherlands and the colony were usually settled with the remittance of silver, and because of the monetary union Dutch silver could freely flow to the Netherlands Indies. The Netherlands Indies thus gradually relieved the mother country of its silver surplus at a time when territorial expansion and the growth of private enterprise boosted its demand for silver enormously.[47]

By now the monetary situation had changed for the better. The last quarter of the nineteenth century saw a more beneficial trading climate. The only thing to do was to enforce national uniformity of the coinage system and incorporate the colonial territory into the Dutch monetary system. This ultimately required a series of currency reforms in Java and the Outer Islands.[48] The first large-scale coinage purge occurred in 1899/1900 when an all-out attempt was made to clear Java and Madura of all remaining *duiten*. Initially it was feared that the indigenous population had become so accustomed to this specific coin that the plan could not be executed.

In July 1899 the Semarang newspaper *De Locomotief* voiced its doubts, writing of 'the strong devotion of the native with regard to his *duiten*'.[49] These fears turned out to be unfounded and, by 15 March 1900, most of the *duiten* had been withdrawn from circulation. A few days earlier, on 9 March 1900, *De Locomotief*, in a mildly critical evaluation, had already acknowledged the success of the purge:

> In general the native seems content with the conversion [...] [he] will benefit a lot by the introduction of cents; he is able, amongst other things, to pay his taxes, buy the necessary salt and get railway tickets without having to change against a premium at the money-changers each and every time.[50]

Purges in 1906 and 1908 were aimed at the coinage system of the Straits Settlements. The dominance of the Straits dollar on the coasts of East Sumatra and West Kalimantan had become a nuisance to the colonial authorities in Batavia who considered it a threat to Dutch sovereignty over this part of the archipelago. Despite the difficulty of such an undertaking in these remote and secluded areas the problem was ultimately solved. For many months 'lonely inspectors would travel quietly from border isle to border isle, collecting old dollars along the length of the frontier and exchanging them for shiny new guilders'.[51] Many purges followed, until the last one had been completed in 1930.[52]

The gold standard was to be upheld until the outbreak of the First World War when it was temporarily suspended. In 1925 the ban on the export of gold was lifted and the gold standard came back into operation. The expansion of the indigenous economy was hardly influenced by all this and monetization proceeded (see Table 5.2 and Figure 5.3). Demand for small change kept rising, but the supply of small coins could not possibly keep up with the needs of a growing and increasingly spendthrift indigenous population. In spite of all the efforts the authorities still failed to match supply and demand for money.[53]

The Great Depression of the 1930s destroyed any hopes of arriving at a short-term solution. The strongly export-oriented Western sector suffered the most, and productive capacity contracted. The indigenous population experienced a great reduction in money income, but the shock was a good deal absorbed by falling costs of living and a partial return to the barter economy.[54] Naturally, there was an accompanying decline in the amount of money in circulation (see Table 5.2 and Figure 5.3). However, the decrease in small change in general and of copper in particular was considerably less than in paper money and coins of greater

Table 5.2: Total money in circulation in the Netherlands Indies, 1855–1940 (million guilders)

1855	44.8	1880	164.4	1905	155.9	1930	518.8
1860	47.6	1885	155.6	1910	202.1	1935	272.1
1865	82.5	1890	160.4	1915	284.6	1940	323.0
1870	102.7	1895	151.4	1920	545.6		
1875	143.9	1900	173.9	1925	489.4		

Note: These data cannot be used in combination with the data displayed in Figure 5.1 since the available sources required different methods of calculation.

Source: Van Laanen (1980: 55, 61, 69–77).

denomination. This indicates that the indigenous economy was less susceptible to outside influences and far from integrated in the world economy. Monetization in the Indonesian Archipelago was not complete.[55]

The monetary situation received a crushing blow with the invasion of the Japanese in 1942.[56] All commercial banks were rapidly liquidated

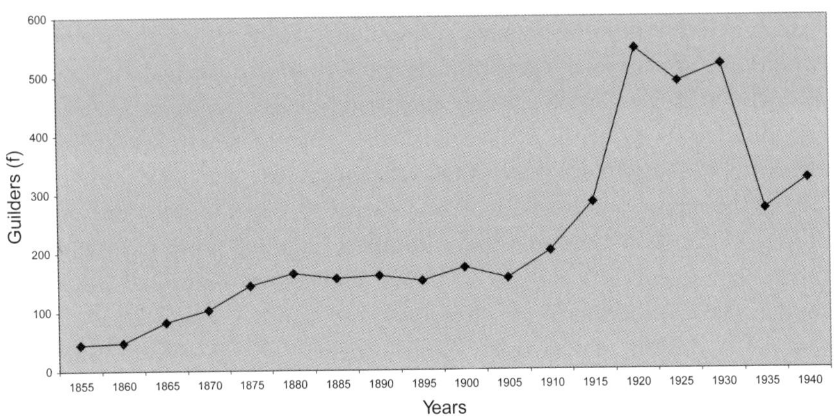

Note: Figure 5.3 shows an almost continuous increase in the total amount of money in circulation. This steady growth was interrupted only by major economic upheavals such as the crisis of 1884 and the Depression of the 1930s. After 1905 the Netherlands Indies entered a new phase which saw a very rapid monetization of the economy as evidenced by the enormous increase in money circulation.

Source: Table 5.2.

Figure 5.3: Total money in circulation in the Netherlands Indies, 1855–1940 (million guilders)

and their role was taken over by several private Japanese banks. DJB (the Dutch bank of circulation) was closed and replaced by the Nanpo Kaihatsu Ginko (Southern Development Bank). Acting as a central bank, it started to distribute invasion money printed in Japan in enormous amounts. In 1945 the total amount of invasion money accounted for more than 4 billion guilders, excluding as much as 2 billion guilders stolen from, amongst others, DJB.

Until March 1946 total money in circulation in the Indonesian Archipelago amounted to 8 billion guilders—an almost sixteenfold increase when compared with the maximum total amount recorded in 1930. This sparked the fall of the monetary value and severely worsened the economic burden.[57] A healthy monetary situation, which could support the economy, was not realized immediately after the surrender of the Japanese in 1945. The prolonged struggle for independence prevented the protracted process of monetization from reasserting itself.[58]

Conclusion

This chapter has shown that monetary developments within the colony were highly erratic. The monetary situation usually trailed the economic conditions. In general, government policy and initiative was geared towards short-term (political and economic) goals. Examples include the introduction of *duiten* in the second half of the eighteenth century which yielded a nice profit for both VOC administrators and local indigenous elites. The same can be said of the measures taken during the advent of the Cultivation System. The authorities required cash payments for the system to succeed and, in so doing, allowed an unlimited inflow of copper coins. Adhering to the (limping) gold standard many decades later was not a decision taken solely for the benefit of the colony, but also took into account the economic needs of the mother country.

Still, it must be concluded that the monetary needs of the population and entrepreneurs were generally served. Creative measures from peasants and businessmen, needed to circumvent the obstacles in place, did put some of the parties involved at a disadvantage. Nonetheless, monetization managed to creep in and the regulated monetary situation towards the end of the colonial era no longer resembled the chaotic situation at the beginning of the nineteenth century.

There appears to have been no real shortage of money in the colony, despite the complaints of merchants, manufactures and planters. The disappearance of silver and other money from circulation during the first half of the nineteenth century did not take place because supply failed to meet demand. This would automatically have resulted in price deflation by driving up the value of the existing coins. However, this seems not to have been the case. In other words, cash imports (mainly in copper) were generally responding to demand, that is, indigenous demand.

The available data even suggest a large unsatisfied indigenous demand for money, which meant that the stock of coins could be increased greatly without having an inflationary impact—a clear indication of the underestimated level of commercialization and monetization of indigenous society. Oversupply did occur in the early 1840s, causing a downward correction of the value of copper money. However, on average the purchasing power of *duiten* appears relatively stable, accounting for the popularity of the coin amongst the population at large.

The sustained scarcity of coins pertained primarily to copper and silver money of much larger value. This explains the complaints from business circles and subsequent gloomy picture of monetary affairs. The currency needs of the larger business of the European private sector differed fundamentally from the needs of the indigenous population. Private-sector imports of Chinese and Spanish-American money obviously did not manage to bring in silver in sufficient quantities. Most of it leaked away to Asia (China and India) in the seventeenth and eighteenth centuries and Europe (mainly the Netherlands) in the nineteenth century. Government measures, hoarding, exporting, smuggling and remittances because of prevailing market conditions accounted for this.

The Javanese *petani* had little to do with this. Complaints about the overabundance of worthless copper coins and the scarcity of coins of larger value came exclusively from the colonial (wholesale) trader. The bad functioning of the coinage system was his problem alone. After all, he was paid in half cents, cents and *duiten*. The accumulation of coins on his desk gave rise to administrative and logistical problems and literally cost him money. When it comes to the local Javanese population, however, the coinage system basically worked, which explains the money paradox. Only, the Javanese population did not write pamphlets, petitions or otherwise voice their opinion on the monetary system in place.

Primary Sources

National Archives Indonesia, Jakarta (*Arsip Nasional Republik Indonesia,* ANRI), *Arsip Muntwezen.*

Notes

1. Wicks, *Money, Markets, and Trade in Early Southeast Asia*, 11, 15.
2. Claver, *Dutch Commerce and Chinese Merchants in Java*, 17.
3. Boomgaard, 'Buitenzorg in 1805'; Boomgaard, *Children of the Colonial State*, 5–6, 109–35; Dick et al., *The Emergence of a National Economy*, 45–53, 58–9, 78–9; Fernando, 'Growth of Non-Agricultural Economic Activities', 77–8, 118; Klein, *The Monetisation of the Dutch East Indies*, 4; Van Laanen, *Changing Economy in Indonesia*, vol. 6, 14; Van Zanden, 'Linking Two Debates', 171.
4. Wicks, 'Monetary Developments in Java', 1986; Wicks, *Money, Markets, and Trade in Early Southeast Asia*, 243–300; Wisseman Christie, 'Money and its Uses in the Javanese States'.
5. Wicks, *Money, Markets, and Trade in Early Southeast Asia*; Dick et al., *The Emergence of a National Economy*, 50–1; Nagtegaal, *Riding the Dutch Tiger*, 107–14.
6. Klein, *The Monetisation of the Dutch East Indies*, 4; Van Laanen, *The Monetisation of the Dutch East Indies*, 14; Van den Berg, *Munt-, Crediet- en Bankwezen*, 107–11.
7. The complex monetary issues the VOC had to deal with are discussed at length in De Bree, *Gedenkboek van de Javasche Bank*, vol. 2, 24–51, 54–8. See also Jacobs, 'De Verenigde Oost-Indische Compagnie', 533–5.
8. For this purpose, Chinese copper and lead coins, so-called *picis* or *kepengs*, were used. These had been introduced into Java in the latter part of the thirteenth century (Van Aelst, 'A South-Chinese Currency Zone', 97–8, 101–5; Wicks, 'Monetary Developments in Java', 243; Wisseman Christie, 'Money and its Uses in the Javanese States'). Blussé details the use of these coins in Batavia and surroundings in early seventeenth century (Blussé, *Strange Company*, 35–48).
9. Klein, *The Monetisation of the Dutch East Indies*, 7; Van Laanen, *Changing Economy in Indonesia*, vol. 6, 15.
10. In 1724 the VOC introduced copper doits (*duiten*) which replaced the *picis* as the preferred petty coin in Java between 1740 and the early 1770s. The production of lead *picis* on the northeastern coast of Java ceased in 1763 because of the popularity of the doits. In 1769 imports of Chinese copper coins to Java were forbidden by the Dutch in order to drive them from the market (Van Aelst, 'A South-Chinese Currency Zone', 109–10). Kwee Hui Kian describes the complex (political) processes underlying this change ('Colonization Creeping in' and *The Political Economy of Java's Northeast Coast*, 97–118).
11. Blussé, *Strange Company*, 48; Kwee Hui Kian, 'Colonization Creeping in', 2.
12. ANRI, *Arsip Muntwezen* 1; Klein, *The Monetisation of the Dutch East Indies*, 5, 7; Van Laanen, *Changing Economy in Indonesia*, vol. 6, 15.

13. Java was a transit station in the flow of silver between the sources of supply in Latin America and the main destination in China. Chinese merchants, controlling much of Java's trade, habitually remitted part of their incomes to China resulting in a negative balance of trade (Van Zanden, 'Linking Two Debates', 177).
14. Boomgaard, *Children of the Colonial State*, 133–4.
15. Zappey, *De Economische en Politieke Werkzaamheid van Johannes Goldberg*; Klein, *The Monetisation of the Dutch East Indies*, 5–6, 11.
16. ANRI, *Arsip Muntwezen* 2, 6; Van Laanen, *Changing Economy in Indonesia*, vol. 6, 16; De Prins, *Voor Keizer en Koning*, 128; Zappey, *De Economische en Politieke Werkzaamheid van Johannes Goldberg*, 110–6.
17. The word 'money' is commonly translated as *uang* into the Indonesian language. When talking about earning a living, the expression *cari uang*—or 'looking for money'—is used. However, in both instances the word *uang* can be exchanged for *duit*, which derives from the Dutch language and dates back to the period of the VOC. Today, the word is used either in the sense of 'money', or in the literal sense of coins and banknotes.
18. Van Laanen, *Changing Economy in Indonesia*, vol. 6, 16; Van den Berg, *Munt-, Crediet- en Bankwezen*, 81; Weber, *Hybrid Ambitions*, 158.
19. ANRI, *Arsip Muntwezen* 12, 13; Van Laanen, *Changing Economy in Indonesia*, vol. 6, 56–7, 59; Klein, *The Monetisation of the Dutch East Indies*, 12.
20. Van den Berg, *Munt-, Crediet- en Bankwezen*, 80.
21. Van den Berg, *Currency and the Economy of Netherlands India 1870–95*, 62; Zappey, *De Economische en Politieke Werkzaamheid van Johannes Goldberg*, 110–6.
22. Van den Berg, *Munt-, Crediet- en Bankwezen*, 80.
23. Van Aelst, 'A South-Chinese Currency Zone', 110.
24. Van den Berg, *Munt-, Crediet- en Bankwezen*, 40.
25. ANRI, *Arsip Muntwezen* 11, 17, 22–3.
26. Van den Berg, *Munt-, Crediet- en Bankwezen*, 83.
27. The Mexican dollar eventually surpassed all in popularity and became the most widely preferred currency in Asia during the nineteenth century (Wolters, *Coins and Credit*, 6–7).
28. Van den Berg, *Currency and the Economy of Netherlands India 1870–95*, xi–xii.
29. ANRI, *Arsip Muntwezen* 11; Scholten, *De Munten van de Nederlandsche Gebiedsdeelen Oversee 1601–1948*; Van Laanen, *Changing Economy in Indonesia*, vol. 6, 16.
30. Van Laanen, *Changing Economy in Indonesia*, vol. 6, 18; Klein, *The Monetisation of the Dutch East Indies*, 12.
31. Van den Berg, *Munt-, Crediet- en Bankwezen*, 85.
32. De Bree, *Gedenkboek van de Javasche Bank*, vol. 1, 165.

33. See De Prins for a description of Commissioner-General L. du Bus de Gisignies' fruitless attempts to solve the monetary situation between 1825 and 1830 (De Prins, *Voor Keizer en Koning*, 126–36).
34. Godée Molsbergen, *Gedenkboek Reynst & Vinju 1836–1936*, 6.
35. Van Zanden, 'Linking Two Debates', 180.
36. Whereas in Java silver in circulation became scarce, this was not the case in Sulawesi or the closely linked regions of Sumatra and Malaya. A useful reminder of the fact that money and monetization do not necessarily have anything to do with states or their policies, I am thankful to Professor D. Henley to draw my attention to the importance of the regional context.
37. Van Zanden, 'Linking Two Debates', 182.
38. ANRI, *Arsip Muntwezen* 29.
39. See Van Zanden, 'Linking Two Debates', 182; Klein, *The Monetisation of the Dutch East Indies*, 12–3, Van den Berg, *Munt-, Crediet- en Bankwezen*, 87; Houben, *Kraton and Kumpeni*, 334–5; Van Laanen, *Changing Economy in Indonesia*, vol. 6, 17–9; 'De Kali Bezaar te Batavia', 154.
40. Dick et al., *The Emergence of a National Economy*, 76–7; Van Zanden, 'Linking Two Debates', 182.
41. Fernando, 'Growth of Non-Agricultural Economic Activities in Java', 78, 88; Klein, *The Monetisation of the Dutch East Indies*, 13–5; Van Laanen, *Changing Economy in Indonesia*, vol. 6, 130–2; Potting, *De Ontwikkeling van het Geldverkeer in een Koloniale Samenleving*, 88–9.
42. Examples of contemporary accounts are the detailed overviews of the Netherlands Indies monetary system in the period before 1850 published by Mees (*Het Muntwezen van Nederlandsch-Indië*) and Steijn Parvé (*Geschiedenis van het Munt- en Bankwezen van Nederlandsch-Indië*). A report on the colonial monetary system written by J. Kruseman in 1823 can be found in ANRI, *Arsip Muntwezen* 10.
43. Houben, *Kraton and Kumpeni*, 336; Van de Laar, *Opperbankier en Wetenschapsman*, 237, 242–55; Vissering, *Muntwezen en Circulatiebanken in Nederlandsch-Indië*, 22–6, 382–8.
44. The use of *duiten* (or *wang* in Javanese) even left its trace in Javanese numerals as the population reckoned on the basis of the old copper coin (Houben, *Kraton and Kumpeni*, 315, 336).
45. The *duiten* still in circulation were in practice equated to the new cents. However, if 120 *duiten* were surrendered at a Public Cash Office one guilder or 100 cents was given in return; that is, only 5/6 of the purchasing power of the original 120 doits at the local market or *pasar*.
46. Francis, *Herinneringen uit den Levensloop van een Indisch' Ambtenaar*, 495–7; Van den Berg, *Currency and the Economy of Netherlands India 1870–95*, xiii; Van Laanen, *Changing Economy in Indonesia*, vol. 6, 20–2.

47. Van den Berg, *Currency and the Economy of Netherlands India 1870–95*, xv; Van den Berg, *Munt-, Crediet- en Bankwezen*, 94–6; Klein, *The Monetisation of the Dutch East Indies*, 16; Vissering, *Muntwezen en Circulatiebanken in Nederlandsch-Indië*, 66–8, 414–7.
48. Van Laanen, *Changing Economy in Indonesia*, vol. 6, 25–7.
49. According to P. Brooshooft—chief-editor of *De Locomotief*—this truism was recognized by everyone. Even *totok*, that is, Dutch, housewives, after having been in the colony for barely a month, knew this. In his own inimitable style: '[…] *het baarste totok-huismoedertje weet dit na een maand verblijf in Indië* […]', *De Locomotief*, 22 July 1899.
50. *De Locomotief*, 22 July 1899 and 9 March 1900; Van den Berg, *Munt-, Crediet- en Bankwezen*, 103–4.
51. Tagliacozzo, *Secret Trades of the Straits*, 169–89, especially 173; Tagliacozzo, *Secret Trades, Porous Borders*, 211; Van den Berg, *Currency and the Economy of Netherlands India 1870–95*, xx; Potting, *De Ontwikkeling van het Geldverkeer in een Koloniale Samenleving*, 105–18.
52. A number of advisory reports on the monetary situation in Sumatra, Borneo, Bali, Sulawesi, Boni and Selayar can be found in Vissering, *Muntwezen en Circulatiebanken in Nederlandsch-Indië*, 101–330.
53. Klein, *The Monetisation of the Dutch East Indies*, 19; Van Laanen, *Changing Economy in Indonesia*, vol. 6, 27–8; Potting, *De Ontwikkeling van het Geldverkeer in een Koloniale Samenleving*, 237–70.
54. Claver, *Capital and Commerce in Colonial Java*, 351–9.
55. Van Laanen, *Changing Economy in Indonesia*, vol. 6, 28–9; Creutzberg, *Changing Economy in Indonesia*, vol. 3, 19–20; Creutzberg, *Changing Economy in Indonesia*, vol. 5, 78–89.
56. Shibata Yoshimasa, *The monetary policy in the Netherlands East Indies under the Japanese administration*, 699–703, 714–5.
57. See http://www.bi.go.id/web/en/Tentang+BI/Museum/Sejarah+Bank+Indonesia/Sejarah+Pra-BI/ historybeforebi5.htm [accessed 20 June 2013].
58. Wolters, 'Decolonizing Money', 123–4.

II

ENTREPRENEURSHIP IN THE COLONIAL AND POST-COLONIAL ECONOMIES

6

John Chinaman Abroad: Chinese Sailors in the Service of the VOC

Leonard Blussé

Tucked away in a portfolio in the print room of the Rijksmuseum in Amsterdam lies this curious drawing that depicts a relaxed group of Chinese loitering around a kettle of food.[1] Who drew this picture and what does it show us? The artist who signed it was Jacob de Vos Wzn. (1774–1844), in daily life a well-known Amsterdam insurance broker. Like his uncle and partner in the family business, Jacob de Vos (1735–1833), he collected drawings and sketches, but he himself was also a gifted artist.[2]

Today, countless groups of Chinese tourists pour forth daily from buses at the Museumplein in Amsterdam. They have become a familiar part of the street scene. However, the group of Chinese visitors depicted in the drawing by De Vos seem to be a different kind of crowd. The caption of the drawing says: 'Chinese matrozen in het Gasthuis' (Chinese sailors in the Guesthouse). It would not seem far-fetched to suggest that in connection with De Vos's work as an insurance broker he must have visited the Dutch East India Company (VOC) wharf in Amsterdam and must have encountered these Chinese sailors, who he then immortalized in this group portrait.

The guesthouse of the VOC was situated on the company's yard in Amsterdam. On the picture we discern seventeen Chinese standing and

'Chinese Matrozen in het Gasthuis' (Chinese Sailors in the Guesthouse), drawing by Jacob de Vos WZ. Collectie Koninklijk Oudheidkundig Genootschap Amsterdam. Courtesy Rijksmuseum-Stichting Amsterdam.

sitting around a big kettle in which food is prepared. In the chimney above the hearth laundry is being dried. The men look quite relaxed: smoking a pipe, lighting a candle, dozing off, slurping with chopsticks from their rice bowls, or busily engaged with cooking. The sketch is quite unique. Chinese were portrayed in seventeenth-century Dutch books, aquarelles and oil paintings of Batavia starting with early Dutch travel accounts such as *De eerste Schipvaart* and Jan Huyghen van Linschoten's *Itinerario*, but this drawing may well be the oldest Dutch picture drawn *naar het leven*[3] of a group of Chinese in Holland itself. The title of the drawing and the relaxed attitude of the people portrayed raise the question how these sailors ended up in Amsterdam and what they were doing there. Were they simply dumped there by the VOC just as Chinese engine room personnel were laid off by bankrupt shipowners in Rotterdam's Katendrecht harbour district in the early 1930s, or were they perhaps a familiar sight on the company's wharf? In fact, as we shall see, the latter was the case. But if the Chinese of Katendrecht arose the interest of anthropologists and social workers, it is surprising how little is known about these oriental visitors to Amsterdam at the end of the eighteenth century.[4]

By the beginning of the 1780s the Dutch East India Company had to contend with a severe shortage of sailors aboard its ships and, in particular, the ships departing from Batavia on the long trip home. As shown by the maritime historian Jaap Bruijn, the quality and health of the personnel of the company in the eighteenth century had not only declined on the way to Asia, but no less important was that many sailors fell victim to the unhealthy conditions in Asia and especially Batavia.[5] Ingrid Dillo and very recently Matthias van Rossum have pointed out that Asian sailors became at the time an essential human element on board the VOC ships on the intra-Asian routes and on the long voyage home via the Cape of Good Hope, the so-called *retourvaart*. She calculated that between 1784 and 1789 the company employed on an annual basis about 2,000 Asian (mostly Chinese and Indonesian) sailors.[6] In the early 1790s this number declined again. Indian (*Moorse*) sailors were recruited without much result in India (Coromandel and Bengal), but at Batavia the company met more success in enlisting Javanese and Chinese sailors. The Javanese turned out to be able sailors on their home turf—that is aboard VOC vessels in the seas of the archipelago or the South China Sea—but they were initially unwilling to embark on oceanic voyages to the Cape or even further to the Low Countries. Consequently, it was the Chinese to whom the company had to turn.

Why it was relatively easy to recruit Chinese sailors for the long-distance voyages to Europe needs to be explained here. First of all, the Chinese maintained a shipping link of their own with Batavia, the junk traffic from Ningbo, Xiamen (Amoy) and Guangzhou (Canton), which every year arrived with the northern monsoon in February and left for home with the southern monsoon. This maritime corridor with the mother country provided a steady supply of sailors. In order to understand where the Chinese maritime tradition somehow fitted in with the Dutch one, it is useful to say a few words about the way in which Chinese crews were organized on their own ships, the two- and three-masted *yang chuan*, or Chinese ocean junks.

The division of labour on board a seagoing trading junk was basically as follows: as on the VOC ships there was a joint command consisting of a skipper and a supercargo. The *nakhoda* (Malay) or *quewij* (Chinese) was in ranking equivalent to the Dutch (*opper*) *koopman*. The skipper and the supercargo were together responsible for the navigation and the trade. Aboard a junk, a pilot and an assistant pilot checked the speed and gauged the depth and watched the compass. The navigators basically played the same role as the mates and the helmsmen on the Dutch ships. A *yaban*, or boatswain, kept order among the crew and was in charge of the cannon. The crew members on junks had specific tasks during the voyage: the helmsman and his assistants steered the junk; the master of the rigging and his assistants looked after the rigging; the three masts and their wing-shaped sails were looked after by three different gangs, each under their own boss.

The rigging was totally different from that of the square-rigged European ships. The anchors were manned by their own crews; two men looked after the *sampan* (boat) that was towed or put on the deck; and a *ya gong* combined the work of the sailmaker and ship's carpenter aboard European vessels. Dutch ships carried a comforter of the sick (*zieken-bezoeker*) who led the crew in prayer and took care of those who fell ill. On Chinese junks an incense master looked after the altar of *Ma-zhu*, the goddess of the sea, burned incense in front of the compass and brought offerings to holy promontories or islands that the ship passed en route. Due to the particular rigging of the junks, crew members did not have to climb into the standing and running rigging as on the square-rigged Dutch ships, but basically carried out all their work on deck, hoisting the extremely heavy battened sails with a windlass and adjusting the sheets of the sail with their hands. This explains why the Chinese crews were adamant about not climbing into the rigging to spread out along the foot ropes slung from beneath the yards to lower or furl the sails. This became such a problem that the decision was taken to hire more Javanese sailors for employment on the homeward-bound ships 'to unbind and bind up the sails, which the Chinese are refusing to do'.[7]

It is important to understand that Chinese labourers, and especially crews sailing overseas, were always hired in gangs (*ploegen*) headed by their own bosses (*mandors*) and not individually, as was the case with European sailors who were generally hired via labour contractors, the so-called *zielverkopers*, by the company in Holland. These Chinese gangs would consist of twenty-six sailors, including their headman.[8] Although the Dutch as early as the 1620s had briefly hired whole junks with Chinese crews for privateering purposes against the Spaniards in Philippine waters, the company could do without Chinese sailors for its own purposes until the 1750s.[9]

For as long as Batavia remained the headquarters of the company on Java, all male Chinese from the age of fourteen living in and around the city were obliged to pay a monthly *hoofdgeld*, a personal poll tax that freed the Chinese from militia service or corvée service. The collection of this poll tax was taken care of by the so-called Chinese officers, the informal leaders of the Chinese community who with their Chinese Council, or *Kong Koan*, basically ruled their own countrymen. The curious collaboration by the company and the Chinese, who constituted the largest ethnic group among the free citizens of Batavia, worked out well for more than a century, until for a variety of reasons a Chinese rebellion broke out in the autumn of 1740. The suppression of this rebellion ended in a terrible massacre of almost all inhabitants of the town, the *Chinezen moord* or Chinese massacre, a black page in the history of Batavia.[10] Here we should note that the main causes of the revolt and the massacre that followed were a crisis in the local economy, rampant illegal immigration and a breakdown in the leadership within the Chinese community. The combination of promoting or keeping a lid on Chinese immigration into town was a continuous headache for the High Government in Batavia and for the Chinese community leaders as well. Great efforts were made to keep a tally of the number of Chinese moving in and out of town with the junks—thousands of people who had to be accounted for, if only for tax purposes.

There were a host of regulations concerning Chinese sailors who sailed on the Chinese junks between Amoy and Batavia. The New Statutes of Batavia spelled out in detail the special laws concerning the Chinese and their junk shipping network.[11] This commerce concerned not merely the Chinese junk shipping to and from China but also navigation within the archipelago. The *nakhoda* of the junk had to hand over a list with the names of all the sailors to the office of the *shahbandar*, or harbourmaster, who then would provide a pass. Those Chinese sailors who were residing in town would have to hand in the *licentiebriefje,* or poll tax certificate, to the *shahbandar,* who would keep it during their absence so that they would not be used by illegal immigrants. Of course, no taxes were owed while at sea. Visiting Chinese such as the sailors and merchants who sailed to Batavia on the northern monsoon—and stayed for four or five months during the trading season before returning home with the southern monsoon—also had to pay a temporary residence tax of twelve *stuivers* per month. Needless to say, this system, which was administered by the Chinese captain and his staff, was continuously undermined.

On 5 July 1756, Governor-General Jacob Mossel was the first to propose employing Chinese sailors in the service of the company. Considering that there was a shortage of European and Moorish (Indian) sailors in the fleet he suggested that it might be a good idea to engage in an experiment to employ a gang of Chinese under the supervision of their own captain in the roadstead of Batavia. This would free a number of European sailors for service on the ships departing for the Indian coast. The experiment worked out well and we know that in subsequent years Chinese sailors were also employed on VOC vessels on short trips throughout the Indonesian Archipelago. Van der Chijs, editor of the *Plakaatboeken*, notes that as of 1771 Indonesian sailors were still 'totally unwilling' to sign on to the company's ships even for relatively short voyages around the archipelago.[12]

The outbreak of the fourth Anglo-Dutch War led to a shortage of sailors from Europe by the summer of 1781. The High Government in Batavia was at a loss as to how to scrape together the crews for the homeward-bound *retourschepen* and now started to toy with the idea of deploying Chinese sailors in the same way as it had been using them in Asian waters over the past decade. This meant that first a proper report had to be made about the current work conditions. On 10 September 1781 the decision was taken to register how many Chinese sailors were serving among the crew of the VOC ships so that the authorities could figure out how much they were consuming in addition to their normal fare and how the cost of that might be deducted from their monthly salaries.[13] Three years later the crewing problem had become a real crisis. The High Government observed that only 420 European sailors were available and 170 of these were in hospital and incapable of doing any work.[14] Why this should be so is quite understandable considering that no less than 1,200 sailors of the total crew of 2,200 sailors of the Batavia-bound vessel that had set sail in 1782 had died en route owing to disease and scurvy.

Chinese sailors now had to be drafted for service in the homeward-bound ships. To entice them into signing up, a monthly salary of ten rixdollars was offered—twice what European sailors received. But what the company gave with its right hand it took away with the left. Originally, Chinese crew members sailing in Asian waters had received extra provisions, just as their European counterparts were provided with rations of salt, bacon and meat. That measure was now repealed because it was too expensive, and probably also because the Chinese had their own culinary demands.[15] Moorish and Chinese sailors in the service of the company at the shipyard in Onrust and on ships in Asian waters indeed received different provisions better suited to their culinary tastes.[16] For the long-distance voyages Dutch sailors also received extra clothing to protect them against the discomforts of wind and weather.

On 6 December 1787 the recruiter of the Chinese sailors, Tan Payko (Chen Peisheng in Mandarin pronunciation), requested that the company give an advance of one or two months' pay so that the sailors could purchase these necessities themselves without going into debt.[17] This request was granted on the condition that the recruiter would pay back the advance in case the sailors he had hired died or ran away. This raises the suspicion that Tan Payko did not hand over the money straight away to the sailors but that he may have made the purchases for them. That the latter was indeed the case is seen in the regulations governing the auction for the annual tax farm, which notes that the then-contractor of Chinese sailors, Tan Khoeko, was allowed to slaughter tax-exempt three pigs per day for these sailors. The chances are that part of the advances and the higher wages for the Chinese sailors ended up in the pockets of this *koppelbaas*. Contrary to the Chinese captain who used to mediate in labour matters, the *koppelbaas* was making a living from these human resource services, which required flexible organization. By 1787, it was mentioned in so many words that more and more Chinese were employed on board of the VOC vessels for no other reason than that there was a lack of European personnel. This made it necessary to keep separate accounts of this contract labour in the company ledgers.

Not until September 1794 do the *Plakaatboeken* give a clear survey of the various regulations concerning the service of Chinese sailors. Many abuses had occurred in the past when payments had been made to returning Chinese sailors:

1. The Chinese should be enlisted and put on a separate payroll in the same way that European sailors were registered.
2. On this list, the *man(da)door* (boss) responsible for the Chinese crew members should be clearly named.
3. What the Chinese would receive during their stopover at the Cape of Good Hope should be carefully noted. The gangs of the Chinese should not be split up *en route*.
4. The Chinese crew should be properly mustered upon departure and arrival.
5. After returning to Batavia, the two months' advance of salary and any additional expenses incurred during the voyage should be deducted before the salaries were paid out to their contractor.
6. Because in 1788/89 already the significant sum of fl. 233500:8:8 had been paid out in salaries to Chinese sailors, it was proposed to make a special entry with the heading 'wages for the Chinese hirelings' in the account books.[18]

This considerable sum on the payroll suggests that several hundred Chinese were employed on the company's ships, and this is confirmed under the list of exemptions from the annual auctioning of the poll tax.

The contractor of the Chinese sailors was allowed to purchase 500 poll-tax forms for only 40 stuivers per person per year, which means that he received a large tax rebate.

The master of the equipment at Batavia, J.D. Schrijver, reported in September 1783 that some 1,066 Chinese in 41 gangs were employed by the VOC in the roadstead, the company wharf, the wharf on the island of Onrust and as crew on various ships sailing in Asian waters. As already mentioned, in the past these people had been contracted via the mediation of the Chinese captain and the Chinese Council of Batavia. Now that gangs were recruited for the long-distance voyages of the homeward-bound *retourschepen,* the company contracted with specialized labour brokers. This initially became the job of one of the sons of Chinese captain Swa Toya (Cai Dunguan), who recruited twenty gangs, and another Chinese broker, Tan Payko (Chen Peisheng) who recruited nineteen gangs. The latter won a monopoly on recruiting all the gangs for the company by agreeing to lower the monthly pay for Chinese sailors from ten to nine rixdollar and, on his unexpected death, the monopoly passed to his younger brother, Tan Khoeko.[19] Using the monthly numbers of Chinese sailors found in the resolutions of the governor-general and council, it is possible to compute that between 1784 and 1793 the VOC employed no less than 1,000 Chinese sailors at sea every year.[20]

Right from the beginning, the High Government of Batavia was much concerned about the treatment on board of the gangs of twenty-five Chinese sailors who would be added to every ship that lacked sufficient manpower. In a resolution of 10 September 1781, they warned ships' officers that the Asian crew members should be treated in a fitting and decent way.[21] The Chinese crews aboard the ships *Java* and *Slot ter Hoge*, which left Batavia in October 1783, felt actually so maltreated that they mutinied even before Cape Town had been reached.[22] In later years no more complaints are heard.

From 1784 onwards Chinese crew members regularly arrived in the Netherlands. Hardly anything is known about their short stay in either Holland or Zeeland. They always had to kill some time while waiting for the return voyage to the Indies with the next departing fleet on which they would be enlisted again. Upon their arrival in Holland, the company allowed them to withdraw two months' wages to be spent on clothing and food. This sum would be deducted from the salary they received upon their return to Batavia. As far as can be ascertained, the Chinese visitors were kept on the precincts of the company's wharf for fear that they would be cheated or might cause trouble if they lodged with landlords or moved around freely in the town. Jacob de Vos's drawing is really the only and telling testimony of the relaxed but likely very boring conditions under which they lived on the company's wharf while awaiting departure on the next fleet.

As the Taiwanese historian Yu Po-ching has shown, the English East India Company for a variety of reasons treated its Chinese crew rather differently when they arrived in London.[23] Let me briefly discuss its contents and point out a few aspects that explain why the residence of Chinese sailors in London created quite a stir.[24] Owing to a dearth of manpower aboard its ships bound home from Canton, the English East India Company (EIC) also started to recruit Chinese sailors in the 1780s. After the enforcement of the Commutation Act in 1784, whereby the import duties on Chinese tea were dramatically lowered, the English tea trade with Canton grew exponentially. The wars with France that followed further increased the demand for Asian sailors on the ships of the EIC and thus large numbers of Chinese were serving on the Canton–London run of the British tea ships. Unlike the VOC, which kept its Chinese crews under contract, the EIC saw less need to look after the sailors that it dismissed once they arrived in England. Special employment laws that served to protect the labour rights of the British sailors made it impossible for the company to employ the Asians soldiers again on the outbound voyage. Its only obligation was to ship them back as passengers.

During their stay in London, the Chinese were lodged in private boarding houses close to the port facilities in town, where they could freely move around—with all the problems that this could cause. Social reformers, among them the famous William Wilberforce, concerned themselves with the often pathetic living conditions of the Asian sailors in London, and a Society for the Protection of Asian Sailors was even established in 1814. From then on, their living conditions improved remarkably. All this serves to show why, contrary to the Chinese sailors in the service of the VOC, the Chinese sailors in London attracted a great deal of attention.

Conclusion

This short exposé shows how the Dutch East India Company began to employ Chinese sailors in its service and made all kinds of special arrangements to make this happen. We may close with the following questions:

What would the Chinese sailors themselves have thought of their recruitment? How did the Chinese community in Batavia consider the company's practice of contracting gangs of Chinese seamen for long-distance voyages? Was the apparently well-paid employment on the VOC ships really that attractive and profitable for the Chinese crews? What were the labour conditions like on the VOC ships? Traditionally the crews of VOC ships were recruited from various European nations, but the Chinese crew must have been rather 'odd man out'. Although they were promised nine to ten rixdollars per month, twice what their Dutch brethren received, one may wonder how much of this salary actually ended up in their hands. The contracting was, after all, in the hands of a monopolist who in turn employed *mandors* to hire and direct gangs of twenty-five men. The *mandors* will certainly have demanded their share of the salaries of the recruited sailors.

Given the dearth of original, reliable sources on the Asian perception of the colonial world, these questions are difficult to answer. But, surprisingly, in this case there is such an answer. It turns out that the idyllic picture of the Chinese sailors in Amsterdam was not representative of the harsh conditions under which they worked on the ships.

According to the anonymous Chinese author of the *Kaibalidaishiji,* the chronological history of the Chinese of Batavia, dating from 1800, the recruiting business of Chinese sailors for long-distance voyages was in such bad odour that it even aroused the ire of the gods—who denied offspring to all Chinese individuals who were instrumental in the contracting of the sailors! That was quite a statement to make, for a lack of descendants is the greatest punishment one can think of in Chinese society, which is well known for its complete devotion to ancestor worship.

But let us give the anonymous author the last word on the recruitment of the Chinese sailors for the long-distance voyages to Holland:

> In the past all the hiring of Chinese crews for the Company's ships was originally controlled by the Chinese Captain [and the Chinese Council] in town. But by 1784, all these affairs came under control of a certain Chen Peisheng [Tan Payko]; but after Peisheng had died his younger brother Chen Genshi [Tan Khoeko] continued to manage the recruitment. Later on this Chen Genshi drew up a contract and made Chen Yuelang act as his agent to manage these affairs. But one year after Chen Genshi has died, a petition was sent by Lieutenant Wu Zanxu [a Chinese officer of the Chinese Council] to the authorities, as a result of which he in turn was able to walk away with the management over all

the [Chinese] recruitment affairs. All these people who were involved in the hiring of Chinese crews for the Company ships acted cruelly and harshly. Yes, they made a lot of profits on the recruitment, but they all remained without progeny.

Is not this very strange? This should be taken as a warning.[25]

Primary Sources

Rijksmuseum, Amsterdam (RM).

Nationaal Archief, The Hague (NA)
- Archives of the Verenigde Oostindische Compagnie, the Dutch East India Company (VOC).

Notes

1. This picture was passed on to me by Jan van Campen, curator at the Rijksmuseum, who discovered it when he was doing his PhD research on the late eighteenth-century Dutch collectioner of things Chinese, J.T. Royer. See Van Campen, *De Haagse jurist.*
2. RM, Jacob de Vos Wzn., *Chinese matrozen in het gasthuis.* 270 × 423 mm. Collectie Koninklijk Oudheidkundig Genootschap Amsterdam. Inventaris number KOG PORT.XVI 23 OF 24. De Vos is best known for a diary that he kept of his happy family life, embellishing it with hundreds of drawings of his four young sons. Eveline Coolhaas-Grosveld has written a lovely bilingual book on Jacob de Vos's illustrated diaries: *Vader & Zoons, Jacob de Vos Ezn. (1774–1844) en de getekende dagboekjes voor zijn kinderen/ Father & Sons, Jacob de Vos Wzn. (1774–1844) and the Journals he drew for his Children* (Hilversum: Verloren, 2001). Wzn. is an abbreviation for Willemszoon.
3. 'The phrase *naer het leven* first used by the seventeenth-century Dutch author Karel van Mander, 'implies that the work gives the impression of being life-like and that natural phenomena are depicted as drawn from life'. Freedberg, *Dutch Landscape Prints*, 132.
4. Van Heek, *Chineesche immigranten in Nederland.*
5. See chapter 9, 'The People on Board', in Bruijn et al., *Dutch-Asiatic Shipping*, vol. 1, 143–72.
6. I was not able to consult the PhD thesis on the subject of Asian personnel of the VOC which Matthias van Rossum defended half a year after this contribution was written. Van Rossum, *Werkers van de wereld.* However, I have gladly made use of the unpublished MA thesis of Chen Lixiong, with whom I exchanged data on Chinese shipping at the time. Chen devoted his research to the Chinese and Javanese working on the shipyard at Onrust, the Asian trading routes as well as the voyages on the ships on the ocean

navigational route between Batavia and the Low Countries. Chen Lixiong, *Chinezen en Javanen*.

7. Resolution GG and Council, 4 October 1794. Van der Chijs, *Nederlandsch-Indisch Plakaatboek*, 17 vols.
8. See for instance the three ships arriving from Batavia in 1790 that all carried Chinese gangs of twenty-six people. Bruijn et al., *Dutch-Asiatic Shipping*, vol. 3, 549.
9. Cheng Wei-chung, *War, Trade and Piracy*.
10. Blussé, *Strange Company*.
11. New Statutes of Batavia were drawn up in 1766. The special laws concerning the organisation of the junk shipping are found in Van der Chijs, *Nederlandsch-Indisch Plakaatboek*, vol. 4, 432–49.
12. Ibid., vol. 7, 186.
13. Ibid., vol. 10, 534.
14. NA, Resolution GG and Council, 14 October 1783, VOC 813.
15. 5 November 1784. Van der Chijs, *Nederlandsch-Indisch Plakaatboek*, vol. 10, 739.
16. NA, Alting collection 67, 'Papieren van eenige speculatie rakende de Chinezen 1781–96'.
17. Van der Chijs, *Nederlandsch-Indisch Plakaatboek*, vol. 10, 982.
18. 'Bepalingen nopens Chineesche zeevarenden in dienst van de Compagnie'. Ibid., 791–2.
19. NA, Resolutie GG and Council, 9 February 1787, VOC 818.
20. Chen Lixiong, *Chinezen en Javanen*, 12–3.
21. NA, 'Op een geschikte en betamelijke wijze behandeld worden', VOC, 811.
22. The detailed study of these mutinies by Klaas van der Tempel, see Bruijn and Eijck van Heslinga, *Muiterij, oproer en berechting*, 134–47.
23. Yu Po-ching, 'Chinese seamen in London and St Helena in the early nineteenth century'.
24. About the early presence of Chinese in English society, see also: Benton and Gomez, *The Chinese in Britain*.
25. A book edition of the annotated English translation of the *Kaibalidaishiji* by Nie Dening and Leonard Blussé is scheduled to appear in 2014.

7

Complementarisasi in the Indonesian Construction Sector in the 1950s

*Freek Colombijn**

Introduction: *Complementarisasi* in the Indonesian Economy

In a study of the decolonization of the Indonesian economy, Thomas Lindblad has adopted and popularized the term *Indonesianisasi* to sketch the multifarious rise of the Indonesian share in the national economy, gaining ground at the expense of Dutch colonial interests. Indonesianisasi indicates the penetration by Indonesians of economic sectors formerly

* I would like to thank Martine Barwegen, who collected part of the data, Liesbeth Dolk who kindly granted me access to papers of NV Associatie, Rosemary Robson, who corrected the English, and Alicia Schrikker and Jeroen Touwen, whose stimulating comments forced me to sharpen my argument. Most research for this article was carried out as part of the Indonesia across Orders programme, funded by the Dutch Ministry of Health, Welfare and Sport. I alone remain responsible for the text. I would like to thank Thomas Lindblad, both as a fellow researcher in the Indonesia across Orders programme, and as one of the supervisors of my PhD thesis two decades earlier. His amiable attitude no doubt helped me a great deal in bringing both intellectual undertakings to fruition.

dominated by Dutchmen and the increased participation of Indonesians in the higher echelons of companies that used to be reserved for Europeans.[1] The process began before the Proclamation of Independence in 1945 and continued long after the Transfer of Sovereignty in 1949, with different sectors of society going through a process of Indonesianisasi at a different pace. The term has now been widely adopted by scholars writing about various aspects of decolonization.[2]

In its narrowest sense, Indonesianisasi sketches a kind of (changing) economic relationship between colonized and colonizer, but it was by no means the only possible relationship between (former) colonizer and colonized people. Another kind of economic relationship developed when Indonesians won economic positions of their own, competing with the Dutch (and other Westerners), but not to take over Dutch positions. A prime example of such a competitive relationship was studied by Lindblad himself, namely the rise of indigenous smallholder rubber cultivation flourishing alongside the might of the Western plantations.[3]

In this chapter I wish to draw attention to a third kind of economic relationship between the Indonesians and the Dutch, which I call tentatively *complementarisasi*. This is an economic relationship between actors from different ethnic groups, in which each side occupies a niche and complements the other. In this third kind of relationship, Indonesians did not take over jobs held by the Dutch (as in Indonesianisasi), did not compete with the Dutch by developing their own methods while steering clear of intense interaction with the Dutch (as in the rubber production), but worked in the same economic sector in which they complemented the work of Europeans, sometimes actively co-operating.

Some historians might wish to add a fourth type of economic relationship, the one between employer–employed (or master–servant). One might also argue that the master–servant relationship was actually a kind of complementarisasi, in which, for example, staff complemented the task of a lady of the house in running a household. However, I would like to reserve the term complementarisasi for economic relations in which each side takes part as an independent economic actor, thus excluding employment. Besides, although the colonial context obviously coloured the relationship between, say, a Dutch landlady and an Indonesian *babu* (female domestic servant) or *kokki* (cook), not all employers were Europeans (nor were all servants Indonesian).

At this point I do not want to get mired down in quibbles about definitions and the conceptual differences between three kinds of economic relationships. My main point is that complementarisasi was an important kind of economic relationship between Indonesians and Dutch during the long decolonization of Indonesia. In this chapter I explore the concept by focusing on a sector in which complementarisasi was definitely essential, not only between Indonesians and Dutch, but even between people from a variety of ethnic backgrounds, namely the construction sector.

Let me state at the outset that ethnicity was not all decisive in determining the economic role that a builder or craftsperson could play in the construction sector. Lists of (ex-)pupils of the technical schools in Bandung and Semarang show that by the 1920s indigenous, Dutch and Chinese boys were already attending school together and obtaining similar jobs. Likewise, the advertisement pages in a brochure promoting the sale of plots of municipal land in Bandung contain advertisements placed by Dutch, Chinese and indigenous builders.[4] Because of this ethnic mixing in specific roles, I believe that an analysis of the construction sector purely in terms of inter-ethnic relations would leave out many interesting economic interactions. Therefore, I shall broaden the scope and sketch the social relations in the construction sector in more general terms. This sort of study of the construction sector has still to be written, despite its economic importance.[5] For practical reasons, I shall limit my study to one city, Medan in the 1950s, occasionally making comparisons with other places and earlier times.

Studying the Construction Sector in Medan

One reason for the dearth of historical studies of the construction sector is probably the lack of readily accessible archival data but, with some effort, interesting material can be found. In my experience lawsuits form an excellent source of information about everyday activities and social relationships that have otherwise left almost no traces in government publications and newspapers. Each court case is a micro-history and the evidence presented by the litigants offers a short description of how things were done, even when the litigants presented diametrically opposed stories and doubts can be cast on the decision of the court,[6] each side must have come up with a credible story, contextualized in the contemporary building practice. The archive of the Pengadilan Negeri (Court of Justice) in Medan contains material that goes back to at least 1950. Medan is also fortunate in having a municipal archive that holds material dating back to the late 1940s (a rare feat in Indonesian cities), although it does not have an inventory, is not open to the general public and its existence is unknown even to most civil servants. This archive material has been complemented with information from more obvious sources such as the annual reports of the Medan Trade Association (Handelsvereeniging te Medan) and the municipal gazette (*Gemeenteblad Gemeente Medan*). Oral history has been another source, but two of the three men interviewed worked most of their time in Jakarta, and it is with some caution that I have used their information to understand the situation in Medan.

It matters a great deal in which city the construction sector in the 1950s is being studied. In Ambon, for instance, 94 per cent of all buildings was destroyed by Allied bombing in the Second World War and reconstruction in the 1950s was hampered by an enormous shortage of both building material and labourers. There was just one electric drill in the whole city and, because of the scarcity of craftspeople, the state used Japanese prisoners of war to do construction work.[7] Jakarta presents the opposite side of the story. Here, builders were close to the stocks of building materials or, very importantly, to the civil servants issuing licences to import material. The ethnic composition of cities could also differ significantly from place to place, making generalizations about complementarisasi impossible for the whole of Indonesia on the basis of one local study.

Medan stands out because of its unusually large share of Chinese in the total population (Table 7.1), built up of migrants who had previously worked on the plantations in its environs. It also had a large Indian population and today still boasts the largest Hindu temple in the archipelago outside Bali. The extremely rapid growth of the urban population in Medan was not exceptional, but was common throughout Indonesia.[8]

Table 7.1: Population size and ethnic composition of Medan, 1930–57 (number of persons, percentages)

Year	*Population Size*	*Indigenous*	*Chinese*	*European*	*Indian and Others*
1930	76,584	53.9	35.6	5.6	4.9
1949	165,659				
1953	363,820	68.7	27.5	0.7	3.0
1957	307,104	66.4	30.0	0.4	3.1

Sources: Colombijn, *Under Construction*, 25, 414; Handelsvereeniging te Medan, *Jaarverslag 1952*, 21; Arsip Medan, Letter K. Rangkuti, Pengetua Usaha Medan, to Kepala Djawatan Kesehatan, province of Sumatera Utara, 1 September 1954, no. 9344/BE-6, and Letter Mohd. Joenoes to Biro Pusat Statistik, 3 October 1957, no. 15445/PE-1. Rounding off percentages may produce a row total that is not 100 per cent.

Medan was also unique among cities of equal size in not having a town plan that could be used as a guideline for the rapid development in the 1950s. In the absence of a town plan, the most important administrative instrument that could be consulted to regulate new buildings was a municipal Building Ordinance promulgated in 1926 and regularly updated thereafter.[9] This Building Ordinance decreed that a house could be neither built nor demolished without a permit from the mayor. The recurrent public announcements reminding citizens of its existence strongly suggest that in the 1950s many people were turning a blind eye to it.[10] The repeated warnings admonishing owners of illegally built houses to demolish their premises, which abound in the municipal archive, also testify to the fact that the municipality was losing control of what was going on in the city. In a notification to some hundred residents, the despairing mayor wrote: 'Over and over again (*telah berkali-kali*) you have been told orally and in written form to demolish your dwelling; this is the final warning, otherwise the municipal government will take steps.'[11] Obtaining this piece of paper was not difficult. As a retired Chinese real-estate developer told me in an interview, when he paid a contractor a lump sum for a new house in Medan, the price also included the effort expended in obtaining a building permit. The state control of whether the work was carried out according to the stipulations in the permit was no more than lip service; as the inspectors were corrupt there was *ipso facto* no control.[12]

A Jakarta-based Chinese owner of a building company (born in West Sumatra in 1926) offered more details about what actually went on.[13] He explained that corruption was rampant in the 1950s, but it did not assume drastic proportions. Civil servants did not ask for a large cash payment under the table (as, he claimed, is the practice today), but were grateful when he offered them something in kind: a dinner, the use of his car for an outing, or an 'official bicycle'. To achieve the desired result, it was important to know the right people to approach: the head of the Public Works Department or the head of the Technical Inspection Service. Once, when he offered a packet of cigarettes to a subordinate official, the man was afraid to accept it. In a nutshell, obtaining a building permit did not form the bottleneck in the construction process in the 1950s.

Contractors and Subcontractors

The physical construction of works of any substantive size was in the hands of complicated combinations of contractors and subcontractors.

It seems that putting out work to a subcontractor was quite common. Most agreements between contractor and subcontractor have faded without a single historical trace, but now and again a glimpse of such an agreement does emerge if a dispute happened to have been fought out in court. For example, in one case discussed in detail below, two subcontractors (Brahmana and Linggar Ginting) promised a contractor to renovate one house (including adding a storey), make some repairs to an army barracks, build a third building, undertake small repairs to another house, improve a guardhouse of the military police, renovate a barracks of the military police, renovate a building of the Public Works Department, clean an engine and repair the military cemetery, all in one deal. The job consisted of nine quite disparate chores.[14]

This sort of agreement between contractor and subcontractor in which several pieces of work were combined in one assignment was not uncommon. In another example the contractor, Asia & Co (head office in Medan), put out a number of construction works in Kabanjahe (North Sumatra) to a man called Hutabarat, who carried out the following tasks: the building of two houses at 5,000 rupiahs each; the building of eight toilets at 250 rupiahs per toilet; and repairs to three houses for 4,837 rupiahs.[15]

One remarkable detail is the fact that the plaintiff, Hutabarat, called himself a trader and not a builder. Probably he was an enterprising person who took on miscellaneous jobs from which he expected to make a profit. The building of new houses and toilets must have required a number of specialists such as carpenters, bricklayers, plumbers and painters, and it is highly unlikely that Hutabarat, not a full-time construction worker himself, had these craftsmen permanently in his employ. So he must have hired the specialists (paid per day?) or sub-subcontracted the work to a number of specialists (paying them an agreed sum). In this case, therefore, at least three layers of (sub)contractors were involved.

Hutabarat was not the only trader who took on construction work. A colonial directory of companies gives numerous examples of firms that combined trade and construction work. The big Medan entrepreneur Liong Sew Kow, who had won the tender to build forty houses for the municipality of Medan, referred to himself as 'contractor and merchant'. The timber yard H. Abdoelrahim and Sons in Bandung advertised that it was available to do light construction work. Other companies were active in the development of real estate and construction, in which the construction was only the first step to exploiting the real estate for an indefinite period. For instance, the Woningpark Arcadië was a firm established in Medan in 1928 for the purpose of building and exploiting houses in Arcadië Park.[16] All these non-specialized builders, no doubt, hired subcontractors who in their turn probably hired sub-subcontractors or an individual specialist to carry out contracted work.

The Jakarta-based owner of a building firm, to whom I have already referred, has provided me with more details about the relationships between contractor and subcontractor in the 1950s.[17] He belonged to a small core of Chinese, indigenous and Eurasian staff permanently employed by a contractor named Siek. They had all received a formal education at a technical school, or, in his case, a technical college (Hogere Technische School) in the Netherlands. Their main task was to supervise the work on the building sites. Siek hired a *mandur* (foreman) for each job. In his turn the *mandur* took on labourers. Some were casual workers, but others, among them a bricklayer, head bricklayer or head carpenter, were higher up in the hierarchy. The electrician and plumber were hired separately. As a rule the *mandur* had no formal training, but ample practical experience.[18]

Lack of skilled labourers was a huge problem. The construction of a 200 m^2 house offered twenty people work for a period of six months. According to my informant, four to five people would have done the same work in the Netherlands and, when he had returned to Indonesia, he at first attempted to mechanize the construction work. Soon he gave up the idea because labour was cheap and the labourers did not have the skill necessary to handle machines. Hence, the machinery he used amounted to only a concrete mixer and a crane. However, he did introduce training for the bricklayers to bring the work up closer to the standard he had seen in the Netherlands. Perhaps with a touch of exaggeration, he told me that the mortar courses between the bricks could be as wide as the bricks, but added that the task of laying bricks was complicated by the fact that locally produced bricks could vary 1–2 cm in size. Walls had to be plastered in order to hide the irregular brickwork.

The contractor did not interfere in the relationship between the *mandur* and the labourers. The contractor paid the *mandur* an agreed sum per square metre of building area and provided the building material. It was up to the *mandur* how much he paid his labourers. If wages rose during the construction work, this was the risk the *mandur* and not the contractor had to run, although the *mandur* would usually request ('*minta*') a pay rise. When this happened, the contractor had to find out whether or not the *mandur* had pocketed too much money for himself. 'By Heavens! (*Potverdorie*!) You had to deal with a *mandur* firmly!', my informant exclaimed. And when the work was well done, the contractor gave the *mandur* a bonus. This type of arrangement, in which a contractor purchased building material and a subcontractor recruited the labourers, was known from at least the 1920s.[19]

Financial Arrangements

Of course, the organizational structure of contractors, subcontractors, and sub-subcontractors gave rise to complex financial arrangements. Table 7.2 gives a (simplified) percentage breakdown of the costs of a housing project in Medan. The Municipal Works Department (*Gemeentewerken*) had commissioned the construction of 140 houses, but provided most of the building material (especially import goods) to which it had easier access than the contractor, Liong Sew Kow.[20] The division of costs presented in Table 7.2 is confirmed by oral history. According to one informant, it was common for wages to swallow up 25–30 per cent of the total costs,

Table 7.2: Percentage breakdown of the construction costs of a real-estate project, Medan 1950 (percentages)

Good/Activity	*Gemeentewerken*	*Contractor*
Brick	20.4	
Cement	6.0	
Tiles	6.6	
Wire nails, zinc, locks and handles, water pipes	6.0	
Paint	1.5	
Light	1.4	
Groundwork, sand, shingle, potash stone (kalisteen)		2.0
Timber		13.4
Mortar, miscellaneous materials		2.1
Wages		32.0
Subtotal	41.9	49.5
Profit constructor		8.6
Total		100.0

Source: Arsip Medan, Letter Directeur Gemeentewerken, S. Ch. Kragt, to Burgemeester Medan, 20 April 1950.

but the proportion of labour costs would increase if more sophisticated work was required. The remainder was set aside for building materials, but this part of a budget included a hidden profit margin of 10 per cent. For example, to the client the contractor listed a bag of cement of, say, 100 rupiahs as costing 110 rupiahs and pocketed the difference between the real and written price as his profit. Naturally a price increase would erode the profit margin of the constructor.[21]

Price increases due to inflation were the order of the day, which meant that contractors often discovered that their profit margin had evaporated into thin air. The survival of the information in Table 7.2 is owed to the fact that the contractor, Liong Sew Kow, politely asked the municipal administration to increase the agreed building sum. He did not demand higher pay but euphemistically 'hoped for assistance', because the state had raised wages twice since he had won the tender. Asked for his expert opinion on the matter, the Director of the Municipal Works Department calculated that wages had actually been raised three times between September 1949 and March 1950, incurring a total rise of 50 per cent for skilled labourers and 60 per cent for daily labourers. The director advised the mayor to compensate the contractor for his loss.[22]

The rapid inflation of the early 1950s was no doubt one of the causes of the lack of capital, a problem recurrently felt by both developers and contractors.[23] When the builder suffered a dearth of capital this could lead to complicated agreements to finance a construction project. For instance, a certain Jan Firman Manik, the owner of a firm in Medan, wanted to develop a plot of land belonging to the Ministry of Education to build shops, but apparently lacked the funds to go ahead with his plan. He agreed with the ministry to erect a school building on one-half of the plot in return for ownership of the full plot; this would allow him to build shops on the other half of the land. However, Jan did not have the capital to build the school and financed the construction by selling the whole plot to a third party, Dari Muda Siahaan, on condition that he, Jan, would surrender the plot vacant. Jan therefore found himself between a rock and a hard place, because this second condition, surrendering the land vacant, conflicted with the stipulation on which he had obtained the land—the building of a school. Vacating the plot was ruled out when the municipal council unsurprisingly refused to issue a demolition order for the new school building.[24]

A dearth of working capital, related to inflation, was also the cause of another conflict about a school. A committee for the construction of a school, and a contractor, Lim Saw Hung, had agreed on the price of

90,000 rupiahs to build the school. However, the work had been interrupted for some unspecified reason and, in the meantime, the price of building materials had gone up. After some negotiation, the two contracting partners agreed that the client would pay the price difference, as the increase in the costs of the building materials was outside the responsibility of the contractor. A revised building sum of 176,000 rupiahs was reached. However, after the client had paid the full sum, the builder Lim Saw Hung still did not complete the work, and the informal, friendly relationship broke down. After being put under pressure by the committee, Lim Saw Hung consented to a formalization of the agreement and both sides signed a contract in the presence of a notary. The contract specified what work remained to be done and the committee arranged a loan of 19,700 rupiahs to the contractor to complete the work. When Lim Saw Hung still did not complete the building, nor did he repay the loan to the committee within the agreed period of three months, the committee began a lawsuit.[25]

A lack of working capital might also have lain behind another recorded dispute, but in this court case the two litigants disagreed on so many essential points that it is hard to decide whose story is actually correct.[26] Nevertheless, some details are similar in both stories and can be accepted as facts. On 12 March 1957, Rapat and Bona Ginting, two brothers who jointly operated a firm of contractors, CV (limited liability partnership) Siwah Sada Ginting, agreed to put out a number of miscellaneous jobs to two men. These two men were S. Brahmana, a 'carpenter' (*tukang kaju*), and Linggar Ginting, who must have been from the same Batak clan as Rapat and Bona, although the court files do not mention any close kinship relation. On 10 April 1958 both sides drew up a contract, covering the list of jobs farmed out to Brahmana and Linggar more than a year earlier. The written contract mentioned a total building sum of 228,765 rupiahs, of which 209,241 had been paid already; the remaining 19,524 rupiahs would be paid upon completion of all work.

In Bona Ginting's version of the story, the lack of capital was the crux of the problem. The two subcontractors, Brahmana and Linggar, did not have the money to pay their labourers to finish the agreed jobs, or to meet the costs of some other jobs they had undertaken. Bona claimed that he had lent the two subcontractors 38,793 rupiahs to help them out and avoid them having to call a halt to the agreed work for financial reasons. This amount was not paid to Brahmana and Linggar as a lump sum, but consisted of eighty-two small payments made erratically from

11 April 1958 to 16 June 1958, listed in an 'overview of receipts' (*daftar kwitansi*). Most of these payments were made to eighteen labourers mentioned by name, but there were also payments for the purchase of fifteen buckets of concrete and other items.[27] The two subcontractors then owed Bona 38,793 rupiahs (the sum lent), minus 19,524 rupiahs (the final payment for the work contracted out), all in all 19,269 rupiahs: this sum was claimed in court by Bona.[28] If this story is correct, the case shows how two subcontractors, Brahmana and Ginting, were tied by a debt relationship to a larger contractor, Bona, because they lacked sufficient working capital.

Formalization

The last two court cases discussed here reveal another recurrent theme. They show the informal way that deals were made, which was all very well as long as there was mutual trust between the contracting partners. However, this informality formed a risk when a good, informal relationship deteriorated causing oral agreements to be reinterpreted. If, during such a breakdown of trust, the partners tried to formalize the earlier oral agreements, it was too late—any attempt to write down earlier arrangements formally in order to resolve the disagreement was counterproductive: simmering tensions flared up into the open and the upshot was a hardening attitude and an open conflict.

The counterproductive effect of formalization after a conflict had emerged is obvious from Brahmana and Linggar's version of the conflict just discussed. They asserted that the first oral agreement, of 12 March 1957, was only made with Bona's younger brother, Rapat, on behalf of CV Siwah Sada Ginting. The agreed sum of 228,765 rupiahs was the remuneration for the labour only; all the building materials were to be furnished by CV Siwah Sada Ginting. When CV Siwah Sada Ginting failed to produce the requisite material, the work was perforce discontinued for fifty-eight days, from 10 April to 16 June 1957 (not counting holidays). Since the work was halted because CV Siwah Sada Ginting had defaulted, this firm had to pay the wages of the labourers of Brahmana and Linggar who were idle for fifty-eight days. This version is an alternative explanation of the eighty-two payments made between 11 April and 16 June.[29]

When the work was near completion in March 1958, Rapat was arrested by the military police for an unspecified reason and, while he was in custody, the flow of payments for work done and for new building materials dried up. Rapat's elder brother, Bona, did not lend a helping hand. In fact, he made matters worse by sending other workers who tried to chase the labourers employed by Brahmana and Linggar away from the construction site. The affair reached its pitch when a fight broke out between the two groups of labourers. On 9 April, Brahmana and Linggar managed to speak to Rapat in jail, urging him to come to a peaceful settlement with his brother Bona. Only then was the formal contract between the two subcontractors and Bona drawn up. The total payment of 209,241 rupiahs, which Brahmana and Linggar had received thus far, had been received from Rapat and not Bona; of the remaining 19,524 rupiahs only 6,500 had been paid by Bona (the first of eighty-two payments in the overview of receipts produced as evidence by Bona), so Bona still owed them 13,024 rupiahs.

Brahmana and Linggar not only denied Bona's accusation, they entered a counterclaim. They had incurred extra costs during the fifty-eight days that the work lay idle: for instance, scaffolding that had been put up but not used; the wages of the labourers; and some damage to walls, doors and tiles because the work had not been rounded off properly. The total extra costs amounted to 17,539 rupiahs. On top of that, inflation added an unexpected wage increase of 24,192 rupiahs. This sort of increase ought to have been paid by the client, or in this case the contractor who had put out the work to Brahmana and Linggar. In total, Brahmana and Linggar claimed 54,755 rupiahs, or the sums of 13,024, 17,539 and 24,192 rupiahs. Bona flatly refuted the whole counterclaim and indicated that he wanted to stick to the written agreement of 10 April 1958.[30] In this case, the contract was written down after a conflict had broken out, when it was clearly too late to come to an amicable arrangement.

Written contracts were also made before the work had begun, as they should have been in order to avoid disputes, but unfortunately contracts were not always exact and could contain errors. One example is a contract deposited in the file of a court case in which a contractor, Wong Tjin, sued two Batak owners of a guest house. The contract stipulated the construction of seven water tanks and the laying of sewerage pipes, worth 24,000 rupiahs in total. One inaccuracy consisted in the spelling of names, with three discrepancies between the spelling in the contract (Wong Tjun, Oberling Tobing) and the court case (Wong Tjin, Oberlin Lumbantobing). More disturbing, though, was the agreed scheme of payments: 60 per cent at the signing of the contract, 30 per cent when half of the work was done and another 30 per cent when the work was completed. Obviously, this payment schedule added up to 120 per cent of the agreed sum! The error is all the more surprising because the payment schedule must have been an important detail in the agreements.[31]

I have found several court cases about overdue payments, but none about any substandard quality of work delivered. In the just given example, technical details of the agreed work were laid down in general terms. All that was said about the water tanks was that they were to have a capacity of 200 litres each. Apart from this, the contractor 'promised to execute the said work to ensure the best possible quality, so as to please [the client]'.[32] A second contract between Wong Tjin and the owners of the guest house concerned the construction of thirty-six bedrooms. The contract covering this more complicated work contained many more technical details. It referred to a building plan (not found in the court file), the height of the walls, the use of chicken wire and mosquito gauze, the kind of timber (*meranti batu* for poles and ordinary *meranti* for other woodwork), the use of Lips locks on the doors and the proportion of cement and water for plastering the walls. This contract also stipulated that the work should be done within sixty days.[33]

The more complicated the construction, the more the formal agreement specified the terms of the construction work, payment and deadline. For instance, the pre-war call for tenders for the construction of a workshop and several company houses for the State Railway Company in North Sumatra was so detailed that it numbered sixty-seven pages.[34] A more modest example is provided by a large house commissioned by an indigenous woman, Zahra Diah, from the constructor Chan Chie in 1953. The house consisted of four rooms, a kitchen, a bathroom, a terrace and an annex with three rooms for servants, another kitchen and bathroom, and one room with an unspecified function. The formal character of the work is demonstrated by the attachment of an official building permit from the government and a fairly detailed blueprint (scale 1:100). The contract stipulated in thirty-two details how the work was done (which parts were to be built in concrete, using floor tiles and so on).

The payment for the work would be handed over in instalments, with a first sum paid at the signing of the contract and the bulk to be paid after completion (Table 7.3). The whole project should have been ready within three months, but the constructor was not obliged to work

Table 7.3: Example of a schedule of payments to construct a house, 1953 (rupiahs)

Task	*Price in rupiahs*
Signing of contract	40,000
Doorposts in place	20,000
Threshold in place	15,000
Roof timbers in place	15,000
Roof tiles laid	15,000
Asbestos, doors, and tiles in place	15,000
Painting done, transfer of keys	100,000
Total	220,000

Source: PN Medan, Sivalingam Chettiar vs Zahara Adil and Chan Chie, Pdt 32/1955.

on holidays or on rainy days. In case of non-completion within the stipulated time, the contractor had to pay a fine of 15 rupiahs per day. Given this relatively small fine (of less than 1 per cent per day) and the excuse of rainy days, completion in time was not high on the list of priorities.[35] When a contractor said that 'Even on rainy days, our work will still continue', it was considered evidence of his diligence and determination to finish his work on time.[36]

The larger the building project, the more the payment was likely to have been divided into smaller portions. For instance, in the construction of a school for the sum of 5.7 million rupiahs, which would take twenty-two months, the payment scheme foresaw nine payments of 10 per cent of the agreed sum every two months, and two payments of 5 per cent in the final four months.[37] If an architect was hired for a project, he usually received 2 per cent of the estimated construction costs (according to two experts giving evidence in a lawsuit). In this particular case, of which more details are known, the architect received 2,000 rupiahs as an advance payment and was entitled to the remaining 7,000 rupiahs of his share if and when the municipality approved of the design and issued a building permit.[38]

Informal arrangements for smaller building projects have left few archival traces, but again another lawsuit gives a glimpse of the everyday past. The case concerns the construction of six basic houses with an earth floor and a roof of palm fronds. The houses were built on a piece of kampong land and the construction was undertaken by one of the landowner's neighbours. In a written covenant, the landowner and the contractor agreed that, after the houses were ready, the builder would transfer three houses to the landowner, while the landowner would transfer half of the land to the builder. In contrast to the written agreements mentioned above, the covenant of this small building project left many details of the agreement unspecified.[39]

Complementarisasi in the Construction Sector

After this overview of the social organization of construction work, it is time to return to the central theme of this chapter, the complementarisasi in the construction sector. The European, Chinese and Indonesian building companies were sometimes each other's direct rivals, but at other times occupied different niches without trespassing into each other's territory. A Chinese informant told me that in the 1950s Dutch-owned firms tended to submit tenders, but Chinese- and Indonesian-owned firms, which were generally smaller, usually did not. A retired Indonesian builder confided to me that in the 1950s Indonesian firms still lacked the expertise for larger projects. As evidence of this lack, he referred to the bend in the Jalan Sudirman (a main road constructed in Jakarta in the 1950s): the bend was caused by the fact that builders had commenced at either end and had failed to draw a proper plan.[40] This unlikely story is possibly not correct, but it does hint at the presumed difference in technological expertise between Indonesian and Dutch firms at that time.

The colonial municipal gazette of Medan provides further insight into the specialization between various firms. To begin with, it is striking that European firms are usually referred to as either 'a construction company' (*bouwkundig bureau*) or 'an engineering firm' (*ingenieursbureau*), but Chinese builders are invariably designated by the term 'contractor' (*aannemer*).[41] The specialization was highlighted even more sharply in 1937 when, after years of grumbling, European firms held a meeting at which they openly complained that the municipality favoured 'Asian contractors' (*Aziatische aannemers*) when it put out work. In response, the Director of the Municipal Works Department, Van Ommen, gave a detailed overview of the works recently commissioned by the municipal government.[42]

Van Ommen denied that the municipality preferred Asian contractors and also shrugged off the suggestion that the contractors bribed civil servants. The reason the municipal government, as did the Deli Maatschappij and other large companies in East Sumatra, usually allotted contracts to Asian entrepreneurs was 'the fact pure and simple that the European contractor cannot compete with his non-European confrères for the said work'.[43] The Asians were 'fully competent' (*alleszins bekwaam*) to undertake construction work and operated more cheaply. European firms found their *raison d'être* in three niches. The first was that they combined construction work and engineering for those medium-sized clients who desired an architect-designed building but could not afford to have their own construction or engineering department. The second was that they took on the largest works, for which scale (more precisely: organization, equipment and purchase of the right building materials) was essential. Finally, they carried out special work, built in iron and reinforced concrete. These niches were enough for the European companies to have won about 70 per cent of the total work (measured in construction costs) farmed out by the municipal administration between 1930 and mid-1937.[44] For very complicated work, even the European firms in Medan were bypassed and the work was given to technically advanced building companies from Java.[45]

The proposition that the European firms could only hold their ground because of their technical expertise is confirmed by an incident in which six Dutch-owned building firms were upset because a municipal technical engineer offered his services to other (unnamed) private contractors. Afraid they would lose their competitive edge in this respect, the firms complained about unfair competition in the winning of the tender for six private projects, including two schools, a swimming pool and a manse. When it came out, the engineer had to stop these activities immediately but was not punished, because allegedly he had not done this work during office hours, nor had he used municipal equipment. Moreover, purportedly he had received only a present and not a cash payment.[46]

How small some of the niches were became apparent during or shortly after the Second World War and the death of engineer Niels Thiele, who had worked in Medan since at least 1929. With his demise, no one competent to undertake large construction work in reinforced concrete was left in all of East Sumatra.[47]

After independence Indonesian contractors played a more prominent role. This change is confirmed by both an old real-estate developer from Medan and by the archives of the NV Associatie.[48] The NV Associatie was a Jakarta-based construction company, which had existed for thirty years before it was set up again as a limited liability company in December 1949. In the first annual reports, the directors complained about the poor performance of the labourers compared to the pre-war standard, a continuing decline in productivity, demands for higher wages and the theft of building material that sometimes meant the loss of 10 per cent of the contracted sum. Nonetheless, despite these worries the company did achieve positive results. However, at the shareholders' meeting in 1955, for the first time the company reported the growing competition from Indonesian contractors.[49] Complementarisasi was gradually giving way to Indonesianisasi.

Conclusion

The construction sector in Medan in the 1930s and early 1950s forms a prime example of what I have dubbed complementarisasi. I propose to reserve the term complementarisasi for economic relationships between independent actors from different ethnic groups working in the same economic sector, in which each side occupied a niche and complemented the work of the other, sometimes having no choice other than to co-operate. Inter-island shipping and urban public transportation are two other important examples of complementarisasi, but the phenomenon is arguably best visible in the construction sector.

Two forms of complementarisasi can be discerned in the construction sector of Medan. The first form was a logical division of the market. Many contractors were Chinese or Indonesian, but there was also room for European contractors who specialized either in big, technically complicated projects or offered technical assistance to medium-sized clients who did not have a technical department themselves. The second form was the chain of contractors and subcontractors who were dependent on each other for the continuation of the construction work, and ultimately needed each other for their own survival.

The concept of complementarisasi needs further exploration. To begin with, the term suggests a parity and a partnership, which might be spurious, hiding the inequality that is inherent in a colonial society. However, in the first form of complementarisasi, a division of the market, Chinese and Indonesian contractors held their ground, contrary to J.H. Boeke's notion of a dual economy. If one wishes to argue that most Chinese and Indonesian contractors did not have structural access to the capital and technical skills necessary to acquire the biggest and most complex construction works, one could just as well state that the European contractors lacked access to cheap labour to penetrate the market of small, routine projects. The second form of complementarisasi, the chain from contractors to subcontractors, implied a co-operation and mutual benefit, which belied Furnivall's notion of a plural society, in which 'one [ethnic] community [is set] against the other'.[50] So, while the colonial society no doubt abounded with examples of economic exploitation, in the cases discussed in this chapter the parity that is suggested by the term complementarisasi seems not unwarranted.

The study of the networks of contractors and subcontractors can be theoretically developed with the help of the concept of 'social capital'. The social capital concept focuses the attention on norms, expectations and trust as indispensable inputs in a productive process.[51] In Medan, the networks of contractors and subcontractors were probably held together by multiple strands, whose financial arrangements and formal contracts have left most historical traces, but trust—a key element in social capital theory—must have been another thread that tied partners together. As studies of institutional economics have shown, trust is especially difficult to achieve in intercultural business networks.[52] Ironically, though not surprisingly, the historian does not get to see the trust itself, but only the void when trust had evaporated and a conflict was brought to court.

Another theoretical question pertains to the processes of formalization; I hypothesize that some actors had an interest in formalization, while others preferred informal arrangements, not because they were supposedly 'backward', but because the informality suited them.[53]

Finally, the question emerges whether the word ending—*sasi*—rightfully suggests that complementarisasi was a gradual, historical process. Unlike Indonesianisasi it certainly was not a historical process leading to somewhere, but perhaps it was a historical development stemming from a colonial situation in which different ethnic groups, in J.S. Furnivall's words, 'live[d] side by side, yet without mingling'.[54] In any case, it should be noted that complementarisasi was a temporary phenomenon, which was ultimately invariably replaced by the Indonesianisasi of the economy.

Primary Sources

Arsip Bagian Umum Kotamadya Medan (Arsip Medan).

Pengadilan Negeri Medan (PN Medan).

Private collection E.C. Dolk.

Notes

1. Lindblad, *Bridges to New Business*, 2–6.
2. See Thee Kian Wie, 'Indonesianization'; Post, '*Indonesianisasi* and Japanization'; Purwanto, 'Economic Decolonization'; Apriyanto, 'Decolonization in Jember'; Marks, 'The Economic Consequences'; Van de Kerkhof, 'Indonesianisasi of Dutch Interests'; Colombijn, *Under Construction*, 40, 58–62.

3. Lindblad, *Between Dayak and Dutch.*
4. Gemeentelijke-ambachtsschool Bandoeng, *Verslag*, 3–6; Technische School Semarang, *Alphabetische naamlijst*; Gemeente Bandoeng, *Prospectus.*
5. There are ample historical studies on (post-)colonial architecture and planning and a few on housing and labour relations, but I do not know of any historical study of the construction business in Indonesia in the mid-twentieth century. For some interesting studies on the operation of the construction sector today, see Kurniasih and Yuwono, 'The Illegal Retribution' and Van der Erve, 'The Diversity of Work'.
6. For example, Pengadilan Negeri (PN) Medan, Radja Bona Ginting and CV Siwah Sada Ginting vs S. Brahmana and Linggar Ginting, Pdt 327/1958.
7. Colombijn, *Under Construction*, 234, 282.
8. The municipal territory was extended from 1,583 to 5,130 hectares in 1951, which partly explains the jump in population size between 1949 and 1953; the decline from 1953 to 1957 can be explained by the fact that 1953 was a rough estimate for the two largest ethnic categories and not a count based on any registration of the population; the 1957 figure seems more accurate than the 1953 figure.
9. Bouw- en woonverordening of 20 January 1926, published in *Javasche Courant*, 30 March 1926, no. 21.
10. For instance, Arsip Medan, Announcement Walikota Medan 5, 2 February 1951; Letter Gubernur Propinsi Sumatera Utara to all Walikota and Bupati, 21 September 1951, no. 17304/4/4.
11. Arsip Medan, Letter Djaidin Poerba to [84 persons], 23 October 1951, no. 5938/KB-8. To exonerate the Medan administration somewhat, people could build a basic dwelling of non-permanent material within days. Arsip Medan, Letter Walikota Medan, A.M. Djalaloe'ddin to Maruli Pangaribuan, 7 August 1952, no. 7803/KB-2.
12. Anonymized interview, Medan, 15 March 2004.
13. Anonymized interview, Jakarta, 27 January 2005.
14. PN Medan, Radja Bona Ginting and CV Siwah Sada Ginting vs S. Brahmana and Linggar Ginting, Pdt 327/1958.
15. PN Medan, A. Hutabarat vs Bukit, owner of Asia & Co, Pdt 725/1952.
16. Arsip Medan, Letter Liong Sew Kow to Walikota Medan, Medan, 20 April 1950; *Handboek 1930*, 1288; Numerous other examples can be found in *Handboek 1930*, and Gemeente Bandoeng, *Prospectus.*
17. Anonymized interview, Jakarta, 27 January 2005. The same structure appears in a report from 1937, *Gemeenteblad 2 Gemeente Medan*, 1937, 33(185).
18. Anthropological research has shown that the division of tasks can be even more complicated than sketched here, with a *tukang* (*kayu*, *batu*, *besi*), *setengah tukang*, *pembantu tukang*, *kepala tukang*, *mandur*, *bas borong*, and *pelaksana*. Van der Erve, *Recruitment and Composition of Construction Labour.*
19. *Gemeenteblad 2 Gemeente Medan*, 1937, 33(185).

20. The municipality referred to the post-war shortages to explain why it provided most building materials itself (with the exception of locally available timber and natural stone), but in 1930 a similar agreement had already been made between the municipality of Medan as client and a Chinese contractor, *Gemeenteblad 2 Gemeente Medan*, 1930, 5(71).
21. Anonymized interview, Jakarta, 27 January 2005.
22. Arsip Medan, Letter Directeur Gemeentewerken, S. Ch. Kragt to Burgemeester Medan, 20 April 1950, and Letter Liong Sew Kow to Walikota Medan, Medan, 20 April 1950. The municipality had hoped to recover the extra costs from the central government, but the latter rejected its request. Whether Medan ultimately paid the extra costs out of its own pocket or whether Liong Sew Kow had to bear the extra costs himself remains a mystery. Arsip Medan, Letter Walikota Djaidin Poerba to Wakil Lembaga Pusat Pembangunan Kembali (Centrale Stichting Wederopbouw), 25 April 1950, no. 1972/RA-1, and letter Pengetua Usaha A.B. Schlette to Pemimpin Usaha Pekerdjaan Kota and Kepala Bahagian Keuangan dan Bea Kota Medan, 28 June 1950, no. 3061/RA.1.
23. Private collection E.C. Dolk, *Verslag over 1950 Associatie*, 3; ibid. *1951*, no pagination.
24. PN Medan, Dari Muda Siahaan vs Jan Firman Manik, Pdt 757/1957.
25. PN Medan, Panitia Pendirian Gedung SGB Negeri 1/II Medan vs Lim Saw Hung, Pdt 458/1958.
26. PN Medan, Radja Bona Ginting and CV Siwah Sada Ginting vs S. Brahmana and Linggar Ginting, Pdt 327/1958. The outcome of the case is unclear. The file contains a writ of sequestration for the houses of Brahmana and Linggar Ginting, indicating that Bona won the lawsuit, but the wrapping of the file bears the handwritten Dutch words '*beschikking tot nader*', suggesting a court ruling had been postponed.
27. An interesting detail is that while most names sound Malay (Ajub, Marbun, Djampi) or perhaps Batak (Djanggun Sembiring), one labourer must have been Chinese (Tam Soon), so apparently the crews were ethnically mixed.
28. PN Medan, Radja Bona Ginting and CV Siwah Sada Ginting vs S. Brahmana and Linggar Ginting, Pdt 327/1958.
29. The overview of receipts (*daftar kwitansi*) is dated 9 April 1958–16 June 1958, and these years confirm the version by Bona and take the edge off the story of Brahmana and Linggar, set in 1957; however, the overview was provided by Bona and no original signed receipts were attached to it, so this piece of evidence must remain inconclusive.
30. PN Medan, Radja Bona Ginting and CV Siwah Sada Ginting vs S. Brahmana and Linggar Ginting, Pdt 327/1958. Bona only added in his defence that Rapat had withdrawn from the firm and had given away his half of it to Bona in December 1958, so only Bona was responsible for the firm.

31. PN Medan, Wong Tjin vs Eddie Muara Lumbantobing and Oberlin Lumbantobing, Pdt 444/1958.
32. '*Pekerdjaan tersebut diatas, [contractor] berdjandji mengadakan kwaliteit jang sebaik²nja sehingga menjenangkan bagi [client].*' PN Medan, Wong Tjin vs Eddie Muara Lumbantobing and Oberlin Lumbantobing, Pdt 444/1958.
33. Ibid.
34. Staatsspoor- en tramwegen, *Mededeelingen.*
35. PN Medan, Sivalingam Chettiar vs Zahara Adil and Chan Chie, Pdt 32/1955.
36. '*[M]aka itu biarpun hari hudjan, pekerdjaan kita djalan terus djuga.*' Arsip Medan, Letter Liong Sew Kow to Walikota Medan, Medan, 20 April 1950.
37. PN Medan, Mak Ping Hong vs Oei Peng Hong (representing Komite Chi Kong Middle School), Pdt 448/1958.
38. PN Medan, Tamin vs Chia Kiat San, Pdt 345/1951; Tamin vs Chia Kiat San, Pengadilan Tinggi (PT) Medan, Pdt 295/1957.
39. PN Medan, Sarinam Djauhari vs Raden Syech Hadji Mohammad Said, Pdt 147/1959.
40. Anonymized interview, Jakarta, 27 January 2005; anonymized interview, Jakarta, 19 April 2003.
41. For example the *aannemers* Ng Gooi Cheong, Oei Chiang Keng, Kwong Tong Seng and Vellasamy, *Gemeenteblad 2 Gemeente Medan*, 1930, 33(363); ibid. 1932, 16(107); ibid. 1936, 19(98), and the firms Bouwkundig Bureau Bennik & Co; G.G. Langereis & Co; Bouwkundig Bureau Meeuwse & Hartog; NV Aannemingsmaatschappij Oost-Indië; Ingenieursbureau Niels Thiele; and Bouwkundig Bureau P.A.J. de Vroom, ibid. 1930, 14(167–8).
42. Ibid. 1937, 33(185).
43. '*het bloote feit dat de Europeesche aannemer voor de bedoelde werken niet kan concurreeren met zijn niet-Europeesche confraters*', ibid. 1937, 33(185).
44. Ibid. 1937, 33(185). It seems that until 1930 the municipality carried out all the work itself, but then began to put out work in response to a request from the *Nederlandsch Indische Aannemersbond* (Netherlands Indies Association of Contractors), ibid. 1930, 2(37); Notulen vergadering Medansche Gemeenteraad, 22 January 1930, no. 1, *Gemeenteblad 1 Medan, Notulen.*
45. *Gemeenteblad 2 Gemeente Medan*, 1938, 28(119).
46. Ibid. 1930, 14(167–8).
47. Arsip Medan, Letter Coordinator O.T.D., C.E. Bekkering to Recomba, Medan, 17 March 1948; *Handboek 1930*, 1288.
48. Anonymized interview, Medan, 15 March 2004.
49. Private collection E.C. Dolk, *Verslag over 1949 Associatie*, 4; ibid. 1950, 4; ibid. 1952, 1; Notulen AV van aandeelhouders, 11 July 1955. *Indonesianisasi* was also visible in the gradual and conscious recruitment of Indonesian staff, which was difficult in 1952, but by 1955 and 1956 the policy to hire

'sons of the soil' (*zonen van dit land*) had begun to bear fruit. *Verslag over 1952 Associatie*, 2; ibid. 1955, 2; ibid. 1956, 2.

50. Furnivall, *Netherlands India*, 459.
51. Coleman, 'Social Capital in the Creation of Human Capital'; Portes, 'Social Capital: Its Origins and Applications'.
52. Crossman and Noma, '*Sunao* as character: Its implications'; Csukas et al., 'The Determinants of Trusting and Reciprocal Behaviour'; Zaheer and Zaheer, 'Trust across Borders'.
53. Boer, '(In)formalization: The Forces Beyond'; De Soto, *The Oher Path*.
54. Furnivall, *Netherlands India*, 446.

8

Commodities Caught in the Crossfire: Java Sugar and Imperial Japan, 1880–1945

Roger Knight

The story of Java sugar and its interface with imperial Japan between the mid-1880s and the end of the Second World War is the story of a commodity caught in the crossfire. From the late nineteenth century through to the mid-1920s, Java's colonial sugar producers—predominantly Dutch-owned companies who did business with Japanese refineries through the agency of European, Japanese and Chinese-Indonesian merchant-houses and banks—came to play an increasingly important part in the emergent Japanese 'sugar empire' in East Asia. Together with its massive export trade to the Indian subcontinent, by the 1920s, sales to Japan and to markets elsewhere in East Asia accounted for virtually all the Java sugar companies' business.

By the mid-1920s, the Java–Japan nexus was under serious strain. In the first place, the Java producers were caught—figuratively speaking—in the crossfire of competition with new suppliers to the Japanese sugar empire, primarily located in Formosa (Taiwan), where Japanese capital was engaged in creating a major world-class sugar industry of its own c.1910 onwards. The second form of 'crossfire' was likewise figurative. This took the form of a trade war between Japan and the Netherlands Indies during which (to pursue the military metaphor) the Java sugar industry suffered serious 'collateral damage'. The third manifestation of 'crossfire' was very literal indeed. It related to the direct impact of warfare on the industry's fortunes, first in China and then in colonial Indonesia itself. Japanese military adventurism in China during the course of the 1930s progressively sealed off most of East Asia's largest market from the Java industry (while creating massive opportunities for imports from Formosa). Japan's military occupation of the Netherlands Indies between 1942 and 1945 added a further and nearly fatal dimension to the 'crossfire'. The military government had little use for Java's sugar *qua sugar*. As we shall see, they had other plans for it.

To write of 'caught in the crossfire' in this context raises, of course, a variety of issues that have emerged in the recent historiography of the political and economic order in East Asia and its international interface, especially during the decades prior to the Second World War. These issues relate, *inter alia*, to the dynamics of intra-Asian trade and its linkages to the world economy; the role of indigenous Asian participants in that trade; and the possibilities (as Akita and Kagotani have remarked) for a 'co-existence of economic interests' that left space for accommodation—as opposed to conflict—in international commercial disputes in East and Southeast Asia in the interwar decades. Last but not least, the crucial long-term issue concerns the continuities, as well as the obvious discontinuities, that characterized economic linkages across the region over the span of a 'long' twentieth century that actually began in the 1880s.[1]

Within these critical parameters, the argument of this chapter is essentially threefold. First, it emphasizes the degree of economic 'complementarity' that characterized the nexus between Java sugar and imperial Japan for much—though by no means all—of the period under consideration.[2] Second (utilizing notable recent work by other scholars), it highlights the extent to which the agencies involved in articulating that nexus were Asian rather than (colonial) European. Third, it outlines a brief analysis of the way in which the nexus became caught up in an international geopolitical conflict (primarily between the United Kingdom, the United States and Japan), leaving open the question of how far the disastrous final outcome was indeed 'inevitable'.

Interregional Trade and the International Sugar Economy: Java's Asia Connection

An inter-Asian trade in industrially manufactured sugar began to grow exponentially in the late nineteenth and early twentieth centuries. The sugar industry on the Indonesian island of Java, almost exclusively owned and run by Dutch-colonial and Chinese-Indonesian interests, played a major part in this development. Java sugar had long enjoyed a connection with Asian markets. Indeed, much of the island's output of sugar had historically gone to other Asian (or Middle Eastern) destinations. Only in the opening decades of the nineteenth century was this trend decisively reversed, with the consequence that Java's rapidly expanding post-1830 output was redirected to European markets. Towards the close of the nineteenth century, however, the previous Asia connection was revived—on a far grander scale than in the past. Whereas in 1880 the greater part of Java's exports had still been consumed in the West (at that stage predominantly in Europe) some forty years later the vastly increased output of the island's factories—it had grown more than sixfold since the 1880s—went almost exclusively to locations in Japan, China and the Indian subcontinent. The tipping point, however, occurred towards the end of that decade when, for the first time, the greater part of Java's sugar output went to markets outside Europe.

The critical development here had to do with the crisis that shook the international sugar economy in the mid-1880s. During the course of 1884, the world price for industrially manufactured sugar effectively collapsed. Although the crisis appeared set to destroy the island's colonial sugar industry, it eventually proved its salvation. What happened was that the steep drop in the price of industrially manufactured sugar—the factory-made form of the commodity often called 'centrifugal'—made it (potentially) available to consumers for whom it had previously been, at best, an expensive and rare luxury. This was particularly the case in Asia, where newly modern people in newly modern cities were looking for equally modern commodities—white, factory-made sugar among them. Those industrial sugar manufacturers able to accommodate themselves to the much lower price, prevailing after 1884, for their product could hope to take advantage of this. Java was one of them.

The Japanese Market and the Zaibatsu

During the 1880s and 1890s most of Java's raw sugar found its prime Asian outlet in the refineries of Hong Kong.[3] By the end of the century, however, the island's colonial sugar factories had also begun to supply newly established refineries in Japan. This was a development that was destined to figure very large in the industry's late colonial history. Until the last quarter of the nineteenth century, Japan existed somewhere near the margins of the intra-Asian commodity trade in sugar. From the 1880s onwards, this situation changed dramatically. There had been a notable growth in imports of primitively manufactured, 'pre-industrial' sugar into Japan, c.1870, initially from southern China, but subsequently from Formosa. Imported refined sugar, increasingly derived from industrially manufactured raw material from Java itself, started to penetrate this market during the 1880s.

Japanese imports of processed sugar from overseas, which had quadrupled in a little over ten years, peaked around the end of the century, and came primarily from the Hong Kong refineries and from the beet sugar industries of Germany and Austria-Hungary.[4] Predominantly, these imports were consumed by Japan's new urban middle classes, a reflection of the fact that it was significantly more expensive than the artisan-made, unrefined sugar imported from either Formosa or other parts of the region.[5] By 1897, Japanese per capita consumption of sugar had doubled within less than a decade to almost five kilos per capita, and continued to rise thereafter.[6] Consequently, Japan was viewed as potentially the most lucrative market in East Asia.

Hardly surprisingly, therefore, Japan's burgeoning sugar consumption had come to attract the attention of the zaibatsu, the big industrial-financial-commercial conglomerates that were indelibly associated with Japan's late nineteenth-century advance into economic modernity. In 1896, for example, it was reported from Hong Kong that Japanese syndicate 'has already sent its emissaries to Europe to study the best methods for [industrial] plant etc'.[7] A couple of sugar refineries were quickly established, one at Osaka and the other in Tokyo, with more to follow.[8] The Osaka refinery had German-built equipment and was said to be capable of producing 100 tons of refined sugar per day.[9] These refineries quickly came to be designated as 'a troublesome competitor' by their British counterparts in Hong Kong,[10] who previously had the East Asian market for refined sugar very largely to themselves. Indeed, plans were mooted (though soon abandoned) to flood the Japanese market with cheap sugar in an effort to deter further investment in domestic refining.[11]

Mitsui and Mitsubishi capital—that is to say, the capital of the two leading zaibatsu—was closely involved in the new ventures. Indeed, sugar was one of the most important items traded by Mitsui through to the outbreak of the Second World War.[12] During much of the 1910s and the first half of the 1920s, however, the biggest name in the country's sugar trade was not one of the established zaibatsu. Instead, it was a (relative) newcomer, Suzuki Shoten. Founded in Kobe in 1874 specifically as a sugar-importing business, by 1914 Suzuki had become a widely diversified conglomerate, with major interests in steel and shipping. It eventually embraced some seventy-eight corporations and rivalled Mitsui itself in terms of paid-up capital and value of traded goods.[13] Nonetheless, sugar remained one of the key facets of its business, and it had its own refinery.

'Complementarity': Java and the Japanese Sugar Empire

Reflected in these developments was the fact that during the opening decades of the twentieth century Japan established what is best described as a 'sugar empire' based on an international web of plantation, manufacture and commerce, at the heart of which lay the refineries of metropolitan Japan. The Japanese refineries, however, were heavily dependent not only on Japan's domestic market but also on their ability to divert 'excess' capacity into overseas markets. Indeed, by the 1920s, they were supplying not only Japan's domestic market but also that of the adjacent Chinese and Manchurian mainland immediately to the west and south. By the early 1930s, moreover, Japanese interests were operating three refineries in the new client state of Manchukuo, and by the end of the decade were also running one in Japanese-occupied Shanghai.[14] By the late 1920s, Japanese sugar interests formed a cartel—as did their counterparts worldwide—designed both to restrain production and maintain the price of the commodity.[15]

The 'empire' drew its raw material from a variety of sources. Its eventual centerpiece was Formosa, which Japan had acquired as a colony in 1895. Nonetheless, its suppliers were as far flung as beet sugar producers in Korea (brought formally under Japanese control in 1910) and cane sugar factories in the mandated territory of the northern Marianas, in Micronesia, which Japan gained in the wake of the German defeat in the First World War. By the mid-1930s, more than 11,000 hectares of cane and six or more large modern sugar factories existed there, worked by a mixture of Japanese, Korean and local labour.[16] The 'empire' also established a beachhead on Java. Around 1920, a handful of the island's factories (5 out of a total of nearly 180) were owned by Japanese interests, including the Dai Nihon refinery company, one of Japan's biggest.[17]

The prime connection between the Java industry and the Japanese sugar 'empire', however, was essentially a commercial and financial one. Japanese interests had very little direct investment in the manufacture of Java sugar, but had huge sums tied up in its purchase and shipment to Japan and elsewhere in East Asia. Developments here dated from around the turn of the twentieth century. In this context, Japanese shipping was to become a very important facet of Java sugar's Asia connection. That connection was greatly accelerated, moreover, by the impact of the First World War and the consequent shifting of the Netherlands Indies out of the European economic orbit and towards the orbits of Japan and the United States.[18] Though the end of hostilities in 1918 brought some return to pre-war conditions, Japanese and associated commercial and financial interests continued to penetrate the Indies economy.[19] Sugar was a prime case. In the ten-year period prior to the sudden termination of large Japanese purchases of Java sugar in 1928 (see below), around one-third or more of the Java industry's sales were made direct to Japanese buyers, with Suzuki and Mitsui well to the fore. Of at least equal significance, Japanese interests were also prominent in the *financing* of the sugar trade over and above the direct purchase of the commodity.[20]

Asian Stakeholders: The Role in the Sugar Trade of Chinese-Indonesian Mercantile Houses

The successful articulation of this key dimension of Java's linkages to the Japanese sugar 'empire', however, was contingent not only on Dutch colonial sugar manufacturers, Japanese sugar refining combines and colonial-based European mercantile houses. Also—and perhaps crucially—it depended on extensive Chinese-Indonesian business concerns. Based in Java but with operations extending from the Indian subcontinent through to Japan, these Chinese-Indonesian businesses drew (among other sources) on Japanese capital to underpin their ventures.[21] Though there were a plethora of such firms, the Semarang-based 'Kwik Hoo Tong Trading Society' (KHT) and the similarly located 'Oei Tiong Ham Concern' (OTHC), together with the latter's 'Kian Gwan' trading arm, were the undisputed leaders.[22] Both firms had long-term links with Japanese financial and commercial interests. Kwik Djoen Eng, who masterminded KHT from the 1910s until its collapse in the 1930s, had major investments on Formosa (as well as Java), where he owned a tea-export company, and had close links with the Bank of Taiwan dating back to the period of its foundation in the very early years of the century. Indeed, it was on Formosa that he died in 1935.

OTHC's commercial profile showed some similar traits. Early in the twentieth century, the firm had opened a branch in Kobe, in addition to those in Hong Kong and Shanghai. Oei Tiong Ham himself, the head of the conglomerate of which Kian Gwan was a part, had close contacts with Japanese capital (and worked hard to promote collaboration between Chinese and Japanese traders and to mitigate the impact in the Netherlands Indies of anti-Japanese commercial boycotts). Close ties to the Bank of Taiwan were also part of his business profile, and like Kwik Djoen Eng, he had a Japanese passport (and hence dual citizenship in the Netherlands Indies), in consideration of his standing in East Asia. The extent to which KHT's and OTHC-Kian Gwan's operations were financed by Japanese capital is difficult to estimate. Certainly, other sources of capital were involved. It looks, for example, as if De Javasche Bank (Java Bank) was a major creditor of KHT.[23] Nonetheless, this hardly detracts from the conclusion that for the better part of a decade prior to 1928, Japanese capital, either directly or indirectly—through Japanese businesses and through links with Chinese-Indonesian 'multinationals'—accounted for the greater part of Java's export trade in sugar.

Java's Marginalization in the Japanese Sugar 'Empire' after 1927

In 1927, the Suzuki Zaibatsu, which had been very big in Java's trade in sugar to Japan over the previous decade, got into very serious difficulties, undermining a sizeable swathe of key Japanese financial institutions, both in Japan itself (where the prime minister and cabinet also fell victim to the crisis), and in Formosa. With close financial ties to the failed zaibatsu, the Bank of Taiwan (BOT) had to close its doors temporarily, and to curtail its subsequent operations.[24]

This was bad news for the Java sugar industry. Moreover, there was worse to come. Driving the evolving situation—one that saw Java sugar rapidly marginalized in the Japanese market—were two underlying factors that spelled very serious, long-term trouble. One was the impact on sugar sales in East Asia of the growing political turbulence in China, something that severely damaged the Java industry's prospects in what had been a growing market.[25] The second was the emergence of Formosa as the new heart of the Japanese sugar empire.

Formosa and Java: Nemesis or Room for Both?

Java sugar's problems in the East Asian market by the 1930s were multiple. Above all, however, what damaged Java sugar's hopes of continued sales to Japan—and vastly complicated its position in the China market—was the emergence of Formosa as a major producer of industrially manufactured sugar. Even so, there might be a case for saying that there was 'room for both'.

Developments in Formosa c.1910 onwards reflected the determination of Japan's leading zaibatsu to create their own, alternative source of supply to that offered by the Netherlands Indies. With strong government backing, Japanese companies began pouring in capital, and importing know-how, to create a network of state-of-the-art sugar factories in Formosa that emulated those of Java.[26] By 1930, Formosa boasted forty-eight fully industrialized sugar factories producing some 571,718 metric tons of sugar from more than 117,000 hectares of cane. By 1940 output amounted to more than one million metric tons, and Formosa had become the world's fourth largest producer-exporter of cane sugar, much of it in the form of so-called 'factory white' well suited to supply the Chinese market since it needed no further refining.[27]

To be sure, matters were far from plain sailing for Japanese sugar interests. From the late 1920s onwards, well before Japan embarked on a full-scale war in China, Japanese military aggression (notably the Jinan Incident of May 1928) and answering Chinese boycotts of Japanese goods and business created considerable problems for the Japanese sugar trade on the China coast.[28] In Shanghai itself, the Japanese-owned refinery was forced to close.[29] It was in this latter market, in particular, that the anti-Japanese boycott had its greatest impact: indeed, by mid-1929 Japanese sugar dealers were resorting to repacking their sugar into the gunny sacks typical of Netherlands Indies production and attempting to sell it as 'crushed Java'.[30]

Nonetheless, the long-term trend favoured the Japanese. As early as 1929 (according to Dutch reports) sugar from the Japanese factories in Formosa was already being smuggled in significant quantities into coastal China on Japanese motor vessels (thereby avoiding heavy duties levied on the legitimate import of the commodity)—and far more was to come during the course of the decade, despite attempts by the (British run) Chinese Customs Service to prevent it.[31] By 1933, Dutch representatives in Shanghai referred to the 'frightful increase' (*schrikbarende toeneming*) in smuggling there, and speculated that around 40 per cent of the sugar coming into China was smuggled.[32] In north China, in particular, sugar smuggling (along with that of other goods) paralleled the growing degree of Japanese entrenchment, c.1930 onwards. By 1936, conditions there—described by one singularly well-placed contemporary in terms of 'an orgy of officially protected smuggling unparalleled even in China'[33]—had created a situation in which the bona fide sugar trade through Shanghai was reduced to a state of 'total disorganization'.[34] In the following year, the outbreak of the Sino-Japanese War meant that in the wake of the Japanese advance, Shanghai itself and its Yangzi valley hinterland were flooded with cheap Japanese goods, sugar included.[35]

The impact of these developments on the Java industry was far-reaching. In the early 1920s, when Formosa industry first began to make significant inroads in the metropolitan Japanese market, Java still supplied about 50 per cent of Japan's requirements. By the end of the decade, however, Formosa (and other Japanese colonial sources) was supplying around 75 per cent and Java only 25 per cent. Moreover, from Java's point of view, worse was to come. At the end of the 1930s, the Dutch colony accounted for a mere 15 per cent or less of Japan's imports, and Formosan sugar totally dominated the Japanese domestic market.

Nonetheless, although the rise of industrial sugar production in Formosa eventually served to marginalize Java in the Japanese sugar empire, at the beginning of the 1930s the demise of the Dutch colonial industry's East Asian markets was far from a foregone conclusion. For all that Formosa took over from Java as the main supplier to Japanese refineries during the course of the 1920s, the colony was not in a position totally to supplant Java in the Japanese sugar empire. Such calculations as are currently available suggest that although Formosa's output was sufficient to supply Japan's domestic market, its factories could not meet all the demands of Japan's expanding empire on the East Asian mainland.[36] Moreover, there seems no doubt that Java's sugar was cheaper to produce than that of its Formosan counterpart—and was hence notionally more attractive to Japan's refineries than the output of their own colonial possessions.[37]

Co-existence and Conflict: Sugar and the Commercial Relations of the Netherlands Indies and Japan during the 1930s

Theoretically, therefore, there remained a place for Java in the Japanese 'sugar empire', despite the rise of the Formosan industry. Attempts to reintegrate Java after the debacle of 1927, however, ran up against a number of obstacles. Chief among them were the conflicted commercial relations between the Netherlands Indies and Japan that developed during the course of the 1930s. Indeed, it was a trade war between the Netherlands and Japan that effectively sank any hopes that the Java sugar producers might find salvation in renewed ties to Japanese refiners and to the Japanese sugar 'empire' in general. Here again, the situation was one in which the possibilities of coexistence were actively explored by both sides for much of the decade. Conflict was not 'inevitable'.

It was a complex situation.[38] On the one hand, Japanese cotton goods manufacturers were anxious to sustain and expand their market in the Indies. In pursuit of this, they appear to have been prepared, had they been able, to sacrifice the interests of the Japanese-Formosa sugar producers as part of a deal that would allow Java sugar into Japan in return for reduced tariffs on Japanese cotton goods imported into the Indies. Understandably, any such proposal met with fierce resistance from Japan's 'sugar barons', represented by the country's leading zaibatsu. To complicate matters further, the latter also had a stake in the cotton goods industry. Even so, there is a strong case for arguing, as does Kagotani, that in general the trade diplomacy of the Japanese government itself was more inclined to accommodate Dutch interests than those of its own industrialists.[39]

On the Dutch side, there were likewise tensions between the interests of metropolitan cotton goods manufacturers, who wanted to keep cheap Japanese cotton goods out of the Indies, and the metropolitan-colonial sugar interest that was prepared to accept Japanese cottons as the necessary trade-off for the entry of substantial amounts of Java sugar into the Japanese arena. The situation was further confused, moreover, by the determination of the Indies government to promote cotton goods manufacture in the colony itself, as part of a larger programme of industrialization in the archipelago. The eventual outcome, over a period of years, went against Java sugar. Japanese cotton goods were (largely) kept out of the Indies, and Java sugar lost a (possible) opportunity of finding a secure market in Japan. Java sugar was thereby sacrificed to competing metropolitan interests. Sugar capital had once been deeply influential in Dutch colonial circles. By the late 1930s, however, other interests had come into play, and the Java sugar producers lacked the heft to prevent the state cutting the industry loose when the demands of a larger colonial-metropolitan economic strategy appeared to require it.[40]

From Sugar to Engine Fuel: Japanese Plans and the Java Industry during the Second World War, 1942–45

Japanese forces overran the Netherlands Indies in the early months of 1942. By the time of Japan's surrender to the Allies in August 1945, output from Java's industrial sugar factories had almost ceased: production was cut back from around 1,700,000 tons in 1941 to a mere 28,000 tons in 1945.[41] The Japanese, already in possession of their own 'sugar colony' of Formosa and, since the beginning of 1942, of the sugar-rich Philippines as well, had no need for Java's output beyond that required to satisfy purely local demand. Moreover, even had they been interested in the possibility of directing Java's production to the East Asian market, the continuing military stalemate in China—in tandem with the havoc wrought by Allied attacks on Japanese shipping—effectively nullified any such expectation.

Even so, there was no rush by the Japanese to close down the industry—not least, presumably, because the occupation authorities quickly became aware of the massive social and economic dislocation that would result. At many factories, production continued on a considerable scale in 1942, reflecting the extensive area that was already being made ready for planting when the Japanese arrived in March–April of the preceding year. Indeed, in many cases it was not until the close of the 1943 sugar campaign that expatriate Dutch factory personnel were finally interned. Even then, the many Eurasian Dutch who worked in the industry as managers and supervisors were left in situ, as were their erstwhile Indonesian subordinates. By the closing stages of the war, however, the number of working factories was reduced from around 80 to no more than a handful.

One of the reasons why the Japanese perpetuated the industry's existence, albeit in attenuated form, was because they had quite radical designs on at least some of its output. Indeed, they aimed to use Java's 'surplus' sugar manufacturing capacity to produce engine fuel, in the form of butane (Dutch: *butanol*). The intention (at least according to what Japanese military officers and civilian officials told the Dutch late in 1945) was to create a crude form of butane that would then be sent on tankers to Japan for refining into fuel that could be used for airplanes. However, the project misfired badly. Very little crude butane was ever produced and even less of it (if any) sent to Japan.

Both ethanol and butane can be manufactured from sugar; in this case, however, the information available is quite specific that it was *butanol* (that is, butane) that was being aimed for.[42] Apparently, the Japanese companies to whom the sugar industry was consigned in Java were to set about the task of manufacturing crude 'butane' (*butanol* 60 per cent, aceton 30 per cent and alcohol 10 per cent) with equipment brought from Japan and garnered from Java's own factories. They also aimed to use locally available organic nitrates in the form of maize and subsequently compressed bean-cake in the fermentation process that 'butane' manufacture involved. At one stage, presumably late in the war, it was planned to refine butane in Java itself, for use locally as aircraft fuel, but the necessary equipment never arrived from Japan. It looks as if very little crude 'butane' was ever produced in wartime Java. By August 1945, some six factories were said to be producing a monthly grand total of 470 tons (Dutch sources were sceptical of even this figure, itself far below the 200,000 tons annually said to have been originally projected). Meanwhile, a number of large and exceptionally well-equipped sugar factories were put permanently out of commission. They include the most ambitious sugar factory ever constructed in Java, which was a total write-off by August 1945. All its manufacturing apparatus, with the exception of the mills for grinding cane, had been removed and replaced with tanks designed for the preparation of butane.[43] A similar fate befell the state-of-the-art Comal factory on the north coast of Central Java, which had been opened with much fanfare only twenty years earlier.[44]

Conclusion

The Java–Japan sugar nexus, one that existed between the 1880s and 1940s, adds significantly to our understanding of international commerce *between* Asian countries. As Kaoru Sugihara has argued, this commerce was of fundamental importance to Asia's modern economic development.[45] Likewise, that nexus highlights the role of indigenous Asian economic actors in interregional commerce, and makes clear that for much of the period concerned here (the 1880s to 1940s) 'complementarity' was as significant a theme as 'conflict'. At the same time, however, the question of continuities—so critical to discussion of the mid-twentieth-century international order in Asia—remains altogether more problematic, in so far as the commodity trade in sugar is concerned. The involvement of Japan in the economic development of colonial-era Indonesia from late in the nineteenth century onwards, evidenced by the formidable role played by Japanese capital in the trade in Java sugar over a period of two decades or more, was indeed one dimension of a history that displayed remarkable continuities across the notional divide that separated the independent Indonesia of the 1950s and 1960s from the Dutch colonial state of the interwar decades. Even so, in the specific case of sugar, the degree of discontinuity was the decisive element. The linkages between sugar production in Java and the refineries and sugar traders of metropolitan Japan, already deeply troubled by the late 1930s, were definitively severed in the decade that followed. Sugar manufacture was resumed in Java after the Second World War (in attenuated form), but in circumstances that quite quickly saw its output disappear from the intra-Asian trade and from international commerce of any kind: the future of Japanese–Indonesian economic ties lay elsewhere.

Primary Sources

Archief Nederlandse Indische Vereniging tot Afzet van Suiker (NIVAS).

Butterfield & Swire Hong Kong (BSHK).

Butterfield & Swire London (Swire).

Nationaal Archief, Den Haag (NA).

Relevant identifying numbers from Elizabeth Hook, *A Guide to the Papers of John Swire and Sons Ltd.* London: The Library, School of Oriental and African Studies, 1977.

School of Oriental and African Studies, University of London, Papers of John Swire and Sons (JSSI).

Notes

1. See in particular Akita and White, 'Introduction: The International Order of Asia in the 1930s and 1950s'; Sugihara, 'An Introduction. In *Japan, China and the Asian International Economy*'; Sugiyama and Grove, 'Introduction. In *Commercial Networks in Modern Asia*'; Grove and Selden, 'Editor's Introduction: New Perspectives on China, East Asia and the Global Economy'. An earlier version of this chapter was presented at a seminar at The Institute for Research in Humanities, Kyoto University, 27 March 2012. I would like to thank the participants, especially Professors Tomoko Shiroyama and Naoto Kagotani, for their comments and suggestions.
2. Akita and White, *The International Order of Asia*, 4.
3. Sugiyama, 'Marketing and Competition in China'; Sugiyama, 'A British Trading Firm in the Far East'; Knight, *Commodities and Colonialism*, 21–8.
4. See the reproduced trade statistics, *De Indische mercuur*, 3.

5. Sugiyama, 'The Structure of the East Asian Refined Sugar Market', 326–9. I am grateful to Kazuhisa Shimada for translating this paper.
6. Mazumdar, *Sugar and Society in China*, 375.
7. BSHK to Swire London, 7 October 1896, JSSI 2/8.
8. "Japan", 322.
9. BSHK to Swire, 18 August 1896, JSSII 2/8.
10. BSHK to Swire, 25 March 1898, JSSII 2/8.
11. BSHK to Swire, 18 February 1898, JSSII 2/8.
12. Sakamoto, 'Diversification: the Case of Mitsui Bussan', 64, 87.
13. Lynn and Rao, 'Failure of Intermediate Forms', 57–70. Morikawa, *Zaibatsu. The Rise and Fall of Family Enterprise Groups*, 123–81.
14. For the refineries in Manchuko, see NHM Kobe to Amsterdam, 16 June 1932/140, NA NHM 9230; for Shanghai, see JV NIVAS 1938–39: 48–53.
15. Sakamoto, 'Diversification: the Case of Mitsui Bussan', 88.
16. Ono and Lea, 'Colonial Towns of the Northern Marianas', 5–9; *Nan'yo: The Rise and Fall*, 123–32; Weitzell, 'Resource Development in the Pacific Mandated Islands', 201.
17. See De Graeff, *Van vriend tot vijand*, 266, as cited in Dick, 'Japan's Economic Expansion', 258; Post, 'Characteristics of Japanese Entrepreneurship', 310–1, Appendix 1: 'Japanese Agricultural Estates in the Netherlands Indies, 1924–25'.
18. Tio Poo Tjiang, 'De suikerhandel van Java', 59.
19. For overviews of the wider commercial context, see e.g., Dick, 'Japan's Economic Expansion', passim.
20. For detailed and documented discussion, see Knight, 'Exogenous Colonialism', 477–51.
21. See Post, 'Japan and the Integration of the Netherlands Indies', 134–65 and Post, 'Japanse bedrijvigheid in Indonesie'.
22. On the history of these firms, and their Japanese links discussed in the following paragraphs, see Post, 'Chinese Business Networks', 154–75; Liem Tjwan Ling, 'Sugar Jing: Oei Tiong Ham', 135–47; Dick, 'Oei Tiong Ham', 272–81; Claver, 'Commerce and Capital in Colonial Java', 292–350; Post, 'The Kwik Hoo Tong Trading Society', 279–96; Lin, 'Overseas Chinese Merchants', 985–1009.
23. Post, 'The Kwik Hoo Tong Trading Society', passim; Claver, 'Commerce and Capital in Colonial Java', 291ff.
24. Lynn and Rao, 'Failure of Intermediate Forms', 62–3. Schneider, 'The Taiwan Government-General', 173.
25. For the China sugar market in the late 1920s and early 1930s, see: Sugiyama, 'Marketing and Competition in China', 143–53. For subsequent developments see: Hill, *Smokeless Sugar: The Death of a Provincal Bureaucrat*, and Shiroyama, *China during the Great Depression*.

26. Factory White was a variety of the commodity produced in the same *factories* in which raw sugar was made (though in practice, because of necessary alterations to the manufacturing process, certain factories generally specialized in its production). It was inferior in colour, taste and texture to the output of sugar *refineries*, but had the critical advantage of being significantly cheaper to produce.
27. Data from: Rosenfeld, 'Een en ander omtrent de suikerindustrie', 1018–29; 'Formosa suikerproductie', 26–7 (which shows Formosa's output in 1931–33 to be composed overwhelming of Factory White); Ho, *Economic Development of Taiwan*, 357.
28. See Goto-Shibata, 'Japanese and British Perceptions', 127–44.
29. See Jaarverslag NHM Agentschap Shanghai 1927: 36 and 1928: 27 NA NHM 5171.
30. BSHK to Swires, 12 July 1929, Sugar Refinery Letters 1929, Swire Papers Box 20, JSSV 1/2.
31. Wright, *China's Struggle for Tariff Autonomy*, 657–91. I am grateful to Dr. Emily M. Hill for kindly directing my attention to this source.
32. JV NHM Shanghai 1933: 52–3, NA NHM 5171.
33. Wright, *China's Struggle for Tariff Autonomy*, 683.
34. JV NHM Soerabaija 1936: 25, NA NHM 5193.
35. JV NHM Shanghai 1939: 22, NA NHM 5172.
36. Geerligs, *Cane Sugar Production*, 67, 69–71; Ho, *Economic Development of Taiwan*, 31.
37. Ho, *Economic Development of Taiwan*, 73–4; Ka Chih-ming, *Japanese Colonialism in Taiwan*, 123–4.
38. For this and the following paragraph, see: Kagotani, 'Japan's Commercial Penetration', 179–206. Taselaar, *De Nederlandse koloniale lobby*, 410–2; Dick, 'Formation of the Nation State', 158–62; Dick, 'Japanese Economic Expansion', 251–5; Booth, 'Japanese Import Penetration', 133–64; Booth, 'Growth Collapse in Indonesia', 79–85.
39. Kagotani, 'Japan's Commercial Penetration', 206.
40. For an overview of the long-term economic nexus between the Indies and its metropolis, see Lindblad, 'The Economic Relationship between the Netherlands and Colonial Indonesia', 109–19.
41. Department van Economische Zaken, Centraal Kantoor voor de Statistiek, *De Landbouw export gewassen*, 57, Table 39: 'Suiker. Ondernemings aanplant en productie'. On developments in the sugar industry during the Japanese occupation (other than references in the text), see also: Postma et al., *De Java suikerindustrie gedurende*; '[NHM] 'Eigen suikerondernemingen. Toestand fabrieken tijdens en na den oorlog', NA NHM 8289.
42. The only account of this entire venture that I have been able to locate is that which appeared in the Indies Government publication, *Economisch*

Weekblad [*Economic Weekly*] for mid-1946 (vol. 12, no. 18, 13 Juli 1946, 143–4).

43. Notulen Handelsvereeniging 'Amsterdam', 2 April 1948/914. NA Archief Handelsvereeniging 'Amsterdam', 2.20.32/7.
44. See JV Tjomal 1941–49: 8, NA Tjomal 29.
45. E.g., Sugihara, 'An Introduction. In *Japan, China and the Asian International Economy*', 1.

9

Entertain People, Accumulate Capital: Indonesian Military Entrepreneurship in the 1950s and 1960s

Bambang Purwanto

Introduction

In colonial Indonesia, the army probably had no significant influence on day-to-day economic life, because at that time political and economic circumstances did not allow the military to get involved institutionally or personally in any profit-making business. In independent Indonesia, on the other hand, the military had a large impact on the economy of the country, because the institutional role of the military was more far-reaching than in colonial times.

There is no consensus on what should be understood by 'military business' in Indonesia. Nor is there agreement on how military business in Indonesia can best be carried out, nor why it has proved so difficult for most scholars to identify the coverage of economic activities by the military. Conceptually there is a distinction between 'military-run industry' and 'business run by military'. Thomas Scheetz, who wrote on military business in Argentina, shows that 'military-run industry' has both import substitution and strategic sector elements, while 'military business' is indicated as an enterprise that has no import substitution notion, is not a profit-oriented corporation, is out of the official budget, is not audited, and is used to increase the personal benefit of the group.[1] Richard Robison supports this idea by pointing out that, historically, the involvement of Indonesian military in business since the beginning of the 1950s was 'primarily to raise extra budgetary revenues for the operation of individual commands and units, as well as for the personal and political needs of individual officers and political factions'.[2]

Apart from its exclusiveness, military business in Indonesia during the first twenty years of independence was also characterized by its deep involvement in illegal economic activities. It applied its control over tools and facilities to exploit economic resources and opportunities to the sole benefit of the military. According to Robison, it was not until after 1965 that the Indonesian military began to formalize its business. The scattered and unco-ordinated economic activities were then unified and managed as corporate business as well as co-operatives, which made it easier for the military to mobilize capital and to earn higher profits under the favourable political climate of the New Order.[3]

Although little has been written on military economic activities in Indonesia in the 1950s and 1960s, and these activities are usually considered to have been less extensive than those in the New Order period, it is hard to deny the existence of military-owned business in the economic history of Indonesia of those periods.[4] Most studies tend to focus either on the illegal nature of military business, such as smuggling and forced purchase, or on the role of the military in big business such as nationalized foreign Dutch plantations and companies, inter-island trade and shipping, oil industry and banking. Not only 'business owned by generals' were run to replenish the funds of the military in those periods, but also other economic activities contributed to the daily economic life of military units and commands. This means that if scholars want to understand the process of economic development and changes that occurred in the military-owned business in Indonesia, they need to know much more than they do at present about the structure of military economic activities in various forms and at different periods.

This chapter is intended to present another form of military economic activities or entrepreneurship, which deals directly with society. I focus primarily on the role of unclassified or informal business activities in capital accumulation as well as the economic aspects of daily life of the armed forces and police units and commands. To what extent were military units and commands able to respond to new economic opportunities created by the increasing need of society towards *entertainment* in the early independence period? To what extent did economic activities affect institutional change? I aim to stimulate a fuller recognition of what is involved in military tasks and responsibilities and, in particular, to show the necessity of a much wider view of the role of the military in the Indonesian economy in the early independence period, by introducing into the economic history of Indonesia what is considered by most Indonesian historians as unconventional events. This chapter also attempts to take issue with the view that economic history is strictly the problem of economic variables, and in so doing challenges a more general view about the military economic activities in historiographical context. However, it is not the purpose to enter into the debate on the causes of rapid growth in military highly capitalized business and its capital mobility within the Indonesian state.

The Rise of Military Economic Interest

The history of the Tentara Nasional Indonesia (TNI) and Polisi Republik Indonesia (Polri), the Indonesian armed forces and the police, has not been treated comprehensively as a part of the decolonization process. Yet they played a remarkable role in the Indonesian nationalist movement: the Indonesia-Dutch war of 1945–49 suddenly transformed the military from a sociological and political non-entity into one of the most important elements in the formation of the image and identity of Indonesian nationhood, as well as in its economic power. The war made the military a new symbol of Indonesian nationalism and, at the same time, positioned them as the new dominant elite of the country.[5] There is overwhelming evidence that TNI and Polri were instruments for a deepening patronage system, and displayed a strong drive to develop a politically and economically strong position.

The organizational and institutional consolidation of the Indonesian military took place during the Indonesia-Dutch war, when the armed forces played a unique role in protecting the independence movement. The military became a corporation that functioned not only as the state institution in the field of protection and defence, but also conducted matters of practical politics and bureaucracy, and played an important economic role. In fact, the decolonization process placed the armed forces and the police in a dominant position. The result was an absence of separation of the roles and responsibilities of the military and the civil powers as part of the principle of the Indonesian military.[6] This dual role was no coincidence, in that it implied a strategy to minimize access to power for others. These factors played a heavy hand in determining the involvement of the military in the economic sphere.[7]

The end of the Indonesia-Dutch war found a military leadership in place and ready to acquire more economic functions. The involvement of the Indonesian military in the control and management of economic resources started when members of the Republic of Indonesia, the armed forces and the police—together with militia—took over strategic economic sources in many areas such as factories, telephone offices, estates, power generators and power installations, transport companies and mines previously managed by the Japanese army. The national oil company Permiri and various oil fields in Sumatra, for example, came into army control.[8] The tendency for the military groups to engage directly in financing the Indonesian revolution was apparent all over the country. The revolutionary period was a rich time for the military, both through direct control of the productive means, and through participation in legal and illegal trading. As a result, during the four years of resistance against the return of Dutch power, the military involvement in Indonesian economy vastly expanded.[9]

After 1950, the policy of takeovers of Dutch companies provided good opportunities for the military to get involved in business. That condition was reinforced by the fact that the government was not able to provide sufficient funds for military operational costs. The military not only functioned as a 'patron', but also became an actor directly involved in economic activities. Using the excuse of routine and military operations and soldier welfare costs as reason to seek more funds, the military business activities, which involved most of the local elite military rulers, developed to become a neat and profitable commercial enterprise.[10] In the early 1950s, the opportunities for soldiers to conduct business activities widened as a result of political conflicts and labour problems, which created uncontrollable security conditions in several areas such as West Java, Central Java, the Moluccas, most of Sulawesi, Aceh and North Sumatra.

The economic activities of the Indonesian military increased as the government announced a state of emergency during the first quarter of 1957, resulting from the appearance of armed movements in Sumatra and Sulawesi, and increasingly uncontrollable labour problems and land conflicts, aggravated by the fall of the elected 1955 cabinet led by Ali Sastroamidjojo in March 1957. The military business ventures gained even stronger legitimacy after the diplomatic failure of Indonesia on the matters of West Papua (New Guinea at the time) in the United Nations, the issuing of the 5 July 1959 Presidential Decree and the start of the confrontation with Malaysia. Since 1957, the conflicts and emergency policy of the state, and the worsening political sentiments towards the Dutch because of the problems with West Papua, had resulted in massive takeovers of Western corporations and corporate interests, especially the Dutch-owned firms, reaching its climax in 1959.[11]

In the nationalization process, the interests of the military and the communists conflicted. This strengthened the economic position of the military in the late 1950s, because the central army command officially ordered the local command to take control over the nationalized Dutch companies.[12] The resulting profit-oriented economic activities of the military not only built up a strong source of income for local military units and commands as well as individual officers, but also generated a large political influence that greatly affected the trajectory of the next period.

The military would not have been nearly as successful in building an economic platform had it not been for this support, which they received directly from the decolonization process. What was even more important, however, was the ability of most military units and commands to exercise control over space, facilities and manpower, while gaining moral support from the people. It was not merely a matter of taking over highly capitalized companies, factories, estates, oilfields or oil refineries, as in the historical narrative described above, but it was also the control over public spaces and the inheritance of tools and facilities of the colonial past and the war. Both the elimination of the colonial regime and the end of the war created huge empty spaces and properties, waiting to be taken by a new master. The Indonesian military played an important role in that process by taking possession of colonial wealth and power as well as the instruments of war. Without doubt this created the circumstances in which other factions were economically subordinated to the military power. As far as capital formation and capital mobility were concerned, the possession of the large firms provided a very strong basis for the Indonesian military to respond to new economic opportunities. To their credit, it can be stated that in the succeeding years of 1950s and early 1960s, the Indonesian military managed to exercise their entrepreneurial capabilities very successfully.

Exercising Military Entrepreneurship

Among their new economic activities, the Indonesian military also took charge of facilitating people dealing with entertainment and event organizing. The military exercised control over space, facilities and labour. They knew how to exploit these sources to raise extra budgetary means, without it being considered illegal, by combining profitable economic activities with philanthropy and the social obligations that stemmed from territorial responsibility. Their main aim in this regard was to gain social support, in connection with providing territorial security and preventing illegal action. Banners were written with slogans such as 'football for charity', 'circus for donation', 'boxing for alms' or 'bazaar for relief', which advertised the various informal economic activities organized by the Indonesian military corps.

The informal economic activities of the Indonesian military took various forms such as fundraising bazaars, fairs, exhibitions, sport events and competitions, music and theatre performances, acrobatics, circus and cinema. Since independence the military seriously attempted to exploit their power to expand informal economic activities to their own advantage. Of course, the financial gains from these activities were relatively low compared with activities in the highly capitalized sectors, such as the plantations and the oil industry.

It is not surprising when a man identifies himself as the third generation of a family that sells various goods in the annual fair organized by local military command in Surabaya of East Java.[13] Previously, both his grandfather and his mother had owned their own temporary *warung* at the annual fair, located at a huge open square owned by the local military command in the middle of the town. This forms an example of how local military units and commands regularly take part in economic activities by exploiting their power and resources. More objective evidence of this can be found in the organization of a fair such as by Persatuan Pegawai Polisi and Mara Wanita in the 1950s. The Jakarta organization of police officers organized a fancy night market 'Pasar Malam Gembira' in the place still known as Prinsen Park from 28 July to 3 August 1951, while a year later the same organization of the Aceh branch organized a charitable night market 'Pasar Malam Amal' for a week in Langsa beginning on 24 July 1952. In April 1952, the female group of the local military command in Medan organized another charitable bazaar 'Pasar Derma' to raise funds.

By organizing such events, the local military units and commands received not only social praise and moral support from society but also found an effective way to raise extra revenue to support the operational cost of the institutions. The police officers' organization in Jakarta, for example, used the event of a fair to change the police image from the enemy of the people—as inherited from the colonial period—to become known as the protector of the people in independent Indonesia. In fact, they also earned a large profit from the sale of admission tickets and the lease of space.[14] In Langsa, the event was able to distribute the profit equally to co-organizers, a football club and Islamic schools of Muhammadiyah and Al-Jamiatul Wasliyah.[15] Although the event was considered to have been a combination of a fair and fundraising bazaar, in fact this military female group in Medan received 90 per cent of the total net income, while only 5 per cent was designated for the invalid and another 5 per cent for other social activities.[16]

A nearly similar occasion took place in South Sulawesi, where a combination of what was called 'fancy fair', exhibition and fundraising bazaar was organized by the local armed forces division to commemorate its anniversary. It provided tremendous financial contribution to the extra budgetary revenue of the division in the early 1960s. For some military officers in this area, where illegal business was a major means by which local military units raised extra budgetary revenue to finance their military operational and social obligations, the fair was then considered as an alternative profitable economic activity rather than involvement in smuggling and providing protection, and illegal levies on businessmen. It was reported that the organizer raised 50,000 rupiahs, and then distributed 23,500 rupiahs to the local people for the construction of conference and meeting places. The rest went into an extra prosperity fund for the battalion.[17]

In the 1950s and 1960s, most military units and commands also made use of sports events to raise revenue. Football was the most popular among these. The local police together with the military command in Medan of North Sumatra, for example, organized a football match between the two most popular football clubs to raise funds in order to construct a new building for social gatherings and meetings of the local police. The organizer was able to raise about 5,000 rupiahs from the match for the construction of the new building.[18] Also, with increased interest towards high-quality football among Indonesians, the army organized national football competitions and friendly international football matches in several big cities such as Jakarta, Bandung, Palembang and Medan. The army even owned a highly qualified football team in the late 1950s. The team sometimes also represented the Indonesia national football team and played against football teams from abroad. National players and trainers such as Saelan, Sailan, Wowo, Jusron, Kiat Sek and Endang Witarsa were also usually associated by the army as members of their football team.

The army event organizer also made a good profit in 1958 and 1959 when international matches against the Red Star Belgrade of Yugoslavia and the Bulgarian national football team were watched by many people who had purchased very expensive tickets, particularly when compared with the Indonesian average income in those years. People paid 75 rupiahs for a ticket for the first-class tribune, 55 and 30 rupiahs for a ticket of second- and third-class seat, while spectators had to pay 15 rupiahs for a ticket with no seat provided.[19] As a comparison, at the same time a skilled worker in the urban area received no more than 20 rupiahs per day, while the daily payment for an unskilled labour in urban factories was about 6 rupiahs, and even less in rural plantations.[20]

Next to football, boxing matches were the second sport that contributed substantially to the financial needs of the military in the 1950s and 1960s. Again, the typical approach of the military organizers to attract more spectators was to make use of philanthropic symbolism. Similar to football, organizers asked people to pay an expensive price for admission tickets to the boxing matches. In the early 1960s, for example, the price of a ticket to watch a boxing match in Surabaya, where many professional boxing matches regularly took place, ranged from 200 and 125 rupiahs for the first- and second-class ticket, to 10 rupiahs for the festival side. The price was far more expensive than the admission tickets to the public entertainment park in the same city, which ranged from only 50 cents to a maximum of 1 rupiah.[21]

The restricted access to wealth caused by economic and political instability in the chaotic period of the late 1950s and early 1960s inspired a productive creativity among the military personnel. As the military controlled the locations, facilities grew, and personal need for entertainment also increased in society, with an increasing number of entertainment events organized by the military. Music, theatre, acrobatics and circus were forms of entertainment that were regularly organized and attracted many spectators. Since the military owned transport facilities such as trucks, ships and aeroplanes, it was relatively easy for them to mobilize a huge number of people, and to transport animals and equipment across land and sea. For other entrepreneurs this was a very expensive and difficult enterprise at that time, so the country was dependent on the military to carry out such activities. As a result, for example, the Indonesian Air

Force was able to donate money collected strictly from flying exhibitions and demonstrations—amounting to 65,000 rupiahs—to the victims of natural disaster in Aceh in the early 1950s.[22]

Besides local circuses and acrobatic groups, the military event organizers also monopolized the economically profitable performances of groups from abroad. In the late 1950s and early 1960s, such groups came from China and Eastern Europe, due to the fact that Indonesia had close international relations with countries of the Eastern bloc. Despite important differences between conditions existing in Java and other islands at that time, these famous and well-known international circus and acrobatic groups from abroad travelled regularly to different places outside Java where infrastructure, facilities and security were a problem. In short, the military managed to control resources that belonged predominantly to the state in order to monopolize the event-organizing business.

Nonetheless, the military did not organize the performances only for themselves but also on behalf of others such as local government, planters and mining companies. Inevitably, this led to a gradual emerging of military dominance that controlled the entertainment activities all over the country. Therefore, the emergence of acrobatic groups, circus and many traditional theatres such as Ketoprak, Ludruk, Makyong, Bangsawan or comedy cannot be separated from the role of the military in post-colonial Indonesia. Although the groups did not officially belong to any military command, the management of the groups was strongly influenced by the interest of military economic activities. A similar development took place in the business of cinema. In the 1950s and 1960s, every military unit and command institutionally or personally controlled at least one movie theatre in the place where they were stationed. The military might not have owned the cinemas, but it was involved in the business and received a regular tribute.

Conclusion

To conclude, I first want to emphasize that military business activities were certainly not solely carried out by generals. Rather, it was also a business of lower commanders and soldiers. Their activities allowed them to accumulate huge amounts of capital, which supported the armed forces and the police, while entertaining the people. The profit was also used to build an image of generosity in society. This type of business affected people beyond the regular capacity of the military and the police in the field of security, and was closely tied to society in economic, social and also political respects. These economic activities were also responsible for the creation of new jobs, the development of an informal economy and a division of labour in society, to the benefit of local people as well as the soldiers and their families in Indonesia. Some activities became legal, but others became illegal and blended with the businesses of the *preman*, a mafia-like organization.

One consequence of the symbiosis between military profit-oriented business and the philanthropic nature of their activities has been the creation of an atmosphere of a more private economic system. The economic activities were bound closely to the personal interests of each military unit and command, but also to individual officers. There is no clear division between the business of the institution in order to gain extra budgetary revenue and the interests of individual military commanders to support their soldiers, to assist surrounding communities and to fulfil their individual needs. These businesses exploited military power, facilities and personnel through formal bureaucracy, but there was hardly ever a formal responsibility, neither officially nor individually. In the case that there was a formal relationship between the military and private business groups, it was developed as a private relationship between these two. These qualities are manifest in the formation of sublimated institutions in the form of cooperative in every military-police unit and level such as Induk Koperasi, Primer Koperasi and Yayasan—economic institutions with a highly political authorization and monopoly.[23]

Entertainment and event-organizing economic activities took a path different from other military economic activities such as the acquisition of the Branjangan rice mills in Demak, the textile factory of Madjatex in Bandung, a shoe factory in Surabaya, and the creation of centralized and incorporated gigantic military companies in 1960s.[24] After the political turmoil of 1965, these economic activities also inherited what has been referred to by Dwi Marianto as 'helmet culture' and '*premanisme*' as referred to by Tim Lindsey—a corrupt regime and criminal state of the New Order military-dominated government.[25] The standard practice was to hide the executive power by replicating a parallel structure and system in ordinary private sectors, despite the fact that it was not uncommon for the military entrepreneurship to practise power abuse. The military became increasingly powerful in relation to capital formation as well as political authority.

Finally, it is not surprising that most laypersons as well as scholars do not recognize and classify these entertainment and event-organizing economic activities as examples of highly profitable military entrepreneurship. Some very popular existing entertainment groups in Indonesia are now in fact military-supported and profit-oriented business activities, which had been started in the 1950s and 1960s. Only since the Reformasi set in after Suharto's fall in 1998, have voices been heard to abolish military business and ask the armed forces and the police to focus on their main task to defend and secure the country. But, in fact, the military-sponsored entertainment and event-organizing business remains uncovered. The hidden businesses are safe: military entrepreneurship is still going on without being threatened by the changing regime. Until now, this was true up to a point. The military continues to be involved in business as usual as there has been little attempt to end the military involvement in profit-making economic activity. There are no structural changes in the pattern of access to and control over critical sources needed to meet personal as well as institutional overall military entrepreneurship ambitions after the 1960s. Thus, 'soldiers never die' in the history of Indonesian entrepreneurship.

Primary Sources

Angkatan Bersendjata, 5 July 1965.

Berita Yudha, 23 January 1963; 29 January 1969; 6 March 1969; 23 March 1963.

Haluan, 24 March 1953.

Harian Operasi, 7 October 1968.

Pedoman Sport, 3 January 1959.

Sapta Marga, 30 January 1969; 6 March 1969.

Utusan Nasional, 2 August 1951; 17 June 1952; 19 April 1952; 24 April 1952.

Waspada, 17 June 1952; 19 April 1952; 24 April 1952.

Notes

1. Scheetz, 'Military Business in Argentina'.
2. Robison, *Indonesia: The Rise of Capital*.
3. Ibid.; Samego et al., *Bila ABRI Berbisnis*.
4. See also Purwanto, 'Economic Decolonization and the Rise of Indonesian Military Business'.
5. Said, *Genesis of Power*; Purwanto, *Gagalnya Historiografi Indonesiasentris?!*
6. Purwanto, *Gagalnya Historiografi Indonesiasentris?!*
7. Purwanto, 'Economic Decolonization and the Rise of Indonesian Military Business'.

8. Lindblad, *Bridges to New Business.*
9. Crouch, 'Generals and Business in Indonesia'.
10. Lindblad, *Bridges to New Business.*
11. Purwanto, 'Economic Decolonization and the Rise of Indonesian Military Business'.
12. Dick et al., *The Emergence of a National Economy.*
13. Interview Surabaya: August 2008.
14. *Utusan Nasional*, 2 August 1951.
15. *Waspada*, 17 June 1952.
16. *Waspada*, 19 April 1952.
17. Sunjoto, *Pradjurit Jon HN 008-LAPRIS Kodam XIV.*
18. *Waspada*, 24 April 1952.
19. *Pedoman Sport*, 3 January 1959; 23 May 1959.
20. Hawkins, 'Labour in Developing Countries: Indonesia': an ILO report on labour conditions in Jakarta in the mid-1950s mentioned that skilled labour received 10 to 20 rupiahs per day, while the daily wage of a skilled mechanic in Bandung was about 20 rupiahs. In the most populated urban centre of Jakarta, the daily payment of bakers and plumbers was 10 rupiahs; bricklayers and carpenters were paid 12.50 rupiahs per day. In the mid-1950s, the structural steel, electrical workers, garage mechanics and truck drivers received slightly higher payments, of about 15 to 18 rupiahs, or a maximum of 20 rupiahs per day, while unskilled labour was paid 5 to 6 rupiahs per day. But in some outskirt urban centres, there was a narrow differential between skilled and unskilled labour in daily payment. The skilled labour received on average 5.36 to 7.90 rupiahs, while the unskilled workers were paid an average of 4.15 to 5.22 rupiahs.
21. *Manifesto*, 17 May 1961; 20 May 1961.
22. *Haluan*, 24 March 1953.
23. *Angkatan Bersendjata*, 5 July 1965; Harian Operasi: 7 October 1968. See also Robison, *Indonesia: The Rise of Capital.*
24. *Berita Yudha*, 23 January 1963, 29 January 1969, 6 March 1969; Robison, *Indonesia: The Rise of Capital.*
25. Vickers, 'The New Order: Keeping Up Appearance'; Lindsey, 'The Criminal State. Premanism and the New Indonesia'.

10

From Tribes to Transaction Costs: How Two Anthropologists of Southeast Asia Anticipated the New Institutional Economics

David Henley

> If capital is to flow freely, if long-range planning is to be possible, and if merchants are to know what they have bought without constantly supervising others and inspecting goods, there must be mutual assurance that contracts will be fulfilled. For the many Javanese who deal with others who are neither kin nor neighbours, there is no effective social structure which can enforce the fulfillment of contracts.
>
> Alice G. Dewey (1962)[1]

> [T]he inability of societies to develop effective, low-cost enforcement of contracts is the most important source of both historical stagnation and contemporary underdevelopment in the Third World.
>
> Douglass C. North (1990)[2]

Towards the end of the twentieth century, the fields of economic history and development economics were revolutionized by the rise of the New Institutional Economics (or New Economic Institutionalism, NEI). This is a school of thought according to which the causes of sustained growth in some economies, and of persistent stagnation in others, are to be found in the realm of politics and law rather than science, culture or natural resource endowments. In the developed countries, market-supporting legal and political institutions have made possible long periods of sustained growth by decisively reducing the risks and costs of economic exchange. Wherever such institutions had not emerged, 'transaction costs'—the costs of negotiating prices and enforcing contracts—have remained too high to permit efficient market exchange, with persistent underdevelopment as a result. Economically inefficient institutions are often stable and persistent because those people who have the power to change them cannot do so without foregoing immediate benefits, or ceding wealth and power to rivals. It is this kind of historical *cul-de-sac* that Douglass North, the most influential exponent of the new approach, refers to as 'path dependence' or 'lock-in'.[3]

The systematic body of theory and knowledge assembled in the 1970s, 80s and 90s by scholars working in the NEI paradigm represented an historic achievement, and four of them—Douglass North, Ronald Coase, Elinor Ostrom and Oliver Williamson—were to receive a Nobel Prize. Yet none of the ideas involved was completely new. That Coase himself had pioneered the theory of transaction costs as early as 1937 (albeit *avant la lettre*—the term itself was not coined until the 1970s), in an article entitled 'The nature of the firm' in which he asked why some transactions were internalized by firms rather than left to markets, is well known.[4] Less well known is that the economic importance of transaction costs was also understood at an early date by anthropologists, not on the basis of speculation regarding the function of modern capitalist institutions, but on the basis of observations regarding the behaviour of individuals in pre-modern economic systems.

In the Southeast Asian context, anthropologists have traditionally paid little attention to economics and politics, other than in terms of the influence of *culture* on economic and political behaviour. Many present-day economic historians of Southeast Asia, by contrast, prefer to see economic and political decisions as rational responses to *institutional* conditions, frequently taking issue with the cultural interpretations of Clifford Geertz and other well-known anthropologists.[5] There are, however, exceptions to the rule that anthropologists of Southeast Asia have been preoccupied with cultural diversity. Two such exceptions are Roy

Franklin Barton (1883–1947), who carried out wide-ranging ethnographic research among recently subjugated and pacified tribal societies in upland Luzon (the Philippines) between 1916 and 1941, and Alice Dewey (b.1928), who studied peasant marketing in Java in the 1950s.

Barton and Dewey resemble pioneers of economic and political anthropology such as Bronislaw Malinowski and E.E. Evans-Pritchard in their aspiration to relate their observations to universal principles rather than cultural specificities.[6] In different ways, Barton and Dewey also anticipated the New Institutional Economics to such a degree that their work can still readily be used to illustrate, and even extend, the insights of that school. By the same token, they can be viewed as precursors of today's economic historians of Southeast Asia. For reasons that will become apparent in the course of this chapter, the two will be discussed below in reverse chronological order, beginning with Dewey.

Alice Dewey and the Origins of Ethnic Commercial Specialization

A granddaughter of the philosopher John Dewey, Alice Greeley Dewey grew up in an American intellectual milieu, studied cultural anthropology and, from 1952 to 1954, took part in the now famous MIT-sponsored, Ford Foundation-funded social science research project in 'Modjokuto' (Pare, East Java) which also involved Clifford and Hildred Geertz, Robert Jay and Edward Ryan. The results of her Pare research were published in 1962 under the title *Peasant Marketing in Java.* An article summarizing her most important theoretical conclusions, 'Trade and social control in Java', appeared in the same year in the *Journal of the Royal Anthropological Institute.* Dewey went on to teach from 1963 to 2005 at the University of Hawaii, where she supervised many PhD students (including Barack Obama's mother, Ann Dunham) but apparently did not further develop the themes and ideas contained in *Peasant Marketing.*

Dewey's brief in Pare was to study 'the native markets' and the primary subjects of her ethnography were Javanese traders operating in the peasant market, or *pasar*, an old and important institution in Java but one previously ignored by both economists and anthropologists.[7] Contrary to common stereotypes, Dewey found Javanese market traders to be industrious, rational and materialistic in their pursuit of profit. That they nevertheless seldom managed to accumulate much capital, or expand the scale of their business operations beyond a petty level, was due mainly to an inability to obtain or extend credit.

> Most loans are made with no security, for the people who need them have few possessions. Thus the lender can compensate for bad debts only by raising his interest rates. There are legal mechanisms for recovering bad debts if the debtor does have property, but many people are unaware of these or simply unused to resorting to court action to settle disputes. In any case, taking legal action would probably prove excessively expensive for most people.[8]

The costs and risks of economic co-operation being high, relations among Javanese traders in the *pasar* were characterized by distrust and individualism. Dewey contrasted this with the relatively co-operative patterns of economic exchange found in their own home villages, where common membership in a permanent community provided exchange partners with powerful informal incentives to behave in a trustworthy way:

> The only social unit of traditional importance to a Javanese farmer is his own village [...]. He is [...] tied to the other members by kin and neighbourhood relationships which define a complex of reciprocal rights and duties between them all. The social, economic, and political structure of the village community supports these rights and obligations, as do the tangible and intangible rewards and penalties which follow from keeping or breaking the rules of conduct. [...] When a man does a day's labour on the fields of a neighbour he need not demand immediate payment or a written receipt. He is reasonably sure that in due course his debtor will do a day's work on his fields or make some other return which is traditionally acceptable. Occasionally the system breaks down, but the risk is low [...]. Within such rural communities deferred payment is part of the pattern of reciprocal duties and obligations. In fact no account is ever closed. It is assumed that an enduring relationship is set up among a stable group of people whose whole life will be spent in a cycle of exchanges.[9]

Dewey's sketch of the village as an economic system in which 'no account is ever closed' anticipates in exact terms the model of efficient but permanently localized exchange developed by later institutional economists, on the basis of game theory, to describe the economics of small, traditional, face-to-face communities:

> The most likely and indeed empirically observable state in which contracts are self-enforcing is that in which the parties to exchange have a great deal of knowledge about each other and are involved in repeat dealings, as [...] with tribal and primitive societies and with small communities. Under these conditions, it simply pays to live up to

> agreements. In such a world, the measured costs of transacting are very low because of a dense social network of interaction.[10]

Again anticipating North, Dewey saw that the extension of exchange beyond the bounds of the local farming community into the realm of long-distance commerce demanded a new set of transaction-regulating institutions which villagers themselves were ill-equipped to provide:

> In order to trade efficiently a rural Javanese must first shake off his obligations to his fellow villagers. Once he has done this his problems are just beginning. When he goes out into the extra-village trading sphere he finds he has not only left behind his obligations to others, but also their obligations to him. Once he starts to deal with people who are not from his village he has gone beyond the reach of his effective social unit and its supporting sanctions. It is the largely informal sanctions which reduce the risk element in credit and contractual relations. These sanctions do not reach out to control the actions of people who live in villages other than his own.[11]

The ultimate and most satisfactory solution to this problem, according to most of the NEI literature and implicitly also according to Dewey, is for the state to replace informal sanctions with a formal, impersonal and impartial system of legal contract enforcement—something which Indonesia had only very imperfectly succeeded in doing in Pare in the 1950s. However, Dewey also observed that there was a very effective alternative or intermediate solution, corresponding to the self-regulating merchant diasporas and trading guilds subsequently identified by North and colleagues as central to the early development of long-distance trade in Europe.[12] This was the management of large-scale commerce by a trade-specialized, diasporic minority group with its own internal social control mechanisms, adapted to minimize the costs of long-distance transactions.

In Java, and elsewhere in Southeast Asia, this economic niche was filled mainly by people of Chinese ethnic origin. But Dewey recognized that the overseas Chinese were only one example of a global category of commercially specialized ethnic minorities, particularly common in underdeveloped economies, which also included Jews in Europe, Indians and Lebanese in Africa, and Arabs in Indonesia itself. Indeed it was the universality of this phenomenon, more than the specificity of its manifestations in Indonesia, which informed Dewey's research, and beyond ethnography her higher goal was to explain the association between ethnicity and commerce in a way which might have universal applicability.[13]

The explanation she arrived at was that because Chinese immigrants in Java were long excluded by legal and other barriers from occupations other than trade, their whole system of social relations became intertwined with their commercial profession to the extent that bad behaviour in business came to mean both social isolation and economic destitution:

> I have indicated that the legal restriction forced most Chinese into commerce. This gave them a common occupational background. The concentration in trade led to their dispersal as they sought opportunities in the various trade centres. They were a small expatriate community against whom considerable dislike and discrimination was directed. [...] In all aspects of life, social, ritual, political, and economic, they had to look primarily to each other for help and protection. If a Chinese did not fulfill his obligations with acceptable regularity in one or more spheres of life he could be cut off from all kinds of support by the Chinese community. It would become difficult for him to find suitable spouses for his children. He would not be given credit. No one would come to his funeral [...]. A man who behaved badly in business could be cut off from all sorts of community activities. If he was cut out of commercial dealings with other Chinese this in effect meant he had been forced out of intermediate trade since it was dominated by Chinese. If he was forced out of the Chinese community this meant almost complete social isolation [...].[14]

The result of all this business-oriented social control in the Chinese community was a consistently high standard of adherence to business ethics. This lowered transaction costs enough to give its members a decisive advantage over Javanese competitors at the higher levels of the rural trading system, where capital and credit were essential for success:

> A merchant who has promised delivery of a certain amount and quality of goods on a particular date will make every effort to fulfill his commitment. Since the buyer is freed from uncertainty and the need for constant supervision of those he deals with, he can go ahead with the resale of the goods knowing they will be available when needed. A man who asks for credit normally gets it, and a man who gives it knows he will be repaid. The Chinese ethical code lowers costs, eliminates duplication of effort, frees the flow of capital, and reduces risks, each trader guaranteeing the others as do the members of a stock exchange.[15]

The hierarchical division of labour whereby co-operative Chinese traders dominated the capital-intensive wholesale business, and individualistic Javanese traders the labour-intensive, atomistic commerce of the *pasar*, was in Dewey's view a rather stable equilibrium. The conditions of each sector suited its incumbents' skills and resources, while discouraging competition from the other group:

> In small scale marketing [...], labour-intensive methods are efficient and Javanese can adjust effectively to the marketing problems. In fact they have been so successful that they dominate market trade. Those advantages enjoyed by the Chinese—larger amounts of capital, and the possibility of using informal sanctions, do not give enough competitive advantage to overcome the lack of personnel with which to carry on labour-intensive operations. Hiring Javanese is unsatisfactory as the absence of controlling sanctions over them makes the risks high and supervision is time—and labour—consuming. At the time there is not enough need in small trading for capital and long term planning to stimulate the development of groups within the Javanese trading class which would be capable of imposing sanctions.[16]

Nevertheless, the situation was not immutable; if this was an example of what would later be called path dependence, then there was evidence that the Javanese path of subordination and poverty—which is what restriction to the lower levels of the trading system implied—could be redirected, both by accident and by design. Indeed, part of the rationale for Dewey's research in Java was that 'Javanese traders have developed more elaborate trading techniques, and handle a larger variety of goods in larger quantities, than do [non-Chinese] traders in Malaya, for example'.[17]

In two cases Dewey was able to document the emergence of new informal exchange-supporting institutions, where none had previously existed, among restricted groups of Javanese traders engaged in penetrating commercial sectors normally dominated by the ethnic Chinese. In the first case, groups of up to eight very experienced Javanese traders pooled their capital—a very rare and risky undertaking outside the Chinese community—to take advantage of an expanding opportunity in the wholesale marketing of onions, a valuable cash crop. Admission to these groups was based on rigorous screening for skill and honesty. Once admitted, traders found membership profitable enough to discourage any behaviour that might lead to expulsion and loss of reputation, so that a system of social control developed, which simulated that found among Chinese traders:

> Once the groups are established it is found that the risk of extending credit and making contractual arrangements with fellow traders is low in relation to profits. In order to continue in association with one's

> fellow traders [...] the separate traders [...] do their best to fulfill their contractual obligations [...]. The existence of this class of traders to whom special facilities were extended gave a basis for economic sanctions among the members of the group. To break faith with the group would probably mean exclusion from future groups [...]. This sanction grew most directly out of the commercial situation and not out of the whole social structure as did the sanctions used between Chinese traders.[18]

In the second such case described by Dewey, a successful class of relatively large-scale Javanese traders emerged after Chinese merchants and retailers were forced to leave rural areas during the Japanese occupation (1942–45) and national revolution (1945–49). Many small local traders and richer farmers soon rushed to take the place of those expelled. Although most were unsuccessful, some eventually managed to develop reputations for reliability, which enabled them to consolidate their businesses by obtaining crucial credit both from farmers and from urban Chinese traders.[19] If the case of the Javanese onion-trading partnerships shows that contract-enforcing institutions may evolve spontaneously in response to economic opportunity, the case of the successful usurpers is a reminder that economic history is nevertheless also a matter of brute politics. It is to the relationship between power, wealth and trade that the next part of the discussion turns.

Roy Franklin Barton and the Commercial Origins of the State

If Dewey was a child of the American intellectual establishment, Roy Franklin Barton was a maverick American autodidact and adventurer. Born in 1883, he trained as a schoolteacher and from 1906 to 1916 worked as a 'supervising teacher' in the colonial Philippines, first in the lowlands and later in the mountains of Luzon among the Ifugao and Kalinga, who had remained independent from the Spanish and were now in the process of pacification by the Americans. Returning to the US, Barton retrained as a dentist, practising dentistry there and in Manila while at the same time writing classic studies on *Ifugao law* (1919) and *Ifugao Economics* (1922). In 1930, for a mixture of political and personal reasons, he moved to the Soviet Union where he lived through the period of Stalin's purges, first continuing to work as a dentist before becoming attached to the Institute of Ethnology of the Russian Academy of Sciences in Leningrad, where he obtained the equivalent of a doctoral degree in 1935. In 1937, using both US and Soviet funding, he conducted further fieldwork in the Philippines. In 1940 he fled the USSR and returned to the Philippines for the last time, just in time to be captured by the invading Japanese. In internment he suffered starvation, beriberi and an infected wound. Never fully recovered, he died in Chicago in 1947. In an obituary, Alfred Kroeber described him as having 'produced some of the most gifted ethnography ever written in English'.[20]

Barton had a humane, but unsentimental, interest in the possibility of order and justice under conditions of political anarchy. His ethnography, making much use of autobiographical reminiscences by elderly informants, takes us back into the violent world of the pre-colonial Philippines—a world in which a homicide record was an essential criterion of social status for men, and crimes (and indeed misunderstandings) sparked off bloody feuds and wars. At the same time, life in this pre-capitalist universe had a disconcertingly economic quality whereby everything, up to and including the life of a murdered relative, had its price. The anger of the bereaved could often be appeased, and vengeance averted, by paying to them an appropriate amount of blood money or 'weregilds' —an Anglo-Saxon term which Barton uses to remind his Western readers that their own ancestors once lived in something like the same way.

Barton's last and most mature work, published posthumously in 1949, is entitled *The Kalingas: Their Institutions and Custom Law*. Although the Kalinga were one of the more egalitarian peoples of Luzon (as well as one of the most violent), two different types of chiefly office existed among them: that of *pangat*, or 'man of rank', and that of *mangdon si budong*, or 'pact-holder'. *Pangat* were also called 'peacemakers' or 'right-determiners', and their main task consisted in the mediation and adjudication of disputes—a highly valued function given that disputes were both common and potentially lethal. Accordingly, one important qualification for the rank of *pangat* was a sense of fairness and an ability to see beyond the interests of one's own kin group—an unusual trait in a society where kinship was the dominant organizing principle. More important still, however, was the need for a *pangat* to be feared, to have 'a reputation as a dangerous man'.[21] This meant that among the Kalinga, the road to stoppage of homicide had to begin with homicide itself:

> The route to pangathood lay as follows: (1) the youth would kill someone in order to get his tattoo and a right to voice his opinions among men; (2) then, seeking dominance, he would kill more people and thus

> inspire fear among the folk; (3) he would intervene to settle disputes between kinship groups [...] and he would be successful because feared by the people; (4) if in these settlements he were fair and acted 'for the good of all the people', [...] then a few of the people would begin to call him pangat.[22]

Wealth was also an asset in this process, since it enabled the killer to pay weregilds to the relatives of his victims, many of whom were typically members of his own community, and in that way to avoid retribution and carry on killing.

Alongside the *pangat*, the second class of political leader among the Kalinga, and the one of greater interest in the context of Barton's relevance to modern institutional economics, was the *mangdon si budong*, or 'pact-holder'. Pact-holders were so called because their task was to enforce the terms of formal peace pacts which they had concluded with foreign regions on behalf of their own community. Essentially, a pact-holder was obliged to punish any inhabitant of his own region, including his own kin, who harmed any inhabitant of the foreign region to which his pact related. Conversely his counterpart in that other region, with whom he was linked by a kind of fictive brotherhood, was sworn to avenge any inhabitant of the first region killed or wounded by an inhabitant of his own. Once again this included his own relatives, to whom, at the ceremony of his inauguration as pact-holder, he addressed the following warning:

> Now that I am a pact-holder, it is an honor to you as well. But though you, my relatives, and you, the relatives of my wife, share the honor with me, you also share the responsibility of restraining anyone from unfriendly acts. [...] Being a pact-holder is a serious business, and I intend to enforce the pact fearlessly and preserve my honor, which is also your honor. You must consider it your duty to me and to our kinship groups to prevent the necessity of my having to resort to extreme measures, for be assured that I shall resort to them even against my own blood if necessary.[23]

Like the *pangat*, then, the pact-holders too were killers. But unlike the *pangat* they killed, and indeed were obliged to kill, only in specific contexts determined by the peace pacts of which they were the guarantors. If they fulfilled their duties properly, inhabitants of the one region travelling in the other would be entirely safe—safer, indeed, than they would have been in their own region.[24] And even if an individual traveller was harmed after all, this still would not result in war between the regions because punishment would be metered out by the local pact-holder and his immediate kin group—which, of course, had to be a strong and feared one—rather than by avenging headhunters from the offended foreign region.

Barton understood the institution of the peace pact as a stage in the evolution of the state. By this, in turn, he understood not just a concentration of political power, but a qualitative shift from the blood tie to the territorial tie as the basis for political community and action. Unusually in a Philippine tribal context, punitive slayings by the Kalinga pact-holder were not acts of private vengeance by one kinship group against another, but 'legal executions' representing 'the police power of a budding state'.[25] The scope of this power was territorially defined. The first article of each standard eight-part Kalinga peace-pact agreement consisted of a precise determination of the geographical region for which each pact-holder was responsible:

> 1. Statement of the boundaries of each region. (These have to be defined whether the region be adjacent to or distant from each other, because they define the people for whom each pact-holder will be responsible.)
> 2. Each pact holder will be responsible for the acts of citizens of his region, and for all acts within his region, that affect citizens of the other region.
> 3. Neither region will pollute the soil of the other with foreign blood (each region will respect the neutrality of the other). [...]
> 4. Each pact-holder guarantees visitors from the other region shelter and food.
> 5. In the event of illness or of accident to citizens of one region within the bounds of the other, the pact-holder where this occurs will return the persons to their home region [...].[26]

With the political territoriality instituted by the peace pact came a concept of regional 'citizenship' and a perception, at least in the context of interregional relations, 'that the citizens of a place are "owned" by the pact-holders'.[27] Barton stops short of postulating a further development in which it is the pact-holders, and not the *pangat* or strongmen, who evolve into kings ruling over regional kingdoms. One reason for his caution on this point was probably that the institution of pact-holdership, as he acknowledges, is not attested to in the ethnography of other tribal peoples.[28] But Barton does note that among the Kalinga, the two types of leadership strongly overlap: the office of pact-holder 'is a road to the rank of pangat if one be not already a pangat, and it raises the pangat's prestige if he has already attained that rank'.[29] This raises the possibility that in other settings the two may not have been differentiated, and that the role of strongmen in maintaining interregional alliances may have been important to their evolution into ruling princes despite its relative invisibility in the historical and ethnographic sources.

Barton's account of the civilizing effect of the peace pact and its enforcers—who for all their ruthlessness served to enable strangers, in an otherwise violent and xenophobic society, to come together on the basis of 'detailed and humane treaties'[30]—offers a radical alternative to the predatory models of state formation often advanced by scholars of Southeast Asian history.[31] More important for the purpose of the present chapter, however, is Barton's account of the historical origins of the peace pact institution, which lay in interregional commerce.

Peace pacts were all about trade. Pairs of brother pact-holders were often individuals who, despite the dangers of travel in hostile regions, had already formed a trading partner relationship (called *abuyog*) with each other prior to the conclusion of the pact:

> Pikut [of Lubwagan], who holds the pact with Kabugao in the Subprovince of Apayao, six days' hike distant, was formerly a very rich and enterprising man. [...] In 1917 or thereabouts, having heard that precious beads were quite cheap in Apayao, he assembled a few kinsmen and, carrying 400 pesos, started for Kabugao, with which, at that time, Lubwagan had no pact. At Salegseg, which had a pact with Kabugao, he hired two men to accompany him in order that they might confer a degree of safety on the party. [...] Arrived at Kabugao, he stopped at the house of Sigon, a wealthy man. Sigon purchased beads for him advantageously; the two agreed to become trading partners. After that, five trips were made by one or another to the town of the other [...]. As happens frequently, the trading partners initiated a pact, with themselves as the pact-holders.[32]

If individual pacts originated in individual trading relationships, Barton believed that the peace pact as an institution had originated in a general category of commercial alliance, also found (unlike the peace pact itself) among the neighbouring Ifugao, whereby trading partners entered into a limited obligation to avenge harm done to each other as individuals:

> Among the Ifugao two men of distant regions sometimes enter into a highly formalized and ritualized pact which makes them *biyao*, trading

> partners, with definite obligations to each other. Each will trade with the region of the other through the other only. Each will avenge the killing of the other or his people accompanying him or sent by him if that killing occurs within certain limits agreed on.[33]

The Kalinga *budong* (peace pact) effectively extended the individual mutual protection of the *biyao* partners to include all traders originating from their respective regions. Among other things this meant first painstakingly negotiating the settlement, by means of weregilds, of all (or at least as many as possible) of the unavenged individual accounts outstanding between any inhabitants of the two regions.

With this accomplished, the way was open to intensive trade. The main economic incentive for an individual to take on the duties and risks of pact-holdership was that the establishment of permanent peace between their two regions was very good for trade, and that the pact-holders were in an advantageous—although seldom monopolistic—position to conduct that trade. In addition, whenever valuable heirloom goods changed hands across regional boundaries, the pact-holders received what was effectively a commission on the transaction.[34] Besides the five articles already listed, which deal in general terms with boundaries, travel and security, Kalinga peace pacts typically also included three further articles dealing specifically with trade:

6. Each pact-holder will assist traders from the other region. If requested, the pact-holder will appoint reliable agents to execute commissions for the visiting trader or will undertake them himself.
7. Money stolen from or lost by a citizen of the one region within the other region will be restored him by a collection from the citizens of the place where this occurred.
8. Pact-holders will facilitate the collection of debts owed citizens of the other region by citizens of his own and seizures (*taliwan*) to cover such debts.[35]

The Kalinga pact-holders, then, were not only guardians of the peace and order on which trade depended; they also provided business introductions and travel insurance for traders, and even served as contract-enforcers with respect to credit transactions entered into by traders with third parties. Their function, in other words, was to reduce transaction costs in the interests of unimpeded commercial exchange, and their concrete personal interest in doing so lay in the fact that they profited directly from that exchange, both as traders in their own right and as recipients of taxes levied on trade.

Viewed in the perspective of the New Institutional Economics, Barton's observations are quite remarkably prescient. Proceeding essentially from the language and concepts of his informants rather than from received theoretical precepts, he describes how Kalinga institutions serve to create both order out of anarchy, and economic interdependence out of isolation. In the process he formulates, however cautiously, a model of the origins of the state itself as an institutional means of reducing the costs and risks of trade. If there is one big surprise it is the ease with which, according to Barton's account, the problem of creating a system of impartial contract enforcement—which North describes as 'a major dilemma in the study of institutional evolution'—was apparently overcome by transparently rational means even in an institutionally simple society dominated by the kinship principle.[36]

Conclusion

The anthropological writings of Alice Dewey and Roy Franklin Barton, both written more than fifty years ago, contain striking anticipations of the New Institutional Economics literature in terms of their understanding of the centrality of transaction costs—determined in turn by institutional structures—to economic development. In Dewey's case, moreover, it is clear that these insights were by no means just her own: in the preface to *Peasant Marketing in Java* she shares the credit for them with leading British economic anthropologist Raymond Firth, without whose help the book 'could not have been written', as well as with economic historian B.S. Yamey and with her fellow Modjokuto researchers, who included the legendary Clifford Geertz.[37] Her advanced ideas, in other words, were part of the common property of the anthropological establishment of her day. In the case of the maverik Barton, whose ideas were above all his own (and those of his informants), this is less obviously the case. On the other hand, Barton's *The Kalingas*, with its startling illustrations of key NEI principles in relation to an obscure tribal institution, indicates the continuing value of the ethnography of that era as a source of empirical material with which to develop the field of institutional economics today.

The canonical texts of the New Institutional Economics were produced in the 1970s and 1980s, when the wealth disparity between rich and poor countries was great, and persistent enough to support the view that if institutional differences were to blame, then institutional change must be an intrinsically slow and difficult process. Today, now that many formerly poor countries are developing at unprecedented speed, this assumption is no longer so tenable. Like North and his colleagues, Barton and Dewey both understood that economically inefficient institutions could be politically stable and therefore resistant to change. But both also provided detailed accounts of how, in the presence of economic opportunity, people in pre-modern societies were capable of overcoming collective action problems to create new and more efficient institutions in strikingly rational ways. It is their insights into the amenability of institutions to deliberate and rapid modification which are perhaps their most valuable potential contributions to the development of the field in the twenty-first century.

Notes

1. Dewey, *Peasant Marketing in Java*, 42.
2. North, *Institutions, Institutional Change and Economic Performance*, 33.
3. Ibid.
4. Coase, 'The Nature of the Firm'.
5. Dick et al., *The Emergence of a National Economy*, 149–50.
6. Malinowski, *Argonauts of the Western Pacific*; Evans-Pritchard, *The Nuer: A Description of the Modes of Livelihood.*
7. Dewey, *Peasant Marketing in Java*, xiii.
8. Ibid., 92.
9. Dewey, 'Trade and Social Control in Java', 178, 183.
10. North, *Institutions, Institutional Change and Economic Performance*, 55.
11. Dewey, 'Trade and Social Control in Java', 180.
12. North, *Institutions, Institutional Change and Economic Performance*, 34–5, 55, 127.
13. Dewey, 'Trade and Social Control in Java', 177–8.
14. Dewey, *Peasant Marketing in Java*, 182–3.
15. Ibid., 47.
16. Dewey, 'Trade and Social Control in Java', 181.
17. Dewey, *Peasant Marketing in Java*, xxi.
18. Dewey, 'Trade and Social Control in Java', 187, 189.
19. Ibid., 188–9.
20. Kroeber, 'Roy Frankin Barton', 91.
21. Barton, *The Kalingas: Their Institutions and Custom Law*, 148.
22. Ibid., 148–9.
23. Ibid., 182.
24. Ibid., 64.
25. Ibid., 199.
26. Ibid., 185–6.
27. Ibid., 208.

28. Ibid., 168.
29. Ibid., 201.
30. Ibid., 146.
31. See for instance: Adas, 'From avoidance to confrontation'; Gullick, *Indigenous political systems of western Malaya*; Scott, *The art of not being governed.*
32. Ibid., 172–3.
33. Ibid., 144.
34. Ibid., 201.
35. Ibid., 186.
36. North, *Institutions, Institutional Change and Economic Performance*, 35.
37. Dewey, *Peasant Marketing in Java*, xvi.

III

TRADE AND ECONOMIC GROWTH UNDER CHANGING REGIMES

11

The External Rice Trade of the Indonesian Republic, 1946–47

Robert Cribb

The economic history of the Indonesian revolution (1945–49) remains a relatively empty page in the economic history of Indonesia. Not only are statistics scarce and unreliable, but the terms on which the economy functioned were very different from those of the eras before and after, when the country was enmeshed in a system of international trade based principally on the production of raw materials and plantation crops. Especially during the early revolutionary years, 1945–47, important parts of the archipelago—notably much of the densely populated and formerly productive islands of Java and Sumatra—were in the hands of the Republic of Indonesia. This new state had declared independence in August 1945, but had not received international recognition and its very existence was challenged politically, diplomatically and militarily by the returning Netherlands Indies authorities. In consequence, and thanks also to an economic blockade by the former colonial power, the republican lands were isolated from the normal channels of international trade. The confrontation between the republic and the Netherlands Indies authorities over the future of the country, moreover, created an unprecedented political frontier within the country. Although that frontier never took on the harsh fortified character of the borders that separated the two

Chinas, the two Koreas or the two Germanies, they created a new economic barrier where none had been before, generating both obstacles and opportunities for Indonesia's people.

No commodity was more important in the political struggle than rice, the preferred staple food for most of the population.[1] As a result of Japanese policies, rice production had languished during the occupation years (1942–45). Particularly important in depressing rice production were the hated Japanese rice requisitions, which diminished the incentive for peasants to grow the crop and prohibited transport of rice across residency boundaries, as well as the lack of consumer goods for peasants to purchase even if they did maintain production.[2] Although the republican and Netherlands and Indies authorities had some confidence in the underlying loyalty of their supporters, they were afraid that lack of access to rice might make those supporters susceptible to blandishments by the other side. Maintaining rice supplies for the public was thus critical, especially in the main cities of Java—Jakarta (Batavia), Bandung, Semarang and Surabaya—which were occupied by Allied forces (British and Dutch) and were cut off from their agrarian hinterlands by demarcation lines laid down by the Allied forces in late 1945 and early 1946. In the formal view of the republic in the hinterland, Allied occupation did not change the status of these cities. Jakarta indeed remained the official capital of the republic until after July 1947. But for practical purposes the occupied cities were now foreign territory and a host of issues hovered over the question of letting rice flow into them.

Rice for the Occupied Cities

In the territories occupied by the Allies were perhaps two to three million people, 90 per cent or more of them Indonesians for whom rice was the preferred basic food. Around the edges of the cities and along the corridor between Jakarta and Bandung, some rice fields and a sprinkling of vegetable gardens and orchards fell within the demarcation line, but the richest of rice-growing regions—the Karawang plain, the volcanic slopes of Cianjur, the valley of the Brantas—lay in republican territory. Only imports from outside Java or trade across the demarcation line could feed the occupied cities.[3]

The dominant feeling in the republic was at first that these cities should not be fed. Clustered along the demarcation lines were *lasykar*, irregular armed units, many of which had sprung up in the cities after the declaration of independence but had been forced out into the countryside by the methodical sweeps of Allied troops through the urban kampungs.[4] Bitter at their defeat and frustrated at their inability to put even a dent in the Allied front line, they quickly adopted what seemed the only immediately effective way to put pressure on the Allies, a blockade of the city. The tightness of this blockade varied from place to place and time to time. Often the nationalists simply enforced the old Japanese regulation banning the transport of rice across residency boundaries in greater quantities than was needed for personal use. On the Karawang front facing Jakarta, for instance, where rice was relatively abundant, the inhabitants of the city were each permitted to take five kilos of rice back into the city. On the Tangerang front, by contrast, which backed on to the rice-poor region of Banten, the ban was absolute. In either case, the control was policed officiously in careful searches of the baggage and belongings of travellers.[5] Some armed units used confiscation at the border as a way of augmenting their own rice supplies, but the main purpose of the blockade was to strangle the Allies.

A rice blockade was in fact a singularly ineffective way of hurting the Allies directly, since many Europeans preferred not to eat rice and those who did generally had access to rice imported from elsewhere in Southeast Asia. The blockade did lead to immediate shortages in the occupied cities, but this affected the Allied authorities mainly in the form of worries over food riots and the uncomfortable spectre of starvation in poorer sections of society. There was never any real question, however, of nationalist forces hermetically sealing the demarcation line against the flow of rice. Demand in the occupied cities was too strong and, more important, the rewards for bringing in rice were too great. Rice could be sold in the cities for cash with none of the troublesome price restrictions of republican markets, and with cash one could buy medicines, tinned food, bicycle tyres and all the other manufactured wonders of the industrial world. At particular times of tension, the borders might be closed effectively for a few weeks, but no long-term closing was possible. The question, then, was not who could stop the rice trade but who would control it.

The *Balai Agung*

The first institution to move significantly into the cross-border rice trade in Jakarta was the republican municipal administration in the city, commonly known as the Balai Agung (town hall), headed by the mayor, Suwiryo, which attempted to provide basic municipal services for the

Indonesian inhabitants of the city. Because of the negotiating process, the central government's diplomatic offices in Jakarta were largely secure for as long as they wished to remain in the city. The city administration, on the other hand, was highly insecure. The Dutch were keen to resume control of the whole of Jakarta in order to begin reconstruction and to use the city as a demonstration both of Dutch legal authority and of Dutch capacity to take effective charge of their colony once more. The Balai Agung for its part was extremely weak financially. Unlike the prewar municipality of Batavia, it could not tax its better-off Dutch residents; nor could it expect significant assistance from its own government. Although it received occasional contributions from the central government, the Balai Agung depended, in fact, for its day-to-day expenses on goodwill and on the meagre income it obtained from market taxes and municipal fish ponds.

The Balai Agung's republican credentials, however, gave it the possibility of breaking the food blockade and thereby simultaneously solving several of its problems. In the first place, importing rice would help to avert malnutrition and perhaps starvation amongst the poorer elements of Indonesian society in Jakarta who were the Balai Agung's responsibility. Second, in doing so, it would reduce the likelihood that the Dutch could buy the acquiescence of the population by being the ones to supply the necessities of life. Third, it would secure the position of the Balai Agung, for the Dutch were at least as alarmed as the republic by the prospect of politically volatile starving mobs in Jakarta and, despite their other objections to the Balai Agung, could be expected to tolerate it if it were fulfilling so useful a role. And fourth, the rice trade offered the Balai Agung the prospect of financial solvency. Rice was cheap in Karawang with its abundant harvests; it was expensive in crowded, hungry Jakarta, and whoever could exploit that difference in price stood to make a handsome profit.

On 19 December 1945, therefore, a full session of the Jakarta city council approved the establishment of a rice-managing organization called BOMA (Badan Oeroesan [Urusan] Makanan, Organization for Food Affairs). BOMA was given an official monopoly of rice imports into Jakarta and it operated by sending officials, armed with copious authorizations, into the interior to gather rice and other food. They received some assistance in collecting food from local republican civil authorities, but the initiative came from BOMA itself. The food was then brought back to Jakarta by train or truck and was distributed to the Indonesian population through outlets organized by the central government's department of economic affairs. BOMA's activities never came close to meeting Jakarta's food needs, but it added a significant margin to the flow of rice into the city and thus contributed to both the security and prosperity of the Balai Agung.[6]

More Trade in Rice

The officials of the Balai Agung, however, were not the only ones to notice the commercial opportunities presented by the rice trade. The lasykar themselves, although they were responsible for the blockade, found it both profitable and necessary to circumvent it. For the demarcation line between Jakarta and Karawang was an unnatural partition of a single economic zone. Just as Jakarta depended on rice from Karawang, so Karawang depended on money from the sale of rice and on the goods that could be bought in the city with that money. Both the army and the lasykar needed access to Jakarta to replenish their material supplies: weapons, clothing, tyres, medicines and the like. Jakarta was also a source of luxury goods such as American cigarettes and lipstick, which could be distributed in the interior by way of patronage. Most of the lasykar and army units in the region, therefore, had their own *badan ekonomi* (economic organizations) whose responsibility was to assemble the money and materials necessary for the survival of the unit. Although these badan ekonomi traded in a variety of commodities, the most significant by far was rice.

Amongst the badan ekonomi, the most powerful was BERI (Badan Ekonomi Rakyat Indonesia, Economic Organization of the Indonesian People), which was established in Karawang in January 1946 and enjoyed the protection of the radical nationalist People's Militia of Greater Jakarta (Lasykar Rakyat Jakarta Raya, LRDR). Its founders claimed that it was formed to reduce the sufferings of the people of Jakarta by supplying rice to the city, and it purported to guarantee that none of the rice it handled reached the Dutch or the Chinese in Jakarta. It not only ignored BOMA's official monopoly but even refused for a time to deal with BOMA, arguing that the Balai Agung, which had by this time established a number of co-operative administrative arrangements with its Dutch municipal counterpart, was virtually working for the Dutch, and that to supply rice to BOMA would thus bolster the Dutch position. It insisted, therefore, on dealing directly with local people's co-operatives in the city and succeeded in establishing a significant flow of rice into Jakarta independent of BOMA. This hard line, however, did not persist. The activities and organization of BERI and BOMA were to a considerable extent complementary and the scale of their respective operations made them logical business partners. The lasykar may have been suspicious of the Balai Agung's flirtations with the Dutch, but it was in the city administration's own interest not to allow that co-operation with the enemy to go too far, and it made sure that it was able to continue to distribute the rice it obtained through its own channels so as to preserve its usefulness to the Dutch. The wary collaboration between lasykar and the Balai Agung helped to sustain both in the face of the looming presence of the Dutch.[7]

The Republic's Rice Policy

The central government of the republic was at first more interested in the rice trade for diplomatic reasons than for financial ones. Britain regarded the issue of food supply as one of the most pressing problems in South and Southeast Asia and, to a considerable degree, it attributed the political turmoil of the post-war period to the disruption to food supplies.[8] A major part of its diplomatic initiative in the region, therefore, focused on co-ordinating the allocation of staple foods, and when in March 1946 it had sent a senior diplomat, Lord Killearn, to the area as Special Commissioner, it was his special responsibility to see to food affairs, although he was also charged with extricating Britain from its awkward military involvement in Indonesia.[9] The question of food supply was therefore an obvious issue on which the republic could aim to manoeuvre the British towards giving it formal recognition.

It was through the Food Commission that the republican prime minister, Sutan Sjahrir, made a bold move intended both to win diplomatic advantage for the republic and to solve the problem of the shortage of consumer goods for its people. On 12 April 1946, he offered the Indian government half a million tons of rice to alleviate a severe famine that then threatened the country.[10] The rice was to be paid for in goods, principally cotton cloth, together with bicycle tyres and agricultural equipment. With the promise of repayment in these valuable goods, the republic hoped that it would be able to solve another problem: how to persuade peasants to hand over rice to the government at reasonable prices. Rice requisitions during the Japanese occupation had caused great hardship and consequent resentment, and the republic could not afford to appear to be emulating the Japanese in extorting produce from the peasants.[11] But in the interior of Java there were few goods that peasants could purchase with the proceeds from their harvests and so the rice market was stagnant. The armed forces had their own means of acquisition, but the republican administration had difficulty functioning without reliable rice supplies. With the promise of Indian goods, the republic could at last hope to extract rice from its peasants in large quantities. Surplus cloth after the repayment would then be available for the republic to make further rice acquisitions for its own purposes.[12]

There were broader diplomatic advantages, too. The offer publicly affirmed the prosperity and administrative efficiency of the republic at a time when the Dutch were attempting to portray it as a ramshackle affair unable even to guarantee the welfare of its own citizens. And it won for the republic the immediate interest of both Britain and India and offered the prospect not only of putting both countries in the republic's moral debt, but of giving the republic some of the formal attributes of sovereignty by establishing it as an international trading partner.

Dutch Reaction

Dutch officials immediately poured scorn on Sjahrir's offer, pointing out that the Netherlands Indies had only once been able to export rice in recent times, in 1941, thanks to an exceptional combination of good conditions, and that the decline in agriculture during the Japanese occupation and the revolution could only mean a decline in production.[13] When the British and Indians showed immediate signs of taking the offer seriously, however, this scorn turned to bitter opposition. The republic's offer was not at all implausible given the known productivity of the regions under republican control. The republic, however, could make its offer precisely because it was not formally responsible for feeding the Dutch-occupied areas on Java and Sumatra nor the Dutch-controlled islands of Kalimantan and eastern Indonesia, where any surplus from Java normally went. In several of the outer islands, as well as in the occupied cities, the Dutch were facing serious food shortages, and they were fearful both of the political consequences of undersupply in the territories they controlled and of the political and economic advantages that the republic stood to win by the proposal.[14]

The preferred solution of the Dutch to this problem was a military operation to seize the fertile rice lands of Karawang. Sjahrir's offer, however, had caught the imagination of the British, and they vetoed any move likely to disrupt the project, although they did persuade Sjahrir on

3 May 1946 to guarantee a regular supply of rice to Jakarta. In return for a promise of 360 tons of rice per day, the British lent the republic seventy-five trucks, with fuel, and arranged for the Dutch to supply cloth, bicycles, nails and other consumer goods as payment for the rice.[15] In fact, no more than 200 tons of the promised rice arrived in Jakarta as a result of Sjahrir's efforts, but the preparations to send rice to India continued. The Indian government sent a special commissioner, K.L. Panjabi, to Singapore and Jakarta to begin negotiations. Dutch opposition to the scheme was unabated, but they were forced to acquiesce by a British threat to remove all their troops from Indonesia if the transaction was not allowed to go ahead. The Dutch were only able to obtain renewed guarantees that the republic would also deliver quantities of rice to them, and that any agreement reached with the republic would not have the character of a formal international agreement. The terms of the agreement finally reached on 27 July between Sjahrir and Panjabi were that the republic would provide India with 700,000 tons of *gabah* (unhusked rice), equivalent to 350,000 tons of milled rice. In exchange, the Indian government would provide cotton cloth, yarn, bicycles and tyres, together with some agricultural and technical equipment. India was also to provide the trucks needed to collect the rice, the sacks needed to pack it and the ships needed to transport it to India. Organization for the rice export, however, preceded the signing of the formal agreement. Collection of rice commenced on a small scale. The trucks were supplied once more through British headquarters in Jakarta and the ships began to arrive in mid-July.[16]

The operation, however, was far from being a success, for the republic proved unable to organize the collection of rice effectively and only about 50,000 tons of gabah reached India.[17] There were various reasons for this. First, although Sjahrir had made his offer at harvest time when rice supplies were abundant, it was not until July that the collection of rice began in earnest and the republic thus missed the most favourable moment for obtaining surpluses. Second, although trucks were supplied for the collection of rice, most of those were very soon requisitioned by local army units who, even if they had no strong opinion on the rice export programme, had a strong sense of their own needs. The warehousing of rice stocks in the major collection ports—Cirebon, Probolinggo and Banyuwangi—also presented problems, as extensive facilities did not exist or had been taken over for other purposes. It was also difficult to find lighters to load the Indian ships, because so many were in use on other lucrative trading activities and on quasi-military operations. In Banyuwangi the shortage of loading vessels became particularly acute after the Dutch navy bombarded the port to destroy small boats which it claimed were being used for infiltration across the strait to Dutch-held Bali.[18]

Ineffective Efforts

The greatest difficulty for the republic, however, was at the point of collection from farmers. The idea of exporting rice to India was not an intrinsically popular one, nor were the advantages to the republic particularly easy to explain outside the diplomatic circles of Jakarta; Sjahrir's diplomatic strategy was in fact distinctly unpopular in much of the interior of Java. Republican radio stations and newspapers attempted to create a sense of momentum by reporting enthusiastic offers of rice from various parts of the country. In the republican rump of the Surabaya residency, the people were reported as being ready to donate 1,000 tons of *beras* (milled rice), although they had none to spare.[19] A radio station sponsored by the Netherlands Indies army (Koninklijk Nederlands-Indisch Leger, KNIL) but purporting to present a nationalist view, on the other hand, emphasized popular resistance to the rice collections.[20]

Officials to collect rice needed to stress the commercial advantages of the deal to the republic in order to establish its credentials. In doing so, however, they ensured that the farmers themselves would see the transaction in a commercial light. The republic, however, was particularly ill-equipped to undertake the large-scale commercial purchase of rice. By July 1946 the government's financial reserves were running low. Japanese occupation currency was still the sole legal tender within the republic and, for obvious political reasons, the government could not increase its funds simply by printing more of this currency. It did obtain some funds through a widely publicized national loan, but most of this went to more urgent aspects of the war effort. A reported *f* 28 million was made available for rice purchases, allowing an average price of around *f* 33 per kg of *gabah*, probably not an unreasonable farm-gate price in the then rapidly depreciating Japanese currency, but this made no allowance for other costs or for the rather extensive loss of money to corrupt or needy officials on the way. In practice, therefore, farmers tended to sell their rice under some degree of duress, and were paid in bonds rather than cash, a practice that created some uneasiness amongst civil servants mindful of the social revolutions that had broken out in many areas a few months previously as a reaction to the compulsory delivery of food during the Japanese occupation.[21]

In most respects, therefore, the republic's rice export programme was an ineffective competitor with the BOMA-BERI operation across the Jakarta demarcation line. The two programmes were in direct competition since the collection port of Cirebon drew principally on the same rice-producing region as did the Jakarta trade. The principal advantage of the republic's operation was its relatively smaller risk, since it did not involve a sometimes perilous crossing of the demarcation line, but this should have been outweighed by the much greater effectiveness of the BOMA-BERI operation in distributing the proceeds of the trade. Yet for some months the Jakarta rice trade showed an apparently serious decline, which was reflected in a deterioration of the Balai Agung's ability to sustain itself, and possibly also in a greater degree of turmoil amongst the Karawang lasykar.[22] (Turmoil being the natural state of affairs amongst the lasykar, it is hard to judge whether turmoil was indeed greater, and even if it were the case it could well be attributable to political rather than economic factors.) The reason for the downturn does not appear to have been directly economic. The actual volume of rice drawn out of the system through Cirebon is likely to have had a perceptible but no more than marginal influence on the volume of rice available, while the meagre amounts of rice brought into the city under Sjahrir's auspices can have made no difference at all. Sjahrir's offer showed a breathtaking disregard not only for the economic base of Balai Agung but also for the political grounds on which it was permitted by the Dutch to survive; if he had been able to supply 360 tons of rice per day he would have done away with the main reason why the Dutch tolerated the Balai Agung in Jakarta. The reason for the slump in the Jakarta rice trade, however, appears in fact to have been political rather than economic.

Sjahrir's offer to the Dutch made sense in terms of his diplomatic strategy of locking the British and Dutch into a de facto recognition of the republic. From the other side of the demarcation line, however, it looked like no more than collaboration with the enemy. One reason why so little came of Sjahrir's arrangements was that it prompted an almost immediate blockade of Jakarta. Sjahrir's agreement aroused such passionate opposition amongst both army and lasykar that the entire rice trade to Jakarta came under suspicion, and the flow of rice dwindled to a trickle. With it dwindled the economic base of the Balai Agung and the lasykar. It is, of course, paradoxical that the lasykar should have tightened an economic noose around their own necks in this fashion. The irregular forces in the Karawang area, however, despite their loose organization under the rubric of the LRDR, were mutually suspicious of each other's loyalty. While each unit may have regarded its own trade as irreproachable, there were always enough other units willing to cast doubt on the destination of a shipment and to refuse it passage across the demarcation line. Nonetheless, while temporary disruption in trade had been common up to this point, what made the blockade stick on this occasion was the attitude of the army.

The republican army commander, General Sudirman, had announced a total blockade of all occupied territories at the end of May 1946, and the army moved to enforce this with considerable enthusiasm. The Indonesian army was not renowned during the revolution for leaping to obey instructions from its high command, but the Jakarta regiment, which was based east of Karawang in the town of Cikampek, had two good reasons for enforcing the rice blockade with vigour. First, in common with large sections of the army, the regiment viewed the government's negotiations with the Dutch with intense suspicion and transferred the suspicion to any other activities that seemed likely to assist the returning colonial power. Second, and probably more important, the army in the Jakarta region was engaged in a competition with the lasykar for military dominance in the region. By attacking the rice trade into Jakarta, the army was able to begin choking off the supply routes that enabled the lasykar to present so effective a challenge to the army. The army, of course, had its own *badan ekonomi* and was involved in the trade across the demarcation line. The location of its headquarters, however, at Cikampek, a considerable distance from the front, together with the more or less fraternal relationship it enjoyed with other army units, gave it the opportunity to develop significant trading links to the east, into republican territory rather than to the west, with occupied Jakarta.

Removal of Impediments

Ironically, the Dutch themselves removed the impediments to the Jakarta rice trade. As the British prepared to leave Java, one of their first steps, in July 1946, was to hand over to the Dutch responsibility for patrolling the demarcation line around Jakarta. No longer restricted by British commanders wishing to avoid incidents, the Dutch forces immediately stepped up patrols and began to press against the demarcation line, forcing the Indonesians to retreat.[23] Although roads and bridges were damaged in the hostilities, the aggressive tactics of the Dutch permitted a greater flow of rice into the city by disrupting Indonesian patrols along the demarcation line. The Dutch navy's shelling of Banyuwangi, too, was a further discouragement to all concerned with the export of rice to India and the project quietly died, freeing limited quantities for the Jakarta trade.

The Jakarta rice trade, however, could not last indefinitely as a useful source of finance for the Balai Agung and the lasykar. In the latter part of 1946 there was a natural downturn in availability of rice as stocks were gradually consumed closer to the point of production. On the Jakarta side, moreover, it became clear that a number of republican officials responsible for co-ordinating the trade were involved in extensive embezzlement of BOMA funds and supplies. The organization was disbanded by the Jakarta national committee (Komite Nasional Indonesia, KNI, in effect the city's local parliament) and was replaced by a Bagian Import Makanan (Food Import Section), directly under the Balai Agung's Department of Economic Affairs, but this effectively deprived the Balai Agung of BOMA's extensive range of contacts in republican territory, and under the circumstances it was unlikely that this network could be rebuilt. It is likely, too, that the rice import business was becoming less lucrative for the Balai Agung. For one thing, rumours had begun to circulate that a cabal of Chinese businessmen working with the Department of Economic Affairs had obtained a virtual monopoly of illicit rice imports into Jakarta.[24] The Netherlands Indies authorities for their part were now better established both in Kalimantan and eastern Indonesia, and in the eyes of the world—and they experienced fewer difficulties in ensuring a flow of supplies to occupied Jakarta. These supplies included not only food but consumer goods, and it was this in particular that turned the balance of payments against the republic, to the acute economic distress of the Balai Agung. Although the Dutch had abolished the Japanese occupation currency when they introduced their own in March 1946, they were forced to tolerate its continued circulation because it was the only currency that could be used to purchase rice from across the demarcation line. Japanese occupation currency, therefore, although depreciating in value as the republic increased the money supply by spending its stocks of unused notes, nonetheless retained significant value, and this value gave buying power to the occupation guilder income of the Balai Agung (which refused to deal in the new Netherlands Indies currency).[25] The large-scale import of consumer goods into Jakarta provided an incentive for the rice trade as a whole, but effectively took it out of the hands of the Balai Agung and placed it in the hands of entrepreneurs with access to Dutch goods.

On the Karawang side of the demarcation line, meanwhile, the blockade whose grip had been loosened in the middle of the year was tightened once more with the republic's initialling of the Linggajati Agreement with the Dutch in November 1946. This agreement, under which the republic acknowledged Dutch authority in Kalimantan and eastern Indonesia, and accepted a federal system and a postponement of international recognition, aroused even more passionate opposition throughout the republic than had the rice agreement—and once more the flow across the border shrank to a trickle. This time, however, the army was determined to make the blockade stick and they maintained an intense regime of patrols along the demarcation line. This monitoring was all the easier because the truce that accompanied the Linggajati Agreement obliged the Dutch to refrain from their previous aggressive pattern of patrols deep into republican territory and thus republican forces were able in turn to patrol more freely. The army's efforts to stifle trade culminated in April 1947 in the establishment of a formal custom post on the demarcation line to give further official weight to the army's restrictions.[26] This programme of choking the Jakarta rice trade was one of the factors leading to armed conflict between the army and the lasykar later in April and the temporary dispersal of the lasykar. Barely, moreover, was this clash over then the Dutch launched their first military action of July 1947 in which they seized most of West Java, including the Karawang Plain. There was thus no longer any possibility that the rice trade in the Jakarta region would significantly support republican organizations.

Conclusion

The post-war partition of the former Netherlands Indies between the Republic of Indonesia and a revived Netherlands Indies created new internal political borders within the archipelago in a way that had not been seen since the early nineteenth century. Then, the imposition of an international border between Dutch and British spheres, running across the island of Borneo and along the Melaka Strait, both disrupted old trading patterns and created new opportunities for lucrative contraband operations.[27] The borders that appeared in late 1945 also created new economic difficulties and opportunities. The isolation of Indonesia's largest cities from their hinterlands created the opportunity for a trade in rice that favoured those with armed force and political connections.

Control of the rice trade became crucial to both the republican authorities in Jakarta and the armed lasykar on the fringes of the city. The republic's central government, too, recognized the political and economic advantages to be had from transporting rice across borders when it offered to supply substantial amounts of the grain to India. The borders that made this trade possible, however, shifted several times even during the short period to 1949, when they came to a complete end.[28] The challenges and potential that they offered proved to be temporary. As Van der Eng shows in this volume, Indonesia rapidly became a major importer of food and the possibility of using rice exports disappeared as Indonesia returned to a more normal pattern of international trade. Within the national economy, however, the army proved increasingly adept at creating and managing internal barriers to free trade. As Bambang Purwanto demonstrates in this volume, these barriers generated their own lucrative opportunities.

Primary Sources

Newspapers

Antara (Jakarta), 16, 26 January 1946.

Berita Indonesia (Jakarta), 7 February 1946; 5 June 1946; 16 October 1946; 10 February 1947.

Djakarta Raya (Jakarta), 16, 26 January 1946.

Merdeka (Jakarta), 8 February 1946; 30 March 1946; 12 April 1946; 2, 9 May 1946.

Ra'jat (Jakarta), 19 December 1945; 19 January 1946; 19, 21 October 1946.

Sin Po (Jakarta), 3 April 1946.

Star Weekly (Jakarta) 3, 10 November 1946.

Archives

Nationaal Archief, Den Haag, Algemene Secretarie te Batavia, Eerste Zending [Alg. Sec. I]

Operatieve rapporten, 12-7-'46 t/m 19-9-'46, box I, file 5, no. 2.

DOBIN [Dagelijks Overzicht Belangrijke Inlichtingen], 2 October 1946, box I, file 21-4/7.

DOBIN, 5 October 1946, box I, file 21-4/6.

AMACAB, Notulen vergadering op 15 juli [1946] in het gebouw Pegangsaan-West no. 22, box I, file 30.

Graaf van Bylandt to Winkelman 2 November 1946, box I, file 30.

'Statement by N.I. Government on food position of Java in connection with Dr Soetan Sjahrir's reported offer to make 500,000 tons of Java rice available for export', 25 April 1946, box XXII, file 16.

Nedinreg to Netherlands Consul-General, Simla, 3 June 1946, box XXII, file 16.

RRI broadcast (Solo), 27 May 1946, box XXII, file 16.

The National Archives, Kew, United Kingdom

Mackereth to FO, 25 April 1946, FO 371/53789.

SAC's 45th miscellaneous meeting, 25 May 1946, FO 371/53797.

Notes on conference re provision of rice, held at HQ AFNEI, 3 May 1946, FO 371/53797.

Memo to Chief of Staff, Joint Planning Staff, 'Transfer of responsibility to the Dutch in Java', 17 July 1946, FO 371/53804.

Mackereth to Wilson-Young (FO), 25 July 1946, FO 371/53806.

SACSEA to Cabinet Offices, 9 August 1946, FO 371/53807.

Private papers

The Diaries of Lord Killearn, St Antony's College, Oxford, Middle East Centre. Private Papers Collection, GB 165-0176, Killearn, Box 6, Diaries, 1945–46, 24 May 1946.

Notes

1. On the place of rice in Indonesia, see Van der Eng, 'Food for Growth'.
2. Shigeru Sato, *War, Nationalism and Peasants.*
3. Van der Eng, *Food supply in Java during war and decolonisation, 1940–1950*, 47–8.
4. Cribb, *Gangsters and Revolutionaries.*
5. For an evocation of the atmosphere surrounding these searches, see Toer, 'Revenge'.
6. *Djakarta Raya* (Jakarta), 16, 26 January 1946; *Ra'jat* (Jakarta), 19 December 1945; *Merdeka* (Jakarta), 30 March 1946.
7. *Antara* (Jakarta), 16, 26 January 1946; *Ra'jat*,19 January 1946; *Berita Indonesia* (Jakarta), 7 February 1946; *Merdeka*, 8 February 1946; Interviews.
8. Tarling, *Britain, Southeast Asia and the Onset of the Cold War*, 122–7.
9. Olver, 'The Special Commission', 286.
10. *Merdeka*, 12 April 1946.

11. See Sutter, *Indonesianisasi*, 300; Vu, 'Of Rice and Revolution', 243–5; Dick et al., *The Emergence of a National Economy*, 156, 165; Lindblad, *Bridges to New Business*, 69–70.
12. See Kasdi, 'Bantuan Beras ke India'.
13. 'Statement by N.I. Government on food position of Java in connection with Dr Soetan Sjahrir's reported offer to make 500,000 tons of Java rice available for export', 25 April 1946, Nationaal Archief, Den Haag, Algemene Secretarie te Batavia, Eerste Zending [hereafter Alg. Sec. I], box XXII, file 16. 'The rice production in Indonesia', 9–12; Vu, 'Of Rice and Revolution', 250. For a detailed and careful consideration of rice production and marketing in occupied Indonesia, see Van der Eng, *Food supply in Java during war and decolonisation, 1940–1950*, 8–25.
14. Lord Killearn, diary, 24 May 1946. Van Mook to Logemann, 7 June 1946, *Officiële bescheiden betreffende de Nederlands–Indonesische betrekkingen 1945–1950*, IV, 420–1. Mackereth to FO, 25 April 1946, National Archives, Kew, FO 371/53789; Graaf van Bylandt to Winkelman, 2 November 1946, Alg. Sec. I, box I, file 30. Interview.
15. SAC's 45th miscellaneous meeting, 25 May 1946, FO 371/53797; Nedinreg to Netherlands Consul-General, Simla, 3 June 1946, *Alg. Sec. I* box XXII, file 16; Notes on conference re provision of rice, held at HQ AFNEI, 3 May 1946, ibid.; *Merdeka* 2, 9 May 1946; Interview.
16. AMACAB, Notulen vergadering op 15 juli [1946] in het gebouw Pegangsaan-West no. 22, Alg. Sec. I, box I, file 30; Overdijkink, *Het Indonesisch probleem: nieuwe feiten*, 163–4.
17. See Van der Eng, *Food supply in Java during war and decolonisation, 1940–1950*, 49–51.
18. Memo to Chief of Staff, Joint Planning Staff, 'Transfer of responsibility to the Dutch in Java', 17 July 1946, FO 371/53804; Mackereth to Wilson-Young (FO), 25 July 1946, FO 371/53806; SACSEA to Cabinet Offices, 9 August 1946, FO 371/53807; DOBIN, 2 October 1946, Alg. Sec. I, I-21-4/7.
19. Radio Surabaya, reported in DOBIN, 5 October 1946, Alg. Sec. I, I-21-4/6.
20. DOBIN, 5 October 1946, Alg. Sec. I, I-21-4/6.
21. See AMACAB, Notulen vergadering op 15 juli [1946] in het gebouw Pegangsaan-West no. 22, Alg. Sec. I, box I, file 30; Overdijkink, *Het Indonesisch problem: de feiten*, 164.
22. RRI broadcast (Solo), 27 May 1946, Alg. Sec. I box XXII, file 16; *Sin Po* (Jakarta), 3 April 1946; *Berita Indonesia*, 5 June 1946.
23. 'Transfer of responsibility to the Dutch in Java', 17 July 1946, FO 371/53804; Operatieve rapporten, 12-7-'46 t/m 19-9-'46, Alg. Sec. I box I, file 5, no. 2.
24. *Ra'jat*, 19, 21 October 1946; *Berita Indonesia*, 16 October 1946, 10 February 1947; *Star Weekly* (Jakarta) 1, nos. 44 & 45 (3, 10 November 1946);

Overdijkink, *Het Indonesisch probleem*, 147–8; Soetopo Soesanto, 'Djakarta Raya pada massa "Pemerintah Nasional Kota" 17 Augustus 1945, 21 Djuli 1947' (Skripsi Sardjana, Universitas Indonesia, 1971), 78–81, 86.

25. See Cribb, 'Political Dimensions'.
26. Cribb, 'Jakarta in the Indonesian Revolution', 182.
27. Tagliacozzo, *Secret Trades, Porous Borders*.
28. In 1949, of course, a new border emerged in the east between Dutch West New Guinea and independent Indonesia, but that is a different story.

12

The Indonesian Economy during the 1950s and Early 1960s and America's Proposal for Economic Aid

Thee Kian Wie

Introduction

At 10 a.m. on 17 August 1945, two days after the unconditional surrender of Japan to the Allied forces, Sukarno proclaimed Indonesia's independence to a crowd of about 100 people in front of his residence at Pegangsaan Timur 56 in central Jakarta.

The independence declaration, drafted by Mohammad Hatta, was formulated as follows:

> We, the people of Indonesia, hereby declare Indonesia's Independence. Matters concerning the transfer of power will be executed in an orderly manner and in the shortest possible time.
>
> In the name of the Indonesian people,
>
> Sukarno – Hatta, 17 August 1945[1]

The proclamation had been drafted in the residence of Rear Admiral Maeda at the pre-war residence of the British Consulate at what was then Nassau Boulevard 1 (now Jalan Imam Bonjol 1). Maeda's residence had been chosen because of his apparent sympathy to Indonesia's nationalist hopes.[2]

On 17 August 1945 the red and white flag, Indonesia's new national flag, was raised on a bamboo pole. This flag had been diligently sewn together by Fatmawati, Sukarno's wife, in the early hours of the morning. After the singing of 'Indonesia Raya' (Great Indonesia), the new national anthem, the crowd started to disperse.[3] This song, which had been composed by W.R. Supratman, had first been sung at the Second Youth Congress in Jakarta on 28 October 1928.[4]

The next day the provisional constitution (which later was referred to as the 1945 Constitution) was adopted. Sukarno and Hatta were unanimously elected by the members of the Preparatory Committee for the Independence of Indonesia (Panitia Persiapan Kemerdekaan Indonesia, PPKI) as the president and vice president of the newly established nation state.[5]

Despite the initial reluctance of the Japanese authorities to yield to the demand to grant Indonesia independence, by early 1945 the Japanese military command realized that they were losing the war. For this reason, on 1 March 1945 the Japanese military commander (*Saiko Shikikan*), Lieutenant-General Harada, announced that a central advisory council would be established, thus allowing prominent Indonesians to participate in the policy-making process. To this end, the Committee to Investigate Preparations for Independence (Badan Oentoek Menjelidiki Oesaha-Oesaha Persiapan Kemerdekaan, BPUPKI) was established.[6]

A few days before the declaration of independence, leaders of Indonesian youth groups (*pemuda*) wanted Sukarno and Hatta to declare independence immediately after hearing of Japan's surrender, and without the approval or tacit consent of the Japanese authorities. To their demand for an immediate declaration of independence, Sukarno argued that a precipitate action to oppose the Japanese directly could lead to a terrible bloodshed and might crush the infant republic at birth.[7] Sjahrir, the third leader of Indonesia's pre-war nationalist movement, got very angry because of Sukarno's adamant stand and, according to a witness, called Sukarno a *banci* (transvestite).[8]

To force Sukarno's hand, the youth leaders decided to kidnap him, not to harm him but to force him to declare Indonesia's independence immediately. In the early hours of 16 August 1945 both Sukarno, accompanied by his wife Fatmawati and their nine-month-old son, and Hatta were in fact kidnapped and driven from their respective homes in

Jakarta to a house owned by a Chinese landowner named Djiauw Sie Kiong, in Rengasdengklok, a small town some 80 km to the east of Jakarta.[9] However, in the evening, one of the pemuda stated that he had been ordered by the Japanese military commander to take Sukarno and Hatta back to Jakarta. As a consequence of this, Sukarno and Hatta were now determined to take matters into their own hands regardless of the consequences. And so the next morning, 17 August 1945, the declaration of Indonesia's independence was proclaimed by Sukarno and Hatta in Jakarta.

This chapter addresses the economic problems that the new nation faced, and asks why the United States decided to propose food aid. This will be discussed in connection to Sukarno's policy orientation and the failure of his economic policy decisions.

The Dutch Refusal to Recognize Indonesia's Independence

Most of the Dutch population, upon learning of Indonesia's declaration of independence, did not take this declaration seriously. They considered the newly proclaimed republic as a 'joke of the Japanese who needed a small compensation for the defeat they had suffered'.[10] In fact, there was a deep fear among the Dutch for the future of their country without the Indies. This fear was reflected in the well-known saying: *Indie verloren, rampspoed geboren* (A disaster would arise if the Indies would be lost).[11] There was also the fear that without Indonesia, the Netherlands would not be viable economically, and that the Netherlands would then 'be relegated to the rank of a country like Denmark'.[12]

The economic importance of Indonesia to the Netherlands was fundamental as to why the Dutch were reluctant to follow the example of the British to leave British India in 1947 and the Americans to leave the Philippines in 1946, and grant Indonesia independence. This was shown, for example, in a confidential memorandum by two Dutch economists, Derksen and the highly respected professor Jan Tinbergen of the Netherlands School of Economics at Rotterdam, which contained their estimate that income from Indonesia amounted to 15 per cent of total Dutch income in the decade from 1925 to 1934. This included income received from profits of private firms, dividends, rents, pensions, and trade in colonial goods and services. In addition, an attempt was made to take into account the 'secondary' or multiplier effects of this income.[13]

A second (and related) consideration was that in the inter-war years the colonial economy became an extremely important source of dollar earnings, mainly because of the rapid growth in rubber exports to the United States. Even with the promise of dollar earnings from massive dollar aid through the Marshall Plan, the Dutch were very reluctant to lose control of their main source of dollar-earning exports.[14]

The Arrival of Allied Troops to Disarm the Japanese Armed Forces

After Japan's surrender on 15 August 1945, British troops landed in Jakarta to disarm the Japanese troops, evacuating Allied prisoners of war and Dutch internees, and maintaining law and order in the main cities. The interlude between the proclamation of independence and the arrival of the Allied forces allowed the republic to set up a rudimentary administrative system. By the end of September 1945 most of Java and Sumatra had joined the republic, and nationalist forces administered many towns and cities, and also ran the public utilities.[15]

The British quickly recognized de facto republican rule, but secured the major cities: Jakarta, Bandung, Semarang and Surabaya on Java, and Medan and Padang in Sumatra. In Surabaya the British troops only gained control after very heavy fighting with republican troops, militias and gangs of pemuda, which started on 10 November 1945.[16] The British took full control of Surabaya after Brigadier-General Mallaby of the British army was killed.[17]

Unfortunately, most Dutch politicians totally misjudged the situation and attempted to impose the restoration of colonial rule. Even before enough military had been mobilized in the Netherlands for transport to Indonesia, the Netherlands Indies Civil Administration (NICA) assumed control of the major cities one after the other. The NICA forces sometimes followed hard on the heels of the British forces. They took over more cities during what they called the First Police Action (*Politionele Actie*),[18] which lasted from 21 July to 4 August 1947. Yogyakarta, the last Indonesian stronghold and seat of the republican government, was occupied by the Dutch forces during the Second Police Action, which lasted from 19 December 1948 to 5 January 1949. Sukarno, Hatta, Haji Agus Salim (Indonesia's minister of foreign affairs) and Sjahrir—without Indonesian troops to guard them—were arrested by the Dutch forces. But Sukarno rejected out of hand a Dutch request that he order the republican forces to cease its resistance.[19]

However, the Dutch military success turned out to be a pyrrhic victory, as it caused US support to shift to the republican side, and led to a full-scale guerilla warfare in the countryside.[20] International reaction was also harsh on the Dutch. In January 1949 Pandit Jawaharlal Nehru, India's prime minister, convened the Inter-Asian Relations Conference in Delhi, with a special focus on Indonesia. This conference sent a set of recommendations to the United Nations' Security Council that the Netherlands should cease its hostilities to the republic.[21]

The Committee of Good Offices of the United Nations, which had been set up to find a solution to the 'Indonesian problem', also reacted negatively to the Dutch occupation of Yogyakarta and to its policy of exiling the republican leaders to Prapat in North Sumatra.[22] As a result, the Netherlands was forced to negotiate the transfer of sovereignty with the republican leaders.[23] This took place at the Round Table Conference (RTC) in The Hague between 23 August and 31 October 1949, and was attended by the Indonesian delegation led by Hatta, Indonesia's vice-president, a delegation of the BFO (Bijeenkomst Federaal Overleg, Meeting for Federal Deliberation), the fifteen puppet states set up by the Dutch to offset the power or attraction of the republic, and the Dutch delegation.[24]

Despite the fact that in the Dutch parliament a minority voted against the draft bill about the transfer of sovereignty, on 9 December 1949 a majority voted in favour of this bill to transfer sovereignty to the United States of Indonesia (Republik Indonesia Serikat, RIS), consisting of the Republik Indonesia and the fifteen BFO puppet states. In Indonesia, on 14 December 1949, a majority in the Indonesian parliament, the Komite Nasional Indonesia Poesat (KNIP), also voted in favour of the draft law on the transfer of sovereignty. Hence, on 27 December 1949 in the Dam Palace in Amsterdam, Queen Juliana signed the act of the transfer of sovereignty, followed by Drees, the Dutch prime minister, and then by Vice-President Hatta in his capacity as Indonesia's prime minister.[25]

In the Paleis Koningsplein (King's Square Palace) in Batavia the events were followed on radio by Lovink, the High Representative of the (Dutch) Crown and by Sultan Hamengkoeboewono IX as the representative of the RIS.[26] On 28 December 1949 President Sukarno returned triumphantly to Batavia, now renamed Jakarta, just like it was called during the Japanese occupation, and was welcomed by a large and enthusiastic crowd.

The Economic and Political Consequences of the Round Table Conference

Although the transfer of sovereignty to Indonesia on 27 December 1949 was welcomed by most Indonesians, this event did not create any euphoria.[27] Many nationalists were quite unhappy with the severe terms imposed by the Netherlands in return for the transfer of sovereignty. The reason was that the transfer had been the result of a negotiated settlement arranged by the United Nations Commission for Indonesia (UNCI). Consequently, the Indonesian delegation at the Round Table Conference was forced to compromise on several issues in order to persuade the Dutch to reach an agreement.[28]

From the outset four controversial issues, two political and two economic, bedevilled the relations between Indonesia and the Netherlands.[29] The first political issue was the Dutch insistence on transferring sovereignty not to the Republic of Indonesian, which had waged the war of independence, but to the United States of Indonesia (Republik Indonesia Serikat, RIS), comprising both the Indonesian Republic and the fifteen puppet BFO states. Forcing the Indonesian nationalists to accept a federal structure was greatly resented, as it was seen as a Dutch ploy to weaken Indonesia. However, this artificial political structure proved to be fragile, as in the ensuing months after the transfer of sovereignty one puppet state after another dissolved itself and declared themselves to become a part of the Indonesian Republic. Hence, on 17 August 1950, the fifth anniversary of Indonesia's declaration of independence, the federal RIS was dissolved to make way for the Unitary State of the Republic of Indonesia (Negara Kesatuan Republik Indonesia, NKRI), which has survived until today.[30]

The second and more intractable political issue concerned West New Guinea—named Irian Barat (West Irian)—by the Indonesian nationalists, which was claimed by the Indonesian nationalists as they considered themselves to be the rightful inheritors of the Netherlands Indies. The Dutch, however, refused to hand over West Irian, arguing that its Papua population was racially, ethnically and linguistically not a part of the Indonesian nation. Moreover, a majority of the representatives of the large Dutch parties in parliament stated that the 'less developed' inhabitants of West New Guinea should not be 'delivered' to Indonesia, as they were not yet able to decide about their future. Moreover, West New Guinea could also become a 'new home country' for the Eurasian community in

Indonesia, which would feel uncomfortable in an independent Indonesia. In short, keeping West New Guinea would serve as a 'painkiller' for the loss of the Netherlands Indies.[31]

The refusal of the Dutch to hand over West New Guinea to Indonesia doomed the prospects of friendly Dutch–Indonesian relations from the outset. It also aggravated the irritation caused by the two economic issues on which the Indonesian delegation at the Round Table Conference had to compromise in order to speed up the transfer of sovereignty. It also enabled more radical nationalists to gain the upper hand at the expense of more moderate, pragmatic leaders.[32]

The two economic issues that rankled Indonesian nationalists were the foreign debt that Indonesia had to take over from the Dutch administration in Indonesia and the continued operations of Dutch business in Indonesia. During the four-year armed struggle against the Dutch (1945–49), the extensive Dutch business interests in Indonesia had gradually realized that hanging on to Indonesia would be futile. Hence, these business interests exerted heavy pressure on the Dutch government to ensure that the Round Table Conference had to yield an agreement with the Indonesian delegation that would safeguard their extensive economic interests in an independent Indonesia.[33]

The Dutch government was also motivated by the need to safeguard the revenues it could obtain from these business interests, which would be indispensable for the depleted Dutch treasury and the revenue it needed for the post-war reconstruction of the Netherlands. Therefore, the unrestricted transfer of profits and dividends of the Dutch enterprises operating in Indonesia had to be legally guaranteed.[34]

Guided by these considerations, the Dutch delegation at the Round Table Conference insisted on discussing those financial and economic issues that could achieve the most profitable outcome. This was ensured in the Financial and Economic Agreement (Financieel-Economische Overeenkomst, Finec). The Dutch delegation was also adamant in refusing to make any significant concessions on the financial and economic issues discussed at the Conference. In return it was prepared to offer political concessions; these, however, were not clearly specified.[35]

Despite the unresolved issue about the status of West New Guinea and the contentious issue of continued economic dominance of Dutch business in the modern sectors of the Indonesian economy, the Round Table Conference nevertheless was successfully concluded on 31 October 1949 with the agreement about the transfer of sovereignty from the

Netherlands to Indonesia, to be held on 27 December 1949. Clearly, the Netherlands had finally realized that holding on to its former colony was no longer possible.

The Achievement of 'Effective' Independence

With the official transfer of sovereignty to Indonesia it had finally achieved its 'effective' or actual independence and sovereignty over the whole territory, with the exception of the still contested territory of West New Guinea (or *Irian Barat*, West Irian). However, the achievement of political independence without economic independence greatly restricted the freedom of manoeuvre of Indonesia's economic policy-makers.

During this period the major problem facing Indonesia's economic policy-makers was reconciling the urgent need to rehabilitate the dilapidated physical infrastructure and the productive apparatus with the strong national aspiration to 'convert the colonial economy into a national economy'. This aspiration was eloquently stated in a pamphlet written by Soejono Hadinoto, chairman of the Indonesian National Party (Partai Nasional Indonesia), entitled *Ekonomi Indonesia—Dari Ekonomi Kolonial ke Ekonomi Nasional* (The Indonesian Economy—From a Colonial to a National Economy). In his pamphlet, Hadinoto pointed out that after independence Indonesia's economy should not be an export-oriented economy any more, but an economy in which the purchasing power of the Indonesian people should be raised as much as possible.[36]

Despite their unhappiness with the continuing Dutch dominance over the Indonesian economy—particularly the modern sectors, including the large estates, the mining sector, the large manufacturing industries, the banking sector and the inter-island shipping industry—the major economic policy-makers during the early 1950s were pragmatic men, and certainly no less nationalistic than their detractors. They included Vice-President Hatta; Professor Sumitro Djojohadikusumo (who, like Hatta, had studied at the Netherlands School of Economics at Rotterdam); Sjafruddin Prawiranegara, who had graduated from the pre-war School of Law (Rechtshogeschool) in Batavia and in the early 1950s became the first Indonesian governor of the Java Bank (Javasche Bank), the bank of circulation during the Netherlands Indies, which subsequently was nationalized in December 1951 by the Indonesian government and named Bank Indonesia, the nation's central bank; and Djuanda Kartawidjaja, an engineer trained at the School of Engineering in Bandung.[37] While most of them were attracted to socialist ideals, none of them adhered to any rigid ideological doctrine. This pragmatism was also evident when Sumitro Djojohadikusumo was Minister of Finance in the cabinet of Prime Minister Wilopo of the Indonesian National Party (Partai Nasional Indonesia, PNI). In a paper that was published by the Ministry of Information on September 1952, Sumitro outlined the basic principles underlying his policies in connection with the present situation. In this regard Sumitro stressed that the whole range of regulations and measures he had taken could be considered as one joint effort to stimulate domestic production and investments; to expand exports; to economize on public outlays of a consumptive character, and to check unnecessary imports. In view of the government's administrative machinery, which was still far below standard as to quality, experience and ability, he stated that the government had to refrain wherever possible from direct interventions. Instead, it should resort to a policy of indirect controls, which should form part of a coherent whole, based on certain strategic concepts.[38]

As mentioned earlier, the approach of most discussions of Indonesia's economic future in the early 1950s stressed that the Indonesian economy should adhere to socialist ideals rather than the thoroughly 'capitalistic' economic structure inherited from the Netherlands Indies. The years after 1953 saw a further growth in the influence of forces that could either initiate an abandonment of constitutional democracy or provoke others to do the same in order to forestall them.[39] Political cleavages also became more rigid than before 1953. Hence, the years between 1953 and 1957 saw both a decline in the influence of those who supported constitutional democracy and an attenuation of the functions that constitutional democracy was able to fulfil for the political system as a whole.[40]

In his classic book *The Decline of Constitutional Democracy in Indonesia*, the Australian political scientist Herbert Feith made a distinction in Indonesia's revolutionary leadership between what he called the 'administrators' and the 'solidarity makers'. The 'administrators' were persons with the administrative, legal, technical and foreign language skills, which were required for the running of a modern state. On the other hand, the 'solidarity makers' might have enjoyed higher Western or Muslim primary or secondary education. They might exercise their leadership on the basis of traditional or charismatic authority.[41] Indeed, such conflicts or differences of opinion were a constant feature of internal struggles in the young republic.[42]

The Break with the Netherlands and the Takeover of Dutch Enterprises

Political relations between Indonesia and the Netherlands steadily worsened during the 1950s, as President Sukarno demanded the return of Dutch-occupied West New Guinea (*Irian Barat*), which he considered to be an integral part of Indonesia. Sukarno based his demand on the fact that Indonesia was the rightful inheritor of the whole territory of the Netherlands Indies.

When the Netherlands refused to hand over West New Guinea, and continually refused to negotiate the status of the region in the course of the 1950s, on 29 November 1957 Indonesia submitted a resolution to the United Nations General Assembly calling on the Netherlands to resume negotiations. This was rejected, however, by a majority in the General Assembly. Consequently, starting in early December 1957 trade unions affiliated with the Indonesian National Party (PNI) and the Indonesian Communist Party (PKI) took over all the Dutch companies, starting with the Dutch inter-island shipping company KPM (Koninklijke Paketvaart Maatschappij, Royal Packet Company). In February 1959 all the Dutch companies were formally nationalized.[43] As there were not enough qualified Indonesian managers to operate these nationalized companies, they were put under military supervision.[44]

The takeover and subsequent nationalization had three unintended consequences. First, it marked the entry of military officers into various businesses, whom post-Suharto governments had difficulties to dislodge (see the contribution by Bambang Purwanto in this volume). Second, it marked the entry of ethnic Chinese businessmen who were now able to enter fields that previously were occupied by Dutch business, and hence became economically more powerful than during the Netherlands Indies or during the early 1950s. In fact, during the Suharto era (1966–98) a number of ethnic Chinese tycoons in cahoots with indigenous Indonesian businessmen, particularly Suharto's children, emerged because of the preferential treament given by President Suharto. This aggravated the public resentment at the perceived economic domination by the ethnic Chinese minority. This public resentment erupted from 12 to 15 May 1998 in the cities of Jakarta, Solo, Surabaya, Palembang in South Sumatra, and Medan in North Sumatra, with widespread looting, burning, rapes and killings.[45]

Third, it also led to the proliferation of the very large numbers of state-owned enterprises (SOEs), as the nationalized Dutch companies were turned into state-owned enterprises. Because of the poor corporate governance and sometimes intervention by political powerholders who used these SOEs as cash cows, many of these SOEs were (and are still today inefficient), and therefore had a poor profit performance.[46]

An increasing need to draw attention away from pressing problems at home prompted President Sukarno's next diversion, namely the 'Crush Malaysia' ('*Ganjang Malaysia*') campaign, launched in September 1963 in response to a perceived threat from the formation of the Malaysian Federation on 31 August 1963, which Sukarno perceived to be a British and American plot to offset the power and attraction of Indonesia. Consequently, Indonesian troops infiltrated the Malayan peninsula and Sarawak and Sabah in Kalimantan. Hostilities at home were directed at Malaysia's Western allies, particularly at the United States, Great Britain and Australia, which sent troops to defend Malaysia against the Indonesian invaders.[47]

Indonesia's confrontation against Malaysia also marked the beginning of increasingly hostile relations with the United States, which actually started with the tacit support of the US in the regional rebellions in West Sumatra and North Sulawesi in 1958. However, in a report to the US government in mid-1965, US ambassador to Indonesia, Howard Jones, pictured President Sukarno to be basically a friend of the US, but whose increasing belligerence resulted from a lack of information.[48]

Sukarno's increasing hostility towards the Western capitalist powers was, however, expressed in his speech in April 1964 when he announced the withdrawal of Indonesia from the United Nations (UN) and its affiliated specialized agencies—this was a strong protest against the election of Malaysia as a non-permanent member of the UN Security Council in 1965, which was supported by Britain and the US. However, this ill-considered step was also one of Sukarno's serious political mistakes, as Indonesia simply increased its isolation from the world community.[49]

The increasingly hostile relations of Indonesia with the US and Britain led to the takeover of at least ninety foreign companies—including British, American, Belgian and Malaysian—by Indonesia's government. In essence, the entire foreign investment sector in Indonesia was seized by the Indonesian government in what was at the time the pinnacle of economic nationalism in modern Asian history. The elimination of foreign investment during the period 1963–65 was the result of a complex confluence of Indonesian domestic struggle and instability, foreign relations and domestic economic policy.[50]

Moreover, the takeovers of the foreign companies, particularly the British and American companies, occurred in separate waves, which until 1965 were not the result of a grand plan of the Indonesian government to eliminate all foreign investment, but instead were targeted at specific groups and ad hoc in nature.[51]

The outcome of these political turmoils was that Indonesia's economic growth during the 1950s and early 1960s was quite low, even resulting in an unprecedented negative real gross domestic product (GDP) per capita growth rate during the early 1960s (Table 12.1).

Table 12.1: Indonesia's average annual growth in real GDP, population and per capita GDP (percentages)

Average Annual Growth Rates	*Real GDP*	*Population*	*Real GDP per capita*
1952–59	3.2	2.0	1.2
1960–65	2.0	2.1	−0.1

Source: Malcolm Gillis, 'Episodes in Indonesian Economic Growth', Table 1, in World Economic Growth—Case Studies of Developed and Developing Nations, ed. Arnold C. Harberger (San Francisco: ICS Press, 1984), 232.

The American Proposal for American Economic Aid to Indonesia

To improve the important relations with Indonesia, which since the late 1950s had become more hostile to the Western countries, particularly the US and Britain, on 1 August 1961 the American ambassador, Howard P. Jones, presented to President Sukarno a report of the US Economic Survey Team entitled 'Indonesia: Perspectives and Proposals for United States Economic Aid'. This report was prepared by the survey team after visiting Indonesia at the request of President Kennedy for the primary purpose of reviewing Indonesia's Eight-Year Overall Development Plan (*Rencana Pembangunan Nasional Semesta Berencana Delapan Tahun*), prepared by Mohammad Yamin, the deputy prime minister in charge of special cases.[52] The survey team was also expected to make specific recommendations regarding future economic assistance to Indonesia. Based on their visit to Indonesia and extensive discussions with several cabinet ministers, senior government officials and senior military officials, the team concluded that Indonesia was still in the early stages of economic development, but moving in the right direction. The native ability of the Indonesian people and Indonesia's rich natural resources made the outlook for progress in economic development promising, once the preconditions of self-sustaining growth are developed. In the metaphor that has become familiar in discussions of economic development, the survey team concluded that 'while Indonesia is not yet ready for the take-off into self-sustained growth, the "plane", that is Indonesia, has only been brought out of the hangar. But this is only the necessary first step. We predict that when the Indonesian economy does take off, it will fly high and fast.'[53]

Based on their survey, the team recommended to provide an aid programme estimated at between US $325 and $390 million. In most cases these costs would cover a five-year period. Of the total, the survey team recommended that programmes involving $125 to $155 million be financed multinationally. The remainder, ranging from nearly $200 million to nearly $235 million, would be financed by the United States through specified grants and loans.[54]

In his letter to President Sukarno, the US ambassador, Howard P. Jones, pointed out that while the team's report contained specific dollar recommendations, that fact did not commit the US government to provide the specified amounts. The ambassador also suggested to President Sukarno that the Indonesian government review and evaluate the team's recommendations. Then, in the common interests of advancing the economic development of Indonesia, the Indonesian and American governments could better co-operate in formulating a programme that would be in the interests of both countries.[55]

Conclusion

America's offer to provide financial aid for Indonesia's economic development programme was the last effort of the US to improve its important relations with Indonesia in order to prevent President Sukarno from turning increasingly to the Soviet bloc for aid. However, under President Sukarno's increasingly strident anti-Western and anti-capitalist policies, economic policy became subordinate to political strategy. Under President Sukarno's slogans of 'completing the national revolution' and building a 'socialist economy *à* la Indonesia', self-reliance and forging closer relations with the socialist countries came first.

Having little grasp of or interest in the serious economic problems facing the country, President Sukarno had little capacity or interest for seeking economic advice or aid, certainly not from the US, which might have enabled the Indonesian government to come to grips with the country's serious economic problems. As a result, the Indonesian economy deteriorated steadily, experiencing an unprecedented hyperinflation of 600 per cent in 1965 and impoverishing the Indonesian people. Thus the early independence period that had started with much hope, ended in economic and social chaos, which led to the fall of a disgraced president, once hailed as Indonesia's 'Great Leader of Revolution', and one of the proclamators (together with Mohammad Hatta) of Indonesia's independence on 17 August 1945.

Notes

1. The year 2605 refers to the Japanese calendar, as Indonesia was still under Japanese occupation. See Hering, *Soekarno. Founding father of Indonesia*, 372.
2. Legge, *Sukarno. A Political Biography*, 197.
3. Hering, *Soekarno. Founding Father of Indonesia*, 373.
4. Abdullah, *Indonesia. Towards Democracy*, 47.
5. Ibid., 1.
6. Yunarti, *BPUPKI, PPKI, Proklamasi kemerdekaan RI*, 39; Hering, *Soekarno. Founding father of Indonesia*, 345.
7. Legge, *Sukarno. A Political Biography*, 198.
8. Mrazek, *Sjahrir. Politics and Exile in Indonesia*, 263.
9. Hering, *Soekarno. Founding Father of Indonesia*, 368.
10. Van den Doel, *Afscheid van Indie*, 89.
11. Wesseling, *Indie verloren*, 285.
12. Baudet, *Nederland en de Rang van Denemarken*, 431.
13. Booth, 'Growth and Stagnation', 402.
14. Ibid.
15. Colombijn, *Under Construction: The Politics of Urban Space and Housing*, 46.
16. Most of the British forces consisted of Indian and Gurkha soldiers.
17. 10 November is now celebrated in Indonesia every year as Hero's Day (*Hari Pahlawan*). See Colombijn, *Under Construction: The Politics of Urban Space and Housing*, 46–7.
18. This Police Action is referred to as *Agresi Pertama* (First Aggression) in Indonesian historiography.
19. Legge, *Sukarno. A Political Biography*, 233.
20. Colombijn, *Under Construction: The Politics of Urban Space and Housing*, 47.
21. Abdullah, *Indonesia*, 186.
22. Legge, *Sukarno. A Political Biography*, 236.

23. Colombijn, *Under Construction: The Politics of Urban Space and Housing*, 47.
24. Abdullah, *Indonesia. Towards Democracy*, 575.
25. Van den Doel, *Afscheid van Indie*, 351.
26. Ibid.
27. In Indonesia, the transfer of sovereignty is described as the Dutch recognition of Indonesia's independence, as Indonesia had already become an independent country after the declaration of independence on 17 August 1945.
28. Thee, *Recollections: The Indonesian Economy*, 5.
29. Dick, 'Formation of the Nation State', 170.
30. Thee, *Recollections: The Indonesian Economy*, 6.
31. Meier, *Den Haag-Djakarta*, 49.
32. Thee, *Recollection: The Indonesian Economy*, 6.
33. Ibid.
34. Meijer, *Den Haag-Djakarta*, 46.
35. Ibid.
36. Hadinoto, *Ekonomi Indonesia*, 36.
37. Booth, 'The Colonial Legacy', 13.
38. Djojohadikusumo, *Facing the Situation*, 21.
39. Feith, *The Decline of Constitutional Democracy*, 577.
40. Ibid., 578.
41. Ibid., 24–5.
42. Ibid.
43. Dick, 'Formation of the Nation State', 184.
44. Glassburner, 'Economic Policy-Making', 92.
45. Purdey, *Anti-Chinese Violence*, 108.
46. Only Indonesia's national airline, Garuda Indonesia, has for the past few years recorded profits. In fact, it is now rated as the best regional airline in East Asia! Gillis et al., *Economics of Development*, 580.
47. Lindblad, *Bridges to New Business*, 205–6.
48. Gardner, *Shared Hopes, Separate Fears*, 207.
49. Abdullah, *Indonesia*, 303.
50. Redfern, *Sukarno's Guided Democracy*, 3.
51. Ibid.
52. Abdullah, *Indonesia*, 302.
53. United States Economic Survey Team to Indonesia, 1963, xi.
54. US Economic Survey Team, *Indonesia*, 15.
55. Ibid., vii.

13

The Ambiguous Position of Economists during the 'Old Order', 1950–65

Farabi Fakih

Introduction

The expert technocrats in present-day Indonesia have an increasingly ambiguous relationship with the wider society. Boediono, the current Indonesian vice president, was attacked during the 2009 Presidential election as representing foreign neo-liberal forces.[1] Economists such as Boediono were important members of the government who wielded power but somehow lacked authority. This was not a new phenomenon. In the 1950s and early 1960s Indonesian economists occupied a contentious position.

A discussion on economists of the 1950s inevitably leads to the problem of decolonization and Indonesianization. Thomas Lindblad has worked much on the economic decolonization and the formation of the national economy.[2] This chapter is part of a larger study that expands Lindblad's work by analysing the discourse surrounding *Indonesianisasi* in management and social sciences during the Cold War struggle between differing political-economic models of society.[3]

Cold War studies on Indonesia have mainly dealt with an American focus. Bradley Simpson's *Economists with Guns* (2008) discusses the development of the Indonesian technocracy but mainly from the viewpoint of American involvement.[4] A range of studies on the American model of modernization has been conducted by Michael Latham and Nils Gilman.[5] This chapter will look from the viewpoint of the Indonesian economists and their detractors during the period. Many of the economists of the Economics Faculty of the University of Indonesia formulated relationships and ideas of power that they saw were necessary for the development of the nation. This chapter will examine the writings of the economists and those of their detractors.

Sumitro Djojohadikusumo and the International 'Community of Scholars'

When Indonesia gained independence there were very few professional economists available within the country. The total number of economics graduates during the time was around fifteen people. Most of the graduates were from the Rotterdam School of Economics. In Indonesia, the only place where training on economics was available was at the School of Law, where they taught Boeke's dual economics and tropical economics.[6] Thus, there were more people working on the problem of the Indonesian economy during the 1950s in Washington than there were in the entire Indonesia.[7]

Sumitro Djojohadikusumo was the son of a well-to-do aristocrat Margono Djojohadikusumo, born on 29 May 1917 in Central Java.[8] After finishing high school in 1935, he went on to study economics at Rotterdam. After finishing his doctorate Sumitro returned to Indonesia in 1946 and became assistant to Prime Minister Sutan Sjahrir and the Finance Ministry. In 1947 he became deputy to L.N. Palar, the Indonesian representative in the United Nations (UN).[9]

Sumitro was known as an institution builder par excellence. Through his international links he built what Benjamin Higgins, one of the main economists working on the United Nations Technical Assistance Administration (UNTAA) Indonesia project, called a '*community of scholars*'. When asked by a reporter as to why foreign experts would be interested in helping Indonesia, Sumitro explained that Indonesia should be a fascinating case for experts as a case of a new country with the problems of development.[10]

In 1948 the University of Indonesia Economics Faculty was created in Makassar, eastern Indonesia. In 1950 it was shut down due to a lack of lecturers.[11] In September 1950, the Economics Faculty of the University of Indonesia was created in Jakarta with Sunarjo Kolopaking as its dean. In 1951, Kolopaking resigned and the students approached Sumitro Djojohadikusumo to replace him.[12] Sumitro occupied the chair of dean until 1957, when he left the country to join the Revolutionary Government of the Republic of Indonesia or PRRI (Pemerintah Revolusioner Republik Indonesia) rebellion against the Sukarno government.[13]

In June 1951, Sumitro went to Europe and the United States as adviser to the Ministry of Economic Affairs in order to obtain six experts to work for the National Planning Bureau (BPN).[14] As part of the early industrialization plan, he wanted to obtain 180 experts. He also wanted to invite scholars and significant experts to dissect and understand the problem of Indonesian development. He had initially pinned his hopes on obtaining Dutch expertise, yet this was a failure.[15] The disappointing trip to Europe was compensated by his success in the United States, where he obtained interest from the United Nations to provide twelve experts.[16]

In 1951, he signed an agreement with Everett Hawkins of the US Economic Cooperation Administration (ECA). They gave a grant for US economists to teach at the economics faculty in Jakarta. His agreement with the Ford Foundation and the University of California-Berkeley had allowed for the sending of some Indonesian economics students to continue their study in the US starting in 1956. Twenty students were sent to various universities.[17]

Sumitro was also central to the creation of the Institute of Economic and Social Research or LPEM (Lembaga Penyelidikan Ekonomi dan Masyarakat),[18] which was also funded by the Ford Foundation and became a centre for research and a place where young social scientists were able to obtain practical experience through internships in the BPN, in which Sumitro was also a founder. In 1955, he also founded the Association of Indonesian Economists or ISEI (Ikatan Sarjana Ekonomi Indonesia),[19] which became a professional organization.[20]

The BPN was created in 1952 under the Office of the Prime Minister. It contained the largest number of experts working on the Indonesian economy within the country. The planning board consisted of members of the Economic and Financial Committee of the Cabinet, or the Finek Committee. Decisions of the committee on issues of economics and finance have the same binding authority as if they were the Cabinet's decisions. One of the major problems with Indonesian development plans has been in co-ordinating development help provided by the UN agencies, the ECA and the Colombo Plan.[21] The BPN was entrusted with the issue of foreign co-ordination.

The presence of foreign experts was also important because it allowed the economists that exist within the BPN to be exposed to the Keynesian ideas that were prevalent during the period; thus its insistence on an expanding state participation in the economy and the formation of a welfare state. The BPN was not only essential in creating experts, it was also important in creating an *esprit de corps*.[22]

One of the most important foreign experts during the period was Benjamin Higgins. He was appointed UN adviser to the Indonesian government as monetary and fiscal adviser to the Ministry of Finance and Economic Affairs and the State Planning Bureau in July 1952. Later, in 1954–55, he came back to Indonesia as director of the MIT Indonesia project within the Center for International Studies.[23] The extent to which Sumitro considered Higgins's advice as crucial was strengthened by the fact that their offices were next door to each other.[24]

The first UN technical mission to the BPN consisted of nine experts, including Benjamin Higgins and Nathan Keyfitz,[25] American labour expert Edgar McVoy,[26] income expert Daniel Neumark, industrial economist Peter Diebold, migration expert D.M. Deane and education specialist T.R. Smith. Many of the UN technical assistance experts were civil servants who held belief in Keynesian economics and Fabian social-democratic ideals. British Fabian values were also the main belief held by the Socialist Party or PSI (Partai Sosialis Indonesia),[27] thus there was ideological affinity between men like Sumitro and Higgins.[28]

There was a perception that foreign experts had become more powerful than local ones. Higgins went abroad to meet and discuss with international donors or partake in international conferences on aid and development planning.[29] One observer wrote that people had mistaken him as head of the BPN, instead of Djuanda.[30] Higgins commented on Indonesian policy-makers:

> In Sjafruddin and Sumitro, the country had a duumvirate on economic policy that few underdeveloped-countries could match for competence and commitment to the national interest. The Wilopo cabinet was composed of extraordinarily able and honest men. In the Planning Bureau and its relationship to other government agencies abroad, the country had an effective instrument for development planning.[31]

In 1951, the Ford Foundation provided a grant to Stanford University to investigate on the state of Asian study in the US and offered eighty-three fellowships to study Asia and the Middle East. In 1953 a research grant of US $125,000 was given to the MIT to study economic development in Indonesia. This was part of a larger research initiative at the Center of International Study, which included research by Walt Rostow into communist societies, and a study of the formation of public opinion in France, headed by Daniel Lerner.[32] The focus of research was on financing economic development, patterns of trade, technological aspects of economic development, management and administrative techniques and quantitative studies.[33]

The Center of International Studies (CENIS) at MIT sent people such as Douglas Paauw to study fiscal structure, Benjamin Higgins to study national income and Guy Pauker to study the political environment. These included economists such as Higgins, Douglas Paauw and William Hollinger, political scientists such as Guy Pauker, Jean Mintz and Ruth McVey, anthropologists such as Clifford Geertz and his field team. The 'community of scholars' also transcended their geographic boundaries and connected places such as the BPN, Faculty of Economics at the University of Indonesia or FEUI (Fakultas Ekonomi Universitas Indonesia), the Boston-Cambridge area, Wisconsin, Ithaca, and Windsor and Montreal in Canada.

CENIS at MIT included sociologist Daniel Lerner, economists such as Paul Samuelson, Evsey Domar and Robert Solow, whose work on economic growth earned him the Nobel Prize in 1987,[34] The 'community of scholars' also included George Kahin at Cornell University; Everett Hawkins, Hans Schmidt and Ted Morgan in Wisconsin; Bruce Glassburner in California; and scholars from McGill University and the University of British Colombia. Especially important was the group's access to President Kennedy's ear. Walt W. Rostow recalled: 'Kennedy sought out and found in CENIS a group whose ardent commitment was to enlarged development aid rather than to party or political personality. He understood this clearly and used us well.'[35] Rostow became what Nils Gilman called Kennedy's 'mandarin of modernity'.[36]

Sukarno and the PKI: Anti-experts

One of the features that tied together the idea of Sukarno and the communists was the dislike towards Western-trained experts. With the destruction of the communist party by Hatta's government during the insurrection of 1948, there had grown deep resentment amongst the communist leadership towards the social democrats of the Socialist Party or PSI and the Muslim Masjumi Party.

The rise of Sukarno's guided democracy and guided economy between 1957 and 1959 was also predicated on this deep dislike towards what he had come to associate as Sumitro's group of experts. One of the major purposes of the guided democracy experiment was to eliminate what it called 'liberal' influences in society. In Sukarno's address at the Bandung Non-Alignment Summit, he expounded:

> I beg of you, do not think of colonialism only in the classic form which we of Indonesia, and our brothers in different parts of Asia and Africa, knew. Colonialism has also its modern dress, in the form of economic control, intellectual control, actual physical control by a small but alien community within a nation.[37]

There was a particular distrust against Western economists. Roeslan Abdulgani, one of Sukarno's ideologues and a member of his tripartite executive said:

> I am no economists, and I have reservations about the purely professional approach of the economist. Particularly, I have reservation about the purely professional approach of the non-Indonesian economists, who, while putting his great skill and knowledge at our disposal, is still outside the stream of our life, our hopes and desires.[38]

Roeslan Abdulgani's explicit dislike of economists can be summed up in one of his quotes. Siding with what he called the 'unprofessionals' as opposed to the professional experts, he said: 'it was these unprofessionals who created and forwarded the Indonesian Nationalist Movement which proved capable of leading the country to shake off the bonds of colonialism [...]. There is no reason why such persons should be any less successful in the task of continuing the Revolution.'[39]

This belittling of the professional was a major theme of Sukarno's speeches, which extolled on the vice of those 'bald headed non-political individuals and text-book thinking teachers'.[40] If the BPN was beholden to the expertise of the Western economists and other social scientists, the new planning agency, the State Planning Board (Dewan Perantjang Negara, or Depernas) was different. It was to be composed of 'ordinary people', politicians and older leadership whose non-technical education provided broad strokes instead of precision expertise: 'Differing from the planning and development boards of yore, who stressed their membership to the expert-intellectuals, the Depernas will stress their membership on the *golongan karya* who are rooted and live in the community without ignoring the advice and opinion of the experts.'[41] The expert intellectuals were motivated only by *careerism* and *professionalism* which, according to Abdulgani, was the root problem of modern bureaucracy. Instead, the membership is of the *cultivated man*: 'a person who has a general education and a wide and forward perspective, who may not be or not yet become a specialist, but who is not yet infected by the disease of modern bureaucracy'.[42]

The assumption of guided democracy development must be seen as an appeal for collectivism and the upbringing of the Indonesian mass as participant in development:

> With the creation of the Depernas we have entered a new phase in the forms of development of our country and nation. This meant that the past experiences must not be replicated again, a development plan that did not involve the masses, but was a purely academic plan that was incomprehensible to the rest of the Indonesian population.[43]

This participatory approach towards development was very different from the elitist, expert and manager-based development that the economists offered.

Similar in tone to Sukarno had been the attack launched by the Communist Party. The PKI always had an ambiguous position in relation to experts and intellectuals. In many communist movements outside of Indonesia, the intellectuals represented a major part of the communist movement, yet in Indonesia this was not the case. [44] For instance, senior leader of the party Dipa Nusantara Aidit conducted studies on the rural condition of Indonesia and attacked Western-trained economists for their misunderstanding of the real conditions of the rural areas. Between February and May 1964, 250 local communist leaders and mass organizations put into the field 3,000 'researchers' (*petugas*) to conduct a study of the rural condition in 124 districts (*kecamatan*) in Java. The research concluded seven archetypes of rural class enemies.[45] What was important about the research was that it was not conducted by university graduates but by the common people of the party.

The communists disliked expert economists. Aidit comments: 'It has occurred for a long while that Indonesian economics experts took on a position of ignorance toward political issues and tried to present the problems of the economy as merely a technical matter, with laws that "are assumed to apply for all ages", stemming from a subjective viewpoint and ignore the objective reality that exists within society.'[46]

Aidit accused Sumitro of siding with imperialism and feudalism by placing the analysis of Indonesian poverty on foreign investment and the lack of savings by the population. According to the communists, it lacked a social component and misunderstood the nature of Indonesian rural society; that the reason lay not in the lack of propensity to save, but as a result of the rent-seeking activities of bureaucratic capitalists, foreign enterprise owners and landlords. He blamed this confusion almost exclusively on Sumitro.[47]

Second Generation Economists and the Military

Social scientists and economists returning from their study in American universities in the late 1950s and early 1960s were able to congregate in a series of institutions before spreading out into the bureaucracy.[48] The formation of the Indonesian Science Council (MIPI) in 1956 was instrumental in this. Research had become an important part of the national development effort as was stipulated in the Eight Year Development Plan of 1961. As a result, the government created the Department of National Research in 1962. In 1960, MIPI had decided to expand the research council, resulting in the formation of seven research institutes. One of them was the National Social and Economy Institute, or Leknas.[49]

In the early 1960s, the universities themselves became the site of contestation between the communists and Sukarnoists on the one hand, and the Sumitro followers on the other hand. The division of the Ministry of Education and Culture into a Ministry of Higher Education and Ministry of Education and Culture in 1960 signalled the shift. Initially, the Sukarnoist Iwa Kusumasumantri was named Minister of Higher Education. He stopped the sending of Indonesians to American universities. He was forced out of office and a more pliable, pro-army man named Tojib Hadiwidjaja replaced him.[50]

Even so, economists had to tread the ground lightly. From 1960 onwards, economists in various universities started researching state-led models in Eastern Europe and China. For instance, Widjojo Nitisastro conducted a series of interviews with Polish planning elites and studied their consumption pattern projections based on West German consumption patterns.[51] Panglaykim contributed wide discussion on various managerial approaches in a variety of Eastern European countries and the People's Republic of China;[52] R. Sardju Ismunandar and Soehardiman, a military manager, went on a study trip to Yugoslavia, Czechoslovakia and Poland and wrote about the economic structure and state enterprises of the three countries in the magazine *Perusahaan Negara* in May 1961.[53]

The problems related to regional development were apparent to those researching on the integration of former rebel areas in places like North Sumatra. J.E. Ismael's visit to the area in 1962 highlighted the enormous problems related to integrating national development planning with regional government capabilities.[54] Mohammad Sadli said that 'regional development was an "ideological commitment" of socialism, at least within the socialism that was practiced in countries ruled by Communists'.[55]

There was a deep realization that economic problems in socialist society were a political-economic problem. Mohammad Sadli asked the question:

> to an economic expert the problem is a question of conscience, meaning does he need to find a 'justification' to all the deviation from resource allocation in accordance to pure economic consideration in a way that the decisions could be accounted for by an economic perspective? Or should he consider these deviations as an unwarranted but unavoidable aspect of his economy, as part of the social cost of economic development, as a necessary waste?[56]

The roots of the answer, according to Sadli, lay in the creation of a development leadership. He pointed out the obvious leaders of the regions during the period: the military.[57]

The idea that military autocracy was a compelling argument to regulate the problem of the political economy was one that was openly announced by economists during the period. Sadli's views were congenial enough to the military elite for Colonel Soewarto of the Seskoad, an old friend of Sadli from his Yogyakarta days, to invite him and his economic friends at FEUI to teach there.[58]

What was assumed here was an extension of military authority to protect the managerial elite, at least in the initial phase in kick-starting economic development. Thus the regulation on regional planning recreated governance within a *Tjatur Tunggal* system that put the military regional commander in power.[59] The idea of the military doctrine on civic action and development was thus very much intertwined. Ibrahim Adjie said this about the army's connection to development: 'war is not the goal of the military, the goal of the military is to uphold the welfare and honor of the nation so as to be at level with the most advanced nation in the world'.[60]

Conclusion

Herbert Feith's discussion on the contention between the administrator and solidarity-maker extends beyond the parliamentary democracy period and reached a high point during the Guided Democracy. A look into the writings of economists during the period showed their willingness to study socialist as well as market economies. The fragility of their position during the period had pushed economists to create tactical relationships with the military. Instead, Sukarno and the communists supported greater participation of the 'people', although much of the earlier effort of the guided democracy state ended up in failure. The discussion and research by economists would eventually help them to determine the type of state–society relations appropriate for Indonesian development. The study of socialist society and traditional culture, not discussed here, was essential for the formation of the New Order corporatist society.

The 'Old Order' period provided a specific environment for the development of Indonesian economists that put the value of pragmatism forward.[61] Economic difficulties under the Guided Democracy and the effort by Sukarno and the communists to limit the role of experts opened up the need to push forth a pragmatic policy with little interference from society. The rise of the military as saviour of the expert managerial class was an important component of the New Order regime.

Not confined to the national economy, Indonesianisasi represented an effort to move away from colonial forms and relations towards Indonesian ones. Yet, the process itself was much internationalized and, in fact, was intermixed with *Americanization*. The reaction to this perceived intrusion has coloured much of the Old Order period but, importantly, the same process was essential in the rise of the New Order regime. Understanding the political economy of twentieth-century Indonesia would not be completely possible without understanding this part of the Indonesianisasi process.

Primary Sources

National Archives, The Hague (NA)

- 2.05.186. Hoge Commissariaat Indonesie. Onderwerp: Internationaal Technische Hulp Verlening. Letter to the Dutch Ministry of Foreign Affairs from

the Head of the Economic Section of the High Commission in Jakarta, Dr. W.J. Kator. 18 June 1951.
- 2.05.61.03. Hoge Commissariaat Bandung.

Arsip Nasional Republik Indonesia, Jakarta (ANRI)
- Departemen Keuangan 1950–69, 294. Report on a Mission to Europe and America. Benjamin Higgins, Monetary and Fiscal Experts, National Planning Bureau.

Newspapers

De Locomotief, 12 July 1951.

Jakarta Post, 16 June 2009.

Notes

1. *Jakarta Post,* 16 June 2009, Moehammad, *Boediono: Islam, neolib dan ekonomi kerakyatan,* v–xi. Ismantoro, *Boediono dan (neolib)eralisme,* 5–8.
2. Lindblad, *Bridges to New Business,* 2–10.
3. Goldman, *Comparative Economic Systems,* 3–8.
4. Simpson, *Economists with Guns.*
5. Latham, *Modernization as Ideology*; Latham, *The Right Kind of Revolution*; Gilman, *Mandarins of the Future.*
6. Panglaykim, 'Some Notes on the Development', 279–80.
7. Bresnan, *At Home Abroad,* 31–3.
8. For more on his biography, consult Katoppo et al., *Sumitro Djojohadikusumo.*
9. Djojohadikusumo, 'Recollection of My Career', 27–39.
10. NA, No. 2.05.186.
11. NA, No. 2.05.61.03. *De Locomotief,* 12 July 1951.
12. Thee Kian Wie, 'In Memoriam: Professor Sumitro Djojohadikusumo', 174.
13. Booth, 'Indonesian Economic Performance', 413–4.
14. Biro Perantjang Negara.
15. NA, No. 2.05.186.
16. NA, No. 2.05.186.
17. Moehammad, *Celebrating Indonesia. Fifty Years with the Ford Foundation,* 48–60.
18. Lembaga Penelitian Ekonomi dan Masjarakat. In 1955, he put Widjojo Nitisastro as head of LPEM.
19. Ikatan Sardjana Ekonomi Indonesia.
20. Moehammad, *Celebrating Indonesia. Fifty Years with the Ford Foundation,* 46–7.
21. NA, No. 2.05.186.

22. Budiardjo, 'Abdi negara', 255. According to Koesoediarso Hadinoto: 'The BPN is effective and productive as a means to create cadres. The experts of the BPN are given the methods to act rationally and capably and also to act on behalf of contributing to the nation and state. These experts were then sent to a variety of government offices and state-owned companies. The emotional bond that have been created amongst them is kept alive and contributes to aiding cooperation between the offices they lead, in accordance to the approach and problem solving methods they've learned during their stay at the BPN.'
23. Higgins, 'Thought and Action', 37–47.
24. Mackie, 'In Memoriam: Professor Benjamin Higgins', 183–8.
25. Webster, *Fire*, 78–9.
26. Edgar McVoy was also famous for introducing the Training Within Industry management programme to Indonesia. He had previously introduced the TWI programme to Japan and Malaya. See Robinson and Schroeder, 'The US TWI Program', 35–56.
27. Feith, *The Decline of Constitutional Democracy*, 130.
28. Webster, *Fire and the Full Moon. Canada and Indonesia in a decolonizing world*, 80–1. 'PSI policies were "remarkably similar" to those being developed by the national CCF in the same period.' The CCF being the Co-Operative Commonwealth Federation of government in Saskatchewan, Canada, which relied on social-democratic planning.
29. ANRI, Departemen Keuangan 1950–69, 294.
30. Webster, *Fire and the Full Moon*, 84.
31. Higgins and Higgins, *Indonesia: The Crisis of the Millstone*, 88.
32. Higgins, 'The Indonesia Project of the Massachusetts Institute of Technology', 151–4.
33. Ibid., 155–7.
34. Whose focus on investment and the big development aid push had become the main target for Communist attack in Indonesia, who re-named it Sumitro's economic ideas. For more on the Harrod-Domar model in relation to aid see Fei and Paauw, 'Foreign Assistance and Self-Help', 251–67.
35. Taffet, *Foreign Aid as Foreign Policy*, 20.
36. Gilman, *Mandarins of the Future*, 115–202.
37. Quoted in Simpson, *Economists with Guns*, 18.
38. Abdulgani, *Beberapa soal demokrasi dan ekonomi*, 36.
39. Abdulgani, 'The Lessons of Indonesia's Experience of Planning', 159.
40. Soemardjan, 'The Changing Role', 114. The particular attack against the Economics Faculty of the University of Indonesia after the PRRI Rebellion and Sumitro's role was directed by the leftist element and President Sukarno. Its relationship with Berkeley and the Ford Foundation made it an even easier target. Bresnan, *At Home Abroad*, 41.

41. Abdulgani, *Sosialisme Indonesia*, 63, 'Berbeda dengan dewan2 perantjang dan pembangunan jang dulu2, jang menitik-beratkan keanggautaannja kepada para intelek-ahli dan intelek-expert, maka Depernas mengutamakan keanggautaannja untuk golongan2 karya jang berakar dimasjarakat dan ditengah-tengah rakjat tanpa mengabaikan nasehat dan pendapat para ahli dan para expert.'
42. Ibid., '...seorang jang berpendidikan umum, dan berpandangan luas serta djauh kemuka, jang mungkin tidak ada atau belum gespecialiseerd, tetapi tidak kena tularan kesempitan pandangan dari penjakit birokrasi modern.'
43. 'Dengan terbentuknja Dewan Perantjang Nasional kita memasuki taraf baru dalam tata-tjara pembangunan negara dan bangsa. Ini berarti, bahwa pengalaman dimasa jang lalu dengan pembuatan rentjana pembangunan tidak boleh terulang lagi satu plan pembangunan jang tidak mendjadi plannja massa, tapi hanja merupakan satu plan akademis belaka jang tidak dipahami oleh sebagian besar Rakjat Indonesia', in *Rantjangan. Buku ke I, Pokok2 Pembangunan Nasional Semesta Berentjana, Djilid I: Pendahuluan*, 56.
44. Hindley, *The Communist Party*, 183–4.
45. *Tuantanah, lintah-darat, tukang idjon, tengkulak djahat, kapitalis birokrat, penguasa djahat* and village bandits.
46. Aidit, *Pemetjahan*, 4, 'Sudah terlalu lama kaum sardjana ekonomi Indonesia pada umumnja mengambil sikap masa-bodoh terhadap masalah politik dan berusaha membahas masalah ekonomi sebagai masalah jang bersifat teknis melulu, dengan hukum-hukum "jang berlaku untuk semua zaman" jang bertolak dari pandangan-pandangan subjektif dan mengabaikan kenjataan objektif jang hidup didalam masjarakat.'
47. Ibid., 12. 'The most significant contributor to this evil analysis is Sumitro, a person that is famous and well known to be rebellious and traitorous to the Republic, but equally traitorous and heinous economic theories has not yet been properly disrobed and is given an important place in our universities and still color the thinking of the officers that man our economic policy apparatuses.'
48. Sadli, '20 tahun perkembangan', 184.
49. 'Laporan tahunan Lembaga Ekonomi', 12–5.
50. Rifai, *Perkembangan perguruan tinggi selama 20 tahun*, 24.
51. Sadli, 'Masalah penentuan roduksi dan masalah bentuk perusahaan dalam sistim sosialisme Indonesia', 107–8.
52. Panglaykim, 'Beberapa aspek struktur management', 126–296.
53. Ismunandar and Soehardiman, 'Isi laporan "team study group"', 261–381.
54. Ismael, 'Beberapa aspek institusionil', 130. 'In Indonesia the National Overall Development Plan has become a reality. Various projects will be built throughout the regions, some are not yet explicitly detailed, others will be built complementary to other projects. As a result, the National Overall Development Plan functions as an index in the initial phase similar to Russia's

Gosplan development plan, all of which in the end would form an integrated regional development plan.'

55. Sadli, 'Beberapa segi masalah pembangunan daerah di Indonesia', 97. 'Pembangunan daerah djuga merupakan suatu 'ideological commitment' dari sosialisme, setidak2nja sosialisme seperti jang diamalkan dalam negeri2 jang dewasa ini diperintah oleh kaum komunis.'
56. Ibid., 94. 'Bagi seorang sardjana ekonomi masalah demikian merupakan suatu "gewetensvraag", artinja haruskah ia mentjari suatu "justification" untuk penjimpangan2 dari resource allocation menurut pertimbangan2 ekonomi jang murni sedemikian rupa sehingga achirnja keputusan2 ini dapat dipertanggung-djawabkan djuga dari segi ekonomi? Ataukah ia harus bersikap bahwa penjimpangan2 ini sebetulnja tidak dapat diharapkan kefaedahan ekonominja tetapi harus diterima sebagai bagian dari "social costs of economic development", jakni jang bersifat "waste" (tetapi "necessary waste").'
57. Ibid., 118–9. 'The military men of the present have power over a wide area. Although they admit to the importance of regional development, they are often unable to collect the funds and forces needed to start this development. Even so, because they are the most powerful group at the present, their potential to play as a role of development leadership is great. Of course, the mental capabilities and understanding, the tools and will power must be attended to. At the moment and as was the case in the last couple of years, they occupied a dubious position. They are in charge of security but not in direct charge of welfare. But increasingly there have been greater realization amongst them that regional security cannot be separated from the welfare of the people and that this cannot be separated from economic development. Thus, lately they have been more responsible to the welfare and wealth of the region. Security is a complex issue and is not purely a military or police problem. If the problem of security has become such a complex issue then everyone is responsible for the general welfare; even in time of military law (SOB), it is not purely the responsibility of the military, as it is not purely the responsibility of civilian during peace times. It requires a collective sense of responsibility, at least between the military and civilian groups on the matter of security, welfare and economic development. Does that mean that the military and civilian, the green and white shirts become pioneers of regional development? The concept of such leadership is autocratic and may not be effective in the long run, but such an autocratic approach may be strong enough to create a momentum to kick start development.'
58. Sadli, 'Mohammad Sadli', 125. Sadli also published a book at CENIS titled *The Influence of the Military on Economic Development: An Analysis Drawn Mainly from Indonesian Experience.*
59. Reeve, *Golkar of Indonesia*, 190.
60. Adjie, 'TNI dan Civic Mission', 13.
61. Prawiro, *Indonesia's Struggle*, 1–13.

14

The Constraints of Economic Nationalism in Early Independent Indonesia, 1945–60

Pham van Thuy

'Branches of production, which are important to the state and which affect the life of most people, shall be controlled by the state; Land and water and the natural riches therein shall be controlled by the state and shall be exploited for the greatest welfare of the people.'[1] This passage forms part of Article 33 of the first Constitution of the Republic of Indonesia, promulgated on 18 August 1945, a day after Sukarno's proclamation of independence. It strongly stressed the importance of state control of the economy, aiming at the prosperity of the Indonesian people. The return of the Dutch to the archipelago and their frequent military threats on the Republic's territories in Java and Sumatra, however, restrained the newly established government from implementing Article 33 of the Constitution. Economic targets took a back seat and were subordinated to the political aspirations and independence. The strategy of the Indonesian government in the late 1940s was to accept foreign control over large segments of the economy in order to secure political independence.[2] It is true that economic concessions made by the Indonesian delegation at the Round Table Conference in The Hague were important factors leading to the Dutch agreement of transfer of sovereignty to Indonesia on 27 December 1949.[3]

With the Round Table Conference agreement, Indonesia at long last obtained political independence from the Netherlands. Now, 'the economic side of the Indonesian revolution has yet to begin', declared Haji Agus Salim, a leading figure of the Indonesian nationalist movement.[4] What happened in the Indonesian economy in the early 1950s must have frustrated Haji Agus Salim and other Indonesian radical nationalists. Very little change occurred in the structure of the national economy; Dutch firms still dominated the most important elements, especially the modern sectors. In 1952, for instance, four leading Dutch trading firms handled 50 per cent of all consumer imports, whereas eight firms controlled 60 per cent of all exports, excluding copra, tin and cinchona.[5] Private banking was largely in the hands of seven foreign banks, of which three were Dutch, three Chinese and one British-owned.[6] By the mid-1950s, Dutch control of the Indonesian economy remained largely intact.[7] Before the Indonesian takeover of Dutch firms in late 1957, it was estimated that about 50 per cent of all estate acreage remained in Dutch ownership and 60 per cent of Indonesia's foreign trade was still Dutch controlled.[8]

The continuing domination of Dutch capital in independent Indonesia has been largely attributed to Indonesian pragmatic leaders who controlled the government in the late 1940s and early 1950s.[9] Believing that an immediate dismantling of the former structure of colonial and capitalist economy would cause economic dislocation and hardship, leaders of the successive Indonesian cabinets in the early 1950s retained the operations of foreign companies in the country.[10] Foreign companies were required to provide the training to Indonesian employees, and capital and technical assistance for the government's projects. Results from attempted co-operation with the Dutch were disappointing, however, adding fuel to the social tensions in Indonesia in the mid-1950s. Anti-Dutch resentments culminated in December 1957 with the takeover of almost all Dutch-owned companies by the Indonesian labour unions, then by the army. Surprisingly, it took a year for the Indonesian government to finally decide on the nationalization of all Dutch enterprises.

What restrained the Indonesian government from ending Dutch economic domination immediately after independence? How did the Indonesian government carry out the pragmatic economic policies in the early 1950s? And, to what extent did these policies support the targets of Indonesian economic nationalism? These are the main questions addressed in this chapter. Without downgrading the importance of the nationalist struggle for independence in the late 1940s and the political strife in the early 1950s, which certainly had a strong impact on the economic decision-making in Indonesia, this chapter nevertheless only concentrates on the economic factors. Two major concepts are used: *Indonesianisasi* and Indonesian economic nationalism. Whereas the former refers to 'a conscious effort to increase the participation and elevate the role of the Indonesian and more particularly the "indigenous" Indonesian in the more complex sectors of the economy',[11] the latter is understood as 'efforts by the Indonesian government to transfer property, or more correctly: productive assets owned by foreigners or foreign businesses, to indigenous Indonesians'.[12]

Legacies of Dutch Colonialism

The immediate factor affecting the Indonesian government's economic policy in the early 1950s was the provisions that the Indonesian delegation signed with the Dutch at the Round Table Conference. In the Financial Economic Agreement (Finec), Indonesian leaders agreed that the Dutch could continue businesses in Indonesia as usual, including the remittance of the profits. There was an obligation for the Indonesian government to consult with the Netherlands on monetary and financial policies likely to have an impact on Dutch economic interests. Nationalization of Dutch enterprises was only permitted if it was essential to Indonesia's national interest and if both parties agreed. The amount of compensation would be determined by a judge on the basis of the actual worth of the nationalized enterprises.[13]

The new nation was forced to take over 4.5 billion guilders (or US $1.13 billion) of the public debt incurred by the Netherlands Indies government to the Netherlands. This amount comprised the entire internal debt of the colonial government of 3 billion guilders and 1.5 billion of external floating debts.[14] The debt ran with an interest rate of 3 per cent per year and, as long as this debt was not fully paid off, the Dutch government had the right to interfere in the Indonesian economic policy.[15] In addition, the Indonesian government was obliged to maintain for two years at European pay scales the positions of 17,000 Dutch officials.[16] It is widely acknowledged that Indonesia paid a high price for independence. No other former colony had to shoulder such a heavy burden as Indonesia from its former colonial ruler.[17]

While under constraints imposed by Finec, Indonesian economic policy-makers had to confront difficult economic conditions in the country after independence. During almost a decade of Japanese occupation and armed struggles against the Dutch, the Indonesian economy had seriously deteriorated. The oilfield areas of Tarakan and Balikpapan in Borneo and Morotai and parts of New Guinea had been targets of Allied attacks during the Second World War. In Java and Sumatra, Allied air strikes caused the sinking of most of the modern inter-island shipping fleets.[18] An estimate by A. Fruin immediately after the war reveals that Indonesia needed at least 2.2 billion guilders (US $800 million) to be able to restore the pre-war economic condition.[19] The four years of armed confrontations between returning Dutch colonial forces and Indonesian revolutionary troops caused additional infrastructural damages and human dislocation. In 1951, for instance, 130 of the existing 134 textile plants in East Java were not operating. In Palembang, seven rubber re-milling plants, employing 5,000 workers, were still shut down. Transport bottlenecks caused the cement factory in Padang to work at only one-third of its capacity.[20]

In the face of difficulties in economic conditions after independence, it was plausible that Indonesian pragmatic leaders gave priorities to economic rehabilitation and stability, rather than economic nationalism. Moreover, in accordance to agreements signed at the Round Table Conference, from early 1950, the Indonesian government started returning agricultural estates and factories, which were seized from the Japanese during the revolution, to their former owners, mostly Dutch.[21] The government also encouraged the continued operations of public services such as local transport and water, gas and electricity, most of which were managed by private enterprises with Dutch owners. In early August 1950, the ANIEM (Algemeene Nederlandsche-Indische Electriciteits-Maatschappij, General Netherlands Indies Electricity Company) and the OGEM (Overzeese Gas-en Electriciteits Maatschappij, Overseas Gas and Electricity Company), the two largest distributors of electricity, accounting for 70 per cent of Indonesia's electrical power distribution, raised their charges by 58 and 48 per cent respectively.[22] The arduous challenge for the Indonesian government was to restore production and employment while ensuring the interests of the Indonesian people before capitalist exploitation by Dutch corporate firms.

Capital and Personnel

The explanations given by pragmatic leaders as to the government's policy to allow the continued operations of Dutch firms in the country often stressed Indonesia's acute lack of capital and skilled personnel. As pointed out by Wilopo, minister of labour in the Hatta cabinet (December 1949–August 1950) and then prime minister (April 1952–June 1953), independent Indonesia faced severe shortages of experts, especially in management, but also outside the economic field. By his calculation, the total number of civil, electrical and other engineers available in Indonesia by July 1950 was no more than 90, whereas at least 4,000 were actually needed. The number of medical doctors, some 1,500, was more favourable, but still far below the minimum of 5,000 required for a total population of more than 70 million.[23]

In the field of government services, the lack of trained personnel was even more critical. A survey of educational backgrounds of Indonesian policy-makers from independence in 1945 to July 1955 reveals that less than one-fifth of the members of parliament were fully trained graduates and almost one-tenth had no more than a primary certificate.[24] Only slightly more than half of the ministers were graduates. The number of civil servants who acquired university certificate was relatively high with 87 per cent, of which 67 per cent were fully trained (Table 14.1). This was a result of the government policy to retain the professional groups of the former colonial authorities. In fact, over one-third of the ministers, about one-third of the members of parliament, and three-fifths of the highest-level civil servants were civil servants before the Second World War.[25] Efforts of the Indonesian government to improve the national education in general and technical training in particular during the 1950s

Table 14.1: Educational level of Indonesian political decision-makers (percentages)

Educational Level Attained	*Cabinet Members*	*Members of Parliament*	*Highest Level Civil Servants*
University	68	27	87
Fully Trained	58	19	67
Partially Trained	10	8	20
Secondary	32	64	13
Senior Certificate	15	32	13
Junior Certificate	17	32	0
Primary Certificate	0	9	0
Total	100 (n = 146)	100 (n = 234)	100 (n = 160)

Source: Soelaeman, *Some Aspects of the Social Origin of Indonesian Political Decision Makers*, 342.

had positive results. By 1959, at the departure of most of the Dutch technicians, Indonesia had organized 248 engineering training organizations with no less than 4,000 teachers.[26]

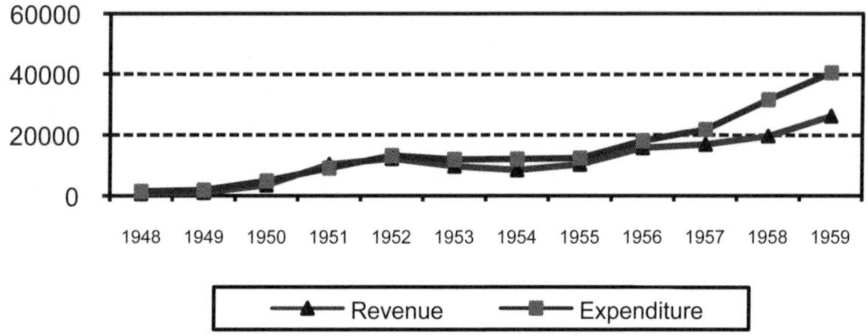

Source: Table 14.2.

Figure 14.1: Revenues and expenditures of the Indonesian government, 1948–59 (million rupiahs)

After independence, Indonesia had a dire shortage of funds. In June 1950, Prime Minister Hatta explained that it was not possible to undertake any nationalization since the government did not have money and was still borrowing from abroad. He stressed that the state budgetary deficit was already high, at 1.5 billion rupiahs.[27] Based on the reports of the Java Bank (later Bank Indonesia), we observe that the republic government indeed experienced a high deficit during the revolution. After the transfer of sovereignty, the deficit was excessively enlarged. Except for one single year, 1951, when the Indonesian government pocketed a budget surplus of 1.2 billion rupiahs as a result of rising revenues from the 'Korean War boom', the deficit greatly expanded during the 1950s, climbing to almost 4 billion rupiahs in 1954 and 15 billion by 1959 (Figure 14.1, Table 14.2). Furthermore, part of the annual budget (5–10 per cent) was reserved to pay debt to the Netherlands.[28] In 1950, the

Table 14.2: Revenue and expenditure of the Indonesian government, 1948–59 (million rupiahs)

	1948	*1949*	*1950*	*1951*	*1952*	*1953*	*1954*	*1955*	*1956*	*1957*	*1958*	*1959*
Revenue	674	1,054	3,517	10,303	12,210	9,707	8,467	10,307	15,733	16,873	19,656	26,322
Expenditure	1,489	1,893	4,901	9,108	13,192	11,947	12,069	12,397	18,031	21,912	31,696	40,602

Source: De Javasche Bank 1950/51, 1952/53; Bank Indonesia 1954/55, 1956/57, 1958/59, 1959/60.

United States granted Indonesia US $100 million, but $60 million was transferred to the Dutch banks.[29] By the time the Harahap cabinet (August 1955–March 1956) abrogated the Finec in February 1956, all but 18 per cent of the 4.5 billion guilders of debt had been paid.[30]

Indonesianisasi and Industrialization

While the presence of foreign capital in the country was considered temporarily inevitable, the Indonesian government's strategy was to promote economic strength of the Indonesians to counter the domination of Dutch and Chinese enterprises. Developing industries and a strong national business class were the main targets in the early 1950s. In an article 'Building up a national economy' published in July 1950, Minister of Prosperity Djuanda stated that 'there is plenty of opportunity for many more branches of industry and for new trading enterprises without interfering with established interests'.[31] This idea was incorporated into an Economic Urgency Program (*Rentjana Urgensi Perekonomian*) or often called the Sumitro Plan. The plan was drafted by Sumitro Djojohadikusumo, minister of trade and industry in the Natsir cabinet (September 1950–March 1951).

The Sumitro Plan was announced in April 1950 under the Wilopo cabinet, where Sumitro served as minister of finance. Its general objective was to increase the economic strength of the Indonesian people by industrialization.[32] Activities embraced credits to small-scale industry, central production and processing units (*induk*) in rural regional centres, and large industrial plants in vital sectors of the economy. All projects were operated under government sponsorship through its agencies. Foreign capital and private Indonesians were allowed to participate in the plan, but under the condition that the government had a dominant control of key industries.[33] This was to be assured by government participation of at least 50 per cent of the capital and two-thirds of preference shares and the control of a majority on the board of directors. Foreigners would serve under management contracts to provide technical assistance and train Indonesians for leading positions in the enterprises.[34]

The Sumitro Plan consisted of short-term projects, to be completed by the end of 1952, connected with the establishment of a wide range of plants for printing, rubber remilling, cement, tyres and textiles. Long-term projects concerned the construction of eleven factories, manufacturing caustic soda, manure, aluminum, iron smelting, plywood, paper, glass, knitting, spinning, tannic acid and coconut flour. The provisional total

Table 14.3: Total cost of the 'Sumitro Plan' (rupiahs)

	1951	*1952*	*After 1952*	*Total*
Laboratories and Institutes	Rp. 3.814.000	Rp. 3.814.000	Rp. 1.552.000	Rp. 7.813.000
Central Production Units	Rp. 14.462.900	Rp. 12.504.100	p.m.	Rp. 26.967.000
Small Industries	Rp. 66.470.500	Rp. 59.500.000	p.m.	Rp.125.970.000
Large-scale Industries (short term)	Rp.106.685.000	Rp. 72.000.000	p.m.	Rp.178.685.000
Large-scale Industries (long term)	p.m.	p.m.	Rp.522.230.000	Rp.522.230.000
Total	Rp.191.432.4000	Rp.147.431.100	Rp.523.782.000	Rp.861.665.500

Source: *Indonesian Review* 1 (1951): 189.

cost of the Sumitro Plan was 861.6 million rupiahs, two-thirds of which was intended for large-scale industries (Table 14.3).

The Sumitro Plan was executed when Indonesia was in extremely short supply of capital. The peak of the 'Korean War boom' had passed by mid-1951 and Indonesia's exports began to decline. Under those circumstances, only projects for supporting small-scale industries, not requiring large investment or skilled labour, could be fully financed. The results of projects for large-scale industries were very disappointing. Only two of the proposed seven remilling factories had been completed by late 1954, and even they were not actually in operation due to the difficulties in finding qualified Indonesian personnel.[35] Little money went into production centres and research and training.[36] Targets were reformulated in the context of the Five Year Development Plan for the years 1956–60. Priority was given to financial support of three major industrial projects, namely the Gresik cement factory, a caustic soda factory in Waru and a cotton-spinning plant in Cilacap in South Java.[37]

The disappointing performance of industrialization in Indonesia also resulted from Dutch hesitance to co-operate with the Indonesian government. Most efforts of the Indonesian government to collaborate with Dutch capital in creating joint enterprises failed, except in aviation. In March 1950, Garuda Indonesian Airways was founded on the basis of a 51:49 shared ownership between the Indonesian government and the national Dutch carrier KLM (Koninklijke Luchtvaart Maatschappij, Royal Dutch Airlines). KLM was required to train Indonesian staff and gradually transfer ownership to Indonesian hands. The contract was made for thirty years with the possibility of nationalization of the aviation within ten years.[38] However, in 1954, Garuda was transformed into a fully state-owned enterprise with the role of KLM limited to providing technical assistance.[39]

The Indonesian government had a specific policy to promote economic strength of indigenous Indonesians by discrimination, namely the Benteng policy. *Benteng* (literally 'fortress') referred to categories of goods that the government reserved for Indonesian importers.[40] In general, the government controlled 60 per cent of total exports. Part of this sum was reserved for highly privileged consumers, such as government institutions, health centres and industrialization; the rest was for the Benteng importers.[41] It is important to note that only ethnic Indonesians were eligible to participate in the Benteng groups. In the views of Indonesian leaders, they were referred to as 'economically weak groups', who were entitled to the government's protection.[42] These protective measures gained results from March 1951, when the Sukiman cabinet (April 1951–February 1952) used foreign exchange certificates as import licenses to monitor imports. A substantial part of the import licenses were reserved for Indonesian indigenous importers. In 1952, 43 per cent of all foreign exchange was allocated to indigenous Indonesian importers, as compared with European firms (31 per cent) and Chinese traders (26 per cent).[43] The number of Benteng importers rose from 250 by the end of 1950 to 741 in April 1952.[44] During the early years of the first Ali Sastroamidjojo cabinet, when the Benteng policy was carried out most aggressively, the number of national trading firms rose to at least 2,111 and possibly 4,000 to 5,000. The percentage of total exchange allocations for imports to national importers increased to 37.9 per cent in 1953 to 80 and 90 per cent in late 1954.[45]

Like what happened to the industrialization efforts, the shortage of capable Indonesian entrepreneurs frustrated the Benteng programme. A large number of persons involved in importing business had no previous commercial experience. The new national companies were frequently *importir aktentas* (briefcase firms), which existed by reselling licences to foreign and Chinese establishments.[46] In early 1955, the head of the Central Import Office estimated that only fifty of the many national importing firms were bona fide establishments, with another 200 concerns on the borderline. About 80 per cent of all licences, which had allocated to national importers, were in fact sold on to non-indigenous traders.[47] Efforts to rationalize the Benteng policy were carried out by the rescreening of persons, who had been accredited as national importers. In the Harahap cabinet, the Benteng was abolished. All businessmen who were citizens of Indonesia, regardless of ethnic origin, were given the same priority.[48]

Efforts to elevate the position of the Indonesians within the Dutch companies also did not obtain satisfactory results. Dutch companies were reluctant to promote Indonesian employees to higher-ranking management positions. They routinely stated that there were not enough qualified Indonesians to replace European expatriates.[49] In order to speed up Indonesianization of Dutch enterprises, in 1952 the Indonesian government introduced immigration quotas, restricting the entry of expatriates from the Netherlands. The number of work permits issued to the Dutch was drastically reduced.[50] As a result, Dutch companies were forced to employ Indonesians to fill the positions vacated by the Dutch, mostly in the lower and middle ranks. In large firms, new positions with relatively high functionaries were created, such as *Staf Indonesia* (Indonesian Staff) in the trading firm Internatio and *mandur* (foremen) in the Dutch Estate Company Oud-Djember (Maatschappij Oud-Djember).[51] These efforts, however, failed to satisfy Indonesia's aspirations. The positions vacated by the Dutch were often taken over by Chinese Indonesians rather than indigenous employees. Moreover, the top management remained exclusively in Dutch hands.[52]

Economic Nationalism

Although priority was given to moderate measures to promote the economic strength and capability of the Indonesians, many attempts were also made by the Indonesian government to seize control and ownership of foreign businesses vital to the national economy. Banking and public utilities were under the strongest pressures. By introducing the new exchange certificate system and a 'monetary purge' in March 1950, the Indonesian government gained significant control of currency. However, the issuing of the official currency, the rupiah, was still in the hands of the Java Bank.[53] Attempts to gain full control of financial policy led to the nationalization of the Java Bank in late 1951. The bank's total capital of 25 million rupiahs was fully paid by the Indonesian government. In 1953, the name of the bank was changed to Bank Indonesia but its primary function as the nation's central bank remained. Sjafruddin Prawiranegara became the bank's first Indonesian governor. It was decided by law that from now on, only Indonesian citizens could sit on the board of managers.[54]

Nationalization also involved public utilities and a number of mines and estates owned by Dutch private corporate firms. According to a report by the Board for Financial Supervision (Dewan Pengawas Keuangan), by the end of 1951 the Indonesian government had obtained a leading share in the Bandung Public Electric Company (73 per cent) and the Surakarta Mineral Water Company (60 per cent), along with the Billiton Mining Company (62.5 per cent) and the Java Private Land Company (75 per cent). In September 1950, the PEPUSKA (Penguasaan Pusat Kapal-Kapal, Central Shipping Foundation) was established, which bought up six large Dutch ships and several smaller ones operating in east Indonesia.[55] The activities of PEPUSKA anticipated the establishment of the PELNI (Pelajaran Nasional Indonesia, Indonesian National Shipping Company) in May 1952. The objective of the PELNI was to wrest control of inter-island shipping from the Dutch KPM (Koninklijk Paketvaart Maatschappij, Royal Packet Company). Due to the lack of expertise in leadership, the operations of the PELNI were not efficient and would never be in a position to challenge the KPM until the takeover of December 1957.[56]

In March 1953, the Indonesian government took over the exploitation of the BVM (Bataviasche Verkeers Maatschappij, Batavian Transport Company). In January 1954, the company was transformed into the state-owned Perusahaan Pengangkutan Djakarta (Jakarta Transport Company). The Indonesian government was required to pay 4 million rupiahs to the Dutch owners.[57] Several branches of OGEM and ANIEM were also brought under the control of the Indonesian government in 1954. The Dutch owners received 15 million rupiahs, far less than their original demand of 52 million.[58] The government had a plan to buy Fuchs & Rens, the main Dutch manufacturer of trains and cars, which owned four assembling plants in Indonesia. The estimated cost was 1.5 billion guilders, payable within five years until 1959.[59] Nevertheless, due to the shortage of funds, no further nationalization of Dutch enterprises, including Fuchs & Rens, was executed during 1956 and 1957.

While all efforts to wrest the economic power from the Dutch had reached an impasse by the mid-1950s, the Harahap cabinet unilaterally abrogated the Round Table Conference agreement. This action was followed by significant changes in the economic leadership as well as the decision-making of Indonesia. In March 1956, Ali Sastroamidjojo, who had sponsored the Benteng programme, returned to cabinet leadership. In May 1956, the cabinet decided not to return the oil installations in North Sumatra to the Dutch—British BPM (Bataafsche Petroleum Maatschappij, Batavian Petroleum Company).[60] Instead, an army-controlled company, Eksploitasi Tambang Minjak Sumatera Utara (North Sumatra Oil Extraction Company), was established, which took control of oilfields in North Sumatra.[61] Attitudes towards Dutch enterprises hardened after the resignation of a leading figure of the pragmatic group, Vice-President Hatta, in December 1956. In March 1957, President Sukarno declared martial law, placing the country under control of the armed forces.[62]

Soon after the introduction of martial law, the military had some sort of preparation for a takeover of the economy. On 24 August 1957, the Ministry of Defence gave an instruction, identifying economic institutions to be under military control.[63] However, while measures for the takeover were being discussed, on 3 December 1957, the trade union of the KPM shipping company took over the head office of the company in Jakarta, marking the beginning of a far-reaching wave of the takeover of Dutch enterprises.[64] During the next few days, a series of Dutch firms were occupied, including three Dutch banks (Escomptobank, Nationale Handelsbank and Cultuurbank) and the 'Big Five' (Borsumij, Geoffrey Wehry, Internatio, Jacobson van den Berg and Lindeteves). By the time the Indonesian government issued an order on 13 December 1957, forbidding further takeover, more than 700 Dutch-owned companies had been seized.[65] The legal status of these enterprises remained in limbo until December 1958, when the Indonesian government officially announced the nationalization of all Dutch-owned enterprises operating within the territory of the Republic of Indonesia.[66] The BPM oil company and Unilever escaped the takeover and nationalization in view of their combined Anglo-Dutch ownership.[67]

Conclusion

The law on the nationalization of Dutch-owned enterprises issued on 27 December 1958 in Indonesia officially ended the fundamental dilemma in the economic thinking of Indonesian nationalist leaders since independence—between the demand of having an independent national economy corresponding to the political independence, and the necessity of retaining Dutch and other foreign capital in the country for the purpose of economic stability and development. Bound by agreements signed at the Round Table Conference, and in the face of economic difficulties of a newly independent country—especially the acute shortage of capital, experts and skilled employees—successive cabinets of Indonesia in the late 1940s and for the most part of the 1950s reluctantly accepted the continued operations of the Dutch and other foreign firms in the country. Attempts to reduce the foreign control of the economy were channelled through pragmatic programmes to promote the national industries, the economic strength and capability of the Indonesians, along with the voluntary nationalization of a number of enterprises vital to the national economy. The apparent failure of these moderate measures to satisfy the Indonesian desire of economic nationalism was one of many reasons leading to the anti-Dutch sentiments in the late 1950s and eventually the takeovers of Dutch-owned firms in December 1957.

It is noted that these takeovers were initially unauthorized by the Indonesian government. The economic situation in the late 1950s shows no significant improvements, given the aggravated deficit and the weakness of the indigenous entrepreneurs. Despite anti-Dutch actions, the Harahap cabinet and second Ali cabinet (March 1956–March 1957) did not express a desire to confiscate or nationalize Dutch companies. The Djuanda (April 1957–July 1959) cabinet also took a fairly moderate approach towards Dutch-owned enterprises.[68] It was only after the Dutch firms had fallen into the hands of the army and trade unions that the government stepped in and assumed control of the seized enterprises. The subsequent re-enactment of the Constitution of 1945, and the official declaration of guided democracy and guided economy in July 1959, reaffirmed the entrenched position of the state in the Indonesian economy. Most former Dutch firms were subsequently converted into state-owned enterprises, which also actively participated in the takeover of the Chinese, British and American enterprises in the early 1960s.

Primary Sources

National Archives of the Republic of Indonesia, Jakarta (ANRI)
- Archives of the Cabinet President of the Republic of Indonesia (KP).

Notes

1. English translation of the Constitution published in *The Voice of Free Indonesia* 1 (1945): 24–6; For the original version, see: *Berita Repoeblik Indonesia*, 15 February 1946.
2. Lindblad, *Bridges to New Business*, 57.
3. Anak Agung Gde Agung, *Twenty Years Indonesian Foreign Policy*, 65–70; Ricklefs, *A History of Modern Indonesia*, 284–5.
4. Higgins, *Indonesia's Stabilization*, 102.

5. Meek, *The Government and Economic Development*, 168; Higgins, *All the Difference*, 168.
6. De Javasche Bank, *Laporan tahun pembukunan 1949/1950*, 43–4; Meek, *The Government and Economic Development*, 164.
7. Lindblad, *Bridges to New Business*, 218; Dick et al., *The Emergence of a National Economy*, 182–4.
8. Golay et al., *Underdevelopment and Economic Nationalism*, 180.
9. The four most influential economic policy-makers in Indonesia in the 1950s were Sumitro Djojohadikusumo, Sjafruddin Prawiranegara, Mohammad Hatta and Djuanda Kartawidjaja. Thee Kian Wie, 'The Debate on Economic Policy', 39.
10. Glassburner, 'Economic Policy-making', 71–3; Dick et al., *The Emergence of a National Economy*, 172.
11. The term *Indonesianisasi* (literally translated as Indonesianization) was first coined by an American political scientist John Sutter in his PhD dissertation defended at the University of Cornell in 1959. The thesis is about the political economy of Indonesia between 1940 and 1954, in which the author discussed various forms of *Indonesianisasi*. Sutter, *Indonesianisasi: A Historical Survey of the Role of Politics*, 2.
12. Thee Kian Wie, 'Indonesianization: Economic Aspects of Decolonization', 19–20. However, it seems that Thee Kian Wie identifies *Indonesianisasi* with Indonesian economic nationalism. The article discusses Indonesianization, but he takes Johnson's definition of economic nationalism as the conceptual framework of the analysis.
13. Dick et al., *The Emergence of a National Economy*, 171.
14. Meijer, *Den Haag-Djakarta*, 536; Clerx, 'De Financiële verhouding', 65; Lindblad, *Bridges to New Business*, 74.
15. Kahin, 'Some Recollections from and Reflections on the Indonesian Revolution', 26.
16. Meijer, *Den Haag-Djakarta*, 196, 536; Dick et al., *The Emergence of a National Economy*, 171.
17. Thee Kian Wie, 'Indonesianization: Economic Aspects of Decolonization', 21; Lindblad, *Bridges to New Business*, 71.
18. Dick et al., *The Emergence of a National Economy*, 168; Dick, *Indonesian Interisland Shipping Industry*, 12.
19. Fruin, *Het Economische aspect*, 47.
20. *Indonesian Review* 4 (1951): 293.
21. Sutter, *Indonesianisasi: A Historical Survey of the Role of Politics*, 696–7.
22. Golay et al., *Underdevelopment and Economic Nationalism*, 144–5; *Indonesian Review* 1 (1951): 71–2.
23. *Indonesian Review* 3 (1950): 14.
24. The date refers to the fall of the first Ali Sastroamidjojo cabinet (July 1953–July 1955).

25. Soelaeman, *Some Aspects of the Social Origin of Indonesian Political Decision Makers*, 345–6.
26. *Berita Indonesia*, 15 November 1959.
27. *Ichtisar Parlemen* 1 (1950): 253–4.
28. *Indonesian Review* 1 (1951): 77.
29. ANRI, Letter of 20 September 1956 about economic co-operation with the United States, KP, 557.
30. Meijer, *Den Haag-Djakarta*, 536; Thee Kian Wie, 'Indonesianization: Economic Aspects of Decolonization', 21.
31. *Indonesian Review* 1 (1950): 8–10.
32. Sumitro, *The Government's Program*, 3.
33. Vital enterprises were specified in the Plan as defense plants, chemical industries, cement plants, power plants, waterworks, and transport enterprises.
34. Sumitro, *The Government's Program*, 186.
35. Sutter, *Indonesianisasi: A Historical Survey of the Role of Politics*, 777.
36. Sumitro, *The Government's Program*, 11.
37. Lindblad, *Bridges to New Business*, 81. For the summary of the Indonesian five year plan (1956–60), see: Paauw, *Financing Economic Development*, 363–92.
38. *Indonesian Review* 1 (1950): 78; Sutter, *Indonesianisasi: A Historical Survey of the Role of Politics*, 894–9.
39. Lindblad, *Bridges to New Business*, 113–5; Thee Kian Wie, 'Indonesianization: Economic Aspects of Decolonization', 26; Daan Marks, 'The Lost Decades?', 85.
40. Mackie, 'The Indonesian Economy', 47–8; Thee Kian Wie, *Recollections: The Indonesian Economy*, 59; Robison, *Indonesia: The Rise of Capital*, 44–6.
41. ANRI, Letter of Dr. Hjalmat Schacht to President of the Republic of Indonesia concerning the problem of economy and finance, 26 October 1951, KP, 262.
42. According to Article 11 of the Finec, the Indonesian government had the right to make regulations necessary to safeguard national interest and protect economically weak groups.
43. Lindblad, *Bridges to New Business*, 131.
44. Sutter, *Indonesianisasi: A Historical Survey of the Role of Politics*, 1021.
45. Feith, *The Decline of Constitutional Democracy*, 9; Bondan, *Nasionalisasi Perusahaan Belanda di Indonesia*, 9.
46. Golay et al., *Underdevelopment and Economic Nationalism*, 171; Thee Kian Wie, 'Indonesianization: Economic Aspects of Decolonization', 32–3; Bondan, *Nasionalisasi Perusahaan Belanda di Indonesia*, 14–5.
47. Amstutz, *The Development of Indigenous Indonesian Importers*, 144.
48. Sutter, *Indonesianisasi: A Historical Survey of the Role of Politics*, 1027; Thee Kian Wie, 'Indonesianization: Economic Aspects of Decolonization', 32–3.

49. Meijer, *Den Haag-Djakarta*, 352; Van de Kerkhof, '"Colonial" Enterprise', 180.
50. Lindblad, *Bridges to New Business*, 167.
51. Van de Kerkhof, '"Colonial" Enterprise', 182; Van de Kerkhof, 'Indonesianisasi of Dutch Economic Interests', 196.
52. Van de Kerkhof, '"Colonial" Enterprise', 183.
53. In the new exchange certificate system, exporters and importers were required to made transactions in the Indonesian currency, the rupiah. In effect, this system allowed the government to reduce the official exchange rate of the Indonesian rupiah from 1:1 to 1:3 to the Dutch guilder. In the monetary reform, it was stipulated that all bank notes with denominations higher than 2.50 guilders were cut in half, one half to be exchanged for a new banknote, the other half for a government bond. In addition, all bank deposits in excess of 400 guilders were reduced to half with the remaining 50 per cent converted into compulsory government loan at 3 per cent interest. By these two policies, Indonesian money no longer depended on the exchange rate system designed by the Netherlands. Moreover, all local monies were demonetized, which meant the unification of the monetary system in Indonesia.
54. Sutter, *Indonesianisasi: A Historical Survey of the Role of Politics*, 997.
55. Dewan Pengawas Keuangan, *Pemberitaan tahun 1951*.
56. Lindblad, *Bridges to New Business*, 116–7; ANRI, Report of the Indonesian Sailor Union, 9 May 1953, KP, 9h.
57. ANRI, Nasionalisasi Bataviasche Verkeers Maatschappij (B.V.M), KP, 1528.
58. Lindblad, *Bridges to New Business*, 119.
59. ANRI, Report by Dr. A.K. Gani, KP, 1579.
60. The status of these oil installations remained in dispute between the Indonesian government and the BPM. As a result of the transfer of sovereignty, the Indonesian government inherited 50 per cent of equity from the Netherlands Indies government. Discussion to nationalization of the oilfields was voiced in the Indonesian parliament in the early 1950s as to whether there were enough Indonesian technical staffs to continue operations without the BPM.
61. Aden, *Oil and Politics*, 161–2; Golay et al., *Underdevelopment and Economic Nationalism*, 159.
62. Sundhaussen, *The Road to Power*, 328.
63. According to the instruction, all companies, departments, and facilities relating to transportation, posts, media, hospital, oil, gas, electricity, and printing were to be under military authority. Four major Indonesian banks, Bank Indonesia, Bank Negara Indonesia, Bank Industri Negara, Bank Rakjat Indonesia, together with mining enterprises, some manufacturing enterprises, and estates would also be controlled by the armed forces. ANRI, Instruction of the Ministry of Defense, 14 August 1957, KP, 1267.

64. Bondan, *Nasionalisasi Perusahaan Belanda di Indonesia*, 61–3.
65. Sundhaussen, *The Road to Power*, 327; Lindblad, *Bridges to New Business*, 184.
66. 'Act No.86 of 1958', 291–5.
67. Aden, *Oil and Politics in Indonesia*, 177.
68. Meijer, *Den Haag-Djakarta*, 584–5; Kenneth and Glassburner, 'Abrogation, Takeover and Nationalization', 163–4.

15

International Food Aid to Indonesia, 1950s–1970s

Pierre van der Eng

Introduction

In a somewhat neglected article in 2000, Thomas Lindblad offered a synthesis of the political economy behind the economic reorientation of Indonesia under President Sukarno.[1] During 1950–65, the country's modest export performance and its significant import dependence caused foreign exchange shortages that were not sufficiently augmented with inflows of new foreign investment and foreign aid. Lindblad argued that this restricted the ambitions of achieving reorientation of the economy desired by the Indonesian government.

Nevertheless, Indonesia was a significant recipient of foreign aid at the time, as the communist and capitalist camps of aid donors tried to outdo each other with economic and military support until 1965.[2] Until then, most of the economic aid to Indonesia took the form of project aid that was not primarily aimed at easing the balance of payment deficits, but at spurring economic development. Foreign aid to Indonesia for the purpose of alleviating the country's precarious balance of payments situation only became a pressing issue in 1967, when an international community of willing aid donors first gathered with representatives of a new Indonesian government to discuss foreign debt rescheduling and ways to increase foreign aid. This International Inter-Governmental Group for Indonesia (IGGI) agreed that project aid would take too long to allay the balance of payments situation, due to its long lead-up time. For that reason, aid initiatives initially focused on forms of aid that could be delivered and absorbed at short notice, including food aid. Increasing quantities of food aid in the form of grants soon started to arrive, to the extent that during the 1970s one-third of Indonesia's imports of rice and wheat consisted of food aid.

This chapter discusses the reasons why food aid to Indonesia increased quickly after the mid-1960s. Little is known with certainty about the factors driving the growth of food aid to Indonesia during the 1950s–1970s. Existing studies of the development of international food aid discuss the motivations of donor countries, focusing on the period since the 1970s when the distorting effects of food aid in global food markets became obvious, or they elaborate the institutional evolution of the multilateral World Food Programme (WFP).[3] Studies of the political economy of bilateral food aid in relation to individual countries are rare.[4] Even less is known with certainty about food aid to Indonesia, even though it was the world's biggest rice importer and also a budding major market for wheat-based food products.[5]

The next section of this chapter discusses the food situation in Indonesia and its growing dependence on grain imports during the 1950s–1970s. This is followed by a section that deals more specifically with international food aid to Indonesia, both rice and wheat. The next section discusses the organization of food aid and its relation to the arrangement of commercial food transactions. The last section explains two lasting consequences of food aid for Indonesia's food markets, and, finally, some concluding remarks.

Indonesia's Food Situation and Grain Imports

During the 1950s and 1960s, population growth in Indonesia accelerated to on average 1.8 per cent per year, and during the 1970s to 2.3 per cent.[6] Due to high population growth, the country's food supply was precariously balanced at a low average level of around 1,750 Kcal per capita during the 1950s and 1960s.[7] Regional rice markets became increasingly disintegrated as a consequence of the increasing degree of control that government agencies, particularly the government's food logistics agency, sought to exert.[8] Control increased, because the agency's operations focused increasingly on purchasing rice at decreasing real prices for distribution to, for example, public servants, the armed forces and state-owned enterprises, rather than stabilizing rice prices and alleviating regional rice shortages. These developments contributed to occasional famines in the late 1950s and 1960s, particularly in Central Java and Nusa Tenggara.

Food imports played a minor role in alleviating the situation. Before the 1930s, Indonesia had become increasingly dependent on rice imports. In the 1880s it imported on average 3 per cent of total rice supply, rising to 12 per cent during the 1920s, largely from Burma, Thailand and South Vietnam. During the 1950s and 1960s the share of imports in total rice supply increased again from an average of 5 per cent in 1951–55 to 10 per cent during 1961–65, as Table 15.1 shows. Foreign exchange shortages caused the government to limit rice imports to an annual average of 5 per cent of total supply during 1966–70. However, increasing oil production and exports, together with rising oil prices since 1974, facilitated an increase in rice imports. From an annual average of almost 800,000 tons during 1971–75 they grew to 1.8 million tons per year during 1976–80, or 10 per cent of rice supply.

Indonesia also imported increasing quantities of wheat flour during the 1950s and since the late 1960s also wheat, which it does not produce. On average wheat-equivalent imports were just 9 per cent of the combined total of rice and wheat imports in the 1920s, rising to 20 per cent in the 1950s, 15 per cent in the 1960s and 29 per cent during the 1970s. Indonesia imported an annual average of 518,000 tons of wheat during the 1970s, rising to an average of 1.1 million tons in the 1980s. Table 15.1 shows that most imported wheat flour and wheat originated from the United States, Australia and Canada.

Since the 1940s, rice and wheat imports were handled by Indonesia's food logistics agency, which held a monopoly on rice imports and later also on imports of other staple foods, including wheat flour and wheat.[9] To compensate for the low real purchase prices that the agency offered domestic rice farmers, its local representatives increasingly co-operated with local authorities and the military in persuading rice farmers to sell surplus stocks to the agency. The agency changed its purchase strategy in 1964 to paying market prices, but in the context of hyperinflation in 1964–65 this change was notional at best, as farmers would not willingly sell for depreciating cash. The system of rice purchase and distribution became largely dysfunctional. Foreign exchange shortages reduced rice imports, and also the ability of public authorities to alleviate occasional regional famines.

Table 15.1: Imports of rice and wheat into Indonesia by country of origin, 1951–85 (1,000 tons, five-year averages)

	1951–55	*1956–60*	*1961–65*	*1966–70*	*1971–75*	*1976–80*	*1981–85*
A. Rice							
Thailand	113	126	255	57	86	538	134
Burma	170	288	256	38	30	158	67
China	0	92	54	8	193	249	30
US	30	20	94	100	2	108	0
Taiwan	4	0	0	0	2	215	106
North & South Korea	0	0	2	63	80	7	
Western Europe	12	47	18	24	2	5	0
Australia	4	0	0	1	9	57	1
Japan	0	0	0	8	33	18	0
Other	79	79	29	40	51	106	8
Commercial imports	411	714	706	277	471	1,532	352
US		61	27	131	223	175	84
Japan			0	0	129	84	53
Western Europe			0	25	3	0	0
Australia			0	3	4	5	2
Other*			158	173	3	14	1
Total food aid		61	185	307	360	278	139
Total imports	411	775	891	584	784	1,810	492
% Imports of supply	5.3	8.8	9.5	5.4	5.5	10.0	2.1
B. Wheat#							
US	39	33	0	0	211	305	608
Australia	113	92	32	37	136	464	488
Canada					29	13	106
Western Europe					38	2	11
Other					6	4	44
Commercial imports	160	160	49	140	419	788	1,258
US		11	21	120	171	145	175
Australia				32	41	29	15
Canada					25	4	11
Western Europe				25	31	10	28
Other			2	9	3	4	5
Food aid		11	24	186	271	191	235
Total imports	160	171	73	325	691	979	1,492
Rice and wheat imports % of supply	7.3	10.5	10.2	8.1	9.9	14.6	8.1

Notes: * 1960s food aid includes rice aid sourced by donor countries such as Japan, US and Australia in other countries, such as Thailand.
Wheat flour imports and aid calculated as wheat-equivalent.

Sources: Commercial imports calculated from *Ichtisar Tahunan Impor dan Ekspor Indonesia* (1951); *Statistik Perdagangan Impor dan Ekspor Indonesia* (1952–53); *Impor dan Ekspor menurut Djenis Barang* (1954–62); *Impor menurut Jenis Barang* (1963–85); food aid 1956–60 rough estimate based on Shakow, *Foreign Economic Assistance*, 332–3 and DeBlois, *12 Years of Achievement*, 91; food aid 1961–69 calculated as the difference between total imports from FAOStat and Indonesia's trade statistics, allocated on the basis of differences between reported country exports to Indonesia for 1962–69 from UN Comtrade and country of origin data in Indonesia's rice imports; food aid 1970–85 from FAOStat; rice production Van der Eng, *Agricultural Growth*.

This situation aggravated famines in Central Java and Lombok in early 1964, and again in Lombok in early 1967. To resolve this situation, the government created an organization aligned to the Indonesian military, the National Logistics Command (Komando Logistik Nasional, Kolognas) in April 1966, and ordered it to assume the tasks of the dysfunctional food logistics agency. In May 1967 Kolognas became the new Board for Logistical Affairs (Badan Urusan Logistik, Bulog). The association with the military meant that Kolognas/Bulog had access to logistical and organizational capabilities that reached across the country, without necessarily being dependent on regional governments. This effectively allowed it to distribute rice more effectively for the purpose of alleviating food shortages. Nevertheless, difficulties in meeting the domestic purchase targets remained and imports continued to be the main source for the domestic distribution of rice. Imported rice comprised on average 71 per cent of the agency's distributed rice during the 1950s, 62 per cent during the 1960s and 77 per cent during the 1970s.

Food Aid: Reasons for Growth

Despite occasional famines in different regions of the country during the 1950s and 1960s, Indonesia did not become a recipient of international food aid until 1966. Indonesia was a member of the Colombo Plan organization since 1953, and was a recipient of foreign aid. However, most aid to Indonesia under this programme consisted of aid and assistance to students for study in donor countries. Donor countries subscribed annually to aid projects put forward by recipient countries. Some of these projects involved food aid. For example, Australia supplied wheat aid to Sri Lanka, India and (East) Pakistan during the 1950s and 1960s. This was not primarily to alleviate famine and malnutrition, but to raise local currency in recipient countries that would be used to pay the local costs of project aid, such as infrastructure projects.[10] Unlike other countries, Indonesia did not request such food aid.

Small amounts of US food aid arrived in Indonesia after both countries signed their first agreement in March 1956 for PL480 deliveries. Established in 1954, the PL480 programme sought to create overseas markets for US farm produce by subsidizing exports of surplus agricultural produce. Recipient countries purchased surplus produce largely on concessional credit, while local currency revenues from the sale of this produce would either benefit the government coffers in the recipient country or cover local expenses related to US development projects.

Much of the US PL480 assistance to Indonesia consisted of raw cotton and tobacco, and small amounts of rice as emergency aid in 1963 and 1964.[11] As PL480 rice was deemed to be of high quality, most of it was likely distributed by the food logistics agency to government employees and the armed forces.[12]

The PL480 programme caused concerns among other countries exporting agricultural commodities. In 1955 they all participated in the Consultative Committee on Surplus Disposal of the multilateral Food and Agriculture Organization (FAO). The committee monitored the disposal of agricultural surpluses—especially by the US—in order to safeguard the interests of other exporting countries that were not in a position in the 1950s to initiate aid programmes akin in scale and intent to the PL480 programme. In terms of food aid, no other donor country had an equivalent programme, so that only US food aid under concessional loans reached Indonesia during 1956–64.

This started to change during the remainder of the 1960s for three reasons. First, in 1963, WFP was established with the task of co-ordinating multilateral emergency food aid. One of WFP's first assignments was the delivery of 10,795 tons of US-donated maize to Indonesia, following the Gunung Agung eruption in Bali in 1963–64. Second, the change of political regime in Indonesia during 1965–67, which opened the door for increased foreign aid to Indonesia co-ordinated by the 'Tokyo Group' of donor countries. The group became known as the multilateral Inter-Governmental Group for Indonesia (IGGI) in 1967.[13] Third, the start of the 'Food Aid Convention' of the multilateral International Grains Arrangement (IGA) in 1968. It obliged signatory countries to provide a minimum amount of food aid. These developments created the institutional framework for other donor countries to counter the rapid growth of the US PL480 programme during the 1960s. For example, the European Union, Australia and Canada emerged since as major aid donors of agricultural produce.[14]

In the late 1960s, Indonesia was one of the first and main beneficiaries of WFP and the 'Food Aid Convention'. IGGI donor countries were interested in helping Indonesia to overcome its economic difficulties as soon as possible through foreign aid. But Indonesia's capacity to absorb foreign project aid at short notice was limited. Food aid therefore became an important part of instantaneous aid that these countries could offer. For example, Australia's food aid programme to Indonesia expanded very quickly as part of Australia's effort to counter the effects of the rapid growth of US food aid to Indonesia in the late 1960s and 1970s.[15]

In general, food aid was provided under multilateral WFP commitments for famine relief and emergency, or it was provided bilaterally as aid in kind, yielding local currency proceeds that were soon used to finance bilateral aid projects.

While President Sukarno's government in the early 1960s only accepted small amounts of emergency food aid, the change of political regime following the coup of 30 September 1965 soon led to informal requests to potential aid donors for food aid to alleviate regional food shortages in Indonesia. For example, in November 1965 government representatives approached foreign ambassadors in Jakarta to discuss emergency credit to purchase foreign rice.[16] Although there was sympathy for food aid to Indonesia within the Australian government, it remained reluctant to consider increasing aid until Indonesia had revoked its belligerent *konfrontasi* policy towards Malaysia and had taken steps towards a programme of economic reform or stabilization.[17]

Following Sukarno's delegation of supreme authority to General Soeharto in March 1966 and the subsequent installation of a new government, Indonesian officials made further representations to potential food aid donors, such as Australia.[18] For example, Ismail, the former Indonesian minister of agriculture, asked informally whether the Australian government could help by guaranteeing payments for rice shipments from Thailand costing US $10 million. Compared with past levels of Australian aid, this was a hefty sum. Therefore, Ismail suggested that the US could perhaps act as a guarantor for Australia if Australia was unwilling to act alone.

The likely reason for Ismail's unusual request was that Indonesia did not yet want any identification with US aid matters in public, as it was only two years since President Sukarno had told the US to 'go to hell with your aid' in March 1964.[19] Nevertheless, the US government arranged shipment of 100,000 tons of Thai rice as US food aid to Indonesia in 1966. The Australian government participated in this deal by financing the US $200,000 shipment of 1,600 tons of Thai rice in May 1966 to flood-affected areas in Central Java, as an indication of goodwill towards and support for its near-neighbour.[20] Like governments of other aid donor countries, the Australian government preferred to wait with making larger commitments until it had received formal requests from the Indonesian government. A major issue was that aid donor countries could not yet be sure that food aid to Indonesia would be distributed appropriately and transparently so as to minimize graft.

While waiting for the first meeting of IGGI to be called, foreign governments thus became familiar with the operations of Kolognas/Bulog since 1966. For example, the Indonesian government engaged Kolognas to transport rice and distribute it in famine-hit areas in Central Java and in Lombok in 1966. In other words, when it came to distributing new food aid commitments, following the two IGGI meetings in 1967, aid donors agreed to Bulog making the arrangements for the delivery and distribution of food aid. The agency's association with the military offered a reasonable guarantee that food aid would be delivered where it was needed, and that it would be accounted for in a reasonably transparent manner.

Food Aid and Food Imports

The existence of a single and ostensibly effective food logistics agency in Indonesia facilitated an ulterior motive that donor countries tacitly pursued with food aid. This was related to the fact that each was also an exporter of staple foods, particularly wheat, wheat flour and/or rice. In the 1950s, Indonesia's rice imports were dominated by supplies from countries in Southeast Asia, while its wheat flour imports largely came from Australia. But in the 1960s, supplying food aid offered a major donor country like the US opportunities to establish and build market share in Indonesia.

To substantiate that point, Figure 15.1 offers an overview of the process by which donor countries delivered food aid to Indonesia. A pre-condition for the process to start was that there would be an agreement between the governments of Indonesia and a donor country for the delivery of food aid. As soon as that was concluded, the donor government would issue (public) tenders among domestic (or in some cases foreign) wholesalers. Companies with successful tenders would then engage a company specializing in foreign trade for the supply and delivery of shipments of rice or wheat flour to Indonesia. The exporting company would deal with a certified private company in Indonesia that conducted the imports, which would secure an import permit from Bulog (in the case of rice, and since 1972 also wheat and wheat flour) and the Department of Trade (in the case of wheat flour and wheat until 1972). The agent in the donor country would be paid by the donor government upon completing the transaction. The agent in Indonesia would receive payment in rupiah from Bulog and/or from wholesalers upon completion of the transaction.

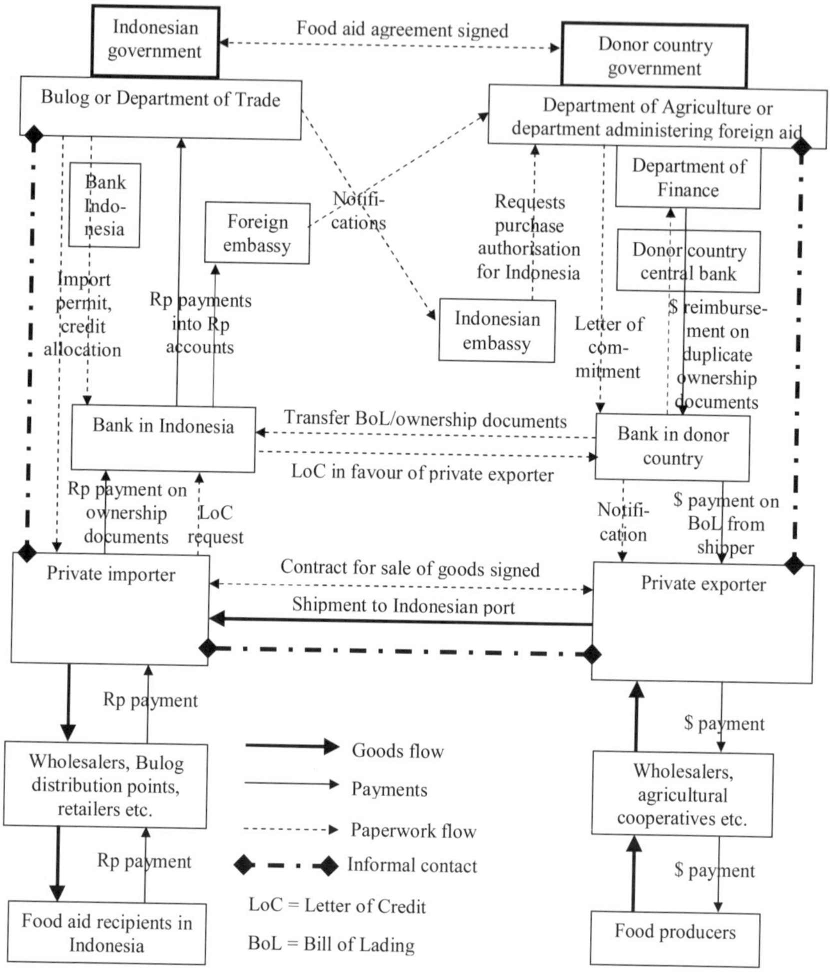

Source: Adapted from Goolsby et al. (1970): 22–4.

Figure 15.1: Paperwork, payments and goods flow in food aid transactions

As Figure 15.1 shows, this system created opportunities for the import and export agents, and/or the wholesalers they were working with, on either side to co-operate in lobbying government agencies and politicians for food aid contracts. The ability to do so would in principle have depended on whether an agent in Indonesia was able to secure an import permit, and whether an agent in the donor country was successful in bidding for a government tender to supply products as food aid. In effect, however, the Indonesian government would submit a formal request for a specific commercial shipment of food products to be regarded as food aid under an existing agreement.

These requests for specific shipments to be accepted as foreign aid could be instigated by Bulog or the Department of Trade. For either to do that, they had to be certain that there was a certified private company in Indonesia to import and handle a shipment of rice or wheat flour on their behalf. In effect, Bulog or the Department of Trade would thus be responsive to requests from Indonesian companies to import and handle food aid deliveries, provided these could be accommodated in an existing agreement for food aid with a donor country. When Bulog or the Department of Trade received Indonesian government approval for specific shipments of rice or wheat as food aid, they would issue the required import permit as well as instructions to private firms for the delivery of shipments in Indonesia. Rice would go to Bulog's warehouses and wholesale distribution points, and wheat flour to wholesalers. The rupiah proceeds of the sales of delivered food aid would then benefit the coffers of Bulog and the Indonesian treasury, and/or the accounts that foreign governments accumulated for local expenditure as project aid.

As Figure 15.1 indicates, the process by which food aid was arranged brought export agents in the donor country in contact with partner firms in Indonesia. At both ends these companies were not only handling government contracts for food aid shipments, but also commercial transactions for foodstuffs. Such commercial transactions tended to be based on an accumulation of mutual trust between private agents at either end. Although they may have been reluctant to concede this, governments of donor countries were effectively facilitating the creation of a potential basis for further commercial transactions of staple foods.

Food aid to Indonesia increased quickly following the IGGI meeting of June 1967, when the Indonesian government submitted a list of projects, including requests for aid in support of its purchases of wheat flour and rice. Food aid shipments paved the way for commercial transactions. For example, a shipment of 6,500 tons of Australian rice aid in October 1969 was soon followed by a commercial order approved by Bulog for 14,000 tons of rice.[21]

Since 1967, IGGI met annually to co-ordinate foreign aid to Indonesia. Its discussions focused on Indonesia's annual requests for bilateral and multilateral project aid, but bilateral foreign commitments of food aid were discussed as well. During occasional regional famines, Indonesia would receive unscheduled emergency food aid, co-ordinated by WFP. Indonesia received most of its food aid in the form of grants of bilateral allocations of rice, wheat flour and increasingly wheat. Occasionally it also received relatively small quantities of other food products as these products became available in donor countries for food aid. Examples are bulgur, processed fish, infant food, butter, skimmed evaporated milk, other dairy products, vegetable oil, sugar and pulses for human consumption, and coarse grains (maize, oats, barley and sorghum) mainly for use as animal feed. Table 15.1 shows that the key donors of food aid to Indonesia were the US in the case of rice, and the US, Australia, Canada and the EU in the case of wheat and wheat flour.

During the 1970s, donor countries agreed to several changes in the principles of their food aid policies and programmes, particularly since the World Food Conference of 1974.[22] However, on the whole, the decade was a period of consolidation of experiences and relative stability for food aid. Only by the mid-1980s did growing criticism of the distortions in food markets caused by the policies of the US and the EU—the largest donors of food aid—lead to changes in the size of international food aid.[23] For some donor countries, Indonesia's eligibility for food aid came into doubt as its oil exports increased, particularly since 1973. Nevertheless, Table 15.1 shows that until the mid-1980s donor countries developed markets and disposed of surplus produce in Indonesia. Significant shares of Indonesia's imports of rice, wheat and wheat flour arrived as food aid. Percentages varied from year to year but, on average during 1966–70, 53 per cent of rice and 57 per cent of wheat imports arrived as food aid, 46 per cent and 39 per cent respectively during 1971–75, 15 per cent and 20 per cent during 1976–80, and 28 per cent and 16 per cent during 1981–85.

Because food aid deliveries were difficult to distinguish from commercial food deliveries, it is almost impossible to establish their end use. Donor countries at times emphasized the arrival or delivery of shipments of food aid in Indonesia for publicity purposes. But it is not possible to gauge whether the bulk of food aid to Indonesia actually alleviated specific episodes of famine and cases of malnutrition. At a macro-level, food aid facilitated Indonesia's increasing dependence on imported food products, particularly rice and wheat. While this improved food supply, the significant increase in per capita calorie supply in Indonesia was largely driven by the 'green revolution' in rice agriculture, which took hold from the late 1960s and reduced Indonesia's need for rice imports to close to zero by the mid-1980s.[24] Notwithstanding changes in international food aid policy, food aid to Indonesia allowed food donors to dispose of excess stocks and build market share by encouraging lasting commercial relations between importers in Indonesia and exporters in donor countries, as they combined handling subsidized and regular food transactions.

Lasting Consequences

Arguably, food aid had two lasting consequences for Indonesia. First, it consolidated Bulog's control over the domestic markets of key staple food crops in Indonesia through its import monopoly, its domestic purchases of products for buffer stocks and its control over distribution networks. After Bulog had demonstrated its relevance by achieving a significant degree of stabilization and integration of rice markets, where that had been lacking in the 1950s and 1960s, its dominant role in domestic markets for a growing number of staple foods enhanced the opportunities for institutionalized corruption during the 1970s, due to the dependence of market operations on the permissions issued by Bulog.

The risk involved in having to deal with Bulog, despite its odious reputation, must have been known to donor countries. Already in 1968, new Trade Minister Sumitro Djojohadikusumo informed the Australian ambassador informally of existing suspicions of Bulog's machinations to argue that the agency be disbanded.[25] In 1969 irregularities in Bulog's rice purchase programme led to proposals in the Indonesian parliament to dissolve the agency. Australian officials also suspected that Bulog had exaggerated Indonesia's need for food aid and had downplayed optimistic rice harvest estimates by the Department of Agriculture.[26] But Bulog's authorities and its involvement in the food markets expanded and were not curtailed until 1998. A possible reason why donor countries may not have pressed for greater transparency in Bulog's operations was that they could deal with Bulog and the Department of Trade (until 1972) as two one-stop agencies to facilitate aid and trade of rice, respectively wheat and wheat flour.

Second, Bulog's import monopoly was extended to other staple foodstuffs. The extension to wheat flour and wheat in 1972 came at a time when Indonesia still imported most wheat on a concessional or grant basis. This placed the agency in a central position to guide the development of the wheat-milling industry, which had started in 1969 through PT Bogasari Flour Mills. This company was owned by Liem Sioe Liong, a long-time business associate of then President Soeharto. When it became operational in 1971, the company had a monopoly on the milling of imported wheat for Bulog and thus service about 80 per cent of the flour market in Indonesia.[27] Starting in 1972, Bulog set the ex-factory wheat flour prices, which were on average 25 per cent higher than the world price due to the inclusion of various charges, such as Bogasari's milling fees. Altogether this resulted in retail prices for wheat flour in Indonesia that exceeded world market prices.

It took until the liberalization of Indonesia's wheat markets in 1998 before Bulog and Bogasari lost their monopolies on import, respectively on the milling of wheat. However, Bogasari's wheat-milling operations expanded over time and came under the control of Liem Sioe Liong's PT Indofood CBP Sukses Makmur Tbk conglomerate. Its operations became so extensive, and its supply chain from imported wheat to final flour-based processed food products so integrated, that other companies were since 1998 only able to commercially challenge the company in the margins of the markets for wheat flour and for flour-based processed foods.

Conclusion

Indonesia experienced growing shortfalls of food supplies during the 1950s, and during the 1960s and 1970s it imported increasing amounts of rice, wheat and wheat flour. In the 1950s, Indonesia received a small amount of US PL480 food aid under concessional loans. Despite occasional famines, and the willingness of countries to supply food aid as grants, Indonesia did not request food aid until 1966. The precarious food situation and reports of famines in Central Java and Nusa Tenggara contributed to the rapid growth of the volume of food aid since then.

This chapter has shown that, apart from cases of famine, the rapid development of food aid is also related to the fact that potential donor countries had food surpluses for the purpose of food aid, at a time when the institutional arrangements for international food aid started to crystallize. Multilateral emergency aid was facilitated by the establishment and operations of WFP in 1963, and the IGA 'Food Aid Convention' obliged member countries to increase food donations after 1967. In Indonesia's case, the donor countries in the IGGI were looking for ways to assist the country in alleviating its balance of payments difficulties. Food aid was a form of foreign aid that Indonesia could absorb relatively quickly, unlike programme aid. The establishment of Bulog in 1967 institutionalized rice aid at the receiving end and offered donor countries and foreign companies the opportunity to deal with single institutions that facilitated aid and imports of rice and wheat.

Donations of wheat flour, rice and other food products started to arrive in Indonesia in 1967 and increased quickly. During the 1970s one-third of Indonesia's imports of both rice and wheat arrived as aid. Initially, donor countries focused on rice aid in efforts to secure shares in Indonesia's growing rice imports. But their focus shifted to wheat aid, in response to opportunities for them to grow Indonesia's market for wheat-based products and secure market share. Food aid helped to alleviate food shortages, but it also strengthened the role of Bulog in Indonesia's food markets until it lost its privileges in 1998.

Notes

1. Lindblad, 'The Political Economy of Realignment in Indonesia', 158.
2. Shakow, *Foreign Economic Assistance*; Mahajani, *Soviet and American Aid*; Boden, 'Cold War Economics'.
3. E.g. Barrett and Maxwell, *Food Aid after Fifty Years*; Shaw, *The UN World Food Programme*; Shaw, *The World's Largest Humanitarian Agency*; Shaw and Clay, *World Food Aid*; Ross, *The World Food Programme.*
4. For example, Latham, *Rice: The Primary Commodity*, does not mention it. Siamwalla and Haykin, *The World Rice Market*, 44, quantified the consequences of country dependence on rice aid for international rice market, using data for 1961–80, to conclude that aid tended to replace rice imports but without detailing why and how that would be the case.
5. McLelland et al., 'Food Aid in Indonesia', investigated the magnitude of US food aid to Indonesia.
6. Van der Eng, 'Bridging a Gap: A Reconstruction of Population Patterns'.
7. Van der Eng, 'Food for Growth: Trends in Indonesia's Food Supply'.
8. Van der Eng, 'All Lies? Famines in Sukarno's Indonesia'.
9. This paragraph and the next is based on Van der Eng, 'All Lies? Famines in Sukarno's Indonesia'.
10. Van der Eng, '"Send Them a Shipload of Rice"'.
11. DeBlois, '12 Years of Achievement', 91, 110.
12. Shakow, *Foreign Economic Assistance*, 336.
13. Posthumus, *Inter-Governmental Group.*
14. The 1967 IGA replaced the 1949 International Wheat Agreement. It contained a 'Food Aid Convention' that specified minimum annual amounts of food aid. The biggest providers were to be the US (1,890 thousand tons), the EEC (1,035 thousand tons), Canada (495 thousand tons) and Australia, UK and Japan (225 thousand tons each). Parotte, 'Food Aid Convention', 12.
15. McLelland et al., 'Food Aid in Indonesia'.
16. National Archives of Australia (NAA) A1838/308 2036/5 PART 7, K. Shann to DEA (16 December 1965).

17. Van der Eng, '*Konfrontasi* and Australia's Foreign Aid Program'.
18. NAA, A1838/280 3034/10/1 PART 27, K. Shann to DEA (22 March 1966), p. 109.
19. See: Thee, 'The Indonesian Economy' in this book for a discussion of the context of the US aid programme to Indonesia.
20. NAA, A4940 C4341 Press statement by J.G. Gorton (27 March 1966); NAA A1838 555/7/142, Draft press statement, Australian embassy Jakarta (5 May 1966). At the same time the US government offered US$8.2 million credit and the UK government US$2.8 million credit for food purchases (Mahajani, *Soviet and American Aid*, 31).
21. During 1968–69, Australian company Ricegrowers' Co-Operative Mills Ltd sought to enter the Indonesian market. Its representatives discussed rice aid and exports to Indonesia with Bulog on several occasions. This contributed to a formal Indonesian request for rice aid to the Australian government. Despite strong reluctance of the aid-administering Department of External Affairs to link aid and exports, the government granted 6,500 tons of rice aid. Due to the urgency of the matter, the company was given the aid contract without tender, and it received additional commercial orders for 14,000 tons of rice from Bulog. NAA A1838 2020/1/32/8 PART 1.
22. Hopkins, 'Evolution of Food Aid'.
23. Clay, 'Review of Food Aid Policy'.
24. Van der Eng, *Agricultural Growth in Indonesia*; Van der Eng, 'Food for Growth: Trends in Indonesia's Food Supply'. See also Frankema, 'The Green Revolution' in this volume.
25. Rice 'Sumitro's role'; NAA A4359 111/5/4 PART 1, M. Loveday to DEA (5 August 1968).
26. NAA A1838 2020/1/32/8 PART 1, 'The rice situation and food aid', Inward Savingram No.56 (14 October 1969), No. 57 (22 October 1969), No. 60 (7 November 1969).
27. Magiera, 'Role of Wheat', 52–3; Sato, 'Salim Group', 414–5.

16

The Green Revolution in Indonesia: A Replicable Success?

Ewout Frankema

Introduction

Indonesia experienced one of the most successful agricultural transitions of the twentieth century. After decades of gradual decreases in domestic per capita food supply and simultaneous increases in food imports and food aid, the acceleration of rice yields in the late 1960s turned deeply pessimistic views on the ability of Indonesian society to overcome mass poverty into hopeful prospects based on tangible improvements in rural income levels.[1] Indeed, few students of the Indonesian economy in the 1960s, if any, had foreseen the speed and depth of the post-1967 agrarian transition. On the contrary, in view of the economic collapse during the final years of the Sukarno regime and the mounting political instability and violence leading up to, and accompanying, the installation of Suharto's New Order, the long-term economic prospects of Indonesia appeared even bleaker to most observers than the Malthusian doom scenarios sketched for other parts of Asia.[2]

This chapter aims to disentangle the complex causal underpinning of the success of Indonesia's 'green revolution' in order to assess which aspects of it are, in principle, replicable in other parts of the world, and which aspects should be attributed to historical and ecological conditions that are too context-specific to be replicated elsewhere. Although rice was certainly not the only (food) crop to witness impressive productivity growth, the discussion here will focus on rice, the key staple of Indonesian agricultural producers and consumers; on Java, the area where the majority of these farmers and consumers lived; and on the period just before and during the so-called 'take-off' of productivity growth.

Despite the fact that the advances in Indonesian agricultural productivity and its long-term welfare effects have been extensively documented and analysed in the literature, I contend that the continuing stress on global agricultural resources, which have sent global food prices through the roof in recent years, justify repeated reassessments of success stories.[3] In particular, with regards to the current prospects of many sub-Saharan African (Africa hereafter) economies, where the lion's share of world population growth in the twenty-first century will occur, the Indonesian example contains some interesting analogies.

First, similar to Indonesia in the 1930s–60s, the majority of African economies have witnessed a long period of stagnating or even declining rates of per capita food production from the 1970s through the 1990s. Some countries have recently shown respectable output and productivity growth in a number of food crops (rice, maize, cassava), but the overall record remains rather fragmented.[4] Second, increasing population pressures in Java have been regarded as a big threat to economic modernization by consecutive colonial and post-colonial administrations since the late nineteenth century. Similar concerns play an important role in the current debate about Africa's long-term growth prospects.[5]

Third, Indonesia's green revolution occurred under a dictatorial regime, which did not shun the use of large-scale violence to consolidate power. African countries have a long legacy of post-colonial conflict, violence and prolonged dictatorships. Fourth, the Asian green revolution unfolded in the context of Cold War politics, where foreign intermingling in terms of financial aid and economic assistance programmes were regarded as legitimate means to pull Suharto into the Western capitalist camp.[6] A similar competition for influence, including massive aid and investment programmes, is presently detectable between the Chinese and several Western powers in sub-Saharan Africa.

The most interesting contrast from an African point of view, however, is the way in which the Suharto regime prioritized rural development and also maintained these policies during the years 1973–79, when spiking oil revenues were releasing pressure. Yet, instead of using foreign reserves to return to cheap(er) food imports and satisfy the demands of

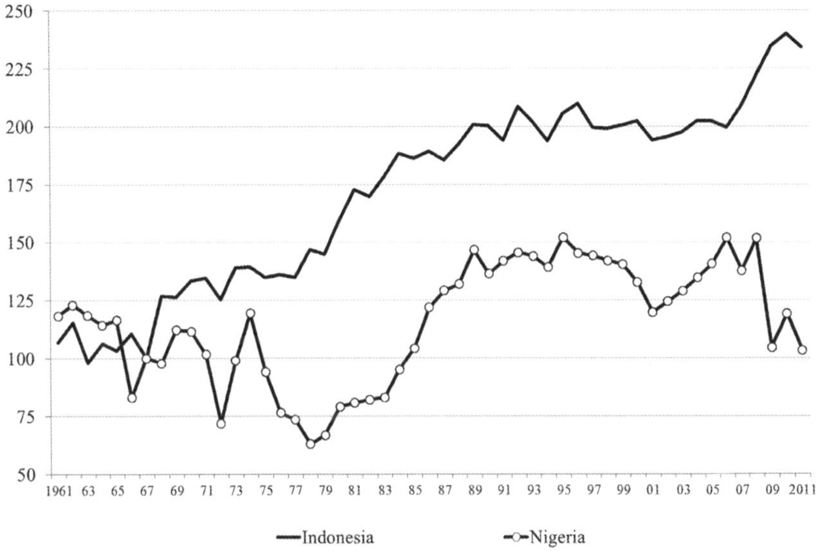

Source: *FAOSTAT* 2013 [accessed 20 August 2013].

Figure 16.1: Index of per capita cereal production in Indonesia and Nigeria, 1961–2011 (1967 = 100)

(urban) consumers at the expense of rice farmers for political gain, the oil money was used to, amongst other things, extend rural credit facilities and extension services, step-up investments in irrigation infrastructure, subsidize the use of chemical fertilizer, expand national fertilizer industry, and strengthen the state monopoly on domestic and international trade in agricultural commodities.

By using oil revenues to revitalize smallholder agriculture, Indonesia posed a striking counter-example to many other major oil-producing countries in the developing world, such as Nigeria, Iran, Saudi Arabia, Mexico and Venezuela. Especially the contrast with Nigeria has raised ample attention, as both countries experienced huge oil windfalls in the 1970s, but spent the money in very different ways.[7] Figure 16.1 shows that in the fifty years between 1961 and 2011, per capita cereal production in Nigeria has recorded a net decline, whereas cereal output per capita in Indonesia more than doubled. Many resource-rich African economies are again enjoying windfall gains from rising world market prices. Since the debt crisis of the late twentieth century has been overcome, these gains could of course be used to jump-start agricultural growth.

Understanding why and how rural investment programmes were implemented in Indonesia will help to reflect on present-day conditions for agricultural growth in Africa.

The discussion is organized in three steps. First, I will argue why Indonesia's green revolution can be rightly called a 'success'. Second, I will introduce a framework to disentangle the causal complex underpinning Indonesia's green revolution and discuss the interaction between five factors: ecology, history, technology, policy and the international environment. Third, the analysis will focus on the nature and timing of the policy-making process during the early years of the take-off. The bottom line of my argument will be that specific historical and ecological conditions make it very unlikely that the Indonesian green revolution can be replicated in sub-Saharan Africa, but that Indonesia's *agricultural policy history* does contain important lessons for African governments aspiring to a 'doubly green revolution'.[8]

What Constitutes 'Success'?

The term 'green revolution' usually refers to a phase of global agrarian transformation between the early 1940s and late 1970s driven by the development and large-scale adoption of 'modern' high-yielding varieties (HYVs) of cereal grains such as wheat, rice and maize. Indonesia followed a typically Asian pattern of this transformation process, in the sense that it was driven by the adoption of new rice varieties that were released since the mid-1960s.[9] It is always questionable to what extent the term 'revolution' offers an appropriate description of historical processes of change, especially since in this case, most of the technological ingredients (the deliberate crossing of varieties, the use of artificial fertilizers, irrigation) had been around for decades, if not centuries. However, if one takes output or productivity growth as a measure of change, there is no denying that the Asian green revolution marked a clear breakpoint in the long-term evolution of Asian agriculture, and for Indonesia even more so.[10]

Indonesian rice yields rose from an average of 1.8 tonnes per hectare (t/ha) in the 1960s to an average of 3.9 t/ha in the 1980s and up to around 5 t/ha at present. Between 1967 and 1985, Indonesian rice production realized an annual average yield growth of 4.7 per cent. Total per capita production of cereals increased by 3.8 per cent, so that imports of staple foods declined up to a point where Indonesia became self-sufficient in rice by 1983–85. Figure 16.2 shows that Indonesian rice

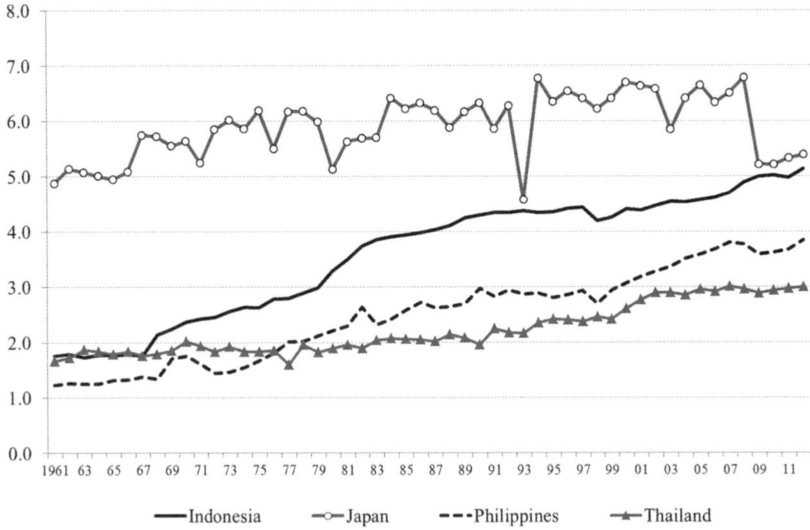

Source: *FAOSTAT* 2013 [accessed 20 August 2013].

Figure 16.2: Rice yields in Indonesia, Japan, the Philippines and Thailand, 1961–2012 (tons per hectare)

farmers, contrary to their colleagues in other major rice-growing economies such as Thailand and the Philippines, produce yields that are comparable to Japanese rice farmers, who can be considered the technology leaders of the twentieth century. Although the pace of rice-yield growth in Indonesia slowed down after 1985, and the sector suffered from the Asian economic crisis in the late 1990s, rice production did recover since 2006 and Indonesia regained self-sufficiency in rice by 2008. Even more important, however, present-day Indonesian rice farmers have adopted ecologically more sustainable production methods than in the early days of the green revolution, which increases the chances that high yield levels can be sustained in the future.[11]

Indonesian cereal production, as shown in Figure 16.3, outpaced the growth rates observed in the rest of Asia by a considerable degree. This adds an extra dimension to the puzzle: why did Indonesian food production grow considerably faster than in the rest of Asia, while all these countries had, at least in theory, access to comparable production technologies? It underscores the notion that the release of modern HYVs was a *necessary* condition for achieving the high-recorded rates of agricultural

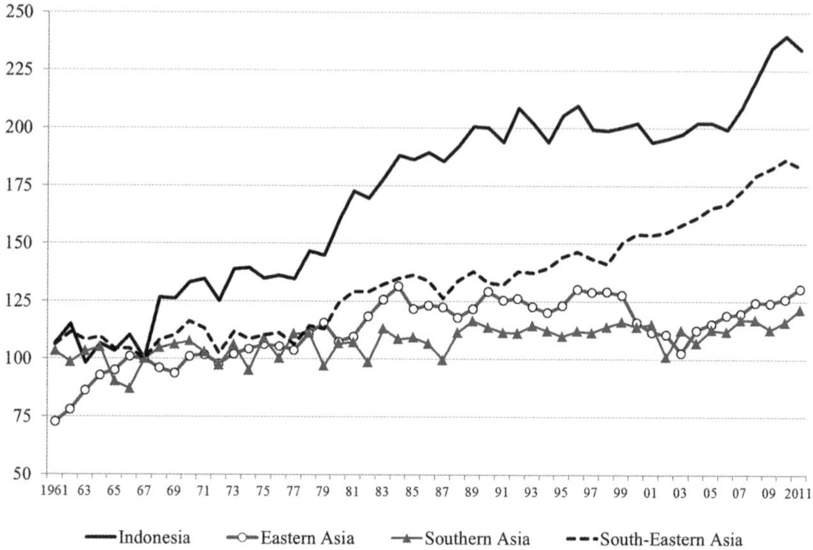

Source: *FAOSTAT* 2013 [accessed 20 August 2013].

Figure 16.3: Index of per capita cereal production in Indonesia and other parts of Asia, 1961–2011 (1967 = 100)

productivity growth, but certainly not a *sufficient* condition. The successful adoption of modern HYVs required complementary public and private investments in land use, water management, disease control and marketing as well as fine-tuned agricultural policies and favourable institutional and macro-economic conditions. Many of these conditions, as we will see further below, were met in post-1967 Indonesia.

Another reason for adopting the term 'success' is that Indonesia's agricultural transition rapidly translated into tangible living-standard improvements. According to the SUSENAS survey, 60.9 per cent of the Javanese were categorized as 'very poor' in 1963–64 and 52.3 per cent in the Outer Islands. By 1984 these shares had dropped to respectively 23.0 per cent and 10.4 per cent.[12] The rice-producing sector was the key driving force of poverty reduction in the 1970s because of its dominant role in domestic production *and* consumption. Moreover, the combination of increasing production and purchasing power created effective demand conditions that lifted both the rural and urban economy from the ground and initiated a process of structural change towards higher value-added industrial and service activities, which in turn resulted in a sustained increase in long-term per capita gross domestic product (GDP) growth rates. The break in GDP growth was striking, jumping up from a long-term annual average of around 0.5 per cent between 1870 and 1967 to an annual average of 3.5 per cent after 1967.[13] Henley's quote of Lipton's one-liner couldn't be more to the point: '*If you wish for industrialisation, prepare to develop agriculture.*'[14]

But the best justification for calling the Indonesian green revolution a 'success' is perhaps that it came so unexpectedly and that it took serious scholarship by surprise. The prevailing view up to the late 1960s was that Javanese smallholders disregarded the potential of modern techniques.[15] David Penny has become famous for his widely quoted statement in 1969 that:

> The reluctance of farmers to buy fertiliser, modern tools, etc., is still so great that it is unlikely that any substantial modernisation of Indonesian peasant agriculture will take place in the next decade or two.[16]

Clifford Geertz explained this resistance to change as the result of a supposed Javanese mentality of 'shared poverty'. According to Geertz, the redistribution of agricultural output growth among a growing pool of surplus labour was a peasant strategy to cope with an increasingly dualistic economy. This dual economy was characterized by rising inequality between a capital-intensive, labour-saving plantation sector and a labour-absorbing impoverished peasantry, without strong intermediate links.[17] For Geertz, it was hard to believe that these peasants were about to become the central agents of the greatest economic turning point in Indonesian history:

> in the absence of any genuine reconstruction of Indonesian civilization [...] pouring fertiliser onto Java's Lilliputian fields is likely, as modern irrigation, labour-intensive cultivation and crop diversification before it, to make only one thing grow: paralysis.[18]

Analysing Causal Complexity

To disentangle the causal complex underpinning Indonesia's green revolution one can distinguish five factors: ecology, history, technology, policy and the international environment (referring to both world market developments and international politics). Their mutual interaction can be analysed according to the scheme presented in Figure 16.4. For the purpose of this chapter it is important to note that the factors of technology

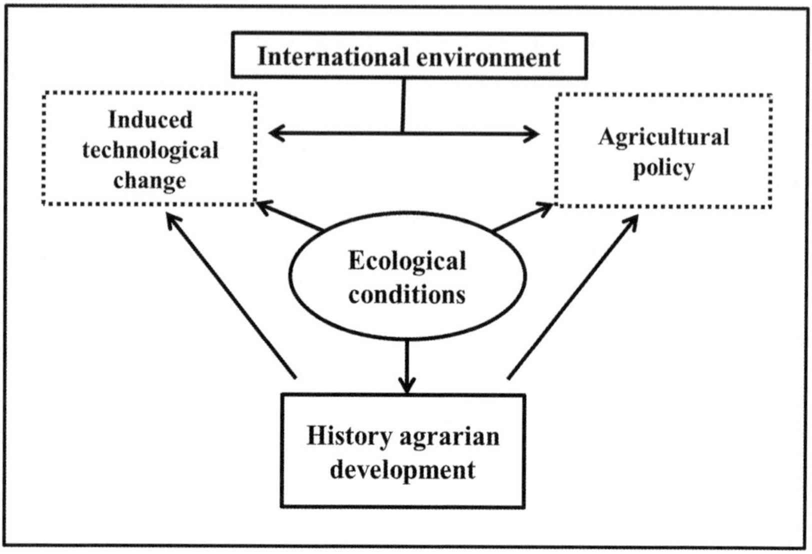

Source: Author's own.

Figure 16.4: A framework to study the causal complexity of agricultural transitions

and policy are, in principle, transferable across time and space, whereas historical development trajectories and ecological conditions are not, while the impact of world markets and international politics are a largely exogenous force to farmers and agricultural policy-makers as well.

At the core of this framework rests the notion that ecological conditions constrain the set of technology and policy options available to rural societies and, thereby, set the boundaries for long-term agricultural development trajectories. The two major ecosystems relevant for the Indonesian Archipelago are: (1) dense lowland rainforest historically suited to shifting cultivation and, at a later stage, to the establishment of capital-intensive plantations producing tropical cash crops such as rubber, coffee, sugar and palm oil; (2) highly fertile, rain-fed volcanic slopes conducive to wet-rice cultivation. The possibilities to grow *padi sawah* on the volcanic soils of Java and Bali and the better irrigated regions of West Sumatra and South Sulawesi have induced great variation in population densities across the archipelago, explaining how Java could emerge as the central polity of the archipelago.

The release of 'modern' high-yielding rice varieties such as the IR8, IR5 and the C4-63 by the International Rice Research Institute (IRRI) in Los Baños, the Philippines, suited the ecological conditions of Indonesia very well. Earlier indigenous hybrid varieties such as the Syntha, Peta and Bengawan had been based on crossing local rice varieties, but none of them proved highly susceptible to chemical fertilizers.[19] The IR8, also called the 'miracle rice', was a hybrid variety based on a crossing between the Taiwanese dwarf variety (DWGW) and the Indonesian Peta variety. The Peta did respond well to nitrogen applications, but the heavier ears had to be bred on the shorter stems of the DWGW in order to prevent the plant from lodging.[20] Hence, with the release of the IR8 in 1966, the IR5 in 1967 and the C4-63 in 1969 a major biotechnological hurdle had been taken: these were rice varieties that effectively transformed high supplies of nitrate and water into a high number of kernels per ear, without falling over. And apart from their improved kernel density, their rapid maturation facilitated multiple annual rice cropping or mixing the rice crops with other commercial crops.[21]

The rapid adoption of modern HYVs after 1967 cannot be understood without a long-term historical perspective of Indonesian agricultural development and the role of the Dutch colonial legacy in particular.[22] According to Anne Booth, Javanese agricultural development can be studied in three consecutive stages of extensification, intensification and modernization.[23] Extensification refers to the *expansion of the cultivated area* to meet demographic growth. Intensification refers to the *growth in cropping ratio* (the ratio of harvested to cultivated area) after the land frontier has been closed. Modernization refers to the use of modern technologies (such as the application of fertilizer-responsive HYVs) to increase *yields per unit of harvested area*. According to Booth, the possibilities of extensive growth had largely run out on Java by 1920. In response to increasing demographic pressures, the Dutch colonial government started to intervene more systematically in food-crop agriculture from the start of the twentieth century onwards, as it had previously done by the forced cultivation of export crops during the 1830s–70s. Substantial public investments in irrigation and drainage infrastructure were complemented by agricultural research and extension services.[24] These government efforts, along with private efforts of smallholders to raise their harvests on gradually shrinking plots of land, led to a phase of intensification that dominated rice farming between c.1915 and 1965.[25] Rising cropping ratios indeed resulted in larger rice harvests, but these gains were insufficient to keep pace with the growing number of mouths to feed.[26]

The closure of the Javanese land frontier and the subsequent phase of intensification resulted in a number of conditions for the successful adoption of modern HYVs. The growing pressure on land resources had stimulated the transition from communal to private property rights to land. This transition had been facilitated by the liberalization of colonial economic policies since the 1870s. Private land ownership made farmers' household income directly dependent on cultivation decisions, creating a favourable incentive structure for experimenting with yield-enhancing techniques. The irrigation infrastructure essential for the adoption of HYVs had been rapidly expanded under Dutch colonial rule to make intensive growth possible. Although parts of the irrigation infrastructure had run down by the 1960s, the framework for successful water management was largely in place.[27] Finally, the increasing population density on Java created favourable conditions for food-market integration, as the lion's share of producers and consumers of rice and other foodstuffs were living close to each other, thus limiting transportation and transaction costs, while enhancing labour specialization.[28]

The role of the state as a co-ordinating institution was also widely accepted and tested in Java before 1967. The great depression forced the Dutch colonial government towards a more structural type of price intervention, building upon centuries of occasional interventions in rice markets in periods of harvest failure. In 1933 the Dutch colonial government started to restrict rice imports in view of the overproduction in Asia, undercutting the incomes of Indonesian rice farmers. In 1939 the colonial state went a step further by setting a fixed rice-selling price and committing itself to clear the market by buying up potentially unsalable supplies against this price.[29] This programme was adopted without significant changes by the Sukarno regime in the late 1940s and the 1950s.

The establishment of a full-fledge state monopoly required an institutional-bureaucratic apparatus that was sufficiently equipped to co-ordinate the rice trade. Seasonal and regional supply fluctuations had to be mediated, rice stocks had to be maintained and market information had to be collected to set the 'right' prices. To let this system function properly, it required a close monitoring of the income effects of price-fixing on both producers and consumers, which made both the logistic part of controlling the monopoly, as well as the collection and diffusion of accurate information, crucial for its success. The Dutch established the Stichting het Voedingsmiddelenfonds (VMF) to carry out these tasks. The organization was continued in the post-independence era under the name JUBM

(Jajasan Urusan Bahan Makanan, Foundation for Food Affairs), to be replaced by Bulog (Badan Urusan Logistik, Bureau of Logistics) in 1967.

According to Peter Timmer, JUBM became a failure because it was lacking the competencies to carry out the fairly complicated co-ordinative tasks.[30] Shortages of foreign reserves hampered the possibilities to stabilize rice supplies via imports in bad harvest years. The mounting budget deficits that sparked-off hyperinflation in the early 1960s derailed the economy and frustrated the functioning of the rice marketing system altogether. As the national rice market crumbled, local administrators started to protect regional supplies and rice price differentials shot up, undermining the attempts of the central government to restore control over this strategic commodity.

Macro-economic mismanagement and the collapse of the rice marketing system also frustrated the structural agricultural development programmes of the Sukarno government. According to Palmer, Java was a 'hothouse' of rural experiments in the 1960s.[31] The implementation in 1959 of a three-year plan to boost rice production included mass demonstration programmes (DEMAS, *mass demonstration*) of fertilizer, pesticides, improved seed varieties, irrigation techniques and the provision of government credit at favourable interest rates. In 1963, attending extension services under the BIMAS programme (*mass guidance*) became mandatory. It remains open to question to what extent the failure of the DEMAS and BIMAS programmes to produce immediate results should be attributed to farmers' resistance to change, the bad management of the programmes (inputs that were not distributed, credits that were not supplied) or the macro-economic conditions (hyperinflation, huge rice price volatility) under which they were implemented or tried out.[32]

It seems clear, however, that these factors reinforced each other. The government allocation of agricultural implements was hampered by a lack of foreign reserves to buy the necessary inputs. The BIMAS programme got the reputation of mismanagement because the promised delivery of agricultural inputs or credit was either delayed, restricted or completely abandoned. Farmers were hesitant to bear the risk of spending substantial parts of their hard-won cash income on high-cost chemical fertilizers, while facing 'unreliable' programme officers. But even if farmers had wanted to consider experimentation with new cultivation practices, they operated in a macro-context of mounting economic insecurity. The hyperinflation that reached its peak in 1966 made their precious cash savings evaporate before they could even spend it on chemical fertilizer or high-yielding rice seed.

Why did New Order Policies Succeed?

Obviously, the success of New Order agricultural policies cannot be explained by a sudden shift in smallholder mentality, or a sudden boost in farmers' education. Indonesian rice farmers did not become 'rational' entrepreneurs from one day to another. In a similar vein, we should not place much emphasis on the fact that Suharto had been the son of a peasant in order to explain his strong personal commitment to rural development.[33] When viewed from a long-run comparative perspective, it becomes clear that the Javanese rice sector was at the top of the political agenda ever since the start of the twentieth century. The goal of food self-sufficiency was no less important for Suharto than it had been for Sukarno, as both leaders knew that their political survival depended on their ability to guarantee food security. In fact, Sukarno had turned rice into an even more important strategic commodity by financing part of the public sector employees in rice allowances. The chapter by Cribb in this volume underlines the great strategic importance of rice during the Indonesian Revolution.

Yet, in comparison to Sukarno, Suharto enjoyed four major advantages, which together can explain the 'take-off'. These four conditions convoluted in the late 1960s were partly coincidental and partly a matter of government agency. The first advantage was this exogenous technology shock: the release of the IR8 in 1966 by the IRRI. What is important for the discussion here is the insight that this modern HYV changed the structure of the rice farmers' cost-benefit calculation. The IR8 raised the expected returns to farmers' investments in chemical fertilizer and irrigation. Village studies have shown that whether that shift in the expected profit margin was immediately acknowledged depended on many other local conditions such as marketing possibilities, access to credit, social structures and potential crop diseases. The bottom line, however, is that these new HYVs tilted the prevailing cost-benefit calculations in which traditional varieties were considered the safest choice.

The second advantage was that Suharto and his economic advisers had themselves experienced how a lack of foreign reserves and foreign political support had destabilized the Indonesian economy, while they did not have to pay the political price for this crisis—yet. In the face of this crisis, Suharto had basically no other option than to break with the economic policies of his predecessor and invest all his efforts in stabilization of the economy.[34] It meant a radical break in international political orientation, shifting away from economic nationalism towards Western capitalism, and this move prevented Suharto from repeating the economic mistakes of Sukarno's 'guided democracy'.[35] The channelling of substantial oil revenues in the 1970s towards rural development programmes becomes much more comprehensible when you realize that the lessons of the crisis of the 1960s were not only still very fresh, but were basically the foundation of Suharto's political position.

The third advantage that Suharto enjoyed is a factor that his government can rightly be credited for: the encompassing price policy conducted by Bulog created favourable conditions for the adoption of modern HYVs. This price policy sought to mediate three sets of parameters: (1) balancing the opposing interests of consumers, producers and traders by setting a floor price for farmers at the state-controlled rice mills and a ceiling rice price for consumers, while leaving sufficient margins for traders to effectively deliver their milling and marketing services; (2) balancing the high costs of expensive agricultural inputs required to grow HYVs (fertilizers in particular) and the additional revenues that farmers expected to make. This balance was achieved by using a simple rule of thumb, the *rumus tami* (the farmer's formula), stipulating that the price of a kilogram of milled rice should more or less equal the price of a kilogram of fertilizer; (3) keeping domestic rice prices within a certain range of world market prices in order to contain the undermining impact of illegal exports (in case of underpricing) or imports (in case of overpricing).[36]

Pierre van der Eng has shown that state intervention in both fertilizer and rice prices helped to cross a long-term threshold. The average ratio of nitrogen fertilizer to rice prices, shown in Table 16.1, indicates that virtual price-parity was reached in the 1970s. In comparison to Japan, the decreasing trend in the relative price of fertilizer in Indonesia lagged behind for about two decades.[37] Micro-studies comparing adoption rates between villages also underscore that the access to fertilizer was one of the key parameters in the decision of farmers to adopt HYVs.[38]

Gonzales et al. demonstrate that Bulog also succeeded in balancing national and international rice prices. Their calculations of the rate of protection for a number of food and cash crops in Indonesia show that, between 1972 and 1988, the nominal rate of protection of Indonesian rice (that is, the ratio of domestic wholesale prices over c.i.f. import prices) fluctuated within a band of around –20 to +20 per cent. Meanwhile, Bulog managed to contain domestic rice price volatility, thereby raising farm investors' confidence.

Interestingly, other crops such as soybeans and sugar were receiving far higher rates of protection, paid by extensive government subsidies.[39]

Table 16.1: Price ratio of chemical fertilizers to rice in Indonesia and Japan, 1900–89

	Indonesia		*Japan*	
	Nitrogen	*Phosphorus*	*Nitrogen*	*Phosphorus*
1900–09			7.6	2.1
1910–19	9.8		6.9	1.5
1920–29	5.5	2.6	3.5	1.2
1930–39	4.4	2.8	2.4	1.3
1951–59	2.4	1.2	1.5	1.1
1960–69	1.9		0.9	0.8
1970–79	1.1	1.1	0.5	0.6
1980–89	0.6	0.6	0.5	0.6

Notes: Prices for Indonesia (1910–19) refer to 1913–19, (1951–59) to 1951–55 and (1960–69) to 1962–69

Source: Van der Eng, *Agricultural Growth in Indonesia*, 116.

The different rates of protection of various crops concurs with Bulog's reputation for abusing its monopoly power in order to make money on the margins that it set between domestic prices and international market prices.[40] Bulog's lack of transparency, together with the limited tenability of expensive subsidy programmes, led to increasing discussions in the 1980s. Especially after the uniform objective of rice autarky had been achieved, and the social returns to high-cost subsidies became less visible, the call for agricultural policy reforms arose. Fertilizer subsidies became an ever-larger drain on the government budget, and the continuing support of the rice sector hampered the diversification of agricultural production, for instance into the tree crops (coffee, cocoa, tea, rubber and palm oil) that were considered important for smallholders in the lesser developed parts of the Outer Provinces.[41]

But let's turn back to the early years of policy success to discuss the fourth, and indispensable advantage of the New Order regime: large-scale international support (see also the chapter on food aid by Van der Eng in this volume). The regime change in Indonesia occurred right at the time that the war in Vietnam was escalating. For the US this war was spinning out of control. Convinced that the impoverished masses in Asia acted as a magnet to socialist propaganda, the US were eager to support Suharto's anti-communist actions by all means.[42] The US had already invested heavily in rural development programmes in their former colony, the Philippines, and quickly grasped the opportunity to build up comparable stakes in Indonesia, which was after all the largest Southeast Asian economy with a considerable geo-political weight.

The Western powers and Japan rescheduled Indonesia's foreign debt and granted ample access to international loans via the International Monetary Fund (IMF) to stabilize the Indonesian economy. In addition, large amounts of development aid started to flow in, soon followed by substantial flows of foreign direct investment.[43] This international assistance cemented the position of Bulog in various ways. Access to foreign reserves secured Bulog's ability to import food, replenish Indonesian rice stocks, and restart to mediate seasonal and regional variations in rice production. Western economic advisers and US-trained Indonesian economists helped to fine-tune agricultural policies and strengthen information collection procedures to guide agricultural policy-making. And, as Suharto successfully withstood the call for renewed economic nationalism, he managed to secure Western support during the remainder of the Cold War. By the time the Iron Curtain fell, Indonesia had become the largest net-recipient of international aid after India and China.[44]

A Replicable Success?

Let's return to the key question of this chapter: is the success of Indonesia's green revolution replicable? The short answer is: No. Indonesia's combination of high demographic pressure, an ecosystem supporting wet rice cultivation, and a long history of intensive state investments in physical and organizational infrastructures for rice production was already fairly unique in Asia, let alone other parts of the world. The new HYVs came very close to a 'silver bullet'-type of innovation. In Africa, such biotechnological innovations are unlikely to have a comparable impact, because of greater ecological (climate, soil types, water resources and so on) and staple crop diversity.[45] This does not imply that rapid productivity gains on a local level based on modern rice varieties are impossible. In fact, in Benin and Rwanda rapid yield-based growth in rice has been recorded after 2000 and there still is a large stock of transferable technology available.[46] It only implies that new rice varieties cannot generate the same scale-effect as the rice revolution had in many Asian countries.

Following the logic of the induced institutional innovation model, which essentially builds upon a Boserupian line of argumentation, demographic pressures pushed colonial agricultural policies in the Netherlands Indies after 1900 in a direction that was very different from the African context of population scarcity.[47] Colonial governments in Africa disposed of (much) smaller government budgets (by itself a function of different agricultural systems and population densities) and prioritized export crops and mining activities instead of food crop production. In this respect, Dutch colonial policies in the mid-nineteenth century resembled the colonial policies in Africa much better than after 1900. African colonial governments and European businesses were bent on solving labour scarcity problems as a result of high land-labour ratios and did not hesitate to withdraw labour from villages, the centres of food production, to support the export sector. Infrastructural investments were geared towards the export of tropical cash crops and minerals as well.[48]

That said, there are a number of lessons we can draw from a closer inspection of Indonesia's *agricultural policy history*, which may actually gain relevance with demographic pressures building up so rapidly in present-day sub-Saharan Africa:

1. The case of Indonesia demonstrates that agricultural transitions can come unexpectedly and can lay at the basis of a fundamental break in income growth and living standards improvements for broad layers of the population. There is no ground for the deep-seated pessimism about African economic development that has dominated the academic literature for a long time, until the sentiment started to change in the late 2000s.[49]
2. The case of Indonesia shows that state co-ordination is crucial by accommodating market imperfections that obstruct the adoption of new cultivation technologies and practices. Governments can accommodate an undersupply of infrastructure, spur the diffusion of knowledge or counter the negative impact of price volatility on investor's decisions. But state development programmes also require time to get a number of necessary conditions right, and should therefore not too quickly be dismissed as ineffective.
3. The case of Indonesia shows that price interventions need to be embedded in encompassing price policy, which has to be continuously evaluated against changing domestic and international market conditions. This requires a certain degree of state capacity and, in case of need, is supported by foreign know-how.
4. The case of Indonesia shows that smallholders, with very little education and small investment potential, can become central agents of change once a number of co-ordination problems are being resolved.
5. The case of Indonesia shows that international economic assistance and aid can help to spur agricultural productivity growth, once there

exists a shared view on development priorities and the policies required to target these priorities.

6. Finally, the last lesson that we can derive from the Indonesian case is that 'time' and 'timing' matter a lot. To explain the absence of a green revolution in Africa to date, it remains a puzzle as to what extent governments failed to support food agriculture because of neglect, or because they were incapable of resolving the weak conditions for a take-off per se? And how are both factors connected? Did weak conditions lead to ineffective policies and, in turn, to governments losing interest in support programmes? And to what extent did the structural adjustment programmes of the 1980s and 1990s generate conditions (austerity measures and trade liberalization) that were almost the opposite of the ample support that Suharto received in the 1970s and 1980s?

In retrospect it seems safe to conclude that the conditions for a green revolution in Africa were indeed suboptimal, to put it mildly. Post-independent governments lacked the state capacity to implement complicated support programmes. Farmers lacked market access, because of weak physical and institutional infrastructures, and low rates of consumer density. Fragile macro-economic conditions lowered farmers' time horizon. And, in a period where world food-market prices were historically low, as a result of green revolutions elsewhere in the world, governments faced an attractive alternative to domestic productivity growth to contain urban riots: cheap food imports made even cheaper by currency overvaluation.[50]

Having said that, it appears that conditions in sub-Saharan Africa reveal increasing similarities to those in Indonesia in the 1960s. The concerns about current rates of African population growth and urbanization are remarkably similar to those voiced some fifty years ago in Asia, and it is bound to change the parameters of agrarian production. Growing urban demand, in combination with higher international food prices, will make investments in local African food production systems more attractive. Colonial investments in railways and harbours connected local economic enclaves to European markets during the first half of the twentieth century, but today's investments in road infrastructure, transport equipment, electricity, and information and communications (ICT) infrastructure allow for a much more fine-grained process of domestic market integration. New communication technologies offer real-time market information to farmers at acceptable costs and facilitate new forms of credit, saving and insurance. Indeed, the tyranny of distance in Africa is rapidly dissolving. Last but not least, current macro-economic conditions in most African countries are far better than they were in the past forty years. There is controlled inflation. Exchange rates are no longer systematically overvalued and the majority of African economies grow at rates of 3–6 per cent per year, despite the severe financial and economic crisis in the industrialized world.[51] Foreign investments are rapidly increasing. In previous periods of global economic crisis, during the Great Depression of the 1930s and the oil crises of the 1970s, African economies did experience serious setbacks. The current recession in Europe does not seem to backfire on Africa. Are these the first signs of a New Order?

Notes

1. See the chapter by Van der Eng in this volume for a discussion of food aid to Indonesia in the 1950s–70s.
2. See a Malthusian interpretation of Asian development prospects in Ehrlich, *The Population Bomb*; Myrdal, *Asian Drama*; and more specifically on Indonesia: Geertz, *Agricultural Involution*; Penny, 'Indonesia. In *Agricultural Development in Asia*'.
3. See a number of key studies in Hansen, *Agricultural and Rural Development*; Booth, *Agricultural Development in Indonesia*; Van der Eng, *Agricultural Growth in Indonesia*; Hill, *The Indonesian Economy*, chapters 7 and 10; Tabor, 'Agriculture in Transition'.
4. See Frankema, *Africa and the Green Revolution*, 2; Tabor, 'Agriculture in Transition'.
5. See an extensive discussion of the threats and opportunities of African demographic growth in Severino and Ray, *Africa's Moment*.
6. See a discussion about the relationship between the Cold war, bio-technological change and the green revolution in Asia in Perkins, *Geopolitics and the Green Revolution* and Cullather, *The Hungry World*.
7. See the Indonesia-Nigeria comparison in Bevan et al., *The Political Economy*; Scherr, 'Agriculture in an Export Boom Economy'. For a broader perspective, see the edited volume by Gelb, *Oil Windfalls*.
8. The term 'Doubly Green Revolution' was coined by Gordon Conway and stresses the need for agricultural transitions based on ecologically sustainable production methods. Conway, *The Doubly Green Revolution*, 31–42.
9. Estudillo and Otsuka, 'Lessons from the Asian Green Revolution in Rice', 18.
10. See a discussion in Frankema, *Africa and the Green Revolution*, 6–8. It is also interesting to note that the term 'green' does not actually refer to what people usually think it refers to, namely 'a field of green plants'. In fact, the term 'Green' was invented by USAID director William Gaud in 1968

(Cullather, *The Hungry World*, 7) to contrast America's foreign policy with the violence associated with Red guerilla movements. 'Green', as opposed to 'Red', referred to the colour of peace. Peaceful scientific progress was presented as the capitalist alternative to combat hunger, poverty and inequality and the Americans actively invested in this strategy, amongst others via the establishment of the IRRI in the Philippines. See Cullather, *The Hungry World*, 7 and Chandler, *An Adventure*, chapters 1 and 5.

11. Mariyono, 'Technological and Institutional Change', 125.
12. Booth, *Agricultural Development in Indonesia*, Table 5.29, 193. See also Hill, *The Indonesian Economy*, chapter 10.
13. Data are from Maddison, *Historical Statistics*. See for an account of the structural change and growth acceleration since 1967: Thee Kian Wie, 'The Soeharto Era'.
14. Lipton, *Why Poor People Stay Poor*, 24: quoted in Henley, *The Agrarian Roots of Industrial Growth*, s25.
15. Geertz, *Agricultural Involution*, 146; Penny, 'Indonesia. In *Agricultural Development in Asia*', 263.
16. Penny, 'Indonesia. In *Agricultural Development in Asia*', 263.
17. Geertz, *Agricultural Involution*, 138.
18. Ibid., 146.
19. Prabowo and Sajoggyo, 'Sidoarjo, East Java, and Subang', 71. See also Dalrymple, *Development and Spread of High-Yielding Rice Varieties*, 47–50.
20. Dalrymple, *Development and Spread of High-Yielding Rice Varieties*, xx; Chandler, *An Adventure in Applied Science*, 104–8.
21. Palmer, *The New Rice*, 110.
22. Booth, *Agricultural Development in Indonesia*; Hayami, 'An Ecological and Historical Perspective'.
23. Booth, *Agricultural Development in Indonesia*, 37.
24. Van der Eng, *Agricultural Growth in Indonesia*, 69–81.
25. Booth, *Agricultural Development in Indonesia*, 101.
26. Ibid., 119–23.
27. See for a survey of colonial investments in irrigation infrastructure: Van der Eng, *Agricultural Growth in Indonesia*, 41–69.
28. Marks, 'Unity or Diversity', 310.
29. Timmer, 'The Formation of Indonesian Rice Policy', 33–7.
30. Ibid., 35.
31. Palmer, *The New Rice*, 21.
32. Ibid., 25–31.
33. On Suharto's biographic relationship to the Indonesian countryside, see Elson, *Suharto: A Political Biography*, 172–3.
34. Papaioannou and van Zanden, 'The Dictator Effect'.
35. See for an overview: Thee Kian Wie, 'The Soeharto Era'.

36. Djurfeldt and Jirström, 'The Puzzle', 47–8; Timmer, 'The Formation of Indonesian Rice Policy', 37–9.
37. Van der Eng, *Agricultural Growth*, 114–7
38. Prabowo and Sajoggyo, 'Sidoarjo, East Java, and Subang', 72.
39. Gonzales et al., *Economic Incentives*, 55–9, 67–72.
40. See Van der Eng in this volume.
41. Tabor, 'Agriculture in Transition', 196–9.
42. Thee, 'The Soeharto Era and After', 205.
43. Ibid., 203–7.
44. Ibid., 206.
45. Larson and Otsuka, *An African Green Revolution*, vi.
46. Frankema, *Africa and the Green Revolution*, 17; Estudillo and Otsuka, 'Lessons from the Asian Green Revolution in Rice'.
47. Hayami and Ruttan, 'An Ecological and Historical Perspective'.
48. See for a comparison of government budgets in the British empire, Frankema, 'Raising Revenue in the British Empire'. See a direct comparison of agricultural policies in Indonesia and the Congo in Booth, 'Varieties of Exploitation'.
49. See for instance Bates et al., 'Lost Decades: Postindependence Performance' or Radelet, 'Emerging Africa'.
50. Frankema, *Africa and the Green Revolution*, 14–6.
51. IMF, *Regional Economic Outlook*.

17

Policy Regimes, Statistics and Unintended Consequences: Transitions in Indonesia's Modern Economic History

Howard Dick

Total output is a figment which would not exist at all, were there no statisticians to create it.

– Joseph A. Schumpeter, 1939[1]

A leitmotif of Indonesia's modern history over the past two hundred years has been the consolidation of a rational bureaucratic state.[2] This perspective was put forward in English writings by Clive Day and J.S. Furnivall before being taken up by many others.[3] Ben Anderson argued that Suharto's New Order could best be understood as a restoration of an atrophied state.[4] Thomas Lindblad with myself, Vincent Houben and Thee Kian Wie made state formation one of the three main threads of our economic history of Indonesia.[5] Thomas is an economic historian who has sought to make what he can of statistics without being beholden to them. So here I want to turn our argument inside out by exploring the relationship between policy regimes and statistics. This approach undermines any narrative of inexorable progress and suggests that the normal situation has been and still is one of muddle, a view with which Day would probably have concurred.

A policy regime has some parallel with Thomas Kuhn's scientific paradigm,[6] but is altogether a more elastic concept: the constituent elements may be identified as an elite of powerholders, a shared mindset or ideology giving rise to specific goals (while ruling out others), and a set of bureaucratic routines to achieve them. These three elements are sufficient to generate a stable, self-reinforcing pattern of knowledge, actions and outcomes with a very specific distribution of benefits and costs. Statistics link knowledge, actions and outcomes and bind them into a self-reinforcing system of government: they are the essential corpuscles for the vitality and effectiveness of a modern state bureaucracy. Economics and economic history, both of which seek to relate causes and consequences, not least by the thread of government intervention, might therefore be expected to pay careful attention to the availability and quality of statistics. Yet although data analysis has come to be seen as the very essence of these disciplines, the statistics themselves are too often taken for granted without much, if any, investigation of their provenance and rationale.

The availability of statistics is both the product and the underpinning of a policy regime: what is to be managed must be measured, and what is measured may also be managed. Yet statistics and analysis cannot just be conjured up. Sometimes the concepts themselves are vague, or the tools and techniques are not available to allow the necessary synthesis. Transition between policy regimes may therefore take a very long time. This chapter explores this proposition by examining two transitions. The first, which took the best part of the twentieth century, was the shift from a regime of colonial exploitation to one of improving welfare for the common people: the goal was proclaimed in 1901 in Queen Wilhelmina's speech from the throne and gave rise to the so-called Ethical Policy. However, not until the nationalist revolution of 1945–49, the introduction of national income accounting, and the consolidation of the developmentalist New Order in the 1970s was there at last a significant alleviation of poverty. The second transition is still ongoing. Developmentalism had the unintended consequence, validated by flaws in statistical coverage, of massive environmental despoliation and destruction. Along with the rest of the world, Indonesia is now struggling to find ways to incorporate environmental accounting into a new regime of sustainable development. The intent traces back to the seminal Club of Rome report of 1972 but, notwithstanding the increasingly harsh realities of climate change, progress over the past forty years has been agonizingly slow.[7] Environmentalism remains an intellectual challenge to the developmental regime, not yet the handmaiden of a new regime of sustainable development.

Indonesia is a rather special case. Colonial conquest made the Indonesian Archipelago a subjugated, peripheral territory. At the same time, colonial rule did provide a channel, albeit a narrow one, for the transfer of much of the technology of the modern European state, including in the nineteenth century some of the mechanisms and routines of the new science of statistics. By 1900 colonial administration was therefore much more modern and empirically based in Indonesia than it was, for example, in imperial China. Tong Lam nicely explains how the Qing administration was then only beginning to conceive of a nation and a society in statistical terms.[8] Yet ironically Indonesia squandered its advantage in the first two decades of independence. Although many of the mechanisms and routines of data collection were perpetuated, the decay of state administration together with economic decline meant that by the 1960s most official statistics were becoming less and less reliable. Nevertheless, by a quirk of history, in the late 1960s a demographer and statistician, Professor Widjojo Nitisastro, became the leader of the group of technocrats who stabilized the economy and set it on a path of economic development. An early imperative was to ensure a reliable system of national income accounting.

This chapter begins with a brief review of the evolution of statistics in the colonial era, and then looks at the impact of national income accounting by the device of comparing the structure of the statistical yearbooks for 1939 and 2009. Next it explores how the limitations of national income accounting have had unintended consequences, most notably in regard to the environment, before outlining recent progress with measures of 'green GDP' (gross domestic product) and sustainable development.

Colonial Statistics

The systematic collection of statistics on the government, people, trade and revenues of the Dutch colonies then known as the Netherlands Indies (Nederlandsch-Indië) may be traced back to the surveys instigated by Governor-General Thomas Raffles during the British interregnum of 1811–16. In this endeavour Raffles acted in the spirit of William Petty

(1623–87), the self-declared founder of the discipline of political arithmetic as a basis for mercantilist economic prosperity. By modern standards, Raffles's enumerations were crude and often improvised, but it was the first attempt to assess the wealth of the new colony as opposed to the Dutch East India Company's (VOC's) preoccupation with exploitation and profit. The returning Dutch civil administration built on these foundations. In the 1820s there began what may be regarded as the first statistical series, on the exports and imports of Java and Madura.[9]

As is well known, the ruinous Java War (1825–30) set colonial administration on a different path through the introduction in 1830 of the notorious, state-controlled Cultivation System, the aim of which was to exploit Java's land and labour in order to restore the public finances of the Netherlands that had been struck a further blow with the secession of Belgium. The modest state apparatus was now directed towards that end with urgent need for accurate local and aggregate statistics on compulsory labour services, crop production, deliveries, exports and revenues. All this, however, skewed state administration away from any rational bureaucratic model with pernicious effects that were not addressed until the introduction in 1870 of a liberal colonial regime committed to private enterprise.

Meanwhile, the government of the Netherlands itself had been placed on a modern basis by the Constitution of 1848, which differentiated civil administration from the royal family and, among many other reforms, set in train comprehensive annual reporting on colonial administration to the Dutch parliament. The first Colonial Report (Koloniaal Verslag) for the year 1849 was tabled in 1851, thereby beginning a century-long series that gradually accumulated statistical appendices. In the early years, however, statistical reporting was still rudimentary and little more than a by-product of administrative reporting. The notable exceptions were the records of public finance, the finely detailed trade statistics and the monitoring of the land, labour and crops involved in the state-directed Cultivation System.

Eventually the compilation of colonial statistics began to reflect the more systematic approach being applied in the Netherlands. From 1887 a separate annual Statistical Abstract for the colonies (*Jaarcijfers voor het Koninkrijk der Nederlanden, Koloniën*) was published by the Vereeniging voor de Statistiek, then from 1892 more formally by the Centrale Commissie (later Centraal Bureau) voor de Statistiek in the Netherlands.[10] Eventually in 1923 responsibility for a more comprehensive annual statistical report was transferred to the recently established Statistisch Kantoor (Statistical Office) within the Department of Agriculture, Industry and

Commerce: the first issue in the new series for 1922/23 was published in two parts in October 1924 as *Statistisch Jaaroverzicht voor Nederlandsch-Indië* (Statistical Abstract for the Netherlands East-Indies). In 1925 the Statistisch Kantoor was elevated in status to the Centraal Kantoor voor de Statistiek (Central Bureau of Statistics) and moved into more spacious premises opposite Pasar Besar on Schoolweg (now Jalan Dr Sutomo and still the site of Badan Pusat Statistik)—in 1933 its controlling department assumed the more succinct title of Economic Affairs (Economische Zaken). Meanwhile, in 1931 the annual Statistical Abstract had become Part II of the annual Netherlands Indian Report (*Indisch Verslag*): from 1935 a condensed, small-format pocket book (*Zakboekje*) was also published for wider distribution.

An interesting feature of this slow evolution of modern statistical reporting was the unit of aggregation. From the end of the Java War in 1830, Java (apart from the princely states) constituted a territorial unit under direct Dutch rule and for statistical purposes was combined with the minor offshore appendage of Madura. The rest of the Netherland Indies, the Outer Territories (Buitengewesten), was an awkward residual. While the Dutch had achieved diplomatic recognition for its sphere of influence, very little of the Outer Islands was as yet under Dutch administration. Customs houses in the few Dutch port towns exercised very little control over the trade of this vast area, which for the most part flowed through Singapore.[11] In 1874 the separate trade statistics for Java and the Outer Islands were at last added up as a notional Netherlands Indies total, but not until the 'pacification' of the last anti-colonial resistance in the first decade of the twentieth century did the Netherlands Indies become a true colonial domain.

Yet even after their complete subjugation, the Outer Territories continued to be an adjunct to Java for most statistical purposes. By the 1920s the logic of aggregation for the whole colony was at least being recognized, but the patchwork of administrative and economic systems militated against the collection of uniform statistics. Only in the case of some more recent statistical collections, such as some criminal and education statistics, was the distinction between Java and Madura and the Outer Territories no longer made by the 1930s. The Netherlands Indies was becoming something more than an archipelago, but it was still a nation-in-waiting.

One notable exception to this statistical disaggregation was the comprehensive household census of 1930. Whereas the results of the modest 1905 census had been reported as an annex to the 1907 Colonial Report and those of the much better 1920 census appeared in 1922 as a separate two-volume work, the 1930 census was published in eight volumes over a six-year period. Only then, in the mid-1930s, did the population of the Netherlands Indies at last become legible as an aggregation of races (European, Chinese and Other Foreign Orientals and Natives) and of geographic and administrative units (villages and towns, districts and provinces). For all that, the data on occupation, socio-economic status and welfare were still crude. Unlike the government of the Republic of China, the Dutch colonial government made little investment in large-scale social surveys, a science that was introduced to China by US scholars during the interwar years and was a useful tool for catching up.[12] Whereas the new republican government sought to redress its lack of knowledge, the Dutch colonial government could rely on a sophisticated and fine-tuned system of administrative reporting. Nevertheless, a few pioneering local surveys were carried out in the 1930s, most notably the Koetowinangun (Kebumen) village study by Ochse and Terra and the municipal labourers ('coolie') survey in Jakarta (Batavia) by Hart and Tan.[13]

The *content* of colonial statistics reflected the functions and bureaucratic routines of the colonial state. A function would be specified and a reporting mechanism set in place with a form to be filled out; at higher levels of government there were procedures to assess the report and collate the information. A prime example was the customs declaration that traders had to fill out for assessment of tariffs and excises to submit at the local customs house for the clearance of goods inwards or outwards—in the colonial era forms also had to be filled out for goods shipped in inter-island trade. Since 1823 these customs forms have provided the raw data that are aggregated at each level of the bureaucratic hierarchy and ultimately measure the balance of trade, subject of course to any errors and omissions from smuggling and false declarations.

It follows from the nature of government itself that, in the absence of some massive disruption such as war or revolution, these statistical routines are stable, almost metronomic, as may be seen in the content of annual statistical yearbooks. For example, the size and structure of the Statistical Abstract for 1929 and the Netherlands Indian Report of 1940 (for the year 1939) was almost identical. The former was 556 pages including index, the latter 549 pages: the chapter structure was identical except that the 1940 report had two new sections, each a single table, on the very last page before the index. That said, various minor improvements had been made: some tables were dropped, others added, some reconfigured.

Table 17.1: Contents by page numbers of the *Indisch Verslag 1940*

1.	Territory	1–2
2.	Meteorology, Seismology and Volcanology	3–12
3.	Population	13–77
4.	Health	78–93
5.	Intellectual state of the population	94–130
6.	Religions	131–149
7.	Justice	150–173
8.	Economic and social condition of the population	175–254
9.	Production	255–334
10.	Commerce	335–355
11.	Prices, index numbers and cost of living	356–364
12.	Currency, banking and Credits	365–383
13.	Communications	384–437
14.	Balance of Payments	438
15.	Organisation of the Government	439–453
16.	Government Finances	454–490
17.	The Native States	491–515
18.	Representative councils	516–535
19.	*Local funds*	536
20.	*Native municipalities*	536–537

Table 17.1 shows the structure of the last Netherlands Indian Report that was issued in January 1941, eight months after Germany had overrun the Netherlands and just a year before the Japanese invasion. The first seven chapters give an overview of the colony's physical geography, population, public health, education, religion and legal situation (justice); the subsequent thirteen chapters all deal in some way with economic matters and public finance.

Noticeably missing from this enormous digest is an overview of the welfare of the population. Chapter 8 ('Economic and social condition of the population') implies such a focus but besides some old data on occupations taken from the 1930 census, the bulk of this 80-page section is taken up by matters of taxation, savings and loans, and co-operatives. While these data do give some insight into the stratification of the population by income and wealth, they by no means equate to modern standard-of-living measures. An assortment of other administrative statistics relate to the availability of foodstuffs, orphanages, homes for beggars, the infirm and the blind, people trafficking, lotteries, guardianships, bankruptcies, trademarks, and weights and measures. At the very end come tables on plantation wages, 'coolie' migration, contracts and complaints (also 'coolie assaults' on 'supervising estate personnel'), recruitment of indentured Javanese labour, labour exchanges, registered unemployment (two new tables reflecting the economic crisis of the 1930s) and, lastly, trade union membership and strikes. There is even a table on the mangrove timber concessions (*panglong*) in the Outer Islands. Some of the detail is exquisite, such as the table on 'Admission tickets on which [municipal] entertainment tax was levied in the municipalities Batavia, Bandoeng and Semarang': eleven price ranges are distinguished for theatrical performances, moving pictures, music and singing performances, dances and cabarets, circuses, matches and open-air games, and exhibitions and lectures. Overall, however, this colonial potpourri offers little insight into the living conditions of the Indonesian population.

This problem is all the more striking because by 1940 almost four decades had elapsed since proclamation of the Ethical Policy. That acceptance of moral responsibility, of a colonial 'burden', led in the first instance to the extensive investigations of the Diminishing Welfare Inquiry (Onderzoek naar de Mindere Welvaart der Inlandsche Bevolking op Java en Madoera), which was carried out in every district over the period 1904–05 and published in multiple volumes and parts over the next decade, including specific volumes on fisheries, poultry, cattle, transport, agriculture, trade and industry, irrigation, law and police, and village economy. Except perhaps for the final volume, there was a marked emphasis on production and very little that nowadays would relate to consumption and welfare as such. By the end of this massive investigation there was much better knowledge of what occupied the population across the archipelago but still very little insight into the original question of whether welfare was indeed diminishing or improving. Much the same could be said of the work of van Ginkel, and Meijer-Ranneft and Huender, in their partial updating of the Diminishing Welfare Inquiry in order to assess the tax burden on the 'native' (*inlandsche*) population.[14] It is easy to criticize Dutch officials and researchers for not devoting more resources and being more diligent in researching changes to the welfare of the 'native' population. The fact remains, however, that until the work of Colin Clark in the 1930s, welfare was still a concept that defied more than crude measurement, anywhere in the world.

National Income Accounting

While the *Statistical Yearbook of Indonesia 2009* bears superficial resemblance to the Netherlands Indian Report 1940, its structure shows what

Table 17.2: Contents by page numbers of the *Statistical Yearbook of Indonesia 2009*

1.	Geography and Climate	3–30
2.	Government	31–72
3.	Population and Employment	73–116
4.	Social and Welfare	117–188
5.	Agriculture	189–282
6.	Mining and Energy	283–298
7.	Manufacturing Industry	299–322
8.	Construction	323–340
9.	Hotels and Tourism	341–362
10.	Transport and Communications	363–390
11.	Banking, Insurance and Cooperatives	391–426
12.	Prices	427–458
13.	Population Expenditure, Food Availability and Consumption	459–484
14.	Foreign Trade	485–542
15.	National Accounts	543–612
16.	International Comparisons	613–625

a revolution had occurred over those seventy years (Table 17.2). The first four chapters similarly address physical geography, population, education, health and crime, but there is a much sharper focus on poverty. Subsection 4.6 (Poverty and Human Development) has five tables that measure numbers below the poverty line, broken down by province and further disaggregated into rural and urban. Education is measured by literacy, attendance and the numbers of schools, teachers and students by each level from kindergarten through to university, though without any metrics for quality. Health statistics are rather more selective but include data on contraception. There are also statistics on house size and owners, water supply, lighting, access to toilets, and type of cooking fuel. Generally, it is just a snapshot of living standards but a much more comprehensive and precise one than was available even at the end of the colonial era. It is supplemented in Chapter 13 by aggregate data on expenditure, food availability and consumption. While the remaining chapters of the 2009 yearbook are, as in 1940, devoted to economic matters, the structure is much tighter. Chapters 5 to 11 correspond with specific sectors of the national accounts: agriculture, manufacturing, construction, hotels and tourism, transport and communications and banking, insurance and co-operatives, followed in Chapter 14 by foreign trade. The last two chapters summarize the national accounts and make international comparisons. In short, the modern yearbook has a coherent structure that relates micro-economic statistics to the macro-economic data of the national accounts.

The watershed may be found in mid-century, around the time of the last Netherlands Indies reports, when John Maynard Keynes called into being macro-economics and macro-economic policy with publication in 1936 of *The General Theory*.[15] This theoretical breakthrough was soon followed by the invention of national income accounting. Colin Clark and (Sir) John Crawford were pioneers in 1938 with their *National Income of Australia*, predating Simon Kuznets et al.'s *National Income and Its Composition, 1919–1938* published by the National Bureau of Economic Research (NBER) in the United States.[16] Meanwhile Clark's protégé, Richard Stone, had been compiling the first national income accounts for the United Kingdom.

Indonesia's first quasi-modern estimates of national income were made in 1943 by Dutch economist J.J. Polak for the years 1921–39, refining previous crude estimates by Meyer Ranneft and Huender (1926) and Gotzen (1933), both of which had sought to quantify the tax burden on the Indonesian population.[17] Polak's estimates were prepared on behalf of the Netherlands Indies government in exile for the Institute of Pacific Affairs and had very restricted private circulation.[18] He did not, however, apply the recent innovations of national income accounting. This was first attempted in 1948 by the Dutch Central Bureau of Statistics in revising Polak's estimates for 1938 and followed closely upon publication of the first modern national accounts by the United States in 1947.

In 1952 the United Nations (UN) with guidance from Richard Stone published the first set of international standards for a System of National Accounts (SNA).[19] Around the same time, Indonesia signed an agreement with the UN to provide expert advisers to establish a State Planning Bureau (Biro Perantjang Negara) with the task of preparing the first five-year plan. Ali Budiardjo, who in May 1953 was appointed Acting Director, later recalled how the first step was to compile basic economic data:

> Apart from data on production and investment, as well as on the agrarian and mining product export trade, which were controlled by major Dutch companies, basic data like population, estimates of population growth, national income, infrastructure, education and so forth were very brief or very difficult to collect.[20]

As part of this effort, UN national income adviser Daniel Neumark compiled a provisional GDP estimate for the year 1951/52.[21] Subsequently, a subordinate Bureau for Economics and Finance was set up, which under Muljatno Sindudharmoko estimated net domestic product (NDP) for the period 1951–59.[22]

National income estimates are no more reliable than the underlying statistical series. In principle, the collation of official statistics was the responsibility of the Kantor Pusat Statistik (KPS), as the Centraal Kantoor voor de Statistiek was now known, whose senior staff had remained Dutch until Sarbini Sumawinata took over as director in 1955.[23] In 1957 as Biro Pusat Statistik (BPS) it was raised to the status of an independent agency reporting to the prime minister.[24] Nevertheless, KPS/BPS was hopelessly under-resourced and until the end of the decade had few staff beyond Jakarta. Publication of the *Statistical Pocket Book of Indonesia* resumed in 1956 but the content was thin.[25] Because the most recent census had been that of 1930, even such basic data as the size and growth of the population and workforce could only be guessed at. Sarbini therefore gave high priority to what became, with a one-year deferral, the 1961 national census. This was followed by the first agricultural census of 1963, the first industrial census of 1964 and the first round of the national socio-economic (household) survey (Susenas) in 1963/64. Sadly little of this was ever published and most of the valuable base-line data seem to have been lost.

In 1960 national income accounting was also transferred to BPS. This effort continued to be supported by UN expert advisers until 1965 when President Sukarno, in a fit of pique, withdrew Indonesia from the United Nations, and also the International Monetary Fund (IMF) and World Bank. By then the chaos of guided economy with hyperinflation, multiple exchange rates, rationing and the spread of black markets was playing havoc with the reliability of economic statistics: the formal sector contracted and the undocumented informal sector proliferated.[26] There ensued the anti-communist bloodletting of 1965–66. These tumultuous events together brought about a hiatus of several years in statistical reporting. Even the pocket book series was suspended after 1963. After consolidation of the New Order government and the appointment of technocratic ministers, in 1968 BPS commenced a new series of GDP estimates according to United Nations guidelines. With countless refinements and periodic backcasting, this series has been maintained.[27]

Unintended Consequences

National income accounting quickly proved to be a powerful instrument of economic policy. In the West its immediate application was in targeting and measuring the impact of the new Keynesian macro-economic policies for full employment, but a subsidiary benefit soon became apparent in focusing attention on the need for development as a means of raising backward peoples out of poverty. Colin Clark had drawn attention to economic disparities in his seminal *Conditions of Economic Progress* (1940). The establishment of the United Nations, the independence of the Philippines in 1946 and of India and Pakistan in 1947, the parlous situation in China and the contest for Indonesia all gave political impetus, as did the worsening Cold War. Because the size of national economies could now be measured according to international conventions, it was practical to focus the rather vague concept of 'development' as 'economic development'. Publication by W.A. Lewis of *The Theory of Economic Growth* (1955) focused it even more narrowly as 'economic growth', that is to say, growth in GDP (or GDP per capita). According to Heinz Arndt, this 'shorthand' made a good deal of sense at the time.[28] For poor countries, the necessity was not Keynesian economic stability with full employment but raising the rate of investment to accelerate economic growth and thereby raise material living standards.

In time, however, the useful 'shorthand' began to constrain rather than assist the raising of what had once been known more simply as economic welfare. The conflation of development with economic growth was compounded by the casual assumption that growth in living standards could somehow be measured by the trend in income per capita, the material availability of goods and services, without regard to the distribution of income or the quality of life. Most people recognized some limitations of this reductionism and were not convinced by assertions that growth would eventually 'trickle down'. Other indicators came into play such as Gini coefficients and poverty lines, but without dethroning economic growth as the prime measure of economic performance.

The most insidious and unintended long-term consequence of the economistic focus on growth has been the neglect of environmental 'externalities', that is environmental inputs to production and consumption that are not valued for national accounting purposes at their true social cost, if indeed they are valued at all. In a resource-rich country such as Indonesia, this flaw in national income accounting has serious consequences. When depletable oil, gas and mineral resources are mined, the addition to GDP includes not just the value added but also part of the environmental capital stock that should, logically, be deducted in a similar way to depreciation. The same goes for forest and marine resources that are exploited beyond their sustainable harvest. Agricultural output should be reduced to the extent that the soil fertility is being depleted or the soil itself being washed away as silt, or aquifers being damaged. Manufacturing output is overstated because of failure to account for pollution, and so on.

The first warning bells for the consequences of unrestrained economic and population growth was sounded as long ago as 1972 when the report 'The Limits to Growth' was issued by the Club of Rome. In the same year, Nordhaus and Tobin argued for a sustainable measure of economic welfare (SMEW).[29] As it happened, the Club of Rome report was soon overtaken almost immediately by the sudden escalation of oil prices by the OPEC cartel. The price restraint on the growth of consumption, accompanied by the now profitable exploitation of offshore oilfields, eliminated any pressing concern as to the sufficiency of the world's oil reserves and the club's modelling came to be derided as a 'doomsday' scenario.

Interest in the Club of Rome's modelling revived around the turn of the century in light of the emerging scientific consensus around the threat of global warming. In Indonesia environmental awareness was much slower to emerge than in Europe or North America and was a matter of many small local streams gradually coming together and being informed by international discourse. Among these streams were deforestation, erosion, siltation and flooding; the deteriorating quality of drinking water; worsening air pollution, especially in Jakarta; annual forest fires in Sumatra and Kalimantan; and so on. As Indonesia's first and long-serving minister for the environment from 1978 to 1993, economist Emil Salim was instrumental in achieving official recognition of environmental problems, bringing about much better measurement of environmental indicators and promoting sustainable development.[30] Nevertheless, and despite his eminence, environmental policy remained marginal to mainstream economic policy throughout the New Order and subsequently.

One indication of the continuing marginality of the environment is the statistical yearbook. As late as 2009, the yearbook contained minimal environmental data. Apart from basic weather records, section 1 (climate and geography) has three indicators of pollution: Table 1.1.7 (status of river water quality), Table 1.2.5 (monthly average of suspended particulate matter in several cities) and Table 1.2.6 (import of materials containing ozone depleting substances). To this may be added in the forestry section Table 5.4.7 (progress of land rehabilitation). Of course, the Indonesian government through the Ministry of Environment does have at its disposal a large amount of environmental statistics down to the provincial and district level. Nevertheless, even allowing for the slow rate at which new statistics come into the format of the yearbook, this low incidence of environmental statistics demonstrates that they are still subsidiary, not yet integrated into the mainstream of economic policy, as indeed might be said of the Department of Environment itself. The explanation is partly political, partly the lack of a statistical method to integrate environmental considerations with the rest of economic and social policy to achieve a gradual shift towards a sustainable path of development.

Environmental Accounting

Though the concept of 'sustainable development' traces back to the Club of Rome, the term itself derives from the Brundtland Commission's report of 1987. Convened in 1983 by the United Nations under the chairmanship of former (and subsequent) Norwegian Prime Minister Gro Harlem Brundtland, the commission brought together the hitherto separate goals of development and environmental stewardship and maintained that they could be mutually compatible. This position was agreed notwithstanding that representatives of developing countries made up the majority of the commission membership: Indonesia was represented by Minister for Environment Emil Salim. It was recognized that progress in alleviating poverty would be illusory if environmental degradation would leave future generations worse off.[31]

While the concept of sustainable development found widespread support, there was no easy way to translate it into practice, not least because of the formidable problems of measuring and valuing environmental resources.[32] The favoured approach, eventually adopted by the United Nations, was to adjust the measure of GDP for environmental inputs and outputs, resulting in a new aggregate that has become known as 'green GDP'. In 1993, one year after the first UN Conference on Environment and Development held at Rio de Janeiro, a draft *Handbook of National Accounting: Integrated Environment and Economic Accounting* was issued and revised in 2003. In 2012 the System of Environmental Economic Accounting (SEEA) Central Framework was adopted as an official standard by the United Nations Statistical Commission with the endorsement of the European Commission, Food and Agriculture Organization (FAO),

IMF, Organisation for Economic Co-operation and Development (OECD) and the World Bank.[33] The new SEEA standard does not replace but supplement the Standard National Accounting (SNA) framework. For the foreseeable future, there will be two measures.

How quickly green GDP will achieve political legitimacy remains to be seen. In 2004 China surprised the world by releasing its first estimates of an adjusted 'green GDP', which, of course, showed that economic growth as conventionally measured was considerably overstated by ignoring the consumption of environmental resources. The initial estimate was to have been further refined, but in 2007 the Chinese government suppressed further publication. The challenge to the legitimacy of the headline conventional GDP and growth figures was too uncomfortable. Among economists there are also strong reservations about green GDP as a single, all-encompassing measure of environmental impact. These reservations were well summarized by the group of experts convened in February 2008 by then French President Nicholas Sarkozy as the Commission n the Measurement of Economic Performance and Social Progress (CMEPSP). Its report issued later that year addressed the limitations of GDP in the round, not only in regard to the environment.[34] Because of its emphasis on production rather than net income (after depreciation), GDP was seen for many reasons to be an inadequate measure of *current* wellbeing, even of material wellbeing. Green GDP seeks to eliminate the exaggeration of GDP by environmental impoverishment, but otherwise suffered similar shortcomings while being constrained by the further difficulties of valuing environmental outputs and the poor calibration with any sustainable growth path for future generations. The CMEPSP Commission argued that no single approach could deal with all the complexities but that, at least in principle, something like an 'extended wealth index', including both human and environmental capital, was needed to determine whether the prosperity of future generations was being enhanced or diminished by current production and consumption.

Nevertheless, at last there is international momentum for proper environmental accounting. In June 2012, twenty years after the historic Rio de Janiero conference and coinciding with release of the revised SEEA framework, the UN sponsored a follow-up Conference on Sustainable Development known as Rio+20. At this forum the World Bank launched a global partnership known as WAVES (Wealth Accounting and the Valuation of Ecosystem Services) to foster a Natural Capital Accounting initiative. Signatories included sixty-two countries plus private firms, non-government organizations (NGOs) and multilateral agencies.[35] WAVES will assist developing countries with institution building to implement natural capital accounting, much as the UN did with national income accounting in the 1950s and 1960s. Indonesia, like China, is not yet a signatory but preparatory statistical work is under way with the support of the national planning agency BAPPENAS.

Conclusion

History puts things in perspective. The past hundred years or so have pivoted around the big events of the mid-twentieth century: the long global depression of the 1930s, the great wars of 1937–45, and the Keynesian revolution in economic thinking and policy. In the case of Indonesia, Dutch rule, seemingly impregnable until 1940, had been swept away by 1950. After a long period of repression, politics now became the dominant discourse. President Sukarno epitomized the attitude that economics was tedious and should be subordinated to revolutionary ends. The unfortunate consequence was that over the first two decades of independence Indonesia became a much poorer country. Fifty years later, this all seems a long time ago. Despite some interruptions, Indonesia now boasts over four decades of rapid economic growth, a prosperous middle class, a modest gain in overall income per capita and a dramatic decline in poverty. As one of the Group of Twenty (G20), Indonesia is recognized as one of the world's twenty largest economies and, as the most populous Islamic nation, also one that is democratic, literate and increasingly prosperous, a nation with especial influence. Were it not for the simultaneous rise of China, Indonesia would be at the forefront of world attention.

None of this was inevitable. The outcomes now accepted as the normal state of affairs were the result of slow and often uncertain transitions, much affected by random shocks. For example, Indonesia would certainly not have achieved its independence in the 1940s had it not been for the great shock of the Second World War, which devastated the Netherlands and, through the Japanese occupation, led to the overthrow of colonial rule. Amidst much bloodshed and cruelty, an 'imagined community' of Indonesia, united in diversity by a common language and shared ideals, was called into being. Likewise, the remarkable economic development of the second half of the twentieth century would surely not have been achieved without the technological breakthrough of national income accounting, which gave structure and substance to what, even for

Keynes, was still a notional macro-economy. The wonderful improvisations of statisticians called into being a macro-economy that was both measurable and manageable.

Perhaps because disciplines lack a common language, the remarkable symmetry between nation and macro-economy has somehow been missed. Ben Anderson's perceptive term 'imagined community' has become popular currency to denote an amorphous national community as an aggregation of citizens regardless of location, age, gender, ethnicity, religion or status.[36] People belong to the nation as much as anything by an act of faith that transcends all other more palpable identities. Yet Joseph Schumpeter's equally valid insight into the national economy is all but unknown. The national economy no less than the nation itself had to be invented and imagined as an act of faith. These two constructs then become self-reinforcing. It is hardly coincidence that the decolonization that gave rise to new nations was accompanied by the application of national income accounting under the umbrella of the United Nations, International Monetary Fund, World Bank and other multilateral agencies.

Yet every solution brings new problems. The metric of national output (GDP) that was once such a useful tool in the cause of raising living standards is now as much a block as an aid to clear thinking and sound policy. GDP has been reified to an extraordinary degree without much regard to its many improvisations, biases and omissions, not least the great neglect of environmental inputs and impacts. GDP no longer just measures but also determines behaviour, locking the world into an outmoded policy regime that threatens the ecological sustainability of the world's bloated population. For statisticians, it is a grand scientific and intellectual challenge. Progress with a much better set of metrics is agonizingly slow. As an archipelago with a large coastal population, Indonesia has as much interest as any country in mitigating global warming, to which it is also a significant contributor. With the benefit of advice from Emil Salim as chairman of his advisory team, President Yudhoyono committed his government to that cause, without necessarily binding future governments. The contested transition to a sustainable economy is likely to continue to be slow.

Notes

1. Schumpeter, *Business Cycles*, vol. 2.
2. My thanks to Anne Booth, Joe Isaac, Pierre van der Eng and the late Thee Kian Wie for their advice and assistance with this chapter. Van der Eng's

Long-Term Macro-Economic Statistics of Indonesia (forthcoming) is a definitive account of the evolution of economic statistics and national accounts in Indonesia and I am most grateful for the opportunity to refer to it.

3. Day, *The Policy and Administration of the Dutch in Java*; Furnivall, *Netherlands India: A Study of Plural Economy.*
4. Anderson, 'Old State, New Society', 477–96.
5. Dick et al., *The Emergence of a National Economy.*
6. Kuhn, *The Structure of Scientific Revolutions.*
7. Meadows et al., *The Limits to Growth.*
8. Lam, *A Passion for Facts.*
9. Edited and collated in the 1930s by CKS director W.F.M. Mansvelt, and in 1975 republished as Volume 1 of the *Changing Economy in Indonesia* series, edited by his former staff member Piet Creutzberg as *Indonesia's Export Crops, 1816–1940.*
10. Creutzberg, *Indonesia's Export Crops, 1816–1940*, 28.
11. Dick et al., *The Emergence of a National Economy*, chapter 1.
12. Lam, *A Passion for Facts.*
13. Ochse and Terra, *Geld-en produktenhuishouding*, and Hart and Tan, *Een onderzoek.*
14. Van Ginkel, *Verslag van den economischen toestand*, and ibid., *Verslag van den belastingdruk*; Meijer Ranneft and Huender, *Onderzoek naar.*
15. Keynes, *The General Theory of Employment, Interest and Money.*
16. Clark and Crawford, *The National Income of Australia*; Kuznets et al., *National Income and Its Compostion.*
17. Creutzberg, *National Income.*
18. Polak's estimate was finally published in 1979 with commentary in the *Changing Economy in Indonesia* series (Creutzberg, *National Income*).
19. *United Nations, A System of National Accounts and Supporting Tables.*
20. Budiardjo, 'Primus Inter Pares', 411–2.
21. Neumark, 'The National Income', 348–91.
22. Van der Eng, 'The Real Domestic Product'; Muljatno, 'Perhitungan pendapatan', 162–211.
23. Thee Kian Wie, *Recollections: The Indonesian Economy*, 108–10.
24. Van der Eng, 'The Real Domestic Product'.
25. The first *Statistical Pocket Book of Indonesia* (sic) was issued in February 1947 by the Central Bureau of Statistics as a belated publication for the year 1941 with some updated appendices.
26. Dick et al., *The Emergence of a National Economy*, chapter 6.
27. Van der Eng (2010) extends the GDP series backwards for the whole period 1880–2008.
28. Arndt, *Economic Development: The History of an Idea*, 51.
29. Nordhaus et al., 'Is Growth Obsolete?'.
30. Thee Kian Wie, *Recollections: The Indonesian Economy*, 204–9.

31. World Commission on Environment and Development, *Our Common Future*.
32. *Wasting Assets* by Repetto was an early and influential work in addressing these issues.
33. United Nations, *A System of National Accounts and Supporting Tables*.
34. Stiglitz et al., *Report by the Commission*.
35. WAVES, *Annual Report 2013*.
36. Anderson, *Imagined Communities*.

Bibliography

Abdullah, Taufik. *Indonesia. Towards Democracy*. Singapore: Institute of Southeast Asian Studies, 2009.

'Act No. 86 of 1958 (Statutes 1958 No.162) Concerning the Nationalization of Dutch-owned Enterprises in Indonesia', *Nederlands tijdschrift voor internationaal recht* [Dutch Journal for International Law] 6 (1959): 291–5.

Adas, Michael. 'From avoidance to confrontation: peasant protest in precolonial and colonial Southeast Asia', *Comparative Studies in Society and History* 23 (1981): 217–47.

Aden, Jean Bush. 'Oil and Politics in Indonesia, 1945–1980'. PhD Dissertation, Cornell University, Ithaca, 1988.

Aelst, A. van. 'A South-Chinese Currency Zone between the Twelfth and Nineteenth Centuries'. In *Wages and Currency: Global Comparisons from Antiquity to the Twentieth Century*, ed. J. Lucassen. Bern: Peter Lang, 2007, 97–112.

Allen, Robert C. et al. 'Wages, Prices and Living Standards in China, 1738–1925: In Comparison with Europe, Japan and India'. *Economic History Review* 64 (2011): 8–38.

Amstutz, Nan L. 'The Development of Indigenous Indonesian Importers, 1950–1955'. PhD Dissertation, Tufts University, Boston, 1958.

Anak Agung Gde Agung, Ide. *Twenty Years Indonesian Foreign Policy: 1945–1965*. Yogyakarta: Duta Wacana University Press, 1990.

Anderson, Ben. 'Old State, New Society: Indonesia's New Order in Comparative Historical Perspective'. *Journal of Asian Studies* 42 (1983): 477–96.

———. *Imagined Communities: Reflections on the Origin and Spread of Nationalism*. London: Verso, 1983.

Anderson, K. *Distortions to Agricultural Incentives: A Global Perspective*. Washington DC: World Bank Publications, 2009.

Angkatan Bersendjata, 5 July 1965.

Apriyanto, Tri Chandra. 'Decolonization in the Jember Estate Economy'. In *Indonesian Economic Decolonization in Regional and International Perspective*, ed. J. Thomas Lindblad and Peter Post. Leiden: KITLV Press, 2009, 107–29.

Aristides Katoppo et al. *Sumitro Djojohadikusumo. Jejak perlawanan begawan pejuang* [Sumitro Djojohadikusumo. Footsteps of resistance of an expert in combat]. Jakarta: Pustaka Sinar Harapan, 2000.

Arndt, H.W. *Economic Development: The History of an Idea*. Chicago: University of Chicago Press, 1987.

Athukorala, P. and C. Manning. *Structural Change and International Migration in East Asia*. Melbourne: Oxford University Press, 1999.

Awaloeddin Djamin. *Ir. H. Djuanda. Negarawan, administrator, teknokrat utama* [Ir. H. Djuanda. Statesman, administrator, primary technocrat]. Jakarta: Kompas, 2001.

Balisacan, A.M. and H. Hill. *The Philippine Economy*. New York: Oxford University Press, 2003.

Bank Indonesia. *Report for the Year 1954/55*. Jakarta: G. Kolff, 1955.

________. *Report for the Year 1956/57*. Jakarta: G. Kolff, 1957.

________. *Report for the Year 1958/59*. Jakarta: G. Kolff, 1959.

________. *Report for the Year 1959/60*. Jakarta: G. Kolff, 1960.

Barlow, Colin and John Drabble. 'Government and the Emerging Rubber Industries in Indonesia and Malaysia'. In *Indonesian Economic History in the Dutch Colonial Era: Monograph Series 35*, ed. Anne Booth et al. New Haven: Yale University Southeast Asian Studies, 1990.

Barrett, Christopher B. and Maxwell, Daniel G. *Food Aid after Fifty Years: Recasting its Role*. New York: Routledge, 2005.

Barton, R.F. *The Kalingas: Their Institutions and Custom Law*. Chicago: University of Chicago Press, 1949.

Baten, Jörg et al. 'The Biological Standard of Living and Body Height in Colonial and Post-colonial Indonesia, 1770–2000'. *Journal of Bioeconomics* 15 (2013): 103–22.

Bates, Robert H., John H. Coatsworth and Jeffrey G. Williamson. 'Lost Decades: Postindependence Performance in Latin America and Africa'. *The Journal of Economic History* 67, 4 (2007): 917–43.

Baudet, H. *Nederland en de rang van Denemarken* [The Netherlands and the rank of Denmark]. Groningen: Instituut voor Economisch Onderzoek van de Rijksuniversiteit te Groningen, 1975.

Benton, G. and E.T. Gomez. *The Chinese in Britain, 1800–present: Economy, Transnationalism, Identity*. Basingstoke: Palgrave Macmillan, 2008.

Berg, N.P. van den. *Munt-, crediet- en bankwezen, handel en scheepvaart in Nederlandsch-Indië. Historisch-Statistische Bijdragen* [Coin, credit and banking system, trade and shipping in Netherlands East Indies. Historical and statistical contributions]. 's-Gravenhage: Martinus Nijhoff, 1907.

________. *Currency and the Economy of Netherlands India 1870–95. A Reprint of 'The Financial and Economic Condition of Netherlands India since 1870 and the Effect of the Present Currency System' with an Introduction by Pierre van der Eng*. Singapore: Institute of Southeast Asian Studies, 1996.

Berita Indonesia, 15 November 1959.

Berita Repoeblik Indonesia, 15 February 1946.

Berita Yudha, 23 January 1963; 29 January 1969; 6 March 1969; 23 March 1963.

Bevan, David et al. *The Political Economy of Poverty, Equity, and Growth: Nigeria and Indonesia*. New York: Oxford University Press, 1999.

Bhagwati, J. and T.N. Srinivasan. 'Trade and Poverty in the Poor Countries'. *American Economic Review* 92 (2002): 180–3.

Blussé, L. *Strange Company: Chinese settlers, Mestizo Women and the Dutch in VOC Batavia*. Dordrecht: Foris Publications, 1986.

Boden, Ragna. 'Cold War Economics: Soviet Aid to Indonesia'. *Journal of Cold War Studies* 10, 3 (2008): 110–28.

Boediono, I.H. and M. Pangestu. 'Indonesia: The Structure and Causes of Manufacturing Protection'. In *The Political Economy of Manufacturing Protection: Experiences of ASEAN and Australia*, ed. C. Findlay and Ross Garnaut. Sydney: Allen and Unwin, 1986, 1–47.

Boer, Leen. '(In)formalization: The Forces Beyond'. *International Journal of Urban and Regional Research* 14 (1990): 404–22.

Bondan Kanumoyoso. *Nasionalisasi Perusahaan Belanda di Indonesia* [The nationalisation of Dutch companies in Indonesia]. Jakarta: Pustaka Sinar Harapan, 2001.

Boomgaard, P. 'Buitenzorg in 1805. The Role of Money and Credit in a Colonial Frontier Society'. *Modern Asian Studies* 20, 1 (1986): 33–58.

————. *Children of the Colonial State. Population Growth and Economic Development in Java 1795–1880*. Amsterdam: Free University Press, 1989.

————. 'The Welfare Services in Indonesia, 1900–1942'. *Itinerario* 10, 1 (1986): 57–83.

Boomgaard, Peter and Hans Gooszen. *Changing Economy in Indonesia*, vol. 11, *Population Trends, 1795–1942*. Amsterdam: Royal Tropical Institute, 1991.

Booth, Anne. 'The Colonial Legacy and Its Impact on Post-Independence Planning in India and Indonesia'. *Itinerario. Special Issue: India and Indonesia from the 1920s to the 1950s. The Origins of Planning* 10, 1 (1986): 1–30.

————. *Agricultural Development in Indonesia*. Sydney: Allen and Unwin, 1988.

————. 'Japanese Import Penetration and Dutch Response: Some Aspects of Economic Policy Making in Colonial Indonesia'. In *International Commercial Rivalry in Southeast Asia in the Interwar Period*, ed. Shinya Sugiyama and M.C. Guerrero. Yale Center for International and Area Studies, New Haven, 1994, 133–64.

————. 'Growth and Stagnation in an Era of Nation-Building: Indonesian Economic Performance from 1950 to 1969'. In *Historical Foundations of a National Economy in Indonesia, 1890s–1990s*, ed. J. Th. Lindblad. Amsterdam: North-Holland, 1996, 401–24.

————. *The Indonesian Economy in the Nineteenth and Twentieth Centuries: A History of Missed Opportunities*. Basingstoke/New York: Macmillan/St. Martin's Press, 1998.

________. 'Growth Collapse in Indonesia: A Comparison of the 1930s and 1990s'. *Itinerario* 26 (2002): 79–85.

________. 'Government and Welfare in the New Republic: Indonesia in the 1950s'. *Itinerario* 34, 1 (2010): 57–76.

________. 'Measuring Living Standards in Different Colonial Systems: Some Evidence from South East Asia, 1900–1942'. *Modern Asian Studies* 46, 5 (2012): 1145–81.

________. 'Colonial Revenue Policies and the Impact of the Transition to Independence in South East Asia'. *Bijdragen tot de Taal-, Land- en Volkenkunde* 169 (2013): 37–67.

________. 'Varieties of Exploitation in Colonial Settings: Dutch and Belgian Policies in Indonesia and the Congo and Their Legacies'. In *Colonial Exploitation and Economic Development: The Belgian Congo and the Netherlands Indies Compared*, ed. Ewout Frankema and Frans Buelens. London: Routledge, 2013, 60–87.

BPS. *Statistical Yearbook of Indonesia 2009*. Jakarta: Badan Pusat Statistik, 2009.

Bree, L. de. *Gedenkboek van de Javasche Bank: 1828–24 Januari–1928* [Commemorative book of the Javasche Bank: 1828–1928]. 2 vols. Weltevreden: Kolff & Co., 1928–30.

Bresnan, John. *At Home Abroad: A Memoir of the Ford Foundation in Indonesia, 1953–1973*. Jakarta: Equinox Publishing, 2006.

Bruijn, J.R. et al. *Muiterij, oproer en berechting op schepen van de VOC* [Mutiny, riots and trials on VOC ships]. Bussum: Unieboek, 1980.

________ et al. *Dutch-Asiatic Shipping in the 17th and 18th Centuries*. 3 vols. The Hague: Nijhoff, 1987.

________. *Commanders of Dutch East India Ships in the Eighteenth Century*. Woodbridge: The Boydell Press, 2011.

Budiardjo, Ali. 'Primus Inter Pares of the Indonesian Expert Staff: State Planning Bureau, 1953–1957'. In *Testimonials of Friends about Widjojo Nitisastro*, ed. Moh Arsjad et al. Jakarta: Kompas, 2008, 409–15.

Campen, J. van. *De Haagse jurist Jean Theodore Royer (1737–1807) en zijn verzameling Chinese voorwerpen* [The Jurist from The Hague Jean Theodore Royer (1737–1807) and his collection of Chinese objects]. Hilversum: Verloren, 2000.

Castles, L. 'The Fate of the Private Entrepreneur'. In *Sukarno's Guided Indonesia*, ed. T.K. Tan. Melbourne: Jacaranda Press, 1976.

CBS. *Statistical Pocket Book of Indonesia 1941*. Batavia: Central Bureau of Statistics, 1947.

________. *Produk Domestik Regional Bruto Propinsi-Propinsi di Indonesia menurut Penggunaan 1983–1991* [Gross Regional Domestic Products of the Provinces in Indonesia based on expenditure, 1983–1991]. Jakarta: Central Bureau of Statistics, 1994.

————. *Produk Domestik Regional Bruto Propinsi-Propinsi di Indonesia menurut Penggunaan 1988–1993* [Gross Regional Domestic Products of the Provinces in Indonesia based on expenditure, 1988–1993]. Jakarta: Central Bureau of Statistics, 1995.

————. *Produk Domestik Regional Bruto Propinsi-Propinsi di Indonesia menurut Penggunaan 1993–1996* [Gross Regional Domestic Products of the Provinces in Indonesia based on expenditure, 1993–1996]. Jakarta: Central Bureau of Statistics, 1997.

————. *Produk Domestik Regional Bruto Propinsi-Propinsi di Indonesia menurut Penggunaan 2003–2007* [Gross Regional Domestic Products of the Provinces in Indonesia based on expenditure, 2003–2007]. Jakarta: Central Bureau of Statistics, 2008.

————. *Statistical Yearbook of Indonesia 1996*. Jakarta: Central Bureau of Statistics, 1997.

————. *Statistical Yearbook of Indonesia 2009*. Jakarta: Central Bureau of Statistics, 2009.

Chandler, Robert F. Jr. *An Adventure in Applied Science: A History of the International Rice Research Institute*. Los Baños: International Rice Research Institute, 1982.

Chen, E. 'The Total Factor Productivity Debate: Determinants of Economic Growth in East Asia'. *Asian-Pacific Economic Literature* 11 (1997): 18–39.

Chen Lixiong. 'Chinezen en Javanen in dienst van de VOC, 1781–1795' [Chinese and Javanese in the service of the VOC, 1781–1795]. MA Thesis, Leiden University, 1990.

Cheng Wei-chung. *War, Trade and Piracy in the China Seas, 1622–1683*. Leiden: Brill, 2013.

Chijs, J.A. van der. *Nederlandsch-Indisch plakaatboek 1602–1811* [Netherlands-Indies Placard book 1602–1811]. 17 vols. Batavia: Landsdrukkerij, 1885–1900.

CKS. *Indisch Verslag 1940: Statistisch jaaroverzicht van Nederlandsch-Indië over het jaar 1939* [Indies Report 1940: Statistical Annual Survey of the Netherlands Indies for the Year 1939]. Batavia: Centraal Kantoor voor de Statistiek, 1940.

Clark, Colin. *The Conditions of Economic Progress*. London: Macmillan, 1940.

Clark, Colin and J.G. Crawford. *The National Income of Australia*. Sydney: Angus & Robertson, 1938.

Claver, Alexander. 'Commerce and Capital in Colonial Java: Trade Finance and Commercial Relations between Europeans and Chinese, 1820s–1942'. PhD Dissertation, Vrije Universiteit Amsterdam, 2006.

Claver, A. *Dutch Commerce and Chinese Merchants in Java. Colonial Relationships in Trade and Finance, 1800–1942*. Leiden and Boston: Brill, 2014.

Clay, Edward J. 'Review of food aid policy changes since 1978'. *WFP Occasional Papers No. 1*. Rome: World Food Programme, 1985.

Clemens, A.H.P. and J. Th. Lindblad. *Het belang van de Buitengewesten: Economische expansie en koloniale staatsvorming in de buitengewesten van Nederlandsch-Indië, 1870–1942* [The Importance of the Outer Islands: Economic expansion and colonial state formation in the Outer Islands of the Dutch East Indies]. Amsterdam: NEHA, 1989.

Clerx, J.M.M.J. 'De Financiële verhouding tussen Nederland en Indonesië opnieuw bezien (1945–1967)' [The Financial relations between the Netherlands and Indonesia revisited (1945–1967)]. *Politieke Opstellen* 11/12 (1992): 59–71.

Coase, R.H. 'The Nature of the Firm'. *Economica* 4, 16 (1937): 386–405.

Coleman, James S. 'Social Capital in the Creation of Human Capital'. *American Journal of Sociology* 94 (1988): S95–S120.

Colombijn, Freek. *Under Construction: The Politics of Urban Space and Housing During the Decolonization of Indonesia, 1930–1960*. Leiden: KITLV Press, 2010.

Conway, Gordon. *The Doubly Green Revolution: Food for All in the Twenty-First Century*. Ithaca: Cornell University Press, 1998.

Creutzberg, P. *Changing Economy in Indonesia*, vol. 1. *Indonesia's Export Crops, 1816–1940*. The Hague: Martinus Nijhoff, 1975.

________. *Changing Economy in Indonesia*, vol. 3. *Expenditure on Fixed Assets*. The Hague: Martinus Nijhoff, 1977.

________. *Changing Economy in Indonesia*, vol. 4. *National Income*. The Hague: Martinus Nijhoff, 1979.

________. *Changing Economy in Indonesia*, vol. 5. *National Income*. The Hague: Martinus Nijhoff, 1979.

Cribb, Robert. 'Political Dimensions of the Currency Question 1945–1947'. *Indonesia* 31 (1982): 113–36.

________. 'Jakarta in the Indonesian Revolution, 1945–1949'. PhD Thesis, University of London, 1984.

________. *Gangsters and Revolutionaries: The Jakarta People's Militia and the Indonesian Revolution, 1945–1949*. Sydney: Allen and Unwin, 1991.

Cribb, Robert and Colin Brown. *Modern Indonesia. A History Since 1945*. London: Longman, 1995.

Crossman, Joanna and Hiroko Noma. '*Sunao* as character: Its implications for trust and intercultural communication within subsidiaries of Japanese multinationals in Australia'. *Journal of Business Ethics* 113 (2013): 543–55.

Crouch, Harold. 'Generals and Business in Indonesia'. *Pacific Affairs* 48, 4 (1975): 519–40.

Csukas, Csongor, Paulo Fracalanza, Tamás Kovács and Marc Willinger. 'The Determinants of Trusting and Reciprocal Behaviour: Evidence from an Intercultural Experiment'. *Journal of Economic Development* 33 (2008): 71–95.

Cullather, Nick. *The Hungry World: America's Cold War Battle against Poverty in Asia*. Cambridge: Harvard University Press, 2010.

Dalrymple, Dana G. *Development and Spread of High-Yielding Rice Varieties in Developing Countries*. Washington: Agency for International Development, 1986.

Day, Clive. *The Policy and Administration of the Dutch in Java*. London: Macmillan, 1904.

DeBlois, Eleanor N. '12 Years of Achievement under Public Law 480'. *ERS-Foreign No. 202*. Washington DC: Economic Research Service, US Department of Agriculture, 1967.

Departement van Economische Zaken, Centraal Kantoor voor de Statistiek. *De landbouw export gewassen* [Department of Economic Affairs, Central Office for Statistics. The agricultural export crops]. Djakarta, 1949.

De Indische Mercuur: Azie–tevens suikernummer [The Indies Mercuur: Asia–also sugar issue], 1903.

De Javasche Bank. *Laporan tahun pembukuan 1949/50* [Report for the financial year 1949/50]. Jakarta: G. Kolff, 1950.

———. *Laporan tahun pembukuan 1950/51* [Report for the financial year 1950/51]. Jakarta: G. Kolff, 1951.

———. *Report for the Financial Year 1952/53*. Jakarta: G. Kolff, 1953.

'De Kali Bezaar te Batavia'. *Het Bijblad van De Economist* [The Kali Bezar in Batavia. Supplement to the Economist], 1862, 153–77.

Dewan Pengawas Keuangan. *Pemberitaan, dewan pengawas keuangan tahun 1951* [Report, the Audit Office]. Jakarta: Dewan Pengawas Keuangan, 1951.

Dewey, Alice G. 'Trade and Social Control in Java'. *The Journal of the Royal Anthropological Institute of Great Britain and Ireland* 92, 2 (1962): 177–90.

———. *Peasant Marketing in Java*. New York: The Free Press of Glencoe, 1962.

Dick, Howard. *Indonesian Interisland Shipping Industry: An Analysis of Competition and Regulation*. Singapore: Institute of Southeast Asian Studies, 1986.

———. 'Japan's Economic Expansion in the Netherlands Indies between the First and the Second World Wars'. *Journal of Southeast Asian Studies* 20, 2 (1989): 244–74.

———. 'Oei Tiong Ham'. In *The Rise and Fall of Revenue Farming*, ed. John Butcher and Howard Dick. New York: St. Martin's Press, 1993, 272–81.

———. 'Formation of the Nation State, 1930s–1966'. In *The Emergence of a National Economy: An Economic History of Indonesia, 1800–2000*, ed. Howard Dick et al. Leiden: KITLV Press, 2002, 153–93.

Dick, H.W., V.J.H. Houben, J.Th. Lindblad and Thee Kian Wie. *The Emergence of a National Economy in Indonesia, 1800–2000*. Sydney: Allen and Unwin, 2002.

Dillo, I. *De nadagen van de Verenigde Oostindische Compagnie 1783–1795* [The latter years of the Dutch East India Company 1783–1795]. Amsterdam: De Bataafsche Leeuw, 1992.

Dipa Nusantara Aidit. *Pemetjahan masalah ekonomi dan ilmu ekonomi Indonesia dewasa ini* [The solving of the current Indonesian economic problem and economic science]. Jakarta: Jajasan Pembaruan, 1964.

Djojohadikusomo, Sumitro. *Facing the Situation*. Djakarta: Ministry of Information, Republic of Indonesia, 1952.

Djurfeldt, Göran and Magnus Jirström. 'The Puzzle of the Policy Shift: The Early Green Revolution in India, Indonesia and the Philippines'. In *The African Food Crisis: Lessons from the Asian Green Revolution*, ed. G. Djurfeldt et al. Wallingford: CABI Publishing, 2005, 43–63.

Doel, H.W. van den. *Afscheid van Indie. De val van het Nederlandse imperium in Azie* [Parting from the Indies. The Fall of the Dutch Empire in Asia]. Amsterdam: Prometheus, 2001.

Dros, N. *Changing Economy in Indonesia*, vol. 13. *Wages 1820–1940*. Amsterdam: KIT, 1992.

Easterly, William. 'Institutions: Top down or Bottom up?' *American Economic Review* 98, 2 (2008): 95–9.

Ehrlich, Paul R. *The Population Bomb*. New York: Ballantine Books, 1968.

Elson, R.E. *Javanese Peasants and the Colonial Sugar Industry: Impact and Change in an East Java Residency 1830–1940*. Singapore and New York: Oxford University Press, 1984.

________. *Suharto: A Political Biography*. Cambridge: Cambridge University Press, 2001.

Erve, Huub J. van der. *Recruitment and Composition of Construction Labour in Semarang, Indonesia* [Urban research working paper 9]. Amsterdam: Free University, 1987.

________. 'The Diversity of Work Relationships in the Construction Sector of Semarang'. In *About Fringes, Margins and Lucky Dips: The Informal Sector in Third-World Countries: Recent Developments in Research and Policy*, ed. Paul van Gelder and Joep Bijlmer. Amsterdam: Free University Press, 1989, 91–111.

Estudillo, Jonna P. and Keijiro Otsuka. 'Lessons from the Asian Green Revolution in Rice'. In *An African Green Revolution: Finding Ways to Boost Productivity on Small Farms*, ed. Donald Larson and Keijiro Otsuka. Dordrecht: Springer Verlag, 2012, 17–42.

Evans-Pritchard, E.E. *The Nuer: A Description of the Modes of Livelihood and Political Institutions of a Nilotic People*. Oxford: Clarendon Press, 1940.

Eyck van Heslinga, E.S. van. *Van compagnie naar koopvaardij: de scheepvaartverbinding van de Bataafse Republiek met de koloniën in Azië 1795–1806* [From Company to Merchant Navy: Shipping connections between the Batavian Republic and the colonies in Asia 1795–1806]. Amsterdam: Bataafsche Leeuw, 1988.

FAO. 'FAOSTAT.' Statistical Database of the Food and Agriculture Organization of the United Nations. http://faostat.fao.org/

Fasseur, C. *Kultuurstelsel en koloniale baten. De Nederlandse exploitatie van Java 1840–1860* [Cultivation system and colonial profits. The Dutch exploitation of Java 1840–1860]. Leiden, 1975.

Fei, John C.H. and Douglas Paauw. 'Foreign Assistance and Self-Help: A Re-appraisal of Development Finance'. *Review of Economics and Statistics* 47, 3 (1965): 251–67.

Feith, Herbert. *The Decline of Constitutional Democracy in Indonesia.* Ithaca: Cornell University Press, 1962.

Fernando, M.R. 'Growth of Non-Agricultural Economic Activities in Java in the Middle Decades of the Nineteenth Century'. *Modern Asian Studies* 30, 1 (1996): 77–119.

Filipina, dan Korea Selatan [The Philippines and South Korea]. Jakarta: The RIDEP Institute, 2003.

Foldvari, Peter et al. 'Indonesia's Regional Welfare Development, 1900–1990: New Anthropometric Evidence'. *Economics and Human Biology* 11 (2012): 78–99.

'Formosa suikerproductie en suikeruitvoer naar China' [Formosan sugar production and sugar export to China]. *Asian Studies* 41 (1933): 26–7.

Francis, E. *Herinneringen uit den Levensloop van een Indisch' Ambtenaar van 1815 tot 1851 medegedeeld in Brieven door E. Francis. Ridder der Orde van den Nederlandschen Leeuw, President der Javasche Bank, Oud Hoofdambtenaar* [Recollections from the life of a civil servant in the Indies between 1815 to 1851 communicated in letters by E. Francis, knight in the Order of the Dutch Lion, president of the Java Bank, former chief civil servant]. Batavia: H.M. van Dorp, 1856.

Frankema, Ewout. 'Raising Revenue in the British Empire, 1870–1940: How "extractive" were colonial taxes?' *Journal of Global History* 5 (2010): 447–77.

________. *Africa and the Green Revolution: A Global Historical Perspective.* Wageningen University: Inaugural lecture upon taking up the post of Professor of Rural and Environmental History, 2013.

________. 'The Green Revolution in Indonesia: A Replicable Success?' In *Promises and Predicaments: Trade and Entrepreneurship in Colonial and Independent Indonesia in the 19th and 20th Centuries*, ed. Alicia Schrikker and Jeroen Touwen. Singapore: NUS Press, this volume.

Freedberg, David Adrian. *Dutch Landscape Prints of the Seventeenth Century.* London: British Museum Publications, 1980.

Fruin, Th. A. *Het Economische aspect van het Indonesische vraagstuk* [The economic dimension of the Indonesian question]. Amsterdam: Vrij Nederland, 1947.

Furnivall, J.S. *Netherlands India: A Study of Plural Economy.* Cambridge: Cambridge University Press, 1944.

Gaastra, F.S. *The Dutch East India Company: Expansion and Decline.* Zutphen: De Walburg Pers, 2003.

Gardner, Paul F. *Shared Hopes, Separate Fears Fifty Years of US–Indonesia Relations.* Oxford: Westview Press, 1997.

Geerligs, H.C. Prinsen. *Cane Sugar Production, 1912–1937: A Supplement to the World's Cane Sugar Industry, Past and Present.* California: N. Rodger, 1938.

Geertz, Clifford. *Agricultural Involution: The Process of Ecological Change in Indonesia.* Berkeley: University of California Press, 1963.

Gelderen, Jacob van. *The Recent Development of Economic Foreign Policy in the Netherlands East Indies.* London: Longmans, Green, 1939.

Gemeente Bandoeng, Dienst van het Grondbedrijf. *Prospectus voor de uitgifte van gronden* [Prospectus for the granting of land]. Bandoeng: Vorkink, 1931.

Gemeenteblad 1 Gemeente Medan [Municipal magazine 1 The Municipality of Medan], 1930.

Gemeenteblad 2 Gemeente Medan [Municipal magazine 2 The Municipality of Medan], 1930–39.

Gemeentelijke-Ambachtsschool Bandoeng. *Verslag betreffende den toestand en de werking van de Gemeentelijke-Ambachtsschool te Bandoeng over den cursus 1929–1930* [Municipal Technical School Bandung. *Report concerning the situation and operation of the Municipal Technical School in Bandung for the course 1929–30*]. Bandoeng: Vorkink, [1930].

Gillis, Malcolm. 'Episodes in Indonesian Economic History'. In *World Economic Growth. Case Studies of Developed and Developing Nations*, ed. Arnold C. Harberger. San Francisco: ICS Press, 1984, 231–64.

________ et al. *Economics of Development.* New York: W.W. Norton & Company, Inc., 1987.

Gilman, Nils. *Mandarins of the Future: Modernization Theory in Cold War America.* Baltimore: John Hopkins University, 2003.

Ginkel, H. Fievez de Malines van. *Verslag van den belastingdruk en den economischen toestand met betrekking tot de inlandsche bevolking in de Buitengewesten* [Report on the burden of taxation and the economic situation in relation to the indigenous population of the Outer Islands]. 4 vols. Batavia: Landsdrukkerij, 1928–30.

Glassburner, Bruce. 'Economic Policy-making in Indonesia, 1950–1957'. In *The Economy of Indonesia; Selected Readings*, ed. Bruce Glassburner. Ithaca: Cornell University Press, 1971, 70–98.

________. *The Economy of Indonesia. Selected Readings.* Ithaca: Cornell University Press, 1971.

Godée Molsbergen, E.C. *Gedenkboek Reynst & Vinju 1836–1936* [Commemorative book Reynst & Vinju 1836–1936]. Batavia: Reynst & Vinju, 1935.

Goenawan Moehammad. *Celebrating Indonesia. Fifty Years with the Ford Foundation, 1953–2003.* Jakarta: Ford Foundation, 2003.

________. *Boediono: Islam, neolib dan ekonomi kerakyatan* [Boediono: Islam, neoliberalism and populist economy]. Jakarta: Cakrawala Lintas Media, 2009.

Golay, H. Frank et al. *Underdevelopment and Economic Nationalism in Southeast Asia*. Ithaca: Cornell University Press, 1969.

Gonzales, Leonardo A. et al. *Economic Incentives and Comparative Advantage in Indonesian Food Crop Production*. IFPRI Research Report 93. Washington DC: International Food Policy Research Institute, 1993.

Goolsby, Otis Halbert, Kruer, George R. and Santmyer, Carolee. 'P.L. 480 Concessional Sales: History, Procedures, Negotiating and Implementing Agreements'. *Foreign Agricultural Economic Report No. 65*. Washington DC: Economic Research Service, US Department of Agriculture, 1970.

Goto-Shibata, Harumi. 'Japanese and British Perceptions of Chinese Boycotts in Shanghai: With Special Reference to the Anti-Japanese Boycotts, 1928–31'. In *Japan, China and the Growth of the Asian International Economy*, ed. Kaoru Sugihara. Oxford: Oxford University Press, 2005, vol. 1: 127–44.

Graeff, A.C.D de. *Van vriend tot vijand* [From friend to enemy]. Amsterdam: Elsevier, 1945.

Granger, C.W.J. 'Investigating Causal Relations by Econometric Models and Cross-spectral Methods'. *Econometrica* 37 (1969): 424–38.

Grove, Linda and Mark Selden. 'Editor's Introduction: New Perspectives on China, East Asia and the Global Economy'. In *China, East Asia and the Global Economy: Regional and Historical Perspectives*, ed. Takeshi Hamashita et al. London: Routledge, 2008, 1–11.

Gullick, J.M. *Indigenous political systems of western Malaya*. London: The Athlone Press, 1958.

Hadinoto, Soejono. *Ekonomi Indonesia. Dari ekonomi kolonial ke ekonomi nasional* [Indonesian economy. From colonial economy to national economy]. Djakarta: Penerbit Grafica, 1949.

Haluan, 24 March 1953.

Handboek voor cultuur- en handels-ondernemingen in Nederlandsch-Indië. 1930 [Handbook for agricultural and trade enterprises in the Netherlands East Indies]. Amsterdam: J.H. de Bussy, 1929.

Handelsvereeniging te Medan. *Jaarverslag 1952* [Trading association of Medan, *Annual report 1952*]. Medan, 1953.

Hansen, Gary E. *Agricultural and Rural Development in Indonesia*. Boulder: Westview Press, 1981.

Hanson, J.R. *Trade in Transition: Exports from the Third World, 1840–1900*. New York: Academic Press, 1980.

Harberger, Arnold C., ed. *World Economic Growth. Case Studies of Developed and Developing Nations*. San Francisco: ICS Press, 1984.

Harian Operasi, 7 October 1968.

Hart, H.M.J. and T.J. Tan. *Mededeelingen van het Centraal Kantoor voor de Statistiek*, no. 177, *Een onderzoek naar de levenswijze der gemeentekoelies te Batavia in 1937* [Reports of the central office for statistics, no. 177, an investigation into the way of life of coolies in municipal employ 1937]. Batavia: CKS, 1939.

Hawkins, E.D. 'Labour in Developing Countries: Indonesia'. In *The Economy of Indonesia: Selected Readings*, ed. Bruce Glassburner. Ithaca: Cornell University Press, 1971.

Hayami, Yujiro. 'An Ecological and Historical Perspective on Agricultural Development in Southeast Asia'. Policy Research Working Papers, 2296. Washington: Development Research Group, World Bank, 2000.

Heek, F. van. *Publicaties van het Geografisch en Sociografisch Seminarium der Universiteit van Amsterdam*, vol. 1, *Chineesche immigranten in Nederland* [Publications of the Geographic and Sociographic Seminary of the University of Amsterdam, vol. 1, Chinese immigrants in the Netherlands]. Amsterdam: JK Emmering's uitgevers Mij, 1936.

Henley, David. 'The Agrarian Roots of Industrial Growth: Rural development in Southeast Asia and sub-Saharan Africa'. *Development Policy Review* 30, 1 (2012): s25–s47.

Hering, Bob. *Soekarno. Founding father of Indonesia, 1901–1945*. Leiden: KITLV Press, 2002.

Hidemasa Morikawa. *Zaibatsu. The Rise and Fall of Family Enterprise Groups in Japan*. Tokyo: University of Tokyo Press, 1992.

Higgins, Benjamin. 'The Indonesia Project of the Massachusetts Institute of Technology–Center for International Studies'. *Ekonomi dan Keuangan Indonesia* 3 (1955).

________. *Indonesia's Stabilization and Development*. New York: Institute of Pacific Relations, 1957.

________. 'Thought and Action: Indonesian economic studies and policies in the 1950s'. *Bulletin of Indonesian Economic Studies* 26, 1 (1990).

________. *All the Difference: A Development Economist's Quest*. Montreal: McGill-Queen's Press, 1992.

Higgins, Benjamin and Jean Higgins. *Indonesia: The Crisis of the Millstone*. Princeton: Van Nostrand, 1963.

Hill, Emily M. *Smokeless Sugar. The Death of a Provincal Bureaucrat and the Construction of China's National Economy*. Vancouver: University of British Columbia Press, 2010.

Hill, Hal. 'Foreign Investment and East Asian Economic Development'. *Asian-Pacific Economic Literature* 4, 2 (1990): 21–58.

________. *The Indonesian Economy since 1996: Southeast Asia's Emerging Giant*. Cambridge: Cambridge University Press, 1996.

________. *The Indonesian Economy*. 2nd edition. Cambridge: Cambridge University Press, 2000.

Hindley, Donald. *The Communist Party of Indonesia, 1951–1961*. Berkeley: University of California, 1964.

Ho, Samuel P.S. *Economic Development of Taiwan*. New Haven: Yale University Press, 1978.

Hopkins, Raymond F. 'The evolution of food aid: Towards a development first regime'. *Food Policy* 9, 2 (1984): 345–62.

Houben, V.J.H. *Kraton and Kumpeni: Surakarta and Yogyakarta, 1830–1870.* Leiden: KITLV Press, 1994.

Houben, V.J.H. and J.Th. Lindblad. 'Towards a historiography of the national economy in Indonesia'. In *Historical foundations of a national economy in Indonesia, 1890s–1990s,* ed. J.Th. Lindblad. Amsterdam: North-Holland, 1996, 3–10.

Huddleston, Barbara. 'Closing the cereals gap with trade and food aid'. *IFPRI Research Report No. 43*. Washington DC: International Food Policy Research Institute, 1984.

Hunter, Alex. 'The Indonesian Oil Industry'. *Australian Economic Papers* 5, 1 (1966): 59–106.

Ibrahim Adjie. 'TNI dan Civic Mission'. *Manager* 4, 37 (1963): 10–5.

Ichtisar Parlemen 1 (1950).

International Monetary Fund. *Regional Economic Outlook. Sub-Saharan Africa: Sustaining Growth amidst Global Uncertainty.* Washington DC, 2012.

Ismael, J.E. 'Beberapa aspek institusionil dalam pembangunan nasional dan daerah'. In *Laporan Kongres Ilmu Pengetahuan Indonesia Kedua, 1962, Djilid ke-sembilan, Seksi E-3 (Ekonomi)* [Some institutional aspects in the national and regional development. In *Report from the Second Indonesia Science Congress, 1962, volume 9, section E-3* (*economy*)]. Archipel: Bogor, 1962, 125–36.

Ismantoro Dwi Yuwono. *Boediono dan (neolib)eralisme* [Boediono and (neo) liberalism]. Yogyakarta: Dwi Pustaka, 2009.

Jacobs, E.M. 'De Verenigde Oost-Indische Compagnie: Een Veelkantig Bedrijf' [The Dutch East India Company: A Multifaceted Company]. *Tijdschrift voor Geschiedenis* 115 (2002): 525–43.

————. *Merchant in Asia: The Trade of the Dutch East India Company during the Eighteenth Century.* Leiden: CNWS Publications, 2006.

'Japan'. *The International Sugar Journal* 2 (1900).

Javasche Courant, 1926.

Johansen, S. 'Estimation and Hypothesis Testing of Cointegration Vectors in Gaussian Vector Autoregressive Models'. *Econometrica* 59 (1991): 1551–80.

————. *Likelihood-Based Inference in Cointegrated Vector Autoregressive Models.* Oxford: Clarendon Press, 1995.

Jones, G.W. 'The Population of Southeast Asia'. *Working Paper Series* No. 196, Singapore: Asia Research Institute, National University of Singapore, 2013.

Ka Chih-ming. *Japanese Colonialism in Taiwan: Land Tenure, Development, and Dependency, 1895–1945.* Boulder: Westview Press, 1998.

Kahin, George McT. 'Some Recollections from and Reflections on the Indonesian Revolution'. In *The heartbeat of Indonesian Revolution*, ed. Taufik Abdullah. Jakarta: Gramedia, 1997, 10–27.

Kaoru Sugihara. 'An Introduction'. In *Japan, China and the Asian International Economy, 1850–1949,* ed. Kaoru Sugihara. Oxford: Oxford University Press, 2005, vol. 1: 1–20.

Kasdi, Aminuddin. 'Bantuan Beras ke India tahun 1946' [The Rice aid for India in 1946]. *Avatara, e-journal Pendidikan Sejarah* 1, 2 (2013) http://ejournal.unesa.ac.id/index.php/avatara/article/view/2357 [accessed 31 May 2013].

Keiko Ono and John Lea. 'Colonial Towns of the Northern Marianas: Rediscovering the Urban Morphology of Saipan and Tinian'. Paper delivered at RMAP series Seminars, 31 May 2001, Research School of Pacific and Asian Studies, Australian National University.

Kenneth, D. Thomas and Bruce Glassburner. 'Abrogation, Takeover and Nationalization: The Elimination of Dutch Economic Domination from the Republic of Indonesia'. *Australian Outlook* 19 (1965): 158–79.

Kerkhof, Jasper van de. '"Colonial" Enterprise and the Indigenization of Management in Independent Indonesia and Malaysia'. In *Indonesian Economic Decolonization in Regional and International Perspective*, ed. J. Thomas Lindblad and Peter Post. Leiden: KITLV Press, 2009.

________. 'Indonesianisasi of Dutch Economic Interests: The Case of Internatio, 1930–1960'. *Bijdragen tot de Taal-, Land- en Volkenkunde* 161 (2005): 181–208.

Keynes, J.M. *The General Theory of Employment, Interest and Money*. London: Macmillan, 1936.

Klein, P.W. *The Monetisation of the Dutch East Indies. A Case of Changing Continuity, 1602–1942*. Wassenaar: Netherlands Institute for Advanced Study in the Humanities and Social Sciences, 1989.

Knaap, G. 'Shipping and Trade in Java, c. 1775: A Quantitative Analysis'. *Modern Asian Studies* 33, 2 (1999): 405–20.

Knight, G. Roger. 'Exogenous Colonialism: Java Sugar between Nippon and Taikoo before and during the Inter-war Depression, c. 1920–1940'. *Modern Asian Studies* 44, 3 (2010): 477–515.

________. *Commodities and Colonialism: The Story of Big Sugar in Indonesia, 1880–1942*. Leiden: Brill, 2013.

Komine, T. and S. Kabe. 'Long-term Forecast of the Demographic Transition in Japan and Asia'. *Asian Economic Policy Review* 4, 1 (2009): 19–38.

Korthals Altes, W.L. *Changing Economy in Indonesia, vol. 15, Prices (non-rice) 1814–1940*. Amsterdam: KIT, 1994.

Kroeber, A.L. 'Roy Franklin Barton, 1883–947'. *American Anthropologist* 51, 1 (1949): 91–5.

Kuhn, Thomas. *The Structure of Scientific Revolutions*. Chicago: University of Chicago Press, 1962.

Kurniasih, Elysabeth Dwi and Prapto Yuwono. 'The Illegal Retribution Faced by the Construction Business: A Case Study in Semarang'. *Kritis: Jurnal Universitas Kristen Satya Wacana* 16, 1 (2004): 1–23.

Kuznets, Simon et al. *National Income and Its Composition, 1919–1938*. Washington DC: National Bureau of Economic Research (NBER), 1941.

Kwee Hui Kian. 'Colonization Creeping in. The Dutch East India Company's Promotion of Petty Coins in Central and East Java, 1740s–1790s'. Unpublished research paper TANAP-project. Leiden, 2004.

———. *The Political Economy of Java's Northeast Coast, c. 1740–1800. Elite Synergy*. Leiden: Brill, 2006.

Laanen, J.T.M. van. *Changing Economy in Indonesia*. Vol. 6. *Money and Banking 1816–1942*. The Hague: Martinus Nijhoff, 1980.

Laar, H.J.M. van de. *Opperbankier en wetenschapsman. Willem Cornelis Mees 1813–1884* [Chief banker and man of science. Willem Cornelis Mees, 1813–1884]. Den Haag: Martinus Nijhoff, 1978.

Lam, Tong. *A Passion for Facts: Social Surveys and the Construction of the Chinese Nation-State, 1900–1949*. Berkeley: University of California Press, 2011.

Laporan tahunan Lembaga Ekonomi dan Kemasjarakatan Nasional [The annual report of Leknas (Institute for national economy and society)]. Jakarta: Leknas, 1964.

Larson, Donald and Keijiro Otsuka. *An African Green Revolution Finding Ways to Boost Productivity on Small Farms*. Dordrecht: Springer Verlag, 2013.

Latham, A.J.H. *Rice: The Primary Commodity*. London: Routledge, 1998.

Latham, Michael. *Modernization as Ideology: American Social Science and 'Nation-building' in the Kennedy Era*. Chapel Hill: University of North Carolina Press, 2000.

———. *The Right Kind of Revolution: Modernization, Development and US Foreign Policy from the Cold War to the Present*. Ithaca: Cornell University Press, 2011.

Leeuwen, B. van. 'Human Capital and Economic Growth in India, Indonesia and Japan. A Quantitative Analysis, 1890–2000'. PhD Dissertation, Utrecht University, 2007.

Legge, J.D. *Central Authority and Regional Autonomy in Indonesia: A Study in Local Administration 1950–60*. Ithaca: Cornell University Press, 1961.

———. *Sukarno. A Political Biography*. Harmondsworth: Penguin Books, 1972.

Leigh, A. and P. van der Eng. 'Inequality in Indonesia: What Can We Learn from Top Incomes?' *Journal of Public Economics* 92 (2009): 209–12.

Lewis, W.A. 'Economic Development with Unlimited Supplies of Labour'. *The Manchester School of Economic and Social Studies* 22 (1954): 139–91.

———. *The Theory of Economic Growth*. London: Allen & Unwin, 1955.

———. *Aspects of Tropical Trade, 1883–1965*. Stockholm: Almqvist and Wiksell, 1969.

Liem Tjwan Ling. 'Sugar Jing: Oei Tiong Ham'. In *Oei Tiong Ham Concern: The First Business Empire of Southeast Asia*, ed. Yoshihara Kunio. Kyoto: Kyoto University, The Center for Southeast Asian Studies, 1989, 135–47.

Lin, Man-Houng. 'Overseas Chinese Merchants and Multiple Nationality: A Means for Reducing Commercial Risk (1895–1935)'. *Journal of Southeast Asian Studies* 35, 4 (2001): 985–1009.

Lindblad, J. Th. *Between Dayak and Dutch. The Economic History of Southeast Kalimantan 1880–1942*. Dordrecht: Foris, 1988.

________. 'De handel tussen Nederland en Nederlands-Indië, 1874–1939' [Trade between the Netherlands and The Netherlands Indies, 1874–1939]. *Economisch- en sociaal-historisch jaarboek* 51 (1988): 240–98.

________. 'Economic Aspects of the Dutch Expansion in Indonesia, 1870–1914'. *Modern Asian Studies* 23, 1 (1989): 1–24. Also published in Paul Kratoska, ed., *Southeast Asia. Colonial History*. London: Routledge, 2001, 132–52.

________. 'Regional Patterns in the Foreign Trade of Java, 1911–1940'. In *Changing Economy in Indonesia*, Vol. 12b, *Regional Patterns in Foreign Trade 1911–1940*, ed. Adrian Clemens et al. Amsterdam: Royal Tropical Institute, 1992.

________. 'The Economic Relationship between the Netherlands and Colonial Indonesia'. In *The Economic Development of the Netherlands since 1870*, ed. J.L. van Zanden. Cheltenham: Edward Elgar, 1996.

________. *Historical Foundations of a National Economy in Indonesia, 1890s–1990s*. Amsterdam: North-Holland, 1996.

________. 'Foreign Investment in Southeast Asia in Historical Perspective'. *Asian Economic Journal* 11 (1997): 61–89.

________. *Foreign Investment in Southeast Asia in the Twentieth Century*. Basingstoke: Macmillan, 1998.

________. 'Indonesian Economic Development in a Time of Globalization'. *Bijdragen tot de Taal-, Land- en Volkenkunde* 154 (1998): 193–217.

________. 'The Political Economy of Realignment in Indonesia during the Sukarno Period'. In *Europe-Southeast Asia in the Contemporary World: Mutual Images and Reflections 1940s–1960s*, ed. Piyanart Bunnag, Franz Knipping and Sud Chonchirdsin. Baden-Baden: Nomos, 2000, 149–72.

________. 'The Late Colonial State and Economic Expansion, 1900–1930s'. In *The Emergence of a National Economy. An Economic History of Indonesia, 1800–2000*, ed. H. Dick et al. Leiden: KITLV Press, 2002, 111–52.

________. 'The Outer Islands in the 19th Century: Contest for the Periphery'. In *The Emergence of a National Economy. An Economic History of Indonesia, 1800–2000*, ed. H. Dick et al. Leiden: KITLV Press, 2002, 82–110.

________. *Bridges to New Business: The Economic Decolonization of Indonesia*. Leiden: KITLV Press, 2008.

________. 'Economic Growth and Decolonisation in Indonesia'. *Itinerario* 34, 1 (2010): 97–112.

Lindblad, J. Thomas and Thee Kian Wie, eds. *Festschrift for A. Booth, Special Edition of Masyarakat Indonesia* 13: 2 (2013).

Lindsey, Tim. 'The Criminal State. Premanism and the New Indonesia'. In *Indonesia Today: Challenges of History*, ed. Grayson Lloyd and Shannon Smith. Singapore: Institute of Southeast Asian Studies, 2001, 283–97.

Lipton, Michael. *Why Poor People Stay Poor: A Study of Urban Bias in World Development*. London: Temple Smith, 1977.

Lynn, Leonard H. and Hayagreeva Rao. 'Failure of Intermediate Forms: A Study of the Suzuki Zaibatsu'. *Organisational Studies* (1995): 57–70.

Mackie, Jamie. 'In Memoriam: Professor Benjamin Higgins, 1912–2001'. *Bulletin of Indonesian Economic Studies* 37, 2 (2010): 183–8.

Mackie, J.A.C. 'The Indonesian Economy, 1950–1963'. In *The Economy of Indonesia*, ed. Bruce Glasssburner. Ithaca: Cornell University Press, 1971, 16–69.

Maddison, Angus. 'Dutch Income in and from Indonesia 1700–1938'. *Modern Asian Studies* 23 (1989): 645–70.

————. 'Historical Statistics on World Population, GDP and Per Capita GDP, 1–2008 AD', 2010. http://www.ggdc.net/maddison/

Magiera, Stephen L. 'The Role of Wheat in the Indonesian Food Sector'. *Bulletin of Indonesian Economic Studies* 17, 3 (1981): 48–73.

Mahajani, Usha. *Soviet and American Aid to Indonesia 1949–1968*. Athens: Ohio University for International Studies, 1970.

Malinowski, Bronislaw. *Argonauts of the Western Pacific: An Account of Native Enterprise and Adventure in the Archipelagoes of Melanesian New Guinea*. London: George Routledge and Sons, 1922.

Manifesto, 17 May 1961; 20 May 1961.

Manning, C. and A. Posso. 'Trade and Labour Market Outcomes: Why have the East Asian Cubs Lagged behind the Tigers?' In *The Rise of Asia: Trade and Investment in Global Perspective*, ed. P. Athukorala. London: Routledge, 2010, 292–308.

Mariyono, Joko. 'Technological and Institutional Changes in the Indonesian Rice Sector: From Intensification to Sustainable Revitalization'. *Asian Journal of Agriculture and Development* 6, 2 (2009): 124–44.

Marks, Daan. 'The Economic Consequences of Decolonization: The "Special" Case of Indonesia'. In *Indonesian Economic Decolonization in Regional and International Perspective*, ed. J. Thomas Lindblad and Peter Post. Leiden: KITLV Press, 2009, 157–74.

————. 'The Lost Decades? Economic Disintegration in Indonesia's Early Independence Period'. *Itinerario* 34, 1 (2010): 77–95.

————. 'Unity or Diversity? On the Integration and Efficiency of Rice Markets in Indonesia, c. 1920–2006'. *Explorations in Economic History* 47, 3 (2010): 310–24.

Martin, W. and P. Warr. 'Explaining the Relative Decline of Agriculture: A Supply-Side Analysis for Indonesia'. *World Bank Economic Review* 7, 3 (1993): 381–401.

Masako Sakamoto. 'Diversification: the Case of Mitsui Bussan'. In *General Trading Companies: A Comparative and Historical Study*, ed. Shin'ichi Yonekawa. Tokyo: United Nations University Press, 1990, 46–91.

McClelland, Donald G. et al. 'Food Aid in Indonesia'. *USAID Impact Evaluation, No. 4*. Washington DC: United States Agency for International Development, 1997.

Meadows, Donella H. et al. *The Limits to Growth: A Report for the Club of Rome's Project on the Predicament of Mankind.* New York: Universe Books, 1972.

Mears, Leon. 'Rice and Food Self-Sufficiency in Indonesia'. *Bulletin of Indonesian Economic Studies* 20, 2 (1984): 122–38.

Mears, Leon A. and Sidik Moeljono. 'Food Policy'. In *The Indonesian Economy during the Soeharto Era*, ed. Anne Booth and Peter McCawley. Kuala Lumpur: Oxford University Press, 1981, 23–61.

Meek, P. John. 'The Government and Economic Development in Indonesia, 1950–1954'. PhD Dissertation, University of Virginia, Virginia, 1956.

Mees, W.C. *Het muntwezen van Nederlandsch-Indië* [The coinage system in the Netherlands Indies]. Amsterdam, 1851.

Meijer Ranneft, J.W. and W. Huender. *Onderzoek naar den belastingdruk op de inlandsche bevolking* [Enquiry into the burden of taxation on the indigenous population]. Weltevreden, Landsdrukkerij, 1926.

Meijer, Hans. *Den Haag-Djakarta. De Nederlands-Indonesische betrekkingen, 1950–1962* [The Hague-Jakarta. The Dutch-Indonesian relations, 1950–1962]. Utrecht: Het Spectrum, 1994.

Meilink-Roelofsz, M.A.P. et al. *The Archives of the Dutch East India Company (1602–1795).* The Hague: Sdu Uitgeverij, 1992.

Mrazek, Rudolf. *Sjahrir. Politics and Exile in Indonesia.* Ithaca: Cornell University Press, 1994.

Muljatno, S. 'Perhitungan pendapatan national Indonesia untuk tahun 1953 dan 1954' [The calculation of Indonesian national income/revenue in 1953 and 1954]. *Ekonomi dan Keuangan Indonesia* 13 (1960): 162–211.

Myrdal, Gunnar. *Asian Drama: An Inquiry into the Poverty of Nations.* New York: Pantheon, 1968.

Nagtegaal, L. *Riding the Dutch Tiger. The Dutch East Indies Company and the Northeast Coast of Java, 1680–1743.* Leiden: KITLV Press, 1996.

Nan'yo, Mark R. Peattie. *The Rise and Fall of the Japanese in Micronesia, 1885–1945.* Honolulu: Hawaii University Press, 1988.

Naoto Kagotani. 'Japan's Commercial Penetration of South and Southeast Asia and the Cotton Trade Negotiations in the 1930s: Maintaining Relations Between Japan, British India and the Dutch East Indies'. In *The International Order of Asia in the 1930s and 1950s*, ed. Shigeru Akita and Nicholas J. White. Farnham: Ashgate, 2010, 179–206.

Neilson, Jeffrey. 'Value Chains, Neoliberalism and Development Practice: The Indonesian Experience'. *Review of International Political Economy* 21, 1 (2014): 38–69.

Neumark, S.D. 'The National Income of Indonesia 1951–1952'. *Ekonomi dan Keuangan Indonesia* 7 (1954): 348–91.

Nordhaus, William D. and James Tobin. 'Is Growth Obsolete?' In *Economic Research: Retrospect and Prospect*, Vol. 5, *Economic Growth*, ed. William D. Nordhaus and James Tobin. Washington DC: National Bureau of Economic Research (NBER), 1972, 1–80.

North, Douglass C. *Institutions, Institutional Change and Economic Performance.* Cambridge: Cambridge University Press, 1990.

Nurhasim, Moch, ed. *Praktek-praktek bisnis militer. Pengalaman Indonesia, Burma, Filipina dan Korea Selatan* [Military business practices: the experience of Indonesia, Burma, the Philippines and South Korea]. Jakarta: Ridep Institute, 2003.

Ochse, J.J. and G.J.A. Terra. *Geld- en produktenhuishouding, volksvoeding en-gezondheid in Koetowinangun* [Money and product economy, food and health of the population in Kutowinangun]. Buitenzorg: Archipel Drukkerij, 1934.

Olver, A.S.B. 'The Special Commission in South-East Asia'. *Pacific Affairs* 21, 3 (1948): 285–91.

Overdijkink, G.W. *Het Indonesisch problem: de feiten* [The Indonesian problem: the facts]. The Hague: Martinus Nijhoff, 1946.

————. *Het Indonesisch probleem: nieuwe feiten* [The Indonesian problem: new facts]. Amsterdam: Keizerskroon, 1948.

Paauw, Douglas S. *Financing Economic Development: The Indonesian Case.* Glencoe: The Free Press, 1960.

————. 'From Colonial to Guided Economy'. In *Indonesia,* ed. Ruth McVey. New Haven: Hraf Press, 1963.

————. 'Economic Progress in Southeast Asia'. *Journal of Asian Studies* 23 (1963): 69–92.

Palmer, Ingrid. *The New Rice in Indonesia.* Geneva: United Nations Research Institute for Social Development, 1976.

Panglaykim. 'Beberapa aspek struktur management/organisasi pada beberapa negara sosialis' [Some aspects of management/organization structure in some Socialist countries]. In *Tata Perekonomian Sosialis Indonesia,* ed. Suhadi Mangkusuwondo. Jakarta: LPEM, 1962, 21–40.

————. 'Some Notes on the Development of Economics and Business Administration in Indonesia'. *De Economist* 113, 4 (1964): 276–91.

Papaioannou, Kostadis. J. and Jan Luiten van Zanden. 'The dictator effect: how long years in office affect economic development'. *Journal of Institutional Economics* (forthcoming).

Parotte, Jean Henri. 'The Food Aid Convention'. *IDS Bulletin* 14, 2 (1983): 10–5.

Pedoman Sport, 3 January 1959.

Penny, David S. 'Indonesia'. In *Agricultural Development in Asia,* ed. R.T. Shand. Canberra: Australian National University Press, 1969, 251–79.

Perkins, John H. *Geopolitics and the Green Revolution: Wheat, Genes, and the Cold War.* New York: Oxford University Press, 1997.

Pitt, Mark. 'Indonesia'. In *Liberalizing Foreign Trade,* Vol. 5, *The Experience of Indonesia, Pakistan and Sri Lanka,* ed. A. Papageorgiou et al. Cambridge: Basil Blackwell, 1991.

Plosser, C.I. and W.G. Schwert. 'Money, Income and Sunspots: Measuring Economic Relationships and the Effects of Differencing'. *Journal of Monetary Economics* 4 (1978): 637–60.

Portes, Alejandro. 'Social Capital: Its Origins and Applications in Modern Sociology'. *Annual Review of Sociology* 24 (1998): 1–24.

Post, Peter. 'Japanse bedrijvigheid in Indonesie 1868–1942: Structurele elementen van Japans vooroorlogse economische expansie in Zuidoost Asie' [Japanese business in Indonesia 1868–1942: Structural elements of Japan's pre-war economic expansion in Southeast Asia]. PhD Dissertation, Amsterdam, Vrije Universiteit, 1991.

________. 'Japan and the Integration of the Netherlands Indies into the World Economy, 1868–1942'. *Review of Indonesian and Malay Affairs* 27 (1993): 134–65.

________. 'Chinese Business Networks and Japanese Capital in South East Asia, 1880–1940: some preliminary observations'. In *Chinese Business Enterprise in Asia*, ed. R.A. Brown. London: Routledge, 1995, 154–75.

________. 'Characteristics of Japanese Entrepreneurship in the Pre-War Indonesian Economy'. In *The Historical Foundations of a National Economy in Indonesia, 1890s–1990s*, ed. J. Th. Lindblad. Amsterdam: North Holland, 1996.

________. 'The Kwik Hoo Tong Trading Society of Semarang, Java: A Chinese Business Network in Late Colonial Asia'. *Journal of Southeast Asian Studies* 32 (2002): 279–96.

________. '*Indonesianisasi* and Japanization: The Japanese and the Shifting Fortunes of *Pribumi* Entrepreneurship'. In *Indonesian Economic Decolonization in Regional and International Perspective*, ed. J. Thomas Lindblad and Peter Post. Leiden: KITLV Press, 2009, 61–86.

Posthumus, Godert Aart. *The Inter Governmental Group on Indonesia (I.G.G.I.)*. Rotterdam: Rotterdam University Press, 1972.

Postma, T.F.H. et al. *De Java suikerindustrie gedurende de Japansche bezetting* [The Java sugar industry during Japanese occupation]. Batavia: Departement van Economische Zaken in Nederlandsch Indie, 1946.

Potting, C.J.M. *De Ontwikkeling van het geldverkeer in een koloniale samenleving. Oostkust van Sumatra 1875–1938* [The development of monetary transactions in a colonial society. Sumatra's East Coast 1875–1938]. Amsterdam: Nederlands Instituut voor het Bank- en Effectenbedrijf, 1997.

Prabowo, Dibyo and Sajogyo. 'Sidoarjo, East Java, and Subang, West Java'. In *Agricultural and Rural Development in Indonesia*, ed. Gary E. Hansen. Boulder: Westview Press, 1981, 68–78.

Prins, B. de. *Voor keizer en koning. Leonard du Bus de Gisignies 1780–1849. Commissaris-Generaal van Nederlands-Indië* [For Emperor and King. Leonard du Bus de Gisignies 1780–1849. Commissioner-General of the Netherlands Indies]. Amsterdam: Uitgeverij Balans, 2002.

Purdey, Jemma. *Anti-Chinese Violence in Indonesia, 1996–1999*. Singapore: Singapore University Press, 2006.

Purwanto, Bambang. *Gagalnya Historiografi Indonesiasentris?!* [The failure of the Indonesia-centric historiography?!]. Yogyakarta: Ombak, 2006.

————. 'Economic Decolonization and the Rise of Indonesian Military Business'. In *Indonesian Economic Decolonization in Regional and International Perspective*, ed. J. Thomas Lindblad and Peter Post. Leiden: KITLV Press, 2009, 39–57.

Radelet, Steven C. *Emerging Africa: how 17 countries are leading the way*. Baltimore, MD: Center for Global Development, 2010.

Radius Prawiro. *Indonesia's Struggle for Economic Development: Pragmatism in Action*. Kuala Lumpur: Oxford University Press, 1998.

Rantjangan dasar undang2 pembangunan nasional semesta-berentjana delapan tahun: 1961–1969 [The basic draft/bill of total-planned national development eight years: 1961–1969]. Jakarta: Dewan Perantjang Negara, 1960.

Redfern, William E. 'Sukarno's Guided Democracy and the Takeovers of Foreign Companies in Indonesia in the 1960s'. PhD Dissertation, University of Michigan, 2010.

Reeve, David. *Golkar of Indonesia: An Alternative to the Party System*. Singapore: Oxford University Press, 1985.

Reid, Anthony. *Southeast Asia in the Age of Commerce*. 2 vols. New Haven: Yale University Press, 1988–93.

Repetto, Robert C. *Wasting Assets: Natural Resources in the National Income Accounts*. Washington DC: World Resources Institute, 1989.

Reynolds, L.G. 'The Spread of Economic Growth to the Third World'. *Journal of Economic Literature* 21 (1983): 941–75.

Rice, Robert. 'Sumitro's role in foreign trade policy'. *Indonesia* 8 (1969): 183–211.

Ricklefs, M.C. *A History of Modern Indonesia since c. 1200*. Hampshire: Palgrave, 2001.

Rifai, Bachtiar. *Perkembangan perguruan tinggi selama 20 tahun Indonesia merdeka* [The development of higher education institutions during twenty years of Indonesian independence]. Jakarta: Departemen Perguruan Tinggi dan Ilmu Pengetahuan, 1965.

Robinson and Schroeder. 'Training, Continuous Improvement and Human Relations: The US TWI Program and the Japanese Management style'. *California Management Review* 35, 2 (1993): 35–56.

Robison, Richard. *Indonesia: The Rise of Capital*. Singapore: Allen & Unwin, 1986.

Rock, Michael T. 'Exploring the Impact of Selective Interventions in Agriculture on the Growth of Manufactures in Indonesia, Malaysia, and Thailand'. *Journal of International Development* 14 (2002): 485–510.

Rodrik, D. *Making Openness Work: The New Global Economy and the Developing Countries*. Washington DC, 1999.

Roeslan Abdulgani. *Beberapa soal demokrasi dan ekonomi* [Some questions on democracy and economy]. Jakarta: Dewan Nasional, 1958.

________. 'The lessons of Indonesia's Experience of Planning'. In *Politik dan Ilmu*. Jakarta: B.P. Prapantja, 1962.

________. *Sosialisme Indonesia* [Indonesian Socialism]. Jakarta: Jajasan Prapantja, 1963.

Rosendale, Phyllis. 'The Indonesian Terms of Trade, 1950–1973'. *Bulletin of Indonesian Economic Studies* 6, 3 (1975): 50–80.

Rosenfeld, Arthur H. 'Een en ander omtrent de suikerindustrie in Formosa' [Some things about the sugar industry in Formosa]. *Asian Studies* 37 (1929): 1018–29. [Reprinted in translation from *The International Sugar Journal* 31 (1929)].

Ross, Sandy. *The World Food Programme in Global Politics*. New York: First Forum Press, 2011.

Rossum, Matthias van. *Werkers van de wereld. Globalisering, arbeid en interculturele ontmoetingen tussen Aziatische en Europese zeelieden in dienst van de VOC, 1600–1800* [Workers of the world. Globalisation, labour and intercultural encounters between Asian and European sailors employed by the VOC, 1600–1800]. Hilversum: Verloren, 2014.

Sadli, Mohammad. 'Beberapa segi masalah pembangunan daerah di Indonesia' [Certain aspects of problems with regional development in Indonesia]. In *Laporan Kongres Ilmu Pengetahuan Indonesia Kedua, 1962, Djilid ke-sembilan, Seksi E-3 (Ekonomi)*. Bogor: Archipel, 1962.

________. 'Masalah penentuan produksi dan masalah bentuk perusahaan dalam sistim sosialisme Indonesia' [The problem of determining production and the form of companies in the Indonesian socialist system]. In *Tata Perekonomian Sosialis Indonesia*, ed. Suhadi Mangkusuwondo. Jakarta: LPEM, 1962.

________. '20 tahun perkembangan ilmu ekonomi di Indonesia' [Twenty years of development economics in Indonesia]. In *Research di Indonesia 1945–1965*, vol. 4, *Bidang social dan budaya*, ed. M. Makagiansar and Widjojo Nitisastro. Jakarta: Departemen Urusan Research Nasional, 1965.

________. 'Mohammad Sadli'. In *Recollections: The Indonesian Economy, 1950s–1990s*, ed. Thee Kian Wie. Singapore: Institute of Southeast Asian Studies, 2002, 119–40.

Said, Salim. *Genesis of Power: General Sudriman and the Indonesian Military in Politics 1945–49*. Jakarta: Sinar Harapan, 1991.

Samego, Indria et al. *Bila ABRI Berbisnis* [If ABRI (Indonesian National Armed Forces) is involved in business]. Bandung: Mizan, 1998.

Sapta Marga, 30 January 1969; 6 March 1969.

Sardju Ismunandar and Soehardiman. 'Isi laporan 'team study group' tentang struktur ekonomi dan perusahaan negara di Jugoslavia, Czechoslovakia dan Polandia' [Report of the 'team study group' on the structure of the economy and state enterprise in Yugoslavia, Czechkoslovakia and Poland]. In *Perusahaan Negara*, November 1961.

Sato, Shigeru. *War, Nationalism and Peasants: Java under the Japanese Occupation 1942–1945*. Sydney: Allen & Unwin, 1994.

Sato, Yuri. 'The Salim Group in Indonesia: The development and behaviour of the largest conglomerate in Southeast Asia'. *The Developing Economies* 31, 4 (1993): 408–41.

Scheetz, Thomas. 'Military Business in Argentina'. In *The Military as An Economic Actor: Soldiers in Business*, ed. Jörn Brömmelhörster and Wolf-Christian Paes. Basingstoke: Palgrave Macmillan, 2003, 18–31.

Scherr, Sara J. 'Agriculture in an Export Boom Economy: A comparative analysis of policy and performance in Indonesia, Mexico and Nigeria'. *World Development* 17, 4 (1989): 543–60.

Schneider, Adam. 'The Taiwan Government-General and Pre-War Japanese Economic Expansion in South China and Southeast Asia, 1900–1936'. In *The Japanese Empire in East Asia and its Postwar Legacy*, ed. Harald Fuess. Tokyo: Deutsches Institut fur Japanstudien, 1998.

Scholten, C. *De Munten van de Nederlandsche Gebiedsdeelen Oversee 1601–1948* [Coins from the Dutch overseas territories, 1601–1948]. Amsterdam: J. Schulman, 1951.

Schumpeter, Joseph A. *Business Cycles: A Theoretical, Historical and Statistical Analysis of the Capitalist Process*, vol. 2. New York: McGraw-Hill, 1939.

Scott, James C. *The Art of Not Being Governed: An Anarchist History of Upland Southeast Asia*. New Haven: Yale University Press, 2009.

Selo Soemardjan. 'The Changing Role of Intellectuals in Indonesian National Development'. In *Culture, Development and Democracy: The Role of the Intellectual: A Tribute to Soedjatmoko*, ed. Kenneth W. Thompson. Tokyo: United Nations University Press, 1994, 111–31.

Severino, Jean-Michel and Olivier Ray. *Africa's Moment*. Cambridge: Polity Press, 2011.

Shakow, Alexander. *Foreign Economic Assistance in Indonesia 1950–1961*. Tokyo: Economic Cooperation Bureau, Ministry of Foreign Affairs, 1964.

Shaw, D. John. *The UN World Food Programme and the Development of Food Aid*. New York/Basingstoke: Palgrave, 2001.

———. *The World's Largest Humanitarian Agency: The Transformation of the UN World Food Programme and of Food Aid*. New York/Basingstoke: Palgrave, 2011.

Shaw, John D. and Clay, Edward, eds. *World Food Aid: Experiences of Recipients and Donors*. Portsmouth NH: Heinemann, 1993.

Shigeru Akita and Nicholas J. White. 'Introduction: The International Order of Asia in the 1930s and 1950s: Contexts, Hypotheses and Scope'. In *The International Order of Asia in the 1930s and 1950s*, ed. Shigeru Akita and Nicholas J. White. Farnham: Ashgate, 2010, 1–13.

———. *The International Order of Asia in the 1930s and 1950s*. Farnham: Ashgate, 2010.

Shinya Sugiyama. 'A British Trading Firm in the Far East: John Swire and Sons, 1867–1914'. In *Business History of General Trading Companies*, ed. S. Yonekawa and H. Yoshihari. Tokyo: University of Tokyo Press, 1987.

________. 'The Structure of the East Asian Refined Sugar Market in the Second Half of the Nineteenth Century'. In *Tokugawa shakai kara no tenbo*, ed. Hayami Akira et al. Tokyo: Dobunkan, 1989.

________. 'Marketing and Competition in China, 1895–1932: The Taikoo Sugar Refinery'. In *Commercial Networks in Modern Asia*, ed. Shinya Sugiyama and Linda Grove. Richmond: Curzon, 2001, 140–57.

Shinya Sugiyama and Linda Grove. 'Introduction'. In *Commercial Networks in Modern Asia*, ed. Shinya Sugiyama and Linda Grove. Richmond: Curzon, 2001, 1–14.

Siamwalla, Ammar and Haykin, Stephen. *The World Rice Market: Structure, Conduct, and Performance*. Washington DC: International Food Policy Research Institute, 1983.

Simpson, Bradley. *Economists with Guns: Authoritarian Development and US–Indonesia Relations*. Stanford: Stanford University Press, 2008.

Soelaeman Soemardi. *Some Aspects of the Social Origin of Indonesian Political Decision Makers*. London: International Sociological Association, 1956.

Soetopo Soesanto. 'Djakarta Raya pada massa 'Pemerintah Nasional Kota' 17 Augustus 1945–21 Djuli 1947' [Greater Jakarta during the 'National Town Government' period, 17 August 1945–21 July 1947]. Skripsi Sardjana, Universitas Indonesia, 1971.

Solow, R. 'A Contribution to the Theory of Economic Growth'. *Quarterly Journal of Economics* 70 (1956): 65–94.

Soto, Hernando de. *The Other Path: The Invisible Revolution in the Third World*. New York: Harper and Row, 1989.

Srinivasan, T.N. and J. Bhagwati. 'Outward-Orientation and Development: Are Revisionists Right?' *Center Discussion Paper* No. 806. Yale University, 1999.

Staatsspoor- en tramwegen. *Mededeelingen aanleg No. 6* [Government rail and tramways. Construction announcements No. 6]. Bandoeng: Nix [1928].

Statistisch Kantoor. *Statistisch Jaaroverzicht voor Nederlandsch-Indië* [Statistical Abstract for the Netherlands East-Indies], 2 parts. Buitenzorg: Statistisch Kantoor, 1924.

Steijn Parvé, D.C. *Geschiedenis van het Munt- en Bankwezen van Nederlandsch-Indië, sedert de Herstelling van het Nederlandsch gezag in 1816, vermeerderd met een Overzigt van de bestaande Muntstelsels in Britsch-Indië, Ceylon, eenige Portugeesche, Spaansche en Fransche koloniën, in China, Cochin-China, Arabië en Perzië* [The history of coinage and banking in the Dutch East-Indies from the restauration of Dutch rule in 1816, with an overview of the existing monetary systems in British India, Ceylon, some Portuguese, Spanish and French colonies, in China, Cochin-China, Arabia and Persia]. Zaltbommel: Joh. Noman en Zoon, 1852.

Stiglitz, Joseph et al. *Report by the Commission on the Measurement of Economic Performance and Social Progress (CMEPSP)*. 2008. www.stiglitz-sen-fitoussi.fr.

Sucheta Mazumdar. *Sugar and Society in China: Peasants, Technology, and the World Market*. Harvard: Harvard University Asia Centre, 1998.

Sumitro Djojohadikusumo. 'Recollection of My Career'. *Bulletin of Indonesian Economic Studies* 22, 3 (1986): 27–39.

________. *The Government's Program on Industries: A Progress Report*. Jakarta: University of Indonesia Press, 1954.

Sundhaussen, Ulf. *The Road to Power: Indonesian Military Politics 1945–1967*. New York: Oxford University Press, 1982.

Sunjoto, R. Soengkono Imam. *Pradjurit Jon HN 008-LAPRIS Kodam XIV 'Hasanuddin'* [Soldier Jon HN 008-LAPRIS Unit XIV 'Hasanuddin']. Makasar: Bataljon Inf. 008 ROI–II/LAPRIS, 1961.

Sutter, John O. *Indonesianisasi: A Historical Survey of the Role of Politics in the Institutions of a Changing Economy from the Second World War to the Eve of the General Election, 1940–1955*. Ithaca: Southeast Asia Program, Cornell University, 1959.

Tabor, Steven R. 'Agriculture in Transition'. In *The Oil Boom and After: Indonesian Economic Policy and Performance in the Soeharto Era*, ed. Anne Booth. Shah Alam: Oxford University Press, 1995, 161–203.

Taffet, Jeffrey F. *Foreign Aid as Foreign Policy: The Alliance for Progress in Latin America*. London: Routledge, 2007.

Tagliacozzo, E. *Secret Trades, Porous Borders. Smuggling and States along a Southeast Asian Frontier, 1865–1915*. New Haven: Yale University Press, 2005. (Also published as E. Tagliacozzo, 'Secret Trades of the Straits. Smuggling and State Formation along a Southeast Asian Frontier, 1870–1910'. PhD Thesis, Yale University, 1999.)

Tarling, Nicholas. *Britain, Southeast Asia and the Onset of the Cold War, 1945–1950*. Cambridge: Cambridge University Press, 1998.

Taselaar, Arjen. *De Nederlandse koloniale lobby. Ondernemers en de Indische politiek 1914–1940* [The Dutch colonial lobby. Entrepreneurs and the Indies government policy 1914–1940]. Leiden: Research School CNWS, 1998.

Technische School Semarang. *Alphabetische naamlijst van de leerlingen der Semarangsche Ambachtsschool thans geheeten Technische School Semarang aan wie een einddiploma voor werktuigkunde of bouwkunde werd uitgereikt* [Alphabetical list of names of the students of the Semarang trade school, presently called Technical School Semarang to which a final diploma for mechanics or architecture was awarded]. Semarang, 1928.

Tham S.Y. and Loke W.H. 'Services Liberalization: The Need for Complementary Policies'. In *Malaysia's Development Challenges: Graduating from the Middle*, ed. H. Hill et al. London: Routledge, 2012, 174–93.

'The rice production in Indonesia', *Economic Review of Indonesia* 1 (January 1947): 9–12. 's-Gravenhage: Martinus Nijhoff, 1978.

The Voice of Free Indonesia, October 1945.

Thee Kian Wie. 'The development of Sumatra, 1820–1940'. In *Economic Growth in Indonesia, 1820–1940*, ed. Angus Maddison and Ge Prince. Dordrecht: Foris Publications, 1989.

________. 'In Memoriam: Professor Sumitro Djojohadikusumo'. *Bulletin of Indonesian Economic Studies* 37, 2 (2001).

________. 'The Soeharto Era and After: Stability, Development and Crisis, 1966–2000'. In *The Emergence of a National Economy: An Economic History of Indonesia, 1800–2000*, ed. Howard Dick et al. Leiden: KITLV Press, 2002.

________. 'Introduction'. In *Recollections: The Indonesian Economy, 1950s–1990s*, ed. Thee Kian Wie. Canberra: Research School of Pacific and Asian Studies, The Australian National University, 2003, 3–43.

________. *Recollections: The Indonesian Economy, 1950s–1990s*. Singapore: Institute of Southeast Asian Studies, 2003.

________. 'Indonesianization: Economic Aspects of Decolonization in Indonesia in the 1950s'. In *Indonesian Economic Decolonization in Regional and International Perspective*, ed. J. Thomas Lindblad and Peter Post. Leiden: KITLV Press, 2009, 19–38.

________. 'The Debate on Economic Policy in Newly-independent Indonesia between Sjafruddin Prawiranegara and Sumitro Djojohadikusumo'. *Itinerario* 34, 1 (2010): 35–56.

Timmer, C. Peter. 'The Formation of Indonesian Rice Policy: A Historical Perspective'. In *Agricultural and Rural Development in Indonesia*, ed. Gary E. Hansen. Boulder: Westview Press, 1981, 33–43.

________. 'Food Price Policy in Indonesia'. Development Discussion Paper, 250. Cambridge: Harvard Institute for International Development, 1987.

________. 'Dutch Disease and Agriculture in Indonesia: The Policy Approach'. Development Discussion Paper, 490. Cambridge: Harvard Institute for International Development, Harvard University, 1994.

Tio Poo Tjiang. 'De suikerhandel van Java' [Java's Sugartrade]. Proefschrift, Nederlandsche Handelshoogeschool te Rotterdam, Amsterdam, De Bussy, 1923.

Toda, H.Y. and T. Yamamoto. 'Statistical Inferences in Vector Autoregressions with Possibly Integrated Processes'. *Journal of Econometrics* 66 (1995): 225–50.

Toer, Pramoedya Ananta. 'Revenge'. *Indonesia* 26 (1978): 43–61.

Tomoko Shiroyama. *China during the Great Depression. Market, State and the World Economy, 1929–1937*. Cambridge: Harvard University Asian Centre/ Harvard University Press, 2008.

Touwen, Jeroen. *Extremes in the Archipelago. Trade and Economic Development in the Outer Islands of Indonesia, 1900–1942*. Leiden: KITLV Press, 2001.

UNComtrade. Statistical database on foreign trade of the United Nations. http://comtrade.un.org/

United Nations. *A System of National Accounts and Supporting Tables*. New York: United Nations, 1952.

________. *System of Environmental-Economic Accounting: Central Framework*. White cover, 2012. http://unstats.un.org/unsd/envaccounting/White_cover.pdf [accessed 28 June 2013].

United States Economic Survey Team to Indonesia. *Indonesia. Perspective and Proposals for United States Economic Aid. A Report to the President of the United States*. New Haven: Yale University Southeast Asian Studies, 1963.

Utusan Nasional, 2 August 1951; 17 June 1952; 19 April 1952; 24 April 1952.

Van der Eng, Pierre. 'The Real Domestic Product of Indonesia, 1880–1989'. *Explorations in Economic History* 29 (1992): 343–73.

________. *Food supply in Java during war and decolonisation, 1940–1950*. Hull: University of Hull, Centre for South-East Asian Studies, 1994.

________. *Agricultural Growth in Indonesia: Productivity Change and Policy Impact since 1880*. New York / London: St. Martin's Press / Macmillan, 1996.

________. 'Food for Growth: Trends in Indonesia's Food Supply, 1880–1995'. *The Journal of Interdisciplinary History* 30, 4 (2000): 591–616.

________. 'Bridging a Gap: A Reconstruction of Population Patterns in Indonesia, 1930–1961'. *Asian Studies Review* 26, 3 (2002): 487–509.

________. 'Indonesia's Growth Performance in the Twentieth Century'. In *The Asian Economies in the Twentieth Centuries*, ed. A. Maddison et al. Cheltenham: Edward Elgar, 2002.

________. 'Productivity and Comparative Advantage in Rice Agriculture in Southeast Asia since 1870'. *Asian Economic Journal* 18, 4 (2004): 345–70.

________. '*Konfrontasi* and Australia's Foreign Aid Program in Indonesia during the 1960s'. *Australian Journal of Politics and History* 55 (2009): 46–63.

________. 'The Sources of Economic Growth in Indonesia, 1880–2008'. *Explorations in Economic History* 47 (2010): 294–309.

________. '"Send Them a Shipload of Rice": Indonesian Famines and Australian Food Aid in the 1950s and 1960s'. Unpublished paper, 2011.

________. 'All Lies? Famines in Sukarno's Indonesia, 1950s–1960s'. Unpublished paper, 2012.

________. *Long-Term Macro-Economic Statistics of Indonesia, 1870–2010*. Tokyo: Toyo Keizai (forthcoming, translated from Japanese).

Verslag over het [eerste-achtste] boekjaar [1949–1957] van de Associatie NV gevestigd te Djakarta [Private collection E.C. Dolk] [Report on the first to eighth administrative year of the Association limited liability company established in Jakarta]. Djakarta, 1950–57.

Vickers, Adrian. 'The New Order: Keeping Up Appearance'. In *Indonesia Today: Challenges of History*, ed. Grayson Lloyd and Shannon Smith. Singapore: Institute of Southeast Asian Studies, 2001, 72–84.

Vissering, G. *Muntwezen en circulatiebanken in Nederlandsch-Indië* [Coinage system and money circulation banks in the Netherlands-Indies]. Amsterdam: J.H. de Bussy, 1920.

Vlekke, B.H.M. *Indonesia's Struggle 1957–1958*. The Hague: Netherlands Institute of International Affairs, 1959.

Vu, Tuong. 'Of Rice and Revolution: The Politics of Provisioning and State–Society Relations on Java, 1945–49'. *South East Asia Research* 11, 3 (2003): 237–67.

Wal, S.L. van der, ed. *Officiële bescheiden betreffende de Nederlands–Indonesische betrekkingen 1945–1950: 4e deel, 31 maart–16 juli 1946* [Official government documents concerning the Dutch-Indonesian relations 1945–1950]. The Hague: Martinus Nijhoff, 1974, IV.

Waspada, 17 June 1952; 19 April 1952; 24 April 1952.

WAVES. *Annual Report 2013*. The Global Partnership on Wealth Accounting and the Valuation of Ecosystem Services, 2013. www.wavespartnership.org/waves/sites/waves/files/images/WAVES-Annual-Report.pdf [accessed 29 June 2013].

Weber, A. *Hybrid Ambitions. Science, Governance, and Empire in the Career of Caspar G.C. Reinwardt (1773–1854)*. Leiden: Leiden University Press, 2012.

Webster, David. *Fire and the Full Moon: Canada and Indonesia in a Decolonizing World*. Vancouver: University of British Columbia Press, 2010.

Weitzell, E.C. 'Resource Development in the Pacific Mandated Islands'. *The Journal of Land and Public Utility Economics* 22, 3 (1946): 199–212.

Wesseling, H.L. *Indie verloren, rampspoed geboren en andere opstellen over de geschiedenis van de Europese expansie* [The loss of the Indies as catastrophe and other essays about the history of the European expansion]. Amsterdam: Ooievaar Pockethouse, 1995.

Wicks, R.S. 'Monetary Developments in Java between the Ninth and Sixteenth Centuries. A Numismatic Perspective'. *Indonesia* 42 (October 1986): 42–77.

________. *Money, Markets, and Trade in Early Southeast Asia. The Development of Indigenous Monetary Systems to A.D. 1400*. Ithaca, New York: Cornell University, 1992.

Williamson, J.G. *Trade and Poverty: When the Third World Fell Behind*. Cambridge, MA: MIT Press, 2011.

Wisseman Christie, J. 'Money and its Uses in the Javanese States of the Ninth to Fifteenth Centuries A.D.' *Journal of the Economic and Social History of the Orient* 39 (1996): 243–86.

Wit, Y. de. 'The Kabupaten Programme'. *Bulletin of Indonesian Economic Studies* 9, 1 (1973): 65–85.

Wolters, W.G. *Coins and Credit. The Monetary System in the Philippines in the late Spanish Period*. Unpublished research paper, Nijmegen University, 2004.

________. 'Decolonizing Money. Central Banks in the Philippines and Indonesia'. In *Beyond Empire and Nation. The Decolonization of African and Asian

Societies, 1930s–1960s, ed. E. Bogaerts en R. Raben. Leiden: KITLV Press, 2012, 109–36.

Wong Lin Ken. *The Trade of Singapore*. Kuala Lumpur: Malaysian Branch of the Royal Asiatic Society, 1960.

Woolcock, Michael et al. 'How and Why Does History Matter for Development Policy?' *Journal of Development Studies* 47, 1 (2011): 70–96.

World Commission on Environment and Development. *Our Common Future: Annex to General Assembly document A/42/427, Development and International Co-operation: Environment, August 2*. New York: United Nations, 1987.

Wright, Stanley F. *China's Struggle for Tariff Autonomy, 1843–1938*. Shanghai: Kelly & Walsh Limited, 1938.

Yoshimasa, S. 'The monetary policy in the Netherlands East Indies under the Japanese administration'. *Bijdragen tot de Taal-, Land- en Volkenkunde* 152, 4 (1996): 699–724.

Yu Po-ching. 'Chinese seamen in London and St Helena in the early nineteenth century'. In *Labour, Law and Empire: Working Lives between the Deck and the Dock*, ed. Maria Fusaro and Richard Blakemore. London: Macmillan, forthcoming.

Yunarti, D. Rini. *BPUPKI, PPKI, Proklamasi kemerdekaan RI* [BPUPKI, PPKI, and the RI Proclamation of Independence]. Jakarta: Penerbit Buku Kompas, 2003.

Zaheer, Srilata and Akbar Zaheer. 'Trust across Borders'. *Journal of International Business Studies* 37 (2006): 21–9.

Zanden, J.L. van. 'Economic Growth in Java 1815–1939: The Reconstruction of the Historical National Accounts of a Colonial Economy'. Working Paper IISG, 2002.

————. 'On the Efficiency of Markets for Agricultural Products: Rice Prices and Capital Markets in 19th Century Java'. *Journal of Economic History* 64, 4 (2004): 1028–55.

————. 'Linking Two Debates. Money Supply, Wage Labour, and Economic Development in Java in the Nineteenth Century'. In *Wages and Currency. Global Comparisons from Antiquity to the Twentieth Century*, ed. Jan Lucassen. Bern: Peter Lang, 2007, 169–92.

Zanden, Jan Luiten van and Arthur van Riel. *The Strictures of Inheritance: The Dutch Economy in the Nineteenth Century*. Princeton and Oxford: Princeton University Press, 2004.

Zanden, Jan Luiten van and Daan Marks. *An Economic History of Indonesia 1800–2010*. Abingdon: Routledge, 2012.

Zappey, W.M. 'De Economische en Politieke Werkzaamheid van Johannes Goldberg' [The economic and political activity of Johannes Goldberg]. PhD Thesis, University of Amsterdam. Alphen aan den Rijn: Samson, 1967.

Contributors

Leonard Blussé is Professor Emeritus in the History of Asian European Relations at Leiden University. As sinologist and historian he has published widely on Asian-European Interaction, with a particular focus on maritime history and early modern Asian port cities. E-mail: vblus@upcmail.nl

Anne Booth is Professor Emeritus of Economics with reference to Asia at the Centre of South East Asian Studies, SOAS, University of London. E-mail: ab10@soas.ac.uk

Alexander Claver holds a PhD from VU University Amsterdam (2006). He has written articles and reviews on Dutch and Indonesian economic history and recently published *Dutch Commerce and Chinese Merchants in Java. Colonial Relationships in Trade and Finance, 1800–1942* (Leiden and Boston: Brill, 2014). At present he is researching the history of the Armenian trading minority in colonial Indonesia. E-mail: alexanderclaver@hotmail.com

Freek Colombijn is Associate Professor at the Department of Social and Cultural Antropology at the Faculty of Social Sciences of VU University Amsterdam. E-mail: f.colombijn@vu.nl

Robert Cribb is Professor at the School of Culture, History & Language, at ANU College of Asia and the Pacific, Australian National University. E-mail: robert.cribb@anu.edu.au

Howard Dick is Honorary Professorial Fellow, Faculty of Business & Economics, University of Melbourne and Conjoint Professor, Faculty of Business & Law, University of Newcastle (NSW). E-mail: h.dick@unimelb.edu.au

Pierre van der Eng is Associate Professor at the Research School of Management and at the Arndt-Corden Department of Economics at the Australian National University, Canberra. E-mail: pierre.vandereng@anu.edu.au

Farabi Fakih is Lecturer in History at Gadjah Mada University in Yogyakarta. He received his PhD in 2014 on *The Rise of the Managerial State in Indonesia: Institutional Transition during the Early Independence Period.* E-mail: farabi.fakih@gmail.com

Ewout Frankema is Professor in Rural and Environmental History at Wageningen University. Frankema's research agenda focuses on the evolutionary history of developing regions (Africa, Latin America, Asia). E-mail: ewout.frankema@wur.nl

David Henley is Professor in Contemporary Indonesia Studies at Leiden University. E-mail: d.e.f.henley@hum.leidenuniv.nl

Hal Hill is the H.W. Arndt Professor of Southeast Asian Economies, Arndt Corden Department of Economics, Crawford School of Economics and Government, College of Asia and the Pacific, Australian National University. E-mail: hal.hill@anu.edu.au

Roger Knight is Associate Professor at the School of History and Politics at the University of Adelaide. E-mail: roger.knight@adelaide.edu.au

Daan Marks received his PhD in 2009 on *Accounting for Services: the Economic Development of the Indonesian Service Sector, ca. 1900–2000* and works at the Dutch Ministry of Finance. E-mail: a.j.marks@minfin.nl

Pham van Thuy is Lecturer in history at Vietnam National University-Hanoi. He received his PhD in 2014 on *Beyond Political Skin: Convergent Paths to an Independent, National Economy in Indonesia and Vietnam.* E-mail: Thuypv@vnu.edu.vn

Alexandra de Pleijt is PhD student at Utrecht University working on the role of human capital in the transition to modern economic growth. E-mail: A.M.dePleijt@uu.nl

Bambang Purwanto is Professor of History at Gadjah Mada University in Yogyakarta. E-mail: purwantougm@yahoo.co.uk

Alicia Schrikker is Lecturer in Colonial and Global History at Leiden University. She has worked on regime change in eighteenth- and nineteenth-century Sri Lanka and is presently looking at political and cultural responses to disaster in colonial Indonesia. E-mail: A.F.Schrikker@hum.leidenuniv.nl

Thee Kian Wie, 1935–2014, was Senior Economist at the Economic Research Centre, Indonesian Institute of Sciences (P2E-LIPI), in Jakarta. He passed away on 8 February 2014.

Jeroen Touwen is Associate Professor in Economic and Social History at the Institute for History at Leiden University. E-mail l.j.touwen@hum.leidenuniv.nl

Jan Luiten van Zanden is Professor of Global Economic History at Utrecht University, the Netherlands, and honorary professor at Groningen and Stellenbosch universities. E-mail: j.l.vanzanden@uu.nl

Pim de Zwart is PhD student at the International Institute of Social History, Amsterdam, working on commodity market integration and living standards in different parts of Asia, c. 1600–1800. E-mail: pza@iisg.nl

Index